Embedded Politics

Embedded Politics

Industrial Networks and Institutional Change in Postcommunism

Gerald A. McDermott

Ann Arbor

THE UNIVERSITY OF MICHIGAN PRESS

First paperback edition 2003
Copyright © by the University of Michigan 2002
All rights reserved
Published in the United States of America by
The University of Michigan Press
Manufactured in the United States of America
♾ Printed on acid-free paper

2006   2005   2004   2003   5   4   3   2

A CIP catalog record for this book is available from the British Library.

Library of Congress Cataloging-in-Publication Data

McDermott, Gerald A., 1966–
    Embedded politics : industrial networks and institutional
change in postcommunism / Gerald A. McDermott.
        x, 295 p. : ill. ; 24 cm.
    Includes bibliographical references (p. 243–281) and index.
    0-472-09803-9 (cloth : alk. paper)
        1. Industrial policy—Czech Republic.   2. Industrial policy—
Czechoslovakia.   3. Post-communism—Economic aspects—Czech
Republic.   4. Post-communism—Economic aspects—Czechoslovakia.
I. Title.

HD3616.C942 M33   2002
338.094371—dc21   2002072422

ISBN 0-472-06803-2 (pbk. : alk. paper)

To Patricia and Kevin,
for giving me the security to attempt the adventure
and
to Sandra,
for guiding me along the way.

Preface

This book is the product of a personal journey. It began with some intellectual questions that took me behind the iron curtain, onward to MIT, back to Prague, through Buenos Aires, and finally up to Philadelphia. In the course of my doctoral studies and the numerous versions of this manuscript, my father passed away, I became an uncle seven times, I lived on three continents, I married Sandra Aidar, and I became a father (and quite a happy one at that). The point is that writing a dissertation and then a book is as much about renewal of the spirit as it is about strengthening of the intellect. My choices of topic and argument as well as my ability to execute these choices have drawn on both my emotional and academic foundations. The story of this book, in turn, intertwines my personal and scholarly journeys as well as the support and lessons from family, friends, colleagues, and advisors. I guess, then, the best way to describe my interests in East Central Europe and institutional change and to thank those for helping me get through this journey is to tell about how the issues came together.

My first significant adventure in East Central Europe was in 1988–89 as a Thomas J. Watson Foundation Fellow. I went to interview managers, bureaucrats, and theorists about the ongoing transformation of industrial and communist governance structures. My professors at Middlebury College and my buddies, like Stefan Sullivan and Dave Blumental, were vital in helping me think about the political and economic changes in the region, win the fellowship, and have the confidence to go into uncharted territory. Czechoslovakia soon became the focus of my interests for two reasons. First, friends and scholars like Dušan Tříska, Kárel Dyba, Lubomír Mlčoch, Aleš Čapek, Vladimír Benáček, Jan Mládek, Roman Češka, Josef Kotrba, Jiří Jonáš, Michal Mejstřík, and Alena Zemplinerová soon helped me learn that despite the apparent orthodoxy of the communist regime, the textbook hierarchical pyramid of command and control was virtually upside down. Managers, workers, and bureaucrats were surviving by diverse social, political, and economic bargaining networks. This perspective quickly influenced the way I began to understand the profound changes taking place throughout the region. Then I met Tony Levitas in Warsaw. Tony began to teach me about how historical, political, and social ties at the micro or everyday level could impact the tenuous position of the communist regimes and the aftermath. His years of experience in Poland, especially on the shop floor, made his perspective appealing, and our friendship gave me the confidence to pursue my intellectual curiosities further, both "in the field" and in a Ph.D. program.

Second, my personal relationships in the region gave me the comfort, strength, and joy to make East Central Europe a key part of my life. People like Wlodek Zieleniec and Stefan Kawalec in Warsaw, Michal Moeller in East Berlin, and Emese Szontagh and Kalman Mizsei in Budapest made me realize I had friends far from White Plains, New York. But my intellectual curiosity in the puzzle of Czechoslovakia, often overlooked because of the fast-paced changes occurring in 1988–89 in Poland and Hungary, was cemented by the enduring personal bonds developed with Kryštof Duchoslav, Daniel and Victoria Spička, Patricie Vláchová, Juraj and Tanie Mihalík, Ivana Mazálková, David Koláček, and, especially, with the Bobeks—Pavel and Marta and their children, Klara and Pavliček. When I was asked why I chose to spend Christmas and New Years in Prague and Bratislava in 1988–89 after just a few months in Czechoslovakia, I replied that this was a time to be with family and close friends. Over the years, I felt like a cousin returning home. They helped me see communism and the transformation through their eyes. They offered me all the support imaginable—from accommodations and contacts to a friendship in which we could share our most personal problems and joys. It may be no coincidence that I was in Prague when my father became suddenly ill, that Sandra and I married in Prague 6, and that Pavel was my best man at the wedding.

But why economic governance institutions? Toward the end of my coursework at Middlebury, particularly with the guidance of my professors, I began to question several of the traditional economic approaches to the theory of the firm and industrial organization. While assumptions of returns to scale limited our understanding of innovation, debates about optimal ownership and contractual structures had difficulty reconciling effective monitoring with decentralized experimentation. Was increased efficiency or productivity based solely on the development of labor-saving methods to produce a widget? Were firms relegated to the choices of becoming large-scale hierarchies or using arm's-length customer–supply relations based on price alone? Given the problems of the modern corporation that I saw in the turbulence of my father's professional life, I took these questions to heart and began wondering whether economic growth was generally incompatible with higher incomes and greater democratic participation in the reconstruction of economic institutions. These questions were put into sharper relief when I went to East Central Europe. I saw not only the wreckage and injustice of the Leninist alternative but also the differences between the ways socialist managers coordinated economic activity and the textbook pictures of communism and planning. Put another way, if the same assumptions that limited our responses to cold war capitalism also failed to capture the contemporary realities of communist planning, then maybe we had to rethink our first principles about political economy.

As this confusion was taking hold of me, Tony Levitas and Dave Audretsch directed me toward the work of Mike Piore and Chuck Sabel. They argued that there were several paths to growth and forms of industrial organization, both of which depended on political struggles over institutional constellations in specific historical contexts. With this introduction into the worlds of possibilities, I began my doctoral studies in political science at MIT. Suzanne Berger, Rick Locke, and Chuck Sabel helped me think long and hard about alternative approaches to political economy, particularly about ways to connect micro-level issues of industrial organization to larger political conflicts within countries. Their guidance led me to take intellectual risks in relating political governance to economic governance—risks that I hope can shed light on new ways of developing public policies and creating business organizations. When I met David Stark, the picture was complete. David, through both his unique work inside Hungarian firms and his big heart, helped me overcome many of the challenges of connecting larger theories of economic sociology to the realities of East Central Europe. Together these four scholars have been a guiding force through the years—intellectually stimulating, compassionate, professionally supportive, and, when needed, very demanding.

Dealing with the pressures of MIT, job searches, and life in general would still have been impossible without the friendship and support of my colleagues in Cambridge and Prague. Ram Manikkalingam, Pablo Policzer, Bob Hancke, Gernot Grabher, Zhiyuan Cui, and Waleed Hazbun really helped open my eyes to new ideas and kept me sane through general exams, fieldwork, and the challenges of marriage. With them I discovered the meaning of collegiality, always helping me renew the confidence needed to follow my intuition. Helen Ray calmed me down with a few simple words over the phone. The folks at the Harvard's Center for European Studies offered me resources and a vibrant forum for debate. And David Woodruff has continually gone above and beyond the call of collegiality, marking up chapters, pushing me forward, and putting up with my rants about academia. In Prague, Michal Mejstřík and Jan Švejnar gave me a base for my fieldwork at CERGE–EI, while Mike Jetton and Blanka Hadová became trusted friends and assistants. Aydin Hayri became my partner in bear-dancing and scholarship. Raj Desai and Mitchell Orenstein helped keep spirits high during gray days in Prague, while their sharp arguments have kept me on my toes. Roman Češka and Jan Vrba opened innumerable doors at ministries and firms for me. Ivana Mazálková helped me all too often in interviewing managers, kicking my ass when I needed it, and being there when I needed someone to talk to. Of course, hardly any of this would have been possible without the generous financial support from the American Council for Learned Societies, the International

Research and Exchange Board, the J. William Fulbright Commission, the Program for the Study of Germany and Europe at the Center for European Studies, the National Security Education Program, and the Institute for the Study of World Politics.

As odd as it may seem, I wrote and rewrote much of these chapters in Buenos Aires (my computer, my wife, and I needed some sun). The Universidad de San Andrés in Buenos Aires was extremely hospitable in allowing me to be a visiting researcher, with full use of their facilities. And then, more recently, IAE, Escuela de Dirrección y Negocios, Universidad Austral took me in as a Research Fellow, providing me ample resources and assistance as well as thoughtful and endearing colleagues.

Finally I landed back in my homeland, when the Management Department of the Wharton School opened its doors to me and allowed me to become part of one of the most intellectually vibrant and collegial settings around. I am truly indebted to all my colleagues here, especially Mauro Guillen, Chip Hunter, Steve Kobrin, and Bruce Kogut, for their support of my work and their insightful comments on revisions. My gratitude would be less than sincere without duly acknowledging as well the very helpful comments from two anonymous referees and the unceasing assistance and patience of Ellen McCarthy, Claudia Leo, and their colleagues at the University of Michigan Press—maybe, one day, we'll figure out the secret of the macros!

I will end this preface sort of where I began. The journey has actually just begun, both professionally and personally. Being an assistant professor at Wharton can often be overwhelming. But I have come this far and know I can fulfill my dreams most of all because of the love of my family and wife. It is not always so easy to trust in God and the intuition He gave me through all the ups and downs, but these people make faith so tangible. My mom and dad, Patricia and Kevin, and my brothers and sister, Kevin, Tom, Karen, and Steve, have truly made my adventure possible. Their devotion and calming advice provided all the foundations necessary to take risks with a courage I never knew was possible.

And then there are Sandra, the true love of my life and my eternal partner, and Miranda, our source of light. Miranda has put a new bounce in my step each day. Sandra is my intellectual debater, my soul mate, my best friend. It was she who moved me forward both as a human being and a scholar. Together, they keep the fire of idealism burning bright inside me. And it is only with them that I can face what's coming around the corner.

Acknowledgments

Grateful acknowledgment is made to:

Cambridge University Press, for permission to reprint Tables 8.3, 8.9, and 8.10 from *The Czechoslovak Economy, 1948–1988: The Battle for Economic Reform* by Martin Myant (New York: Cambridge University Press, 1989);

Kluwer Academic Press, for permission to reprint Tables 4.7 and 6.6 from *The Privatization Process in East-Central Europe: Evolutionary Process of Czech Privatizations* (Boston: Kluwer Academic Publishers, 1997), edited by Michal Mejstřík;

Oxford University Press, for permission to use significant parts of my 1998 article coauthored with Aydin Hayri, "The Network Properties of Corporate Governance and Industrial Restructuring: A Post-Socialist Lesson," *Industrial and Corporate Change* 7, no. 1: 153–93;

the editors of *Finance a úvěr*, for permission to reprint Tabulka č. 2 from Jozef Makúch's 1988 article, "Bankový úvěr v podminkách intezifikáce ekonomiky," *Finance a úvěr* 38, no. 11: 737–44;

Josef Valach of the Prague School of Economics, for permission to reprint Tabulka 6.1 and 8.5 from *Financie podnikov a odvetvi* by Milan Majcher and Josef Valach (Praha: SNTL, 1989);

and to Alena Buchtiková and Vladislav Flek, for permission to reprint parts of their tables from pp. 19 and 23 of their unpublished article, "The Impact of Deconcentration and Indirect Industrial Policy on Structural Development and Export Performance in Czech Republic (1989–1992)." Paper presented for the ACE Workshop in Vienna, 1993.

Contents

Tables

Figures

Abbreviations

Countries and Categories
CMEA—Council for Mutual Economic Assistance
CPE—Communist Political Economy
CR—Czech Republic
ČSR—Czech Socialist Republic
CSFR—Czecho-Slovak Federated Republic
ČSSR—Czechoslovak Socialist Republic
DDR—Delegated Deliberative Restructuring
GDR—German Democratic Republic
IPC—Investment Privatization Company
USSR—Union of Soviet Socialist Republics
VHJ—Výrobní Hospodačský Jednotck (Industrial Association for
    Economic Planning)

Government Institutions
CNB—Czech National Bank (Central Bank)
EBRP—Enterprise Bank Restructuring Program (of Poland)
FNM—Fund for National Property of the Czech Republic
KOB—Consolidation Bank, s.p.
ME—Ministry of Economy of the Czech Republic
MF—Ministry of Finance of the Czech Republic
ML—Ministry of Labor and Social Affairs of the Czech Republic
MPO—Ministry of Industry and Trade of the Czech Republic
MP—Ministry for the Administration of National Property and Its
    Privatization of the Czech Republic
SBČS—State Bank of Czechoslovakia

State and Private Companies; Associations
ČMKOS—Czech Moravian Confederation of Trade Unions
ČS—Česká Spořitelna, a.s.
ČSOB—Československá Obchodní Banka, a.s.
IB—Investiční Banka, a.s. (after June 1994, Investiční Poštovní Banka, a.s.)
KB—Komerční Banka, a.s.
PPF—První Privatizační Fund, a.s.
SST—Svaz výrobců a dodavatelů strojírenské techniky
TST—Továrny Strojírenské Techniky, VHJ

CHAPTER 1

Introduction

The Embedded Politics
of Institutional Change
in Postcommunism

What kinds of institutions help countries restructure their economies, improve growth, and promote democracy? And how do countries actually construct them? Perhaps there is a single *right* set of institutions that can be implanted in any society. If so, then we may want to focus analysis on whether political leaders select the proper institutional design and garner enough power to put it in place. Or maybe deep social forces beyond the reach of individuals will directly determine a country's institutional characteristics and its ability to adjust to new political and economic challenges. If this is the case, then we should be concerned with historical continuities and whether a specific country has the *right* social structures.

The events of recent years in the former communist countries of East Central Europe offer a unique opportunity to examine this debate on the creation of governance institutions. Since the middle of 1989, citizens of these countries have witnessed rapid, fundamental changes in their institutions and economies. In a matter of months, democratically elected parliaments replaced the rule of Communist party Politburos. Freedoms of travel, expression, the press, and political organization replaced oppression by the secret police. Rigid, suffocating central planning gave way to entrepreneurship and free markets. One of the most-cited cases of these discontinuities was Czechoslovakia, and particularly the Czech Republic (CR).[1] Within twelve months after the collapse of one the most orthodox communist regimes, the new political leaders initiated national and municipal multiparty elections, dismantled the institutional controls of the Communist party over society and economy, and launched the most extensive market liberalization and privatization program in the region. The hallmark of this process was a powerful team of technocrats privatizing over 1,800 firms in less than four years. Many scholars indeed held the Czech case as proof that a transforming society was a tabula rasa upon which new institutions could be rapidly built and as a model for other countries, from Russia to Mongolia, to follow.[2]

Alongside this evidence of discontinuity, however, one also finds strong continuities and legacies of the past in the region. At the most basic level, people's routines and traditions continued—be they the organization of working hours, cultural festivals, or their social calendar. From the western manager who complained about the work habits of his local employees and his failure to penetrate the local cliques of bankers, to the citizens and academics who observed the enrichment and continued power of former apparatchiks, the cry was heard, "Nothing has changed!"[3] Compared to Poland and Hungary, the Czech Republic had poor economic growth, as many large, communist-era industrial conglomerates and banks remained intact and failed to restructure.[4] Despite their advocacy of free market forces, successive Czech governments continued to intervene into the economy and by 1999 had constructed a new agency to help manage the restructuring of several leading industrial concerns. Some scholars have attributed the economic problems and cases of asset theft to the reproduction of old industrial networks. Others have noted, rather, that the interwar history of Czech democracy and the transformation of its past economic networks into new investment funds lent the Czech Republic the norms of compromise necessary to maintain the course of political and economic reforms.[5]

In this book, I seek to account for change and continuity in the formation of new economic governance institutions in the Czech Republic by analytically linking the macropolitics of state policy with the micropolitics of industrial restructuring. In so doing, the book attempts to advance an alternative approach for the comparative study of institutional change and industrial adjustment.

I argue that the development of new institutions is not simply a product of the ability of the state to impose an optimal institutional design or the result of a path defined by a particular social structure from a past regime. Rather, the creation and execution of institutional and organizational strategies are the products of the specific conflicts that emerge from the interaction between the micro-level attempts to reproduce past *sociopolitical* networks and the macro-level attempts to impose state policy designs. Firms and banks are embedded in communist-era sociopolitical networks that can continue to shape and constrain individual strategies. But changes in a country's political regime can alter the cohesion and distribution of resources within an existing network. In this *embedded politics* view, institutions emerge as experiments with new forms of public and private governance within the social and political space where the state and society meet. In this space, conflicts over the reorganization of past sociopolitical networks of firms, banks, and regional government councils define the possibilities for public and private actors to learn from and monitor one another effectively.

On the one hand, past economic and social relationships can define the set of initial organizational and restructuring strategies of member firms as well as their relative bargaining power vis-à-vis one another and the state. But under new economic uncertainties, the cohesion of the network is stressed as members try to reposition themselves, pursue different business strategies, and assert control over common assets. On the other hand, the establishment of new private property rights or the existence of old social ties is insufficient to facilitate cooperation among members. Firms and their regional bank branches and Communist party councils politically constructed the authority structures of industrial networks. Changes in the political context—such as the dissolution of the Communist party, efforts to centralize policy powers, and public sector reforms—weaken or remove key actors that once helped resolve intranetwork conflicts.[6] As new state actors experiment with different transformation policies, they can exacerbate or help resolve the intranetwork struggles to control assets and reorganize firms. In turn, the different patterns of intranetwork conflicts and their resolutions create different conditions for the way institutional rules are rewritten, resources redistributed, and the roles of both public and private actors redefined.

Using an embedded politics approach to analyze postcommunist transformations helps us identify how certain factors of change and continuity impact the development of both micro- and macro-level institutions of economic governance.

Consider first the debate on the creation and evolution of business organizations that has informed approaches to institution building. Some scholars emphasize the determining impact of sectoral factors, such as transaction costs, resource dependencies, and technology, while others emphasize the stability and path dependent nature of past social structures.[7] Yet in the Czech Republic, as in other postcommunist countries, groups of firms within the same industry chose distinctly different privatization and restructuring strategies that were also unstable.[8] A good comparative example comes from two groups of firms associated with Czech communist-era concerns, Škoda Plzeň and Továrny Strojírenské Techniky (TST), which the *Wall Street Journal* cited in mid 1996 as among the major corporate leaders and agents of change for East Central Europe.[9] Despite their common roots in mechanical engineering, these groups had contrasting definitions of firm boundaries, rules of asset control and risk sharing, and relationships with government agencies and banks. Moreover, the networks of firms and plants around Škoda and TST experienced fundamental changes in their structures of asset control and decision making. Past social relationships did little to resolve restructuring conflicts within the two groups. Instead, firms and plants in these cases depended on the Czech government to mediate disputes and become a financial partner, an issue that left the *Economist* a bit confused in its analysis of the turnaround at Škoda Plzeň.[10]

An embedded politics approach reintegrates factors of change and continuity into industrial organization by understanding the inherited socioeconomic relationships as sources of both future asset value and restructuring conflicts that are politically constructed. The tight technical and financial interdependencies between specific firms and banks are the bases for product development and risk sharing. Yet while high uncertainty limits contractual solutions to the collective-action problem, historical bonds are also ineffective in mediating conflicts over asset control and the selection of reorganization strategies. From an embedded politics perspective, any aspects of associationalism and authority were derived from past alliances between certain firms and political-institutional actors controlling key public resources. In turn, organizational change comes from alterations in the political buttressing that once supported the balance of power and internal cohesion within the network. For instance, key firms within the networks associated with Škoda and TST lost their authority and access to resources when the centralization of policy-making power eliminated formerly allied regional councils, and financial reforms gave Czech banks little incentive to finance restructuring. The combination of the ensuing turmoil and the needed intervention of new public actors to share risk and create negotiated resolutions to intranetwork conflicts changed the distribution of power and the rules governing asset control.

Consider also the double challenge of institution building for transforming political economies: countries must simultaneously create ways to govern the rule-making process and determine which types of institutions will, hopefully, enhance the performance of economic assets.[11] Whether one advocates the sanctity of private ownership or the need for government intervention, the common solution to the double challenge often begins with the necessity of concentrated control, be it over policy-making powers or economic assets, and clear boundaries, be they between firms or the state and society. The Czech Republic vindicated this view initially by forming a powerful "change team" that was cut off from society and that rapidly implemented policies of market liberalization, mass privatization, and rule-based recapitalization of banks. Yet the ensuing events should cause us to pause in accepting the importance of concentrated control and speed. Firms and banks became deadlocked in conflicts about reorganizing production and dividing old debts. Where restructuring advanced, boundaries of the state and between firms remained blurred. Government agencies reengaged banks and groups of firms to forge structures that facilitated negotiated solutions to restructuring conflicts and the definition of governance rules.

An embedded politics approach makes sense of the new roles taken by Czech government agencies by emphasizing that sustainable restructuring emerges from deliberative governance structures that help public and private actors learn from and monitor one another, not simply divide them. In this view, sociopolitical networks cause institution building and asset reorganization to be two intertwined experimental processes.

Return for a moment to the cases of the Škoda and TST networks. State actors simply defining their own new rules of the game or enforcing agreements made solely by private actors did not advance restructuring. Rather, government agencies helped resolve restructuring conflicts initially by delegating authority to certain network actors, bearing some of the financial risk, and sponsoring structured deliberations among the parties. Akin to workout procedures in the West, these government-backed negotiations helped network members to share information and risk with one another. At the same time, state actors began to learn from their own policy experiments what roles they could play in fostering innovation and growth. As joint control over assets remained, iterative deliberations between representatives of public agencies and the distinct networks of firms defined the rules of economic governance and the role of the state.

Clearly, in this realm of joint control and frequent negotiation, the opportunities for adverse selection, moral hazard, and outright collusion are present. Indeed, the Škoda and TST firms have followed an all-too-familiar pattern of industrial restructuring in postcommunist countries: near collapse, collaborative restructuring through state-backed negotiations, state withdrawal, self-dealing, and renewed state intervention. But these threats have been present in the evolution of a variety of public-private institutions in advanced industrialized countries that aid firm reorganizations, limit systemic financial risk, and promote innovation and investment.[12] Simply assuming away the public-private realm will not aid us in the study of transformations. Rather, specification of the social and political forces underpinning asset restructuring can aid one to determine the conditions of self-dealing, mismanagement, or productive collaboration.

In the rest of this chapter, I develop my argument about the impact of sociopolitical networks on restructuring strategies and institution building. I assess the main approaches used to explain the formation of economic governance orders in postcommunist countries and particularly the Czech Republic. I then discuss my own argument in detail. Finally, I outline the structure of the book and the key findings of subsequent chapters. In this book, I refer often to the development of economic *governance orders*. By this term, I mean the particular constellations of institutional rules, norms, and resources that help public and private organizations divide risk and asset control, coordinate transactions, monitor economic activity, and provide dependable methods of conflict resolution. This definition goes beyond the level of *firm* to capture the development of the rules and norms that govern a particular firm or bank as well as the relationships between different actors—firms, financial entities, and government agencies.[13]

Explaining Institutional Change in Postcommunist Transformations

Discontinuity and the Importance of Depoliticization

Much of the debate about institutional and economic transformation in general, and in East Central Europe in particular, has centered around two apparently contrasting theories of economic development. Advocates of economistic/property rights theories argue that the decline of communism is largely due to the cancerous bargaining relationship between firms and the protectionist state. Only when this umbilical cord is cut by the rapid withdrawal of the state from the economy, the liberalization of markets, and, especially, the mass privatization of assets, will firm managers be disciplined by private owners and creditors, assets restructured, and resources invested.[14] Advocates of developmental statist theories argue, in contrast, that since postcommunist societies are late-developers, markets are too weak and lack an entrepreneurial class to organize the necessary investments for restructuring. In turn, the state, with its superior control of resources and information, must intervene strategically with a rule-based industrial policy.[15]

Although these two theories appear to differ radically about what particular economic policies transforming countries should pursue, they share a common understanding of communism and a common approach to building new governance orders. These theories view a communist country as essentially comprised of a unified Party-state hierarchy commanding atomized firms or individuals.[16] Transformations are moments of profound discontinuity—a leap from one complete set of organizing principles to another, in which the state alone can define and impose a new set of institutions upon a tabula rasa of atomized, self-interested actors.[17] Politics here is limited simply to whether the state has the will, power, and autonomy to enact the so-called right set of rules and incentives that guide economic actors toward restructuring and that gain their acceptance for consolidating the new order.[18] With these assumptions, approaches stressing discontinuous change can maintain the idea that institutional creation and restructuring are and should be depoliticized affairs—processes that require virtually no serious discussions between state and societal actors about how to create and revise the rules of economic governance.[19]

The proponents of property rights and developmental statist theories embody this approach of discontinuity and depoliticization in two critical ways. First, both theories emphasize the importance of creating an insulated and powerful policy-making state apparatus that cuts off rent-seeking actors from infecting the design of the new rules. The economistic approach is most explicit in the aim of depoliticization.[20] Its proponents advocate the consolidation of power into a team of reformers, such as a special agency to privatize assets that has the legal powers to design and implement the new rules without the interference of politicians, special interests, and distributional coalitions.[21] The liberalization of prices and trade, rapid divestment of state ownership, and the creation of a system of private property eliminate the further possibility of state and private actors bargaining over allocation of resources and favors. Statists are no less sanguine about the depoliticization strategy.[22] But to limit capture by entrenched interests, the state must create a powerful, disciplined, and internally coherent policy apparatus that is buffered from society to design and implement clear, rule-based policies that help finance restructuring.[23]

Second, the immediate implementation of clear new rules supposedly provides the incentives for complete, technical solutions to restructuring conflicts. That is, the new institutions are sufficient to resolve restructuring conflicts and promote investment in such a way that social and economic actors will not need to engage government actors to revise the baseline rules and incentives for economic governance. For instance, economists such as Boycko, Shleifer, and Vishny, as well as lawyers such as Frydman and Rapaczynski, argue that after private property rights are delineated and a legal framework established, self-interested stakeholders to assets, such as managers, workers, local governments, and banks, will resolve restructuring and investment conflicts through typical complete contract methods, such as buyouts, foreclosure of delinquent debtors, and switching of suppliers and customers.[24] For statists, industrial or financial assistance policies may include more institutional details, but at the limit the constituent rules and incentives are set by state actors and imposed on private actors. For instance, the work of Amsden and her collaborators shows how the state should discipline capital and facilitate investment by designing subsidy incentive contracts with banks and firms.[25] The rules and incentives of an industrial policy are defined a priori by state actors and according to a country's place on the path of technological development. The industrial policy and the design of the attendant governance orders, in turn, become a complete, clearly enforceable contract, which needs no revision through negotiations between societal and state actors.[26]

For those emphasizing discontinuity and urging state-imposed, depoliticized transformation, the Czech Republic was a textbook case.[27] In contrast to the regimes in Hungary and Poland, the communist Czechoslovak regime was one of the most orthodox in the region since the repression of Prague Spring and had barely experimented with market-oriented reforms. The communists left the country with a relatively stable macroeconomy, low budget and trade deficits, virtually no organized social or political groups, and a state with full ownership of over 96 percent of assets. Vaclav Klaus took advantage of these starting conditions and led three post-1989 governments to implement policies of rapid liberalization, stabilization, and mass privatization.[28] To limit the blocking power and rent seeking of entrenched interests, the Czechs eliminated veto powers of labor councils, slashed bureaucracy, and organized a disciplined, coherent, insulated team of state technocrats to control policy. This state apparatus, centered on the Ministries of Privatization and Finance and the Fund for National Property (a special state organ for the administration of assets to be privatized), was guided by clear laws and deadlines. By most measures, it effectively and quickly privatized over 1,800 firms, liberalized prices, cut off subsidies, established clear laws, and created independent banks.[29] Mass privatization combined give-aways (vouchers) and foreign direct investment (FDI) with incentives for banks, mutual funds, and foreign investors to become active agents of industrial restructuring. The state apparatus also set special rules for FDI and bankruptcy, targeted well-defined debt write-downs, and promoted the break-up of large firms to invigorate further restructuring and investment.

Given the ability of the Czechs to design and implement such policies, the subsequent restructuring stalemates, financial crises, and policy reversals, however, undercut the depoliticization approach.[30] First, the legal and financial incentives failed to induce industrial restructuring. Despite the delineation of ownership and a legal framework, firms and banks refused to settle disputes through buyouts, break-ups, and foreclosures. Instead, an intractable stalemate emerged between creditors and debtors, owners and managers, and suppliers and customers. Even when the state provided direct incentives and financing to promote the break-up of large firms, bankruptcy, and bank-led restructuring, the firms and banks virtually ignored these actions. These recurring stalemates threatened the stability of the Czech financial system in 1992–93 and again in 1996, forcing the Czech government to reverse policy and collaborate with distinct groups of firms and banks to resolve the impasses.

Consequently, a second and perhaps more troubling aspect of the Czech case for the advocates of depoliticization is that certain firms and their creditors made significant advances in reorganizing production and debts despite the fact that state boundaries and ownership rights remained blurred. From engineering to steel to truck and aircraft manufacturing, stalemates were broken as government organs shared asset control and risk with distinct groups of banks and firms.[31] Rather than impose an ownership or restructuring design, the Czech government became both a financial partner and conflict mediator with the parties to facilitate negotiated solutions. The parties, including the government agencies, frequently traded control rights and responsibilities and, in turn, revised original privatization plans and cooperation agreements.

Historical Continuity and the Path Dependence of Communist-Era Social Structures

A second dominant approach for analyzing the transformation of institutions begins with the sound observation that the countries of East Central Europe are not generic tabulae rasae. Rather, these countries have different histories of institutional development that grew out of distinctive organizational sources of power and norms. These legacies of political and social structures continue to determine policy choices and institutional paths of countries during the transformation period.[32]

The recent work of David Stark and his collaborators is probably the most prominent in applying this approach to the issues of economic governance and restructuring in the region.[33] They argue that the different paths of property reform between East Central European countries are determined by the different paths of extrication from the former communist regimes and the different attributes of social networks of firm-level actors created under communism. The Czech's ability to impose strict macroeconomic reforms and rapid privatization is a product of the capitulation of the Czechoslovak communists in 1989 and the utter lack of institutions of civil society due to the repressive policies of the earlier regime. The relatively strong meso-level economic networks under communism were the foundations for complex webs of cross-ownership and cross-lending among new large investment funds (IPCs) and the main Czech banks. While these ties helped spread risk for needed organizational experiments, they possessed inherited norms of reciprocity and associationalism that enabled the IPCs and banks to coordinate their actions and govern firms. Indeed, Stark and Bruszt use the Czech case as the prime example where network relationships have been best preserved and translated into sound formal governance institutions writ large by a responsive government.

This approach is extremely useful in moving the starting point of analysis from simplifications about atomized actors to the complex social structures left by communism. It directs comparative analysis away from the use of idealized images of modern capitalism as benchmarks for reform to the use of mid-range analytical categories that help highlight the distinctive patterns of economic organization created during transformation. For instance, Stark's work on the continuing embeddedness of firms in communist-era socioeconomic networks helps explain why privatization did not lead Czech firms to pursue plant closures, break-ups, and bankruptcies. Because of the use of mid-level industrial associations and endemic shortages during communism, distinct groups of Czech firms inherited tight production and financial interdependencies. The interdependencies made it too risky for a single firm to suddenly foreclose on one of its few customers or break relations with one of its only potential collaborators for product development. In turn, Stark's work also suggests that these interdependencies would shape initial firm privatization strategies and the emergence of new governance structures, perhaps more so than technological or sectoral factors would.[34] Czech industry indeed shows two different patterns of strategy and resulting governance orders. One pattern that led to state-backed holding companies can be found across the Czech engineering, steel, and truck and aircraft manufacturing sectors. Moreover, within the Czech mechanical engineering sector, one finds not only the holding company model but also an alternative model of an indirectly state-supported network of small and medium-sized firms. These two models are exemplified by the groups of firms associated with the communist-era *koncerns*, Škoda Plzeň and TST, respectively.[35]

On the other hand, Stark's emphasis on the stability of reproduced social structures and attendant norms of reciprocity fails to help us explain why the Czech industrial networks often radically changed their composition and needed government assistance to resolve internal conflicts. For instance, in all the holding company models, regardless of their sector, and especially in the cases of Škoda and TST, interlinked firms and banks were unable to cooperate over restructuring but required government agencies to help them create new rules of asset control and risk sharing. This combination of conflicts and government intervention substantially changed the authority structures and organization of such long-standing manufacturing networks as the ones associated with Škoda and TST.

Such analytical limitations of the continuity approach become even more evident when one examines more closely its own assessment of the Czech case. First, in stressing the enabling social relationships of past networks, Stark's analysis of Czech IPCs and banks tends to portray associative ties as being fully reproduced during transformation and sufficient for governing economic activity. This appearance of stable, self-governing or self-correcting social groups is quite common in much of economic sociology, and adherents resort often to using vague concepts such as *adaptive fitness* to explain the selection of particular strategies or governance rules.[36] As a result, Stark's own analysis lacks discussions of intranetwork conflict, and he must avoid completely the critical issue of how firms select within a set of restructuring strategies.[37] Moreover, if reproduced, long-term social ties were sufficient to guide restructuring, we would expect that the IPCs and their banks would have been able to overcome collective-action problems on their own and would have invested into the corporate governance and restructuring of complex cases, such as in manufacturing. But as in the cases of Czech industrial networks, the evidence to date shows that Czech IPCs failed to invest, severely mismanaged firms and banks, and, in some instances, engaged in corrupt asset stripping.[38] Then the question becomes not whether networks are reproducing themselves but how reproduction occurs to make networks more likely to produce socially beneficial restructuring or wholesale corruption.

A second explanatory dilemma for Stark and his collaborators is common to the utilization of path dependency analysis—a disjunction between the causes of change and continuity.[39] Stark and Bruszt argue that restructuring via networks is optimal when societies construct "deliberative associations," which are institutional forms that facilitate accountability, longer-term strategies, and risk sharing. For them, the Czech case stands out as one in which deliberative associations are strongest because autonomous political institutions constrain the arbitrariness of executive power.[40] While I am sympathetic to such arguments, as I will show, Stark and Bruszt have difficulty using networks and path dependency to demonstrate how such institutions may come about. On the one hand, they argue that the constrained executive was a consequence of the continued use of the Czechoslovak constitution and the breakup of the political movement Civic Forum. On the other hand, their path dependent analysis of the adoption of the voucher method of mass privatization points to a strong, independent policy-making apparatus and a weak civil society.[41]

The common weakness of both the tabula rasa/depoliticization approach and the continuity approach leads to a theoretical point of departure to connect aspects of continuity and change in the analysis of institutional development in postcommunist countries. Both approaches tend to treat micro-level social structures and macro-level political changes as mutually exclusive.[42] For instance, in the models advocating depoliticization, the creation of the so-called right institutional rules is determined by the political will and the power of the elite change teams. In approaches stressing continuity and path dependence, the continuing impact of past social structures appears disconnected from changes in political institutions and policy.[43] We are left with transformation approaches that focus mainly on the state or on society, taking as given the less emphasized variable. Hence, the failure to show how macropolitical and microsocial forces can mutually influence one another ends up depicting transformations as solely epochal changes or reproductions of old structures.

An Embedded Politics Approach

In my alternative approach to institutional development, I attempt to capture the interaction between micro- and macro-level political economic factors by emphasizing how firms are embedded in *ongoing social and political relations* both during and after communism. Rather than focusing mainly on the central state or on the socioeconomic structures, I focus on the political and social space that blended the bureaucratic and economic domains during communism and becomes the staging ground for institutional construction during transformation. Within this space, one identifies distinct sociopolitical networks of firms, regional state bank branches, and regional Party council actors that emerged during communism. During the transformation period, these networks are the raw materials that can shape action and decision-making power and can be reshaped by conflicts and their resolutions.

Using sociopolitical networks helps one define the nature of restructuring conflicts and the conditions of the bargaining between certain public and private institutional actors to resolve these conflicts. The specific patterns of conflicts and their negotiated resolutions produce new economic governance orders—the rules of asset control and risk sharing and the distribution of resources. For instance, network ties constitute channels of power, resources, and communication that mediate relations between particular economic and political actors. They define the key parties to certain assets, endow them with variety of roles, resources, and worldviews, and highlight the points of common and potentially conflicting interests. But the power and interests of constituent network actors are not fixed, since the political alliances constructed between constituent economic actors and local public officials during communism helped define the network authority structure. As interlinked plants and firms initiated conflicting restructuring strategies during transformation, attempts by new political leaders to replace communist political-economic institutions with new ones threw the authority structures into flux and inhibited intranetwork cooperation.[44] A reconstitution of the rules governing assets becomes, in turn, a political project of government agencies resolving the conflicts among the interlinked firms and banks over control of assets.[45] By analyzing the formation of different networks and their divergent patterns of conflict and resolution, one can then account for the way public authority and resources are used by actors, how public and private monitoring rules become cocreated, and why different governance orders can emerge within a single national or industrial setting.

By attempting to connect political and social factors, this approach in part draws on the work of Karl Polanyi, who emphasized both the embeddedness of economic activity in society and the roles of high politics and the state in constructing the institutional conditions of economic development.[46] But an embedded politics approach departs from Polanyi in his understanding that the construction of market institutions necessarily destroys the social fabric, which the state must replace as the principle motivation of regulation.[47] If institutions can be both embedded in society and the product of politics, then they are the vehicles of governance and the transmission of resources and information between that which is public and private. By focusing on the sociopolitical networks that occupy this public-private space, one can begin to determine the role of the state and the definition of institutions not so much according to efforts that mitigate market failures but, rather, according to efforts to mitigate the failures of inherited sociopolitical relations to resolve the new conflicts of restructuring. New institutions are not created simply by state designs or by state validation of previous network structures. Rather, new roles for government agencies and economic actors are created simultaneously by the way these agencies attempt to resolve intranetwork restructuring conflicts and directly help network members create new rules for their economic governance. In other words, institutions emerge through the efforts of public and private actors to reconstruct politically the social fabric vital for economic activity.

Thus, rather than focusing exclusively on factors of structural change or inertia, my embedded politics approach attempts to clarify how these factors mutually influence one another at the micro and macro levels of analysis. In doing so, I present a framework for the study of institutional development that is less concerned with "critical junctures" or "lock-in effects" and more concerned with the way that economic institutions are socially and politically constructed and reconstructed through an evolution of organizational and governance experiments.[48] In this view, actors are strategic in the sense that they consciously try to bend the structural and institutional constraints that they confront.[49] Strategy is an experimental process of recombining their inherited organizational and political resources in different ways so as to hedge the uncertainties of their means and ends during periods of more or less malleability. The eventual selection of a limited number of production and organizational experiments, and thus the implicit rules that govern them, occurs through the conflicts between network actors over their competing strategies to control assets and the ways that government agencies align themselves to pursue a negotiated resolution.

The Network Properties of Assets
and the Politics of Institution Building

Actual historical experience of the development of most institutions and business organizations often defies the analytical concepts of punctuated disequilibria, lock-in effects, or wholesale replacement.[50] This has led scholars from such diverse schools of thought as rational choice, strategic choice, and historical institutionalism to call for greater emphasis on the sociopolitical roots of the cognitive frameworks and bargaining power of actors.[51] In this regard, the Czech Republic is a case in point. Those promoting the depoliticization agenda and those apparently entrenched in the former regime both eventually pursued negotiated solutions that transformed initial institutional designs, organizational forms, and the distribution of public and private authority. How does an embedded politics approach help identify the sources of continuity and change in the strategic choices and power of both political and economic actors? And how can it clarify the bargaining conditions for these actors? To answer these questions, I will first outline my definitions of *embeddeness* and *sociopolitical networks*. This discussion will then lead to an illustration of how these concepts can help one capture the interaction between the macropolitics of state designs and the micropolitics of interfirm restructuring conflicts.

Defining the Network Properties of Assets

In the 1980s, scholars identified two major processes that opened a political and social space between the state and private society within the rigidities of centrally commanded hierarchies of communist political economies (CPEs).[52] One was bureaucratization through accommodation.[53] Following the turbulence of the late 1960s, communist officials attempted in different ways to reassert the political primacy of communism and reorganize the economy. To enact these experiments, central authorities depended on subordinates with local knowledge and granted them greater autonomy to enlist the cooperation of other societal actors. At the level of execution, formally distinct vertical command structures, such as regional administration and industrial planning, overlapped.[54] Such actors as firm managers and local Party officials held potentially conflicting roles agents of the center and mediators of local or sectoral interests.[55] The effect of shortage economy was the other major process that helped open a political and social space between the state and private society during communism.[56] Shortages in factor markets and rigidities of the bureaucratic rules led firms and regions to become self-sufficient and, thus, created tight interdependencies between managers and work groups, customers and suppliers, as well as firms and Party councils. These actors created extensive informal relationships and rules of reciprocity to coordinate bargaining within firms, with the planning center, and with other regions and industrial conglomerates.[57] As distinct constellations of vertical and horizontal ties emerged to form quasi-autonomous domains, actors introduced unofficial ideas and organizational initiatives into their daily routines.[58] In turn, formal institutional structures and policies could take on a variety of uses and thus be transformed.[59]

Although this pathbreaking research mainly focused on more liberal CPEs, like Poland and Hungary, recent research reveals that formal and informal attempts to adapt the ineffective institutional structures guiding the economy were taking place in such orthodox communist countries as the German Democratic Republic (GDR), the USSR, and communist Czechoslovakia (ČSSR).[60] Following the suppression of Prague Spring, ČSSR Party-state officials sought to improve productivity and return social and political order to the economy through a series of financial and industrial planning experiments that focused on increased use of industrial associations (výrobní hospodářské jednotky, or VHJs)—meso-level planning structures that managed particular industrial sectors.[61] The use of VHJs had grown out of an ongoing debate since 1956 about the inadequacies of orthodox Soviet-type directive planning for the ČSSR with its own historical forms industrial organization. I argue that VHJs became the centers of durable and distinct sociopolitical networks that merged formal institutions with informal rules and norms of economic coordination and conflict mediation.

VHJs integrated firms with related production to increase technological synergies and decrease the number of unfilled interfirm orders. As VHJ directorates gained greater responsibilities to guide production, firms gained greater independence from the state. At the same time, territorial administrative reforms effectively brought vocational training, housing, health care under the comanagement of VHJ managers and regional Party officials.[62] To meet the central directives, the VHJ director had to balance the needs of the plan, of its constituent firms, and of the Party councils. This balance, in turn the changing constellation of political and social ties, allowed legally similar VHJs to forge distinctly different patterns of bargaining channels, economic organization, rules, and authority within the VHJ and between the VHJ and the state and Party organs.

I am not able to capture and quantify each VHJ network arrangement. By 1985, for instance, there were 71 VHJs encompassing 542 firms and over 1.6 million employees under ČSSR federal ministries for engineering, steel, and electronics. But from my own field research on industrial adjustment in the Czech engineering, steel, and aircraft industries, I have derived two

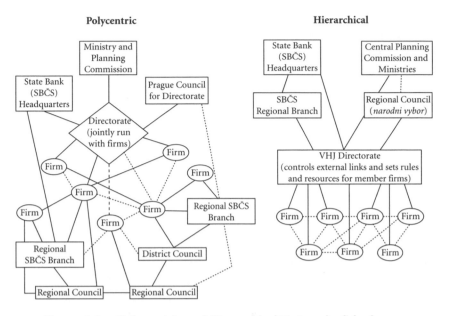

Figure 1.1.   Polycentric and Hierarchical Networks (ideal types of VHJ networks)

Note: Solid lines denote strong channels of communication and coordination; broken lines denote weak channels.

ideal-typical arrangements—hierarchical and polycentric.[63] These ideal types help us to organize what may initially appear to be an endless variety of network arrangements and to illustrate how particular contextual features and ongoing sociopolitical relationships shape restructuring conflicts in distinct ways. These types of VHJ networks have both unusually broad upstream and downstream production capabilities as well as financial and technical interdependencies between the *core members*—VHJ directorate, firms, and plants. Certain core members constructed bargaining channels with *external members*—particular regional and district Party councils and central bank branches—to share the economic and political risks of maintaining autarky and redundancy as well as create a reliable internal authority structure.[64] That is, the relationships with external members provided certain core members with economic and political resources to limit direct intervention of central state authorities and to bolster their bargaining power with both other core VHJ members and central bureaucrats.

The VHJ networks differ, however, in their traditions of production, nodes of power, distribution of informal decision-making rights, and strength of bargaining channels within VHJs and between VHJs and regional Party councils and bank branches. Figure 1.1 depicts these differences for the ideal-typical networks. In hierarchical networks, decision-making power is concentrated largely in the hands of the VHJ directorate and lead firm. This power is mainly derived from the ability of the directorate and the lead firm to monopolize political and economic relations with the regional bank branch and Party council. While the lead firm's tradition of tight vertical and horizontal integration creates tight production linkages among other member firms and plants, the latter bargain with one another within the terms set by the directorate and lead firm. In contrast, the member firms of a polycentric network have greater decision-making and financial autonomy and reach decisions with one another and the VHJ directorate largely through consensus. Member firms also have mainly horizontal production relationships. This more decentralized authority structure is largely derived from the ability of several member firms to develop direct links to regional bank branches and regional and district administrative-Communist party councils.

This view of embeddedness is not unique to the former Czechoslovakia. It also reflects recent research on advanced industrialized countries and other Communist bloc countries that demonstrate how social and political relationships constructed within regions and past industrial associations continue to shape the creation of business organizations, restructuring strategies, and financial institutions.[65] Networks have qualitative features and patterns of interaction that can distinctively shape the way members perceive government policy and resolve production and restructuring problems.[66] Administrative and industrial planning experiments during communism allowed key elements of property rights to devolve into distinct networks of firm, bank, and local actors. As actors try to reproduce these relationships in the period of transformation, they have with them the ability to reshape the new official institutional order proposed by the state, even if they do not block state policies outright.

In this view, the *unit of analysis* of economic activity and institutional renovation in the Czech Republic is the distinct former VHJ network that continues to mediate between firms and between the market and the state.[67] Members are bound together by tight financial and production links and the sociopolitical bargaining capital (e.g., inherited decision-making authority, control over resources, and perceived legitimacy) that lubricated the flow of resources. Even if members conflict over restructuring strategies, individual discretion is constrained by economic interdependencies—such as subcontracting, joint production programs, and intertangled debts—and the ongoing sociopolitical relationships that define the authority to change the rules governing the use and recombination of assets.

The relational and structural features of former VHJ networks help then to identify the principal factors of continuity and change in the restructuring and reorganization assets. First, both the *value of assets* and the *rules and rights governing their use* are bound up in the inherited social and economic ties. In as nascent and highly concentrated a market as the Czech Republic, the constituent firms, plants, and banks of a network are mutual suppliers and customers, creditors and debtors. Their mutual cooperation underpins the restructuring of liabilities and the reorganization of production and, hence, the value of assets. These are also the same actors, with whom one must negotiate to reorder the new rules and rights over assets. Thus, the renovation of firms and banks and the defining of property rights are simultaneous.

Second, the ability of network members to cooperate voluntarily or by the force of a few is uncertain because these networks can not be reduced to an individual resource or a holistic group. Within networks, core members are torn between the need to cooperate and the pursuit of individual restructuring strategies; the bargaining and economic strengths of members are derived from both the cohesion of the group as a whole and one's position in the group. The strength and goals of the network and the individual members then are bound together but in potential conflict. With new uncertainties and opportunities, reawakened aspirations for individual autonomy and conflicting visions of future production specializations clash with inherited social and economic links that bind the network actors together. For instance, new economic uncertainties brought on by liberalization and privatization can alter the importance of a particular supplier or customer. Moreover, the uncertainties on the return of a particular restructuring strategy undermine the ability of interlinked firms to cooperate via standard contractual methods, such as effort-reward provisions, side payments, or buyouts.[68]

Some scholars on networks and institutional creation would argue at this point that continuity would win the day. The preexisting social capital of former VHJ networks would mitigate new conflicts. The norms of reciprocity or the distribution of resources constitutive of past social structures and relations would directly determine the new bargaining outcomes and new rules of governance.[69] Change is minimal because social structures with long histories are largely self-governing or self-correcting and are viewed as autonomous from the political environment.

In contrast, my embedded politics approach highlights a third, political, aspect of past networks that is a source of change in both the bargaining conditions and potential for cooperation among interlinked actors. The political constructionist view emphasized in my approach takes into account the authority structure and relationships of a network as being constructed through alliances with public officials and thus subject to change under new political contexts.[70] For instance, conflicts within former VHJs over the distribution of resources and production strategies arose frequently from the uncertainties of shortage and new demands of the planning system. But their resolution was based on an informal system of bargaining rules and the distribution of power. Power and the authority structure of VHJ networks were derived not only from one's position a key parts supplier or final assembler but also from the alliances made by certain core members with regional and district councils and state bank branches. The dismantling of the communist political and economic structures dissolves these past alliances. For instance, in the Czech Republic, firms often lost their authority and access to resources when the centralization of policy-making power virtually eliminated regional and local councils and when the rapid privatization of banks and the new financial regulations gave the banks little incentive to finance restructuring. The stress here is also, although not solely, on the role of politics in shaping interests, tactics, and the power to realize them.[71]

To sum up, the tensions created by the joint control of network assets—between the need to cooperate and the distribution of power and resources that impedes cooperation, between the restructuring needs to maintain common production programs and the contrasting visions of each member about recombining assets—make the loyalties, interests, and goals of both the network as a whole and each member a priori indeterminate. The inherited sociopolitical relationships and structures give actors worldviews and resources that help them define possible courses of actions. But intranetwork fights, in the face of new privatization and economic policies, redefine goals and strategies and redistribute asset control. At the same time, organs of the communist system that once informally supported the network authority structure are eliminated.

Two Levels of Politics Defining Worldviews and Governance Orders

Earlier I described how the Czech government stood out among its neighbors in effectively implementing the depoliticization approach. This approach, however, led to a series of financial crises that forced the government to change course and pursue negotiated solutions to restructuring firms. As a result, the Czech government became a partner to distinct groups of firms and banks in creating new public-private governance orders that differed from one another according to their definitions of firms boundaries, the rules of asset control, and the roles of specific government agencies, firms, and financial institutions. An embedded politics approach can begin to make sense of these changes and their implications for institution building by highlighting first how the depoliticization agenda can undermine the resolution of restructuring conflicts.

Consider the debate over privatization, which has been central to policies for redefining the boundaries between the public and the private as well as the creation of new institutions for economic governance.

A political commitment to privatization means a commitment to two related goals: the delineation of private ownership and the guarantee that the assets to be transferred have value. The latter goal is often implicit but no less salient. Otherwise, private recipients would receive useless assets, and popular support for transformation would collapse.

The economistic/property rights view emphasizes that the rapid delineation of property rights will allow firms and banks to resolve restructuring conflicts via standard complete contractual means, such as effort-reward agreements, buyouts, and liquidation of problem debtors and loss makers. The developmental statist view emphasizes, in contrast, that asset value must first be supported by the state because market signals and private contractual regimes are too weak. Therefore, the state must provide investment and restructuring incentives via another form of complete contract—a clear, rule-based financial-assistance program to banks and firms that the state defines and monitors on its own. Although these two views conflict about whether governments should restructure assets or delineate property rights first, they share a common view that building asset value and clarifying private property rights are mutually exclusive issues that can be addressed separately at both the levels of public policy and firm strategy. This assumption is closely wedded to the common depoliticization approach they share. For instance, for both theories, institution building and restructuring policy are reduced to single legislative acts and decrees to define and transfer private ownership and creditor rights, to set financial and legal incentives for banks and foreign investors to lead restructuring, and so on. The state can then maintain its autonomy from society and avoid negotiations with private actors about defining and revising governance rules and restructuring criteria.

The previous discussion about the network properties of assets gives a contrasting perspective. First, the building of asset value and the clarification of property rights are interdependent and simultaneous. That is, the preservation of asset value depends on the ability of the network actors to cooperate, which demands that the actors periodically reorder the rules of asset use and risk sharing through negotiated incomplete contracts.

Second, building asset value and utilizing private property rights are in potential conflict. For instance, the main Czech commercial banks attempted to clean their portfolios (i.e., asserted their rights as independent creditors to punish debtors) but also had to maintain troubled industrial firms as their future client base. Firms and plants tried to assert their autonomy and pursue new production experiments to gain new market niches and cash flow, but they could not ignore the potentially conflicting financial and production needs of their few collaborators involved in their own experiments or existing joint programs.

Third, private workouts of these conflicts are not forthcoming but, rather, holdups abound. The many financial uncertainties for a restructuring project inhibits the ability of a network firm to give credible guarantees to another firm or an outside financier, be they for a joint production project or a buyout. Past social capital, say, of the former VHJ networks fails to mediate the conflicts since, as discussed previously, the change in financial regulations and the elimination of regional and local councils altered the authority structure of networks. Reliance on the courts is fraught with delays, if not corruption, as much research has shown.[72] A potential solution is a government-organized workout regime akin to Chapter 11 that ties financial and operational restructuring together with a renegotiation of property rights. But such a scheme, like the Enterprise-Bank Restructuring Program launched in Poland in 1993, demands that the government become an extended partner to certain firms and banks in sharing risk, adjudicating conflicts among the parties, and monitoring their agreements. This would violate the principle of a clear boundary between state and society that is paramount to the depoliticization approach. Moreover, any notion of subnational governments playing such a role, as was also the case in Poland, does not exist. The centralization of power into an insulated state apparatus effectively removes local or regional public organs, as in the Czech case, from playing any new version of their traditional role as providers of financial and political capital to mediate restructuring disputes among network actors. In turn, deadlocks can then ensue, assets sit idle, and value drops potentially to the point that all connected parties will crash.

From an embedded politics point of view, then, one would expect that a government's pursuit of the depoliticization approach would exacerbate intranetwork conflicts and lead to stalemates. In attempting to centralize power and cut itself off from society, the Czech government effectively removed traditional public organs from aiding restructuring disputes. In addressing the issues of creating asset value and clarifying property rights separately to maintain its insulation, the government offered only complete contract resolutions to conflicts. These types of resolutions are antithetical to the sharing of risk and control among internal and potential external network actors. In this view, for instance, the Czech policies to invigorate restructuring and decrease interfirm and bank debt with rule-based, one-time bank recapitalizations and factoring subsidies failed not because of traditional incomplete market problems.[73] Rather, they failed because simply the injection of new funds did not help banks and interlinked firms jointly repair the inherited authority structures that underpinned their ability to cooperate and share risk. In short, banks and firms were not about to reveal private information on finances and commit funds to one another without some means to credibly monitor one another.

How then would network firms begin to cooperate if the use of standard contractual methods or past norms is insufficient? An embedded politics approach suggests that they can try to create organizational forms that resemble incomplete contracts—frameworks that allow the parties to agree to some initially broad criteria about restructuring and division of property rights, while clarifying them over time. Such frameworks are not unique to East Central Europe but have been at the heart of current debates on the stability of manufacturing alliances and joint ventures, multiparty product development projects, responsive regulatory regimes, and purposely-vague legal agreements.[74] The difficulty is that such frameworks limit the ability of purely private actors or bright-line laws to support them. To sustain such frameworks, for instance, members of former VHJ networks attempted to reposition themselves and gain new external partners to provide new resources. But the ambiguities of incomplete contracts give private external partners few guarantees to protect their investments.

The question then becomes how a production network obtains outside partners to share risk and help mediate internal disputes. In other words, how can the core and potential external network partners commit resources to restructure jointly controlled assets while gradually clarifying individual property rights and thus bridge the incomplete contracts? In order to fulfill the dual goals of privatization and not face popular unrest, the government would have to violate its tenets of depoliticization and play a key, but new, role here.[75] Because cooperation is central to the value of assets, the government can support value preservation by moving beyond the role of enforcer of private contracts or the role of a first mover that injects cash or leads debt write-offs.[76] Rather, the government can become: (1) a mediator to forge compromises over the definition of control rights and restructuring strategies and (2) a financial partner to show its commitment to both network actors and outside private investors.

Therefore, an embedded politics view argues that sustainable restructuring demands that network actors utilize organizational forms that resemble incomplete contracts, which requires third-party (government) mediation and finance. Such actions foster negotiations with both government agencies and networked firms about rewriting the rules of asset use and risk sharing. These negotiations are dynamic and may not define completely all aspects of new governance institutions. Rather, they indicate the directions to which the roles of public and private actors, the rules of governance, and the organization of production and finance are heading.[77]

The recent research on development and industrial adjustment shows that delegation with deliberation includes the roles just mentioned and is distinct from pure ownership and state-imposed solutions in two ways.[78] First, the private parties receive partial control rights and restructuring authority, and the government holds them accountable for their actions. Linking the delegation of authority with general agreements on compensation and risk sharing makes the government a sponsor and participant in structured deliberations over the definition of control rights and restructuring strategies. This dual process of delegation and deliberation forces the private parties to demonstrate concrete results and to account for difficulties in meeting them. In doing so, they reveal information to one another as well as points of further negotiation and problem solving. The private parties and the government monitor one another as well as trade control rights and risk.

Second, although the delegation agreement has blurred property rights, it is in no way under the complete discretion of the government. To maintain its own bargaining credibility, the government allows the private parties to improvise on the agreement and makes itself more accountable. As a partner and mediator, the government can be subjected to continual scrutiny by the delegates so that they are treated fairly—together and separately.

In this role, the government, as the seller of and an inherent party to the assets, helps bridge the incomplete contracts by using its public authority to foster structured deliberations among the network actors—deliberations that fuse the defining of property rights with the risks and benefits of restructuring.[79] In the Czech case, stalemates were gradually broken as the fights between the Czech government organs, banks, and groups of firms and plants turned into forums, in which these parties continually negotiated over the division of control rights, financing, debt reduction, and product development. Such political compromises in many ways reversed Czech government policy and set the foundations for new patterns of government-supported governance orders. Deliberations broke down the forced boundaries between government and private actors, allowing the initial designs of governance institutions to be rewritten.

However, because networks play such a critical role in this process, the different structures, substance, and histories between networks can give rise to distinct patterns of conflict and resolution. In other words, the specific conditions of the government's participation in negotiated solutions—the ground rules, the use of force or compromise, and its recognition of worthy bargaining partners—are the products of the different patterns of intranetwork struggles for asset control. For instance, in chapters 4 and 5, I will show how within the mechanical engineering sector inherited hierarchical and polycentric networks shaped the initial strategies of members, subsequent patterns of conflict, and conditions of resolution in different ways. These conditions included the identification and roles of public and private participants, the issues of bargaining, and the relative bargaining powers of participants. The results were new, divergent sets of rules of asset control and risk sharing for both government agencies and network actors.

Notice that the embedded politics approach presented here is attempting to specify the points where government agencies must re-engage economic actors. In doing so, it helps clarify which agencies will take the lead on negotiations. The likely candidates are those that are most closely positioned to the nexus point of the network and those that can begin to provide the social and political capital necessary to reconstruct the authority structure of the network at the moment when the intranetwork conflicts externalize into systemic financial crisis. This approach also helps clarify the way new public-private governance rules get constructed—through delegation and deliberation that open rule making and role making to the ongoing social structures and organizational experiments within distinct networks.

Notice also that the dual learning processes between government agencies and interlinked banks and firms are constrained by two factors. Ideally, government agencies are learning which rules they should adopt to adequately monitor network actors and facilitate restructuring, while the network actors are learning which governance and reorganization strategies they should follow. But the delegation of partial authority to specific network actors constitutes public legitimacy and thus added power for the delegate to influence the negotiating processes both with the government agencies and with other network members.[80] Thus, although deliberative governance structures can improve monitoring, the political impact of designating a particular actor as a restructuring delegate can limit the extent to which that actor can be punished or simply thrown out of the game.

Moreover, since deliberation is the main mechanism to fuse monitoring and learning for both public and private actors, impediments to the government agencies becoming more indirect, though active, interlocutors would degrade accountability, information flows, and trust building.[81] Government agencies need to learn from their various projects with different industrial networks to adjust policies and establish more generalized means of monitoring or assisting restructuring and institutional development. Clearly, continued adherence to a tightly centralized state and political system could block resources for and voices of alternative restructuring projects, such as those initiated by local government or opposition parties. If the preoccupation with centralized government is not confronted directly, then typical problems like unchecked bureaucratic turf battles and splits in coalitions can easily make the political incentives for a return to concentrated control overwhelming.

Such actions undermine accountability and adaptation, and they make conditions ripe for self-dealing, corruption, state capture, and organizational and production lock-in effects.

An Empirical Application of the Embedded Politics Approach

In the remainder of this book, I analyze in detail the evolution and impact of industrial networks on the formation of the institutional orders governing restructuring in the Czech Republic. In using sociopolitical networks as the guiding unit of analysis, the book tells the Czech story from two different angles and during two different time periods.

In chapter 2, I trace in detail the formation and evolution of industrial VHJ networks in the ČSSR, particularly in the mechanical engineering sector (ISIC [International Standard Industrial Classification] 29 and 292). I argue that the peculiarities of Czechoslovak industrialization and planning experiments in the 1970s and 1980s led to distinct meso-level VHJ networks. Throughout the analysis, I compare and contrast the alternative networks of two dominant mechanical engineering VHJs, Škoda Plzeň and TST. They represent the two ideal types—hierarchical and polycentric, respectively—that I outlined earlier in this chapter. In showing the development of these networks and the different ways managers reproduced them, my account of the ČSSR reflects analyses of industrial and political adjustment in Western Europe that treat institutional change as a subtle process of shifting power and responsibilities within the existing framework.[82]

Chapter 3 shifts attention to the current transformation period, and I examine first how the apparently prudent adherence by the Czechs to the standard reform approaches of depoliticization during 1990–92 failed to initiate the restructuring of banks and industrial firms and produced a financial stalemate. Using a network approach, I outline how the Czech policy toward privatization and bank reform failed to help resolve the basic holdup problems common to the issues of debt restructuring, bankruptcy, and investment. In particular, the legal and financial policies left the main banks, equity investment companies, and foreign investors to bear alone the risks of leading the restructuring, breakup, or bankruptcy of firms. As these actors refused such risks and the Klausians refused to alter policy, most of the proposed joint ventures between Czech and foreign industrial firms collapsed in 1992–93.

In chapters 4 and 5, I analyze the restructuring stalemates that led to the crises of 1992–93 and 1996 and their resolutions from the level of the former

VHJ networks. First, I show how the members of inherited networks were unable to resolve on their own their internal conflicts over asset control and production strategies, which in turn prevented them from replacing previous external allies with new private partners. Conflict resolution required multi-party deliberations between network actors and government agencies that defined simultaneously the role of the agencies and the rules of economic governance. Second, I show in these chapters how the two ideal types of inherited networks had contrasting impacts on the formation initial privatization and restructuring strategies and the subsequent conflicts. The combination of government reaction to these conflicts and the different ways the inherited networks conditioned the negotiating power of firms and banks reshaped the networks and led to two distinct, nascent governance orders.

I utilize two sets of cases in these chapters, drawing on a methodology well established in comparative analysis.[83] I formed the structured case studies by examining sectoral and national financial, production, and privatization data and by conducting approximately 200 structured and unstructured interviews with relevant ministerial, bank, and firm managers mainly from 1993 to late 1996. The first set of cases analyzes how one ideal type, the *hierarchical network,* reproduced itself in the form of a holding company and led to a similar pattern of conflict resolutions, state policy reversals, and governance orders across different industries—steel (Poldi), mechanical engineering (Škoda Plzeň), as well as truck (Avia and Liaz) and aircraft (Aero) production. The second set uses matched pairs of divergent, ideal types of network politics and structures—*hierarchical versus polycentric*—within the mechanical engineering sector, the historical backbone of the Czech economy.[84] These ideal types are represented by the former VHJs, Škoda Plzeň, and TST, and allow me to control for alternative explanatory variables, such as technology, unit labor costs, former legal organizational category, and labor union. The demonstration of similarities in restructuring strategies and conflicts across different industries and then the emergence of different governance orders within the same sector helps strengthen my arguments about the role of network politics and control for alternative explanations. The two governance orders differ in terms of their definitions of firm boundaries, methods of subcontracting and debt resolution, division of asset control, monitoring mechanisms, as well as the links to and roles of the main Czech commercial banks and government agencies.

The sixth and concluding chapter has two parts. First, in reviewing the book's main findings, I examine the implications of an embedded politics approach for future research in comparative political economy, namely on institutional change and creation. By emphasizing how sociopolitical networks emerge during the breakdown of old governance institutions and then mediate between private and public actors during the construction of new governance institutions, one can better specify the distribution of power and the conditions of cooperation for industrial adjustment in East Central Europe. Second, I then argue that institutions of deliberation, an often overlooked, but key, component to democracy, are central to the renovation of economies and the creation of effective financial and monitoring structures. The Czech case is contrasted with that of Poland, which appears to have been able to sustain and improve the learning and monitoring capabilities of public actors by allowing both central and regional governments to assist firms and banks in complicated workouts.

Institutional Experiments and the Emergence of Industrial Networks in Communist Czechoslovakia

Beginning in 1948, the central authorities of the Party-state in Soviet-dominated Czechoslovakia (ČSSR) introduced a particular model for the mobilization and control of economic resources. Industry was to be organized according to the principles of mass production and scientific management. The central planning commission would command subordinate, atomized firms and control the use of resources and information through a strict bureaucratic hierarchy. This model, whether fully implemented or not, has largely been accepted by many approaches to institutional transformation as constituting the essential characteristics of Communist Political Economies (CPEs).[1] Comparative analysis of CPEs mainly considered official reforms toward greater political freedoms and use of the market, such as those in Hungary from the late 1960s onward and Poland in the 1980s, as indicators of any type of departure from this model.[2] From this perspective, the ČSSR of the 1980s was a classic CPE. The ČSSR was a heavily industrialized economy with over 96 percent of gross domestic product (GDP) produced by state-owned firms and, especially since the repression of Prague Spring in 1968, had no evidence of dismantling the levers of central planning and control by the Communist party.[3]

In this chapter, I argue that despite its apparent orthodoxy and relatively high level of industrial development, the ČSSR resembled neither a classic mass-production regime nor a classic hierarchy controlling atomized firms or individuals. Rather, the ČSSR is better understood as a complex set of distinct sociopolitical networks, in which actors with often conflicting roles and interests were bound together by both vertical and, more importantly, horizontal ties. The frequent attempts by the ČSSR Party-state to standardize production and improve planning actually allowed for an expanded use of sociopolitical networks to coordinate economic activity and for changes in the institutional composition of the ČSSR without a major shift in or collapse of communist Party-state doctrine. The centerpiece for ČSSR experiments in industrial planning and for the emergence of sociopolitical networks was the development of industrial associations (VHJs).

An analysis of the evolution of VHJs reveals two related aspects of CPEs that have largely been overlooked. First, most models of economic bargaining in CPEs define the interests of managers as ones of investment hunger to grow their firms and maintain prestigious programs.[4] But one finds that managers were equally interested in maintaining autonomy, especially vis-à-vis central authorities. Maintaining autonomy meant that managers would not only seek autarky within their firms and VHJs but also that they would have to develop horizontal ties to other political and economic actors. In turn, analysis of VHJs shows the different patterns of linkages between firms, plants, and the state banks as well as the variation in alliances certain firms had with regional and district Communist party councils. These linkages and alliances allowed VHJ networks to develop highly autarkic and broad production capabilities as well as divergent patterns of power distribution, coordination rules, and sociopolitical bargaining channels. This chapter will focus on two ideal types of industrial networks (hierarchical vs. polycentric) in the ČSSR mechanical engineering industry.

First I set the background for the formation of VHJs and the central role they played in debates and organizational experiments from the 1950s into the 1970s. These debates and experiments centered on the ability of the ČSSR Party-state to develop an efficient mass-production system and maintain political and social control.

Second, I examine one consequence of these experiments. The VHJ organizational principles and the exigencies of ČSSR growth and trade policies undermined the formation of standardized mass production. Firms adapted their traditional methods of universal production to enhance self-sufficiency. Distinct groups of firms developed close production interdependencies and were able to produce a broad range of final goods and parts in relatively small batches, albeit at a substantial economic cost.

Third, I analyze the other main consequence of these experiments. Policies aimed at both improving industrial performance and maintaining Party-state control through VHJs allowed for a de jure and de facto decentralization of decision making as well as the creation of alternative patterns of VHJ networks. Despite the creation of one legal form of VHJs for most industries in 1979–80, the earlier forms of VHJ structures and their varying relationships to the state banks and territorial administrative councils allowed constituent firms and plants to create alternative sets of informal governance rules and vertical and horizontal bargaining channels. The partial decentralization of decision making to bank branches and councils during the 1980s made the different patterns more pronounced, as bank branches and councils became partners with certain VHJ actors for sharing political and financial risk of increasing autarky, limiting central intervention, and maintaining an authority structure within VHJs.

Fourth, I examine the resilience of the VHJ networks after the formal dissolution of the VHJ system in 1987–88. It shows how the different patterns of power distribution and associationalism of the two ideal-type networks shaped the contrasting ways VHJ firms reorganized themselves in the face of new uniform economic and planning laws.

This chapter focuses on the Czech mechanical engineering industry for two reasons. First, as the cornerstone of industrial and military development for the Austro-Hungarian Empire and then as the engine for some of the highest industrial growth rates in Europe during the interwar period, the mechanical engineering industry was at a highly advanced stage of development, especially in comparison to the levels of industrial development in such neighbors as Poland and Hungary.[5] In turn, for the standard theories of CPEs, one would expect to find a highly developed system of mass production for the ČSSR.[6] Moreover, this industry continued to be a major focus of ČSSR policy. Between 1970 and 1989, mechanical engineering consistently accounted for approximately 33 to 40 percent of net industrial output, 21 to 25 percent of industrial value added, 25 to 28 percent of industrial employment, 48 to 56 percent of total exports, and 14 to 19 percent of industrial investment in the ČSSR.[7]

I will use the VHJ mechanical engineering *koncerns*, Škoda Plzeň and TST, to control for the sectoral and legal factors while examining the formation of the hierarchical and polycentric networks. Into the 1980s, both Škoda Plzeň and TST were dominant producers in ČSSR industry and shared similar technologies, employment profiles, and formal planning laws, as well as domestic and export markets. However, they contrasted with one another in terms of their rules guiding production and bargaining, their distribution of decision-making rights, and their structures of the financial and sociopolitical linkages within the *koncerns* and with outside institutional actors.

The Debate over Planning—VHJs and the Legacy of Universal Production

It has been well established that communists from Lenin to Stalin embraced the Taylorist or Fordist principles of scientific management for mass production to provide the organizational and economic bases for state central planning. Stalin himself once defined "the essence of Leninism" as "the combination of Russian revolutionary sweep with American efficiency."[8] Mass production provided a model of industrial organization that permitted a fusion of central state ownership of assets with high levels of growth. Mass production is the attempt to produce a single good at the highest possible volume to reduce costs through economies of scale. Taylorism focused on ways to enhance efficiency and growth by narrowing the range of final goods and inputs, specializing producers of standardized parts, and creating long production runs for both final goods and parts.[9] Unimpeded by the laws of capitalist competition, the Party-state could achieve unprecedented economies of scale by rationalizing, standardizing, and specializing production through vertical integration of component production and horizontal integration of similar final production into large-scale firms. This model of growth and organization often led analysts to equate the Party-state as the ultimate modern, hierarchical corporation.

Moreover, Lenin and Trotsky saw in scientific management the means to heighten hierarchical control of industry and the Party and to militarize workers.[10] When combined with a relatively narrow range of standardized, predictable parts and final goods, the segmentation of work into specific tasks could allow central authorities to control each stage of the production process—planning each through-put with an increase in output—by a unified, command hierarchy.

Standard views of CPEs took for reality the model of the Party-state apparatus vertically commanding atomized firms and plants through a strict hierarchy and scientific management of mass production.[11] For instance, totalitarian theories saw strict command hierarchies as the vital structures for the Party-state to maintain its coercive policies. Economic theories equated the planning hierarchies with those of the modern capitalist corporations. Pluralist and modernization theories argued that mass production and scientific management were the defining features of CPEs. These views would appear all the more reasonable for the ČSSR given the belief that the advanced development of society's industry was equated with the development of Taylorist mass production and, in turn, could facilitate the creation the Leninist-Stalinist CPE model.[12] Relative to neighboring communist countries, 1948 Czechoslovakia appeared to have such an advantageous starting condition. Bohemia and Moravia already had been the bases of rapid growth in industrial and military production for both the Austro-Hungarian Empire and interwar Czechoslovakia. Moreover, the country had one of the highest levels of industrial concentration in the region.[13]

Yet despite the initial embrace of the Soviet model in 1948,[14] officials from the Czechoslovak Communist Party (KSČ) and industry were already calling for the reform and potential removal of the adopted Soviet model of directive central planning by the mid-1950s. As early as 1954, even Jaromir Dolansky, the minister of planning, publicly urged "a consistent decentralization in planning to be carried out in all planning bodies, in the State Planning Office, in the ministries and in their chief administrations."[15] This view was reiterated in the 1956 KSČ conference that called for an immediate overhaul of planning and industrial organization that stressed increased decision making, independence, and responsibility of lower-level organs as the keys for enhancing economic growth and building socialism.[16] While Stalin's death opened the possibility for a reconsideration of policy, the fall in industrial productivity and output, the exhaustion of material and human resources, and a decline in export performance offered added incentives to revise the planning system. The uprisings in Poland and Hungary in 1956 only reinforced the fears in KSČ leaders that economic stagnation could turn to social and political instability.[17]

The criticisms were not a rejection of the leading role of the KSČ or of central planning and mass production, per se. Rather, Party and ministry leaders were concerned about reorganizing industry and planning so as to *create* a system of scientifically managed mass production. Critics argued that naive installation of Soviet methods and directive planning ignored and was potentially incompatible with the existing organization of production in the ČSSR.[18] Detailed central planning could function as long as a classic mass-production system was in place. But the ČSSR had inherited an advanced industrial structure, in which Czech manufacturers had developed alternative organizational and production methods that had focused as much on scope, flexibility, and variation as they did on scale, segmentation, and standardization. These methods contrasted with Taylorist mass production in two ways.

First, in order to penetrate new export markets after World War I, Czech manufacturers utilized their existing production capabilities geared toward heavy engineering and armaments to produce a broad scope of customized engineering and machinery products in small batches.[19] For instance, the Škoda Works in and around Plzeň was able to expand commercial production from 20 percent to 60 percent of output between 1919 and 1922 by offering new customers a variety of designs and qualities of machines, power-generation equipment, locomotives, and steel.[20] In machine tools and forming machines, approximately twenty medium-sized firms in Bohemia and Moravia were able to produce 210 different models by 1939.[21] As Czech firms sought to adapt and vary their basic designs to customer wishes, they internalized parts production, and norms became company specific. After 1948, such production scope and variation in norms for components impeded efforts by central planners to standardize and narrow production, rationalize and integrate units, and resolve bottlenecks.

Second, Czech machinery and engineering firms organized production according to so-called *universal* or *technological* principles, rather than final-product-specific assembly lines common to Taylorism.[22] A typical mass-production firm focused on large volumes of a relatively unchanging, narrow range of parts that fed an assembly line producing large batches of a single final product for a well-established market. In contrast, Czech shops using universal principles focused on adapting their given technological capabilities to produce a wide range of components in a few classes. A final or intermediate product either was assembled in a particular shop, which received specified components from nearby supplying shops; or the product moved from beginning to end through the various shops, which produced and attached the specified components or made the needed changes. Among other things, such universal production clearly impeded the division of labor necessary for planners to maximize capacity utilization uniformly, specialize shops and plants for a particular standardized product, and control worker productivity and wages. An example of this was in 1951–52 when managers and workers rejected the "shock workers" policy that attempted to promote a detailed division of labor and the production of high volumes of standardized parts.[23]

The ensuing debates over reforming the planning system focused on new organizational forms that could maintain state control and reflect the management traditions of the country.[24] Authorities recognized the limits of centralized detailed planning for coordinating production and rationalization, yet were concerned about maintaining enterprise responsiveness to the state. However, both managers and ministry officials were split over the level of centralized decision making in firms. Those trained in the management traditions of Tomas Baťa argued for firms and plants to be semiautonomous and revenue-sharing centers.[25] Managers from heavy engineering centers, such as Škoda and ČKD, argued for centralized firms with no legal or financial autonomy for plants, because orders for specified parts in low series production and enforcement of interunit supplies had always flowed from the directorate to the tightly nested units.[26] The result was a compromise—VHJs.

Industrial associations, or literally "production economic units" (VHJs), were created in 1958 as middle-level management bodies to help decentralize planning and reorganize specific branches toward a mass-production system. VHJs would help simplify planning directives, integrate plants and firms into fewer and larger production units, and eliminate redundancy.[27] They reflected the two Czech management traditions in that they were to be tightly integrated production organizations with decision-making powers partially decentralized to the top directors.[28] There were three main principles guiding the formation of VHJs—consolidation, variation in organizational structures, and decentralization.

First, consolidating firms and plants with related production profiles into a single VHJ was to improve planning and productivity by a rationalization of production and a decrease in the number of firms.[29] In turn, central planners would have a simpler task with fewer firms to control and directives to administer. This rationalization process, in turn, increased the concentration of both VHJs and firms. Table 2.1 shows the decrease in the number of firms as a result of the new VHJ system in 1958. Tables 2.2 and 2.3 show the shift in the structure of engineering employment towards large firms between 1955 and 1974. For instance, engineering firms with 500 to 5,000 employees captured 80 percent of the growth in engineering employment by 340 thousand. As table 2.4 shows, over 1,000 firms were integrated into only 101 VHJs.

Second, since VHJs had to reorganize the branches, they had to partially take account of the different existing forms of industrial organization.[30] In turn, the different methods of integration and thus VHJs structures reflected the contrasting inherited methods of organizing firms and plants, just mentioned. Tables 2.1 and 2.5 give a sense of the variation in the sizes and organizational forms of VHJs. In the VHJs called *branch national enterprises,* a large single, highly integrated firm was associated with one or a few relatively large

TABLE 2.1.   Reorganization of Industries into VHJs in 1958

Industry Ministry	Number of Firms before 4/1/58	New Organization (VHJs) after 4/1/1958			Total Number of Firms, including those in VHJs
		Total	Trusts	Branch National Enterprise	
Total	1,417	383	67	316	929
Fuel	90	12	5	7	73
Energy	54	39	—	39	50
Metallurgy, ores	76	23	1	22	42
Chemicals	98	37	1	36	41
Heavy engineering	138	23	4	19	75
Precision engineering	69	27	2	25	62
Motor vehicle and agricultural machines	90	25	7	18	64
Construction	77	32[a]	22[a]	10	72
Consumer goods	287	45	10	35	181
Food	322	40	14	26	178
Transport	32	32	—	32	32
Health	25	9	1	8	20
Finance	1	1	—	1	1
Agricuture and forestry	36	38	—	38	38
Administration of water economy	22	—	—	—	—

Source: Rosický (1983, 39).

Note: The number of enterprises excludes marketing organizations, nonindustrial enterprises, enterprises under construction, and research institutes.

[a] Includes eighteen regional (kraj) associations of Ministry of Constructions, which concentrate both construction and industrial firms.

TABLE 2.2. Employment in ČSSR Engineering Sectors, 1955 to 1974 (grouped by firm size)

Size Class (Number of Employees)	1955	1960	1965	1974
1–499	75,359	78,569	69,019	74,160
500–999	95,744	102,854	102,795	133,663
1,000–2,999	178,824	242,573	271,728	336,489
3,000–4,999	38,709	62,586	97,476	114,604
5,000–9,999	103,152	107,697	101,694	121,761
Over 10,000	27,916	73,940	67,545	77,198
Total	519,704	668,219	710,257	857,875

Source: Vácha (1978, 21)

TABLE 2.3. Number of Firms in ČSSR Engineering Sectors, 1955 to 1974 (grouped by firm size)

Size Class (Number of Employees)	1955	1960	1965	1974
1–499	339	326	281	294
500–999	136	145	145	190
1,000–2,999	109	142	157	196
3,000–4,999	10	17	26	30
5,000–9,999	15	16	15	19
Over 10,000	1	5	4	5
Total	610	651	628	734

Source: Vácha (1978, 21)

TABLE 2.4. Number of Industrial, Construction, and Agricultural VHJs under Federal and Republic Ministries, 1974

Ministry (federal and republic)	Number of VHJs	Number of Subordinate Firms
Total	101	1050
Federal ministry of fuel and energy	9	121
Federal ministry of metallurgy and heavy engineering	15	173
Federal ministry of universal engineering	13	214
Ministry of industry (ČSR)[a]	24	225
Ministry of industry (SSR)[a]	7	96
Ministry of construction (ČSR)	6	57
Ministry of construction (SSR)	2	33
Ministry of agriculture and food (ČSR)	13	78
Ministry of agriculture and food (SSR)	12	53

Source: Rosický (1983, 60)
[a] ČSR denotes Czech Socialist Republic; SSR denotes Slovak Socialist Republic.

firms involved in a particular product. While the associated firms were financially independent and received commands from central planners, the lead
firm directed common services and strategy for the related production area
and was the principal manager and monitor of plans for the whole VHJ.
Plants within the lead firm had no autonomy. An example is the Škoda VHJ.
By 1975, Škoda Plzeň not only directed its own twenty existing plants and
production areas but also coordinated research and development (R&D),
production, investment, and some procurement for three newly associated
firms involved in turbine and boiler equipment. VHJs called *trusts* attempted
to integrate several geographically dispersed, medium-sized firms within the
same product group that could not consolidate and rationalize on their own.
While trust firms maintained much of their legal, financial, and production
independence, the VHJ directorate coordinated plan drafting and fulfillment,
specialization and rationalization among finalists and parts producers, and
supplier-customer relations, as well as sales and procurement of raw materials. As can be seen in table 2.1, most trusts in 1958 were in food processing,
construction and consumer goods. The trust for machine tool and forming
machine producers, TST, was one of the few trusts in engineering. The geo-
graphical dispersion of its firms and their Baťa traditions allowed it to gain
greater internal decentralization.[31]

Third, decentralization focused on streamlining planning while increasing
the capabilities of VHJ directorates to manage their respective branches and become intermediaries between central planners and firms.[32] VHJ directorates
absorbed many of the responsibilities and decision-making rights previously
held by firms and central planning authorities, as a smaller central planning
bureaucracy used fewer, broader, and longer-term planning indices.[33] At the
same time, the governance of the directorate was to be strengthened by expanding the membership of its board—the VHJ director and VHJ enterprise
managers, as well as representatives from the regional and district Party/ad-
ministrative councils, the labor union, and the relevant industrial ministry.
This board composition would open up new channels of information for the
VHJ directorate.

Through the 1960s, analysts inside and outside the ČSSR viewed VHJs as
the focal point of innovative organizational and management experiments.
Several observers of the time noted that VHJs were a clear break from the
unified hierarchy of classic CPEs because the economy depended on specific
low-level decisions, linking enterprises into concrete and self-perpetuating
supply-and-demand networks.[34] The use of VHJs was seen as "an attempt to
introduce multiple partitioning and overlapping hierarchies in the form of
interstitial agencies, where the administrative structure became a network
rather than a hierarchy."[35] This network arrangement was strengthened dur-

TABLE 2.5. Structure of Individual Engineering VHJs According to Number of Employees, 1974

Name of VHJ	Number of Production Firms in VHJ	Number of Production Firms in the VHJ, According to Size Class (number of employees)				
		< 1,000	1,000–2,500	2,501–5,000	5,001–10,000	> 10,000
Škoda Plzeň[a]	1					1
ČKD Praha	2				1	1
ČS. Vagónky	3		1	2		
ZTS Martin	10	1	4	2	1	2
Chepos Brno	11		6	3	2	
Sigma Olomouc	12	3	8	1		
Ivtas Chrudim	5		1	2	2	
Vzduchotech-nika Praha	4	1	2	1		
ZSE Praha	23	1	10	11	1	
TESLA Praha	22	2	11	4	4	1
ZPA Praha	15	3	7	4	1	
Chirana Stará Turá	6	3	2	1		
Elitex Liberec	11	1	9	1		
TST Praha	22	2	8	7	5	
Aero Praha	12	2	7	3		
Prago-Union Praha	18	3	12	3		
Strojsmalt Bratislava	15	7	4	4		
ZVS Brno	13	2	5	4	2	
ČAZ Praha	25	1	5	10	6	3
Zbrojovka Brno	11	3	2	4		2
ZVI. Považská Bystrica	9	2	5	1	1	
ČKD Dukla Praha[a]	1			1		
ZES Brno[a]	3	3				
Total	254	40	109	69	26	10

Source: Vácha (1978, 23)

[a]In early 1970s, the production in energy equipment was being reorganized in anticipation for the new program in nuclear plant equipment and facilities. In 1975, the Skoda VHJ incorporated three associated firms, which were previously independent.

ing the liberalization period of 1965–69 by further consolidating VHJs, increasing their decision-making autonomy over certain investments and interfirm relations, and allowing the state bank to directly monitor and finance inventories.

The reforms linked to VHJs and bank finance were not lost even after Prague Spring, as the orthodox communists saw in these reforms a way both to avoid previous mistakes of overcentralization and to improve the discipline of firms.[36] While the Husak regime brutally repressed open political dissent and discredited market-socialist reforms, its so-called normalization policies sought to restore Party-state order and to stabilize the economy by intensive growth, that is, greater efficiencies through rationalization and technological development. Continued focus on strengthening VHJs was the vehicle to achieve these familiar aims. First, Party leaders were quick to criticize the so-called excesses of both liberalization and the centralism that brought on the crises in the 1950s and the recession of 1964. The 1970 Party congress made it clear that the 1958 reforms saw "more progressive proposals from the enterprises than from central directives" and that attempts to return to the "old system of [pre-1958] management" in 1963 offered no solutions.[37] Second, rejuvenating the ideas of 1958 also meant the inclusion of several aspects of the reform debates during 1965–69, namely those centered on the roles of VHJs and the state bank. The increased powers and consolidation of VHJ were aimed to resolve key problems of the "dictatorship of suppliers" lie in the "intransparent networks of customer-supplier relations," which central organs only worsened.[38] State bank credits continued from 1967 to be the main source inventory finance to control inflation.[39] Third, as opposed to the reform movements and uprisings in 1956 in Hungary and in 1980 in Poland, Prague Spring was more of an intraelite conflict within the KSČ, with state institutions surviving the conflict virtually intact.[40] Stabilization and demobilization required more an elimination of market and political reform supporters than a complete rebuilding of institutions. Thus, drawing on parts of the reform was legitimate in the eyes of the normalizers.

The 1970s marked a return to Party-state order but also the renewal of experiments with VHJs and bank finance. Combined with the decentralization of the territorial administration system, these experiments would unwittingly allow VHJs to graft durable, informal methods of governance and production onto the formal institutional system. I will examine how planning experiments and the VHJ structures shaped the social and political relationships of the very networks they were designed to bring under control later in this chapter. But first, let us examine how the legacies of universal production and the continued primacy of VHJs fostered an alternative form of production through the 1970s.

Broad Production Scopes, Low Uniformity, and Redundancy

Although ČSSR officials aimed to build economies of scale through increased concentration, rationalization, and standardization, international trade policies, the shortage environment, and the VHJ organizing principles undermined these efforts. Instead, by the 1980s a typical engineering VHJ and its firms had become a highly autarkic, tightly interlinked production network of a relatively broad range of final goods and nonstandardized inputs.

Trade policy had two major impacts on ČSSR industry. On the one hand, as the ČSSR became one of the main providers of engineering and machinery products for the CMEA and COMECON, the Communist bloc trade regimes, it was forced to produce an expanding assortment of final and semifinished products, in turn undercutting the ability of engineering and machinery VHJs to narrow and standardize their production.[41] Socialist countries accounted for over three quarters of ČSSR exports, most of which were machinery and related equipment (see tables 2.6, 2.7, and 2.8). By the mid-1980s over 80 percent of ČSSR exports of engineering products and machinery went to socialist countries.[42]

On the other hand, with its high dependency on imported raw materials and limited hard currency, the ČSSR restricted imports of machines, equipment, and advanced components, be they from capitalist or communist countries. For instance, even as late as the mid-1980s, over 70 percent of ČSSR machine tools and forming machines were exported, while only 20 percent of machine tools and forming machines, including their inputs, were imported. In contrast, for France comparable figures were 44 percent and 78 percent, respectively; for the USSR, 7 percent and 46 percent; for the United States, 19 percent and 78 percent; for the Federal Republic of Germany (FRG), 62 percent and 60 percent.[43] This caused increased autarky for engineering firms and slow development of the automation needed for rationalization and large series production. As ČSSR engineering firms invested heavily into repairing, modernizing, and expanding existing equipment, little went toward automation and streamlining.[44] Into the 1970s, ČSSR heavy engineering had only twenty-five automated production lines and a very high share of handwork in the dominant machining and assembly steps of production.[45] By the 1980s, about 70 percent of all machines and equipment in the ČSSR were produced domestically, only about 13 percent of machines in ČSSR firms were fully automated, and the average age of machines and equipment (twelve years) and fixed assets (twenty-two years) became very high.[46]

While the import constraints and broad export demands on engineering forced ČSSR VHJs and firms to produce an expanding number of parts and products without advanced dedicated machinery, the VHJ structure and the shortage environment only undermined the development of Taylorist mass production. Planners integrated an increasing number of firms and workers into relatively few VHJs, which then grew to cover ever more industrial branches and product groups (see table 2.9). Rather than narrowing the division of labor, producers tended to stress scope and self-sufficiency, adhering to the Czech saying of the time, "Either new needs are satisfied by a greater

TABLE 2.6.   Czechoslovak Foreign Trade Balance in the 1970s, in Millions of Kcs

	Socialist Countries		Nonsocialist Countries	
	1970–72	1973–79	1970–72	1973–79
Total	+3,433	−9,267	+168	−16,937
Machinery	+15,707	+44,676	+120	+8,135
Fuel and mineral raw material	−9,216	−54,891	+3,589	+6,731
Food	−6,338	−15,652	−2,099	−8,421
Consumer goods	+5,896	+22,470	+3,205	+14,010
Other materials	−2,616	−5,870	−4,647	−21,122

Source: Myant (1989, 191)

TABLE 2.7.   Changes in Trade Balances with Socialist Countries in Early 1980s, in Millions of Kcs

	1976–80	1981–85	Difference
Balance—of which:	−13,517	−15,963	−2,446
Machinery	+41,910	+104,653	+62,743
Mineral, raw materials	−54,885	−143,939	−89,054
Food	−11,250	−12,778	−1,628
Consumer goods	+20,265	+37,726	+17,461
Other	−9,557	−1,625	+7,932

Source: Myant (1989, 204)

TABLE 2.8.   Structure of Czechoslovak Exports, 1951–85 (average share in total exports)

	1951–55	1956–60	1961–65	1966–70	1971–75	1976–80	1981–85	1985
Socialist	71.0	68.9	73.5	70.5	70.3	72.6	74.5	77.0
USSR	32.9	32.2	37.4	33.5	32.0	34.8	41.4	43.7
Machinery	37.6	42.7	47.1	49.8	48.7	51.0	55.7	57.0

Source: Myant (1989, 205)

variety of products or old needs are satisfied by a variety of new methods."[47] In turn, as VHJs produced a greater variety of final goods, they reacted often by creating completely new production designs and models. For instance, in Škoda Plzeň, the credo was that "each turbine must be a new and different prototype." Its 50MW turbine had only two production runs in medium-sized batches.[48]

At the same time, the broadening of main production programs forced VHJs to expand upstream operations.[49] Given the import restrictions, the shortage environment, and the ineffective central coordination of inter-VHJ deliveries, VHJs and their members found it easier to produce on their own as

TABLE 2.9.   Number of Branches/Product Groups Covered by an Engineering VHJ

	Number of Different Branches/Product Groups (3-Digit ISIC)					
	1965		1970		1973	
Name of VHJ	Total	Those with Volume > 100 Million Kcs	Total	Those with Volume > 100 Million Kcs	Total	Those with Volume > 100 Million Kcs
ČKD Praha	52	13	62	13	65	13
Chepos Brno	53	9	56	10	58	11
Ivtas Chrudim	38	4	46	7	49	9
Sigma Olomouc	34	3	41	6	43	6
Vzduchotechnika Praha	12	1	13	1	15	2
TST Praha	61	7	66	11	69	13
Škoda Plzeň	45	8	60	13	62	13
ZSE Praha	66	8	60	12	62	13
Tesla Praha	55	9	59	11	66	13
ZPA Praha	31	3	34	5	40	4
ZES Brno	33	2	34	2	38	5
ČKD Dukla Praha	10	1	11	3	12	3
ČS Vagónky Praha	14	2	14	3	15	4
ČAZ Praha	88	13	90	13	94	13
Zbrojovka Brno	34	6	42	8	46	8
ZVS Brno	69	5	74	8	80	12
Prago-Union Praha	64	5	74	8	82	9
AERO Praha	38	2	40	2	47	3
ZTS Martin	66	7	71	11	78	12
Strojsmalt Bratislava	—	—	56	7	66	8
Elitex Liberec	11	1	15	2	16	3
Chirana Stará Turá	11	1	13	2	14	2
ZVL Považská Bystrica	45	—	49	5	53	6
VSS Košice	14	—	15	—	15	1

Source: Vácha (1978, 25)

many parts, and as many machines to produce those parts, as possible. The upstream diversification was intensified by the fact that most engineering and machinery VHJs supplied whole production facilities and systems as well as machines and equipment.[50] Autarky became a vicious cycle, and redundancy of parts and machine production became pervasive. For instance, Jirásek showed that despite a slight narrowing in the number of main production programs in engineering firms and VHJs, the number of complementary programs increased beyond those of the main programs.[51] Kareš showed that during 1960–65, the rapid increase in the number of machine tool producers came from new units providing mainly single-purpose machine tools for their particular VHJ.[52] By 1970, parts and machine purchases from outside the average engineering firm accounted for only 20 percent of production.[53] By 1986, Škoda Plzeň VHJ covered ninety-two product groups, most of which were for small-batch, upstream production.[54] Such autarky-cum-diversification maintained almost bizarre levels through the 1970s and 1980s: the assortment of ČSSR engineering production covered approximately 80 percent of the internationally classified product groups (i.e., 3-digit ISIC); about 53 percent of the ČSSR assortment was designated main production programs, while the rest was complementary.[55]

The existence of forced substitution, redundancy, and expanding upstream and side production in firms is not new to the analysis of CPEs.[56] But in focusing on such production habits as failures of the planning system, scholars may have overlooked how the emphasis on autarky and product variety may have undermined the production and management regimes crucial for hierarchical control in three ways.

First, as table 2.2 suggests and other recent research on both the Czech Republic and USSR has shown, industry lacked many giant firms and the economies of scale that advanced capitalist countries found necessary to build mass-production regimes.[57] Conversely, data show that piece, low, and medium batches accounted for a disproportionately high share of production in engineering and machinery, relative to that in Western Europe.[58] For instance, between 1939 and the mid-1960s, the number of different types of machine tools and forming machines increased from 120 to 420, and the volume of production rose from 5,000 units to 30,000 units. The assortment grew immensely, but production runs per model remained relatively low.[59] Table 2.9 also shows that into the 1970s, as the number of branches and product groups within a VHJ increased, the majority of production programs focused on small to medium-sized batches of either final or complementary products. Only thirteen of the sixty-two product groups covered by Škoda Plzeň were produced in large volume; for TST only thirteen of sixty-nine.

Second, there was little progress in the standardization of parts, vital for systemic rationalization and integration. Industrial VHJs and their firms did not standardize parts according to the national classification system but rather to their own norms.[60] ČSSR industry had very few specialized plants for standardized parts, the production of which was very low in comparison to advanced capitalist countries as well as the other communist countries.[61]

Third, the broadening of production capabilities developed with the prevalence of so-called nested or associated organizational forms of plants and shops, reflecting the traditional organization of universal production methods.[62] In contrast to standardized assembly production, shops and plants operated semiautonomously from one another and were organized according to their technologies and production abilities rather than according to a specific final good or input. They were nested in the sense that the exigencies of shortage, trade policy, and VHJs deepened the production links between them. That is, plants and shops became highly interdependent for particular inputs and the sharing of workers. As Jirásek observed, the needed concentration, specialization, and standardization still demanded a "new system of plants," since "today's plants are still built on the universal principal, incorporating all phases of the engineering production process—iron foundries, forges, pressing centers, machining centers, departments of surface/finishing modifications, assemblies, etc."[63] Even when advances were made in design and productivity, production was not taking expected forms. For instance, when Škoda Plzeň made advances in the production of its heavy horizontal boring machine, the design was module-based. While one shop focused on the core components and the base of the machine, other shops would modify it with various spindle accessories.[64] Also, although the ČSSR had become one of world's the top producers of machine tools by the 1960s, TST firms produced usually in short series and with universal, rather than dedicated, machinery well into the 1980s.[65]

Into the 1980s, VHJs and their firms continued to direct investment into repairing machinery for existing uses and adding new, nonautomated machines for additional parts or modified inputs, rather than rationalize operations and shift to automated assembly lines for achieving economies of scale for standardized parts.[66] VHJs appeared more like collections of tightly linked workshops exploiting economies of scope utilizing a broad range of production capabilities for short production runs. Diverse export demands, shortage, and the VHJ organizational structure led VHJ managers to increase their production scope and autarky, but at the cost of growing underutilization of capacity and redundancy. Yet the ČSSR economy did grow without high inflation or budget deficits and without a complete collapse of central planning. If planners and managers did not have a Taylorist mass-production regime with its simplified division of labor to set tasks and control inputs, then how did VHJs govern themselves and acquire the resources to frequently adapt their manufacturing methods and support their redundant, broad production programs? The answer, as I will explain, can be found in the way VHJs developed their sociopolitical networks.

Expansion of VHJ Networks and Partial Reforms

In not conforming to the principles of Taylorist mass production, firms created continual problems for the effectiveness of central planning.[67] As the product group profiles of VHJs broadened, the number and variety of inputs, and in turn customer-supplier relationships, grew ever more complex.[68] The frequent changes in product composition, design, and production methods undermined the use by central planners of fixed quantitative targets to coordinate deliveries between VHJs. As inter-VHJ relationships persistently broke down and firms failed to rationalize and standardize their production, firms and plants within a particular VHJ increasingly turned to one another to create supplementary supply links. The internalization of supply lines made VHJs less transparent. Central planners, in turn, frequently had to intervene directly in firms and revise short-term plans in order to open bottlenecks. This led to more planning and production instability.

Through the 1970s, economic policymakers initiated a set of organizational and financial experiments in different industrial sectors with the hope of improving planning and performance. These experiments culminated in a series of broad reforms beginning in 1979 that focused on strengthening three interconnected meso-level institutions: VHJs, the state bank (SBČS), and territorial administrative councils *(narodni vybory)* that also functioned as key parts of the Communist party infrastructure. The reforms not only granted these entities greater decision-making rights on various issues but also allowed them to coordinate economic and social programs directly with one another. The SBČS and its branches would become directly responsible for credits, inter-VHJ payments, and inventories, relieving the central planners and the state budget of these burdens. The regional and district councils would directly manage certain social programs with VHJ managers.[69]

The following subsections show how the planning reforms and the enhanced roles of the SBČS branches and *narodni vybory* contributed to the creation of VHJ sociopolitical networks during the late 1970s and 1980s. On the one hand, the institutions of planning and finance took on uses beyond the intentions of partial reforms because of the ways VHJ managers used their enhanced autonomy to adapt to the exigencies of shortage while avoiding the intervention of central planners. The increased discretionary powers gave VHJ members more room to define on their own formal and informal rules of internal decision making and bargaining. The strengthening of VHJs, SBČS branches, and the *narodni vybory* system allowed VHJ members to create new horizontal channels of political and financial risk-sharing with relevant bank and council actors. The channels offered VHJ managers access to new resources to support their autarky. The channels also supported an intra-VHJ authority structure that influenced the way bargaining rules were created and revised.

On the other hand, the different patterns of bargaining, authority, and strong or weak linkages grew out of different VHJ histories of production and organization that had been in existence more or less from 1958 until the late 1970s—when the reforms were fully enacted. As will become evident in the cases of Škoda Plzeň and TST, which represent my ideal-type hierarchical and polycentric networks, these histories provided different norms of management and power distribution over both assets in the VHJ and links to outside institutions.

Organizational and Planning Reforms

In 1979–80, the ČSSR initiated two sets of reforms to strengthen the internal cohesion and autonomy of VHJs—the creation of the *koncern* form of VHJs and the simplification of planning directives (see table 2.10).[70] First, while the new laws strengthened the position of VHJs (as opposed to firms) as the basic business unit, many VHJs were converted into *koncern* forms, the majority of which were in industry. In replacing most of the existing forms of VHJs, the heavily centralized *branch national enterprises* and decentralized *trusts,* the *koncern* form was legally and organizationally between the two. The *koncern* VHJ as a whole, rather than individual members, was the subject of taxation, plan targets, and technical development. The directorate of the *koncern* was the primary legal, planning, and financial body of VHJ, while member *koncern* firms had limited legal autonomy and reported directly to the directorate. The directorate was the main interlocutor between members and outside organs, be they central planners or other VHJs, and developed and managed short- to medium-term plans. Member *koncern* firms still maintained their own financial accounts, had legal authority over their plants, and could directly engage in certain commercial relations outside the VHJ.

Second, reformers argued that the VHJ directorate also required certain discretionary powers vis-à-vis central planners over finances and production plans, because the "formalities and over-quantitative approach of central planning" ignored the frequent firm-level qualitative changes in production and product composition.[71] In turn, VHJs obtained greater managerial discretion, as planning indicators were broadened and decreased, five-year plans established the main targets, binding annual plans were abolished, and counterplans from VHJs became the basis for planning criteria. These changes essentially allowed the VHJ to define many of the key indicators on its own, as the necessary information about production flowed upward and five-year plans were revised regularly.

How indicators actually became defined, plans revised, and resources redistributed depended on two levels of internal bargaining and rule making. At one level, member firms and plants bargained over sharing resources, machine use, and labor, as well as more qualitative issues such as standards for parts and the terms of subcontracting and reciprocity.[72] Here, the directorate could participate in various ways—mediating conflicts, enforcing compliance on its terms, or delegating these responsibilities to a few favored plants or firms. The greater its discretion over the plan and resources, the more bargaining chips it

TABLE 2.10.   Structure of VHJs in ČSSR Industry, 1985

Jurisdiction	Total	In Which the Following VHJ Form			
		Trust	*Koncern*	Branch Firm	Directly Managed
Federal ministries[a]					
a[b]	71	12	28	3	28
b[b]	542	182	355	5	—
c[b]	1,607	600	927	49	31
ČSR government					
a	62	19	11	17	15
b	384	222	111	51	—
c	800	430	205	152	13
SSR government					
a	35	18	1	5	11
b	183	166	9	8	—
c	353	329	7	10	7

Source: ČSSR Statistical Yearbook

[a]There were three main federal industrial ministries: Ministry for Steel and Heavy Engineering, Ministry for Universal Engineering, and Ministry for Electro-technical Industry. All principal engineering fims and VHJs in the ČSSR were under the first two federal ministries.

[b]a = Number of VHJs; b = number of subordinate firms in VHJ; c = number of employees (in thousands)

had to fulfill this role. But the role and discretionary powers of the directorate, and in turn those of the member firms and plants, were largely defined at a higher level of bargaining, namely within the board of the VHJ. The board became the forum where the interests and relative power of the VHJ members and of outsiders met. The board included directors of *koncern* firms, relevant ministries, the labor union, and the *narodni vybory*. It essentially set the bargaining framework for the VHJ—the rules of bargaining, the distribution of formal and informal authority, and thus the method of settling internal disputes. The framework was defined, and sometimes redefined, simultaneously with the organizational rules and structure of the VHJ.

The framework became a function of the shifting distribution of power— the concentration of legal rights and links to outsiders, such as councils, the SBČS, or the ministry, and the position of a member firm or plant within the VHJ production system (e.g., as a critical supplier or end producer).[73] That is, the way certain details of the *koncern*'s organizational or governance rules were interpreted or how rules over resources and coordination were implemented depended on the context, particularly the relative political strength of certain board members at the point of *koncern* creation and the preexisting organizational structure of the VHJ. Thus, although such VHJs as Škoda and TST formally became *koncerns* in 1980 and were subjected to the same planning laws, their actual organization and bargaining framework developed quite differently.

Škoda had been a branch national enterprise VHJ, with highly centralized powers in the hands of the directorate of Škoda Plzeň.[74] Converting Škoda into a *koncern* was to limit the dominance of the old primary firm, Škoda Plzeň, allowing the many plants and associated firms to become *koncern* firms, thus increasing their transparency and independence. Yet while a few former associated firms became *koncern* firms, the group of units in and around Plzeň remained plants under the direction of the *koncern* firm Škoda Plzeň. Such firms as Ejpovice, which was originally a *koncern* firm, and Stankov, a unit of a firm just outside of Plzeň, were soon incorporated into Škoda Plzeň as plants as well. Although a new separate VHJ directorate was created in Plzeň mainly to oversee the energy engineering programs, the dominance of Škoda Plzeň within the VHJ production process allowed it to assert its own centralized management traditions. Moreover, by having the resources of many units under one large firm in Plzeň, the councils for Plzeň and the region western Bohemia could bargain exclusively with Škoda Plzeň to fulfill social programs; otherwise, they would have to compete with other regional and district councils over resources, if the Škoda Plzeň plants were *koncern* firms. The Plzeň and western Bohemia councils revealed the limits of their influence, however, when in 1984 Škoda Prague, previously a plant in Škoda Plzeň's energy equipment program, became a *koncern* firm with the help of the Prague council.[75]

As the strongest member firm with numerous operations and control of ties to the regional councils, Škoda Plzeň's top management dominated the VHJ directorate and the way resources were distributed and bargaining rules defined.[76] On the one hand, the directorate permitted flexible terms for member firms and plants to bargain directly over machining and labor sharing, subcontracting, and so forth so as to utilize the excess capacity and close proximity of members. On the other hand, the directorate facilitated the expansion of the production profiles of Škoda Plzeň's forge, foundry, electrotechnical, generator, and gearbox plants to supply its own machining, transport, and energy equipment programs and limit the unreliable supplies from outside Plzeň. When the nuclear power equipment program was developed after 1979, Plzeň was able to force the program to be developed as part of its Turbine plant, not as a new *koncern* firm or part of the other *koncern* firms. This action gave Plzeň leverage over the other *koncern* firms and limited their autonomy. Moreover, the directorate clearly favored certain programs and plants, such as Locomotive, Turbine, and Hut (steel programs), which Škoda Plzeň deemed critical for its autarky and prestige in ČSSR industry. These plants essentially had greater bargaining power with respect to other member firms or plants.

TST had been a trust form of VHJ. The legal and financial primacy of geographically dispersed member firms and the lack of legal rights for the trust directorate allowed the firms to maintain their own final product lines and autarky and produced weak, uncoordinated interfirm production relations.[77] Transforming TST into a *koncern* form was to reverse this trend by empowering the new directorate to rationalize production and to act as the sole body in dealings with central planners and other VHJs. Yet, in contrast to Škoda, TST retained much of its decentralized structure. Member firms resisted allowing the directorate to unilaterally consolidate firms and plants, as it contradicted with each firm's traditions, production, and organization. The several relevant regional and district councils assisted their efforts, as a more decentralized structure facilitated the access councils had to firm resources. In turn, the twenty TST firms directly became *koncern* firms with greater autonomy over finances, production, and inter-VHJ relations. At the same time, members with the largest production programs, such as Šmeral, ZPS, and Kurim in Moravia and Čelákovice and Kovosvit in Bohemia, shared managerial authority with the directorate and became managerial hubs overseeing the development of smaller firms in their respective regions.[78]

Since TST's organization of formal and informal authority was more dispersed, the directorate had less command power and was more of a mediator or facilitator.[79] An example was in the directorate's attempt to rationalize and standardize production. The profiles of various foundries, Kurim's production of screws and spindles, and Rakovnik's and Vrchlabi's production of hydraulics were expanded to supply many of the TST firms. There were limits, though, as to how far the directorate could push member firms. The new numerically controlled (NC) machinery installed in five TST firms failed to produce the expected specialization and large series production. The firms instead spread the machinery through shops to modify steel castings and produce a variety of parts in small batches for themselves and informally for other TST members. Meeting the firms halfway, the directorate ended up helping members to share machine time or subcontract. Yet the result of this power distribution was the continued lack of integrated supply lines between member firms, expansion of firm-level production of parts and end products, and redundancy. By the late 1980s, the firms still produced a significantly broad range of machine tools and forming machines, covering 23 percent of the known assortment. By 1986–87, intra-TST supplies accounted for only 10 percent (on average) of the output of a TST firm, whereas in Škoda it was about 50 percent. Foreign and local analysts noted that TST firms exhibited a high degree of flexible job-shop production, based on modularity, but lacked the level of automation, production flows, specialization, and interfirm integration common in the West.[80] By guarding their autonomy, TST firms continued their respective final product specializations according to class and size, and in turn, continued producing and adapting most of the inputs within their own plants.[81]

Financial Channels and VHJ Networks

Financial reforms were to improve VHJ and firm self-financing and accountability.[82] A key criticism during the 1970s was that the relatively high dependence of firms on the state budget contributed to excessive central intervention and inefficient use of investment. Beginning in the late 1970s, central authorities began reform experiments by cutting budgetary expenditures to firms and large centrally planned investment projects. By 1980, the share of state budget expenditures in the economy dropped to just 42.9 percent, the lowest since 1953, and continued to remain low through the 1980s.[83] To maintain stable growth and limit budget deficits, the ČSSR enacted in 1980 a dual-track financial reform. First, VHJs directorates and member firms gained greater discretion over internal transfer prices, retained earnings, loan negotiations with the SBČS, and planned funds, which were consolidated and often mixed to finance smaller investments.[84] Second, the SBČS and its branches, as opposed to central planners, directly administered an increasingly large proportion of VHJ investments, inventories, and operating costs.

In the standard view of a CPE, these reforms would appear to do little to transform the institutional relationships of the ČSSR.[85] In this view, bargaining is a zero-sum game between the planning center and the firm only over a stock of resources (i.e., subsidies and investments), where firms are only interested in growth (prestige) and sucking resources from the center. As the state-center weakens in its bargaining position, budget deficits increase along with inflation. These were the main arguments about the collapse of market socialism in Poland, Hungary, and the USSR.[86] The fact that the ČSSR ran marginal state budget deficits and kept inflation low would indicate that the ČSSR maintained an orthodox planning system and kept firms on a relatively tight leash. Yet during the periods of low budget deficits and inflation, and sustained cuts in planned credits, investments, and budget expenditures in the 1980s, the ČSSR experienced real growth in enterprise expenditures and the money supply.[87]

Several Czechoslovak analysts suggested that the conventional theories of CPEs misunderstood bargaining as a zero-sum game between rent-seeking firms and the center over a stock of funds.[88] Rather, bargaining around VHJs was particularly concerned with building horizontal links to coordinate economic activity and avoid central intervention. Managers were interested as much in maintaining autonomy and avoiding negotiations with superiors as in growth. Money was not simply a stock of resources to be sucked from the center but a flow of funds to be recycled and used to lubricate horizontal channels. Indeed, Bulíř suggests that the use of money as flows to support elaborate horizontal bargaining relationships without significant increases in centrally allocated resources helps explain the high velocity of money from the late 1970s through the 1980s in the ČSSR.[89] In turn, the formal institutional framework may have largely stayed the same, yet a decoupling was taking place between the central Party-state apparatus and the institutional alterations occurring at lower levels of society.

The aggregate data on financial flows show how VHJs were depending less on central state expenditures and subsidies and more on bank credits, retained earnings, and interfirm debt particularly for financing investments and current operations (see tables 2.11–2.14). Viewing money as flows helps one not only see *who* was governing VHJ finances (the VHJs themselves and the SBČS) but also *how* VHJ members could use a relatively fixed stock of centrally allocated resources to maintain internal and external bargaining channels.[90]

First, the effective decentralization of direct negotiations between VHJs and the SBČS, coupled with the growth in interfirm debt, strengthened the links between the VHJs and SBČS system.[91] For both the five-year plan and counter plans, the VHJ directorate and the industry department of the SBČS formulated a framework agreement for the various loans provided to the VHJ. The actual settling of the loan contracts took place between the VHJ firms and their regional branches. Current account loans were of particular importance, because their defined uses could be blurred and thus used by VHJ directors and member firms to maintain supply channels or bargaining positions within the VHJ or with the regional council. By 1985, current account loans became the most important type of loans, accounting for almost 50 percent of operating loans.[92] Moreover, with reforms on loan maturities and retained earnings, VHJ managers were more likely to receive supplementary loans.

Second, VHJ members could support side production and strengthen their internal bargaining relations without having to solicit more resources from central planners and incite intervention. Depending on the formal and informal rules of the VHJ, member firms and the directorate could mix the resources of different internal budgets and use the added cash flow and retained earnings accommodate ongoing barter arrangements with one another (i.e., sharing of labor and machining time) and settle intra-VHJ conflicts.[93] For instance, VHJ firms had full discretion on the creation and use of new *limit investments* (up to 2 million Kcs), and could be increased (via other VHJ funds and supplementary loans) according to guidelines set by the VHJ directorate. Such investments were mainly for repairs and modifications to

TABLE 2.11. Credits Granted to State Economic Organizations (noncooperatives)

	Operating Loans		Investment Loans		Total Loans	
Year	Billion Kcs	Percentage Change	Billion Kcs	Percentage Change	Billion Kcs	Percentage Change
1970	121.4	—	53.3	—	174.7	—
1975	178.7	47.2	75.0	40.7	253.7	45.2
1980	256.3	43.4	102.0	36.0	358.3	41.2
1982	283.5	10.6	103.3	1.3	386.8	7.9
1985	323.8	14.2	110.4	0.1	434.2	12.3

Source: Majcher and Valach (1988, 175)

TABLE 2.12. Structure of Operating Loans, in Percent

	1981	1982	1983	1984	1985	1986
TOZ[a]	36.32	39.53	40.39	32.08	35.46	34.4
Risk currency[b]	10.22	9.55	7.29	5.87	5.92	5.09
Other[c]	53.46	50.92	52.32	57.45	58.62	60.17

Source: Makúch (1988, 739)
[a]TOZ stands for long-term revolving inventory loans
[b]Classified as loans made in "undesired" currency
[c]Other stands for current account loans toward general operating expenditures

TABLE 2.13. Sources of Current Operating Finances in State Economic Organizations (noncooperatives)

	1977		1982		1985	
Indicator	Billion Kcs	Percent	Billion Kcs	Percent	Billion Kcs	Percent
Own sources	134	27.6	158	23.6	178	22.5
Bank credits	194	39.8	269	40.1	323	40.8
Payables	159	32.6	243	36.3	290	36.7
Total	487	100	670	100	791	100

Source: Majcher and Valach (1989, 235)

existing equipment or installation of new machines, typical for maintaining forced substitution and autarky. The autonomy that VHJ actors had over limit investments allowed them to maintain internal reciprocity and coordination without haggling with central planners. Indeed, limit investments came to account for 40–80 percent of all investments in industrial VHJs.[94]

As much as the reforms in VHJ finance and banking enhanced the autonomy of VHJs and their relations with the SBČS, the different existing informal and formal distribution of authority within VHJs shaped the control over internal bargaining and the discretion VHJ members had in negotiations

TABLE 2.14.   Structure of Sources Financing (large) Construction Investments,
State Economic Organizations (noncooperatives), in Percent

Year	State Budget	Own Sources	Investment Loans
1955	50.8	49.2	—
1960	48.8	47.6	3.6
1965	55.0	42.1	2.9
1968	20.9	43.7	35.4
1971	35.1	44.3	20.6
1975	29.2	44.5	26.3
1980	24.7	45.6	29.7
1981	14.3	60.5	25.2
1982	14.8	56.7	28.5
1983	15.1	56.2	28.7
1984	9.4	68.6	22.0
1985	11.6	63.1	25.3

Source: Majcher and Valach (1988, 282); Horský (1988, append. 1)

for supplementary loans and overdrafts. A clear difference emerged between Škoda and TST.[95]

In Škoda VHJ, where power and accounts were centralized, the directorate set the rules of transfer pricing and financial bargaining, allowing plants and *koncern* firms to manage their barter and subcontracting relationships largely by themselves, as in-house supplies and interunit debts grew. But in controlling the directorate and, in turn, negotiations with the SBČS and its regional branch, Škoda Plzeň management was the principal arbitrator of funds. It used them to favor its large plants and force the compliance of lesser plants and *koncern* firms. Other *koncern* firms had to go through the directorate to negotiate with the SBČS, curtailing their formal rights and the management of their own accounts. The plants of Škoda Plzeň had no rights to directly interact with the bank. By controlling channels to the SBČS, Škoda Plzeň thus increased its power over the VHJ.

In contrast, TST firms, despite having similar sizes and production needs as those of many of Škoda Plzeň's plants, had significantly more power and autonomy than even the *koncern* firms of Škoda VHJ. In TST, directorate and firm managers managed internal prices and funds relatively jointly. Managers met every month to review internal price ranges and regulate abuses to the mutual labor, material, and subcontracting exchanges, which supplemented formal payments. Within these norms, firms bargained directly with each other and tried to avoid direct intervention by the TST director. But TST polycentric distribution of authority was most prevalent in limit investments and banking. Since member firms had the right to manage their own accounts, the TST directorate had limited resources to force the compliance of members to its wishes, notably for increased integration and rationalization. Moreover,

virtually all supplementary loans and overdrafts were directly negotiated between the firms and their regional branches. The VHJ directorate monitored
the additions to the original frameworks in regular meetings with the SBČS
and the VHJ board, and became responsible for any large investment loan or
operating loan that exceeded available funds in the regional branch. The direct
access TST firms had to bank branches strengthened their positions in their
respective regions or districts and vis-à-vis the TST directorate.

Up to now, I have focused mainly on how the financial and banking reforms affected VHJ actors. But in becoming an external member of a VHJ
network, an SBČS branch changed its role.[96] To balance the increased VHJ
autonomy in credit relations, the reforms in the 1980s made branches the
local monitors of firm inventories and of customer-supplier relations between firms and units of different VHJs. Branches had the discretion to assess
penalties and renegotiate terms of loans, while repayment of loans received
preferential treatment over all other firm expenditures. In turn, the branch
was no longer a simple bookkeeper for the SBČS but rather had the authority
to regulate firm cash flow and inventories and mediate payment disputes between firms and units.[97] But as a branch became a financial and political risk
sharer with certain VHJ actors, the network structures complicated its loyalties and effectiveness.

The most striking example is the growth of interfirm debt in the 1980s.[98]
The combination of stagnating economic growth, cuts in state subsidies, and
the declining rate of growth in total loans had a gradual negative impact on
aggregate VHJ cash flow. In turn, firms used their production networks to
build financial cushions through interfirm debt. Since firms had relatively
few main customers and suppliers, the constraints were too great to avoid
being hooked into the channels of payment arrears. Between 1980 and 1988,
interfirm debt rose steadily from 4 billion Kcs to 40 billion Kcs and became
an increasingly important component of operating funds (see also table
2.13). As reports of the SBČS reveal, branches were caught in a compromising
situation.[99] They were obligated as representatives of SBČS to discipline the
delinquent payments of firms. However, because they were also responsible
for the financial stability of their respective regions and under pressure from
the regional councils, they were reluctant to take a hard line against firms. A
hard line could lead to a string of rising financial problems for firms in the region. This problem was exacerbated since the different arrangements of VHJs
prevented a uniform solution.

For instance, the interfirm debts of Škoda Plzeň were kept on one set of
accounts and thus simplified bank-firm relations for the Plzeň regional
branch.[100] Yet the centralized accounts made plant and most inter-*koncern*
firm finances intransparent and difficult to monitor. Since such a large and

complex firm as Škoda Plzeň had considerable financial impact in and beyond the region, and maintained close links to the regional council (see the
following), the bank branch often submitted to the authority of Škoda's top
management. In contrast, the relatively decentralized TST firms, each with its
own financial accounts in addition to those of the VHJ as a whole, severely
impeded a coordinated financial policy among the various branches that
were linked to these geographically dispersed firms.

Territorial Administrative Councils and VHJ Networks

I have noted frequently in this chapter that the overlapping, meso-level institutions that managed ČSSR economic and political affairs allowed their
members to build horizontal negotiating channels and alter their respective
roles and governance rules. I have discussed the general impact of the regional and district councils of the *narodni vybory* system on the alternative
forms of *koncern* VHJs. I will now focus on how the ability of VHJs and councils to comanage social welfare programs transformed the role of councils
from being simply a monitoring arm of the KSČ to a critical external financial and political partner of certain VHJ members.

Regional and district councils had primary responsibility for social welfare planning and KSČ mobilization. Each of the 10 regions *(kraj)* of the ČSSR
(7 in the CR) and the 2 leading cities (Prague and Bratislava) had a ruling
council, under which stood councils of the 112 districts (75 in CR).[101] The organizational structure and rule making of regional and district councils resembled the VHJ system, yet these councils were grouped territorially and reported to the ministries of Labor and Social Welfare and Health as well as to
the KSČ. From the point of view of the councils, linkages between the councils
and the firms developed for three main reasons. First, as the representatives of
the KSČ, the councils could influence the promotion and demotion of managers in their respective jurisdictions. Second, councils largely depended on
VHJs and firms (i.e., from the social cultural funds and from wage taxes) for a
large part of financing social welfare programs.[102] Third, councils were responsible for coordinating the firms and VHJs in their respective jurisdictions
to participate in the maintenance of these programs and in the KSČ elections.[103] However, as much as councils were able forge collaborative alliances
with firms, the incongruence between the territorial organization of councils
and the various forms of VHJ organization complicated the tasks of the councils and caused their roles as bargaining partners for firms and VHJs to vary.

The sizeable Czech sociological literature on the administrative council
system shows that the interdependence between regional/district councils
and VHJs/firms in their jurisdiction led to the formation of strong relation-

ships between managers and council members.[104] Managers and council members sought to protect one another from central ministerial and KSČ intervention and to coordinate services and the flow of goods within and between communities and VHJs. The region or district depended on the local firms or VHJ to provide resources and often facilities for social services, housing, and employment. Managers often depended on the council leaders to run these services, to assist SBČS branches balance interfirm debt with the continuance of supplementary loans, to lobby council superiors and VHJ directorates for additional resources, and to aid the acquisition of inputs from distant suppliers (within and outside the VHJ). District councils could assist local firms in securing payments, finances, and supplies by directly negotiating with the relevant firm or VHJ directorate or, more commonly, by using their own contacts in other district councils and superior regional councils to apply pressure and diplomacy where needed. Informal relations were reinforced as firms and councils shared employees. For instance, Premusová reports that over 60 percent of council employees in northern Bohemia and Moravia were former or current employees of the VHJs in these regions.[105] These relationships became further solidified as districts and regions created joint committees in the 1980s to coordinate the pooling of financial and material resources and their bargaining with superiors, be it through industrial or territorial administrative channels.

Yet getting firms from different VHJs to contribute limited resources to regional or district projects led councils to tailor their bargaining methods to the different organizational forms and informal rules of the VHJs. Inversely, the distribution of control of channels from the VHJ to the councils was a source of added power for certain VHJ actors. In turn, as councils sought the collaboration of firms and VHJs, the way councils were connected to VHJs shaped the maintenance of authority in the broader VHJ network. For instance, the relationship between the regional council for western Bohemia and Škoda Plzeň was rather straightforward.[106] Because of Škoda Plzeň's dominance in the VHJ and its centralization of resources, the regional council had direct negotiations with the firm, rather than indirect coordination of resources through district councils. Yet this collaboration was limited by the bargaining leverage Škoda Plzeň had due to its size and impact on the whole region as well as to the fact that health care facilities, many apartments, and vocational training centers for the outlying communities were "owned" by Škoda. In turn, a somewhat symbiotic relationship grew. The alliance between the regional council and Škoda's top management allowed the two parties to draw on one another's power to affirm one another's authority—helping the council run the region and Škoda top management maintain its hierarchical order over VHJ members.

The channels between councils and TST firms arose differently.[107] Although TST had its headquarters in Prague, TST was not as vital for the city council as was Škoda for Plzeň and western Bohemia. Prague had the status of the seat of the Party-state and was the home to numerous firms and industries, while TST had simply its directorate and a few firms in the capital. The various regional, and particularly district, councils were dependent on local TST firms and plants, but they faced coordination problems with the relatively decentralized and geographically dispersed organizational form of the *koncern*. In turn, the social and political ties between the firms and districts developed in two ways. First, as both the district councils and the firms had an interest in increasing the firm's employment, wage bill, and discretionary finances, the district and respective regional councils collaborated with one another to support manager initiatives in the TST board to enhance the formal and informal independence of firm decision-making rights and finances. Second, since TST firms were responsible for many of their own supplies and purchases outside the VHJ, councils assisted firms in mediating conflicts in these relationships, be it with suppliers or customers within or outside of the district. Councils also assisted firms in their negotiations with the SBČS branches and in coordinating their interfirm debts.[108] Thus, in contrast to the network pattern at Škoda, TST firms drew on their alliances with their respective regional and district councils to coordinate the flow of resources and maintain a decentralized or polycentric VHJ order.

Reproducing Networks after VHJs

By the late 1980s, VHJs had become the hubs of alternative sociopolitical networks that enabled firms to adapt to shortages and to limit central control. Forced substitution coupled with demanding industrial and trade policies had led firms and units within VHJs to form strong financial and technical links and broad production capabilities. The internal bargaining regimes of VHJs provided a sense of order in limiting central intervention, coordinating improvised customer-supplier relations, and expanding channels to the SBČS and administrative councils for the additional flow of resources. But the different production and organizational legacies of VHJs shaped the different patterns of VHJ networks during the implementation of new legal forms for VHJs *(koncerns)* and partial reforms in planning finance and territorial administration.

Škoda represents what I call a *hierarchical* VHJ network (see fig. 2.1). Formal and informal management and financial powers were centralized in the hands of the VHJ directorate, dominated by top management of Škoda Plzeň.

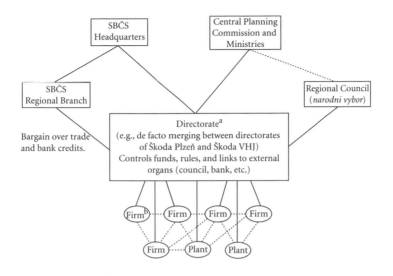

[a] Directorate sets rules of production and bargaining; commanding some member firms and plants, favoring others.

[b] Member firms have tight production links; within framework, they bargain mainly over barter items and production standards.

Figure 2.1.   Hierarchical Network (e.g., Škoda VHJ)

Note: Solid lines denote strong channels of communication and coordination; broken lines denote weak channels.

While the directorate controlled critical horizontal channels to the regional council and SBČS branch, it also had virtually full discretion over resources and the writing of governance rules. In so doing, it could command and favor certain members regarding production changes and program development. With limited powers and resources to protect their autonomy, member firms and plants developed strong, mutual sub-contracting links and bargained directly through barter and changes in standards. In contrast, TST represents what I call a *polycentric* VHJ network (see fig. 2.2). The TST directorate and the member firms jointly held formal and informal management and financial powers. Member firms developed close relationships with their respective regional or district councils and SBČS branches. These dispersed channels provided firms political and financial resources to protect their relative independence and limit the directorate's attempts to alter production and rationalize integral parts and input production. The directorate facilitated and did not impose cooperation within TST. The various SBČS branches and regional/district regional councils supplemented the relative weakness of the directorate by aiding firms to coordinate the flow of resources.

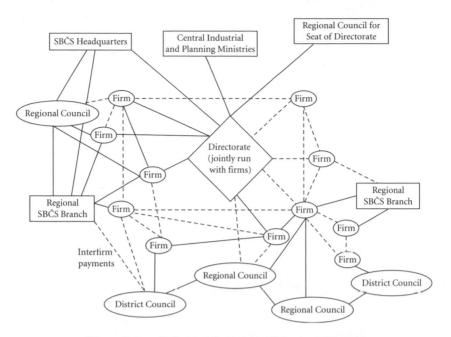

Figure 2.2.   Polycentric Network (e.g., TST VHJ)

Note: Strength of technical links varies; direct bargaining among firms and directorate over rules, resources, and external customer-supply relations. Solid lines denote strong channels of communication and coordination; broken lines denote weak channels.

Directorate manages relations with central government organs and basic trade relations with other VHJs and FTOs. Councils and SBČS branches aid firms in district and region with interfirm payments and limited trade or bargaining relations with other VHJs or firms.

By the mid-1980s, the distribution of power, and in turn economic coordination, no longer emanated from the formal VHJ structures but rather from the political and social relationships that grew up within the distinct VHJ networks. The strength of these relationships can be seen in how the VHJ networks reproduced themselves in the face of the state's attempt in 1987–88 to break up and dissolve VHJs.

In late 1987, the ČSSR government enacted reforms to liberalize the economy gradually with new wholesale price and tax systems, indicative planning, two-tier banking, partial foreign investments, a consolidation of ministries, and full self-financing for firms.[109] At the center of the reform was the reorganization of industry through the dissolution of VHJs. The aim was to increase competition by breaking up VHJs and large firms into many new and smaller state enterprises as independent legal entities. However, amendments were added to the criteria of recombining assets, the linking of relevant branch foreign trade organizations (FTOs), and the creation of voluntary associations by legally independent firms. Managers and administrative councils subsequently were able to reproduce their links in at least two major ways.

First, as indicated by the increase in industrial concentration, managers merged firms and plants, and in many cases converted virtually whole VHJs into single state firms.[110] As tables 2.15 and 2.16 show, the number of industrial firms actually decreased by one-third, and employment per firm increased. Between 1987 and 1989, the number of Czech engineering firms, for instance, dropped from 175 to 109, as the employment in firms with over 5,000 employees jumped from 140,000 to 236,000. Along with the major steel firms, Škoda Plzeň is a case in point of the fight to limit fragmentation.[111] In June 1988, the VHJ officially became the state firm Škoda Plzeň. After two large *koncern* firms in Moravia and southern Bohemia fought to become independent, the regional and city councils aided Škoda Plzeň in retaining plants and making three other *koncern* firms, including Škoda Praha, subsidiaries. Moreover, as FTOs became state joint-stock companies, Škoda Plzeň incorporated the previously independent Škoda Export as a subsidiary.

The second main form of reproduction was allowing *koncern* firms to retain their plants, become independent state firms, and create a weaker directorate through a voluntary association.[112] If the first form showed the dominance of a single firm over the network and a region, the second showed a more dramatic struggle between firms, the VHJ directorate, and the councils. Along with chemical and heavy pump manufacturers, TST is representative. With the aid of already decentralized financial accounts and their various regional and district councils, TST firms pushed to become independent state firms. However, because each firm alone lacked financial strength and direct foreign trade experience, the firms formed the association SST, or "the Union of Manufacturers and Suppliers of Engineering Technique," in which each firm held membership shares (eventually equity). The TST directorate was converted into the SST directorate, whose board was composed of SST firm directors. The SST directorate was responsible for common domestic and import procurement, export and R&D strategies, facilitating joint ventures with foreign firms, and obtaining investment loans for joint or individual production programs. Moreover, in 1987 TST used similar arguments as Škoda Plzeň and obtained 50 percent of the equity of their main FTO, Strojimport. These shares remained pooled within SST, and the SST director represented its members in Strojimport as chairman of the board.

Despite the dissolution of VHJs and legal changes, the two ideal-type networks remained, perhaps pushing toward their extreme points. For instance in Škoda's network, top management consolidated both legal and informal power by converting the VHJ into a single firm with plants, which it

TABLE 2.15. Number of Industrial State Firms and Employment, 1987

Sectors	Number of Firms	Within Employment Size Category					Number of Employees in Thousands	Within Employment Size Category				
		<500	501–1,000	1,001–2,500	2,501–5,000	>5,000		<500	501–1,000	1,001–2,500	2,501–5,000	>5,000
						ČSSR						
Total	884	89	179	399	163	54	1,843	28	133	648	565	474
Steel A[a]	16	—	1	5	2	8	128	—	1	9	8	110
Steel B[a]	19	4	6	5	3	1	31	2	5	8	10	6
Chemicals and rubber[b]	67	12	19	23	11	2	109	3	13	38	41	14
Engineering	226	24	48	101	33	20	507	7	36	168	112	184
Electronics	52	1	7	33	9	2	109	0	5	54	37	13
						ČSR						
Total	630	60	122	292	117	39	1,333	18	91	468	404	352
Steel A[a]	12	—	1	4	1	6	98	—	1	7	4	86
Steel B[a]	15	4	5	3	3	—	21	2	4	5	10	—
Chemicals and rubber[b]	46	10	16	15	3	2	63	2	11	26	10	14
Engineering	175	17	35	84	24	15	391	5	27	138	81	140
Electronics	33	—	3	23	6	1	72	—	2	35	27	8

Source: ČSSR Statistical Yearbook
[a]Steel A includes ferrous metals; Steel B includes nonferrous metals
[b]Includes chemicals and rubber manufacturing

TABLE 2.16. Number of Industrial State Firms and Employment, 1989

Sectors	Number of Firms	Within Employment Size Category					Number of Employees in Thousands	Within Employment Size Category				
		<500	501–1,000	1,001–2,500	2,501–5,000	>5,000		<500	501–1,000	1,001–2,500	2,501–5,000	>5,000
ČSSR												
Total	588	54	114	243	109	68	1,855	17	87	401	378	972
Steel A[a]	16	—	1	5	3	7	123	—	1	9	11	102
Steel B[a]	17	5	4	4	3	1	26	2	3	6	10	5
Chemicals and rubber[b]	32	4	6	10	6	6	132	2	3	16	23	88
Engineering	134	7	33	53	20	21	486	2	23	89	72	300
Electronics	32	3	6	15	5	3	111	1	5	25	20	60
ČSR												
Total	430	48	84	175	74	49	1,344	15	63	283	257	726
Steel A[a]	12	—	1	4	2	5	94	—	1	7	7	79
Steel B[a]	13	5	4	1	3	—	16	2	3	1	10	—
Chemicals and rubber[b]	24	4	5	9	2	4	57	2	3	14	7	41
Engineering	109	5	26	43	17	18	386	1	18	69	62	236
Electronics	20	3	3	9	3	2	34	1	2	16	13	55

Source: ČSSR Statistical Yearbook
[a]Steel A includes ferrous metals; Steel B includes nonferrous metals
[b]Includes chemicals and rubber manufacturing

ruled. In TST's network, member firms used their political and financial powers to increase their independence but still create SST. Managers ran SST jointly and did not have to worry about a directorate with independent political or resources channels to the central Party-state or regional councils.

Concluding Remarks

In this chapter, I have argued that, despite its relatively high level of industrialization and apparently orthodox communist regime, the ČSSR evolved into distinct sociopolitical networks because of the interaction of two levels of politics. First, at the macro level, the ČSSR Party-state attempted to maintain political-economic control and develop a system of mass production by creating and strengthening middle-level, overlapping institutions—namely VHJs for industrial management, SBČS bank branches for financial management, and regional and district Party councils for territorial administration. At the micro level, VHJ managers attempted to meet the increasing industrial needs of the ČSSR and the CMEA and adapt to the shortage environment by increasing their self-sufficiency and broadening their production scope. This strategy demanded the creation of formal and informal rules within VHJs to coordinate production and access to resources but with limited intervention by central ministries. The partial decentralization of decision making attendant to the strengthening of the middle level-institutions gave VHJ managers the opportunity to build direct, horizontal bargaining channels with SBČS branches and councils. These relationships enabled VHJ managers to share political and financial risk, coordinated production, and build an authority structure within their semiautonomous VHJs. That is, the channels spread financial risk by enabling VHJs to access needed funds to support their broad production capabilities and internal bargaining regimes without soliciting aid continually from the planning commission or ministries. The channels spread political risk by enabling certain VHJ managers to combine their authority with that of councils and bank branches to limit the intervention of central state authorities and create rules to maintain the flow of production and resolve conflicts within VHJs. In turn, a VHJ became a sociopolitical network or coalition of particular VHJ managers, SBČS branch officers, and regional or district representatives that together acquired state resources and created rules and authority structures to govern production.

Second, this interaction between the two levels of politics allowed for distinctly different VHJ networks to emerge, despite the attempts by the central Party-state authorities to create a single type of VHJ *(koncern)* and implement partial reforms uniformly. Two ideal types of VHJ networks—hierarchical and polycentric—emerged within the mechanical engineering industry. The two ideal types grew out of contrasting histories of industrial and planning organization. These histories interacted with the strengthening of the middle-level institutions to shape in different ways the formation of VHJ networks—the formal and informal governance rules, authority structure, production organization, roles of members, and channels to councils and SBČS branches. Škoda and TST represented the respective hierarchical and polycentric VHJ networks.

Finally, I showed how these networks reproduced themselves despite the formal dissolution of the VHJ system and the attempts to break up firms and liberalize the economy. The patterns of financial and production interdependencies between member firms and plants clearly shaped the way VHJ networks reproduced themselves. But the ability to maintain order and support the different methods of production in the face of shortage and new laws depended largely on the patterns of sociopolitical relationships forged between certain VHJ managers, SBČS branches, and councils.

In the following chapters, I analyze how these sociopolitical relationships impacted the formation of new institutions for economic governance after the so-called velvet revolution in 1989. I will compare and contrast how the former VHJ networks attempted to reproduce themselves and interacted with the new government's attempts to impose its owns designs for governance institutions.

State Designs for Defining Property Rights and Maintaining Asset Value in the Czech Republic

Although Czechoslovakia remained a holdout of orthodox communism until late 1989, it would soon become a post-communist leader in market-oriented reforms. While countries such as Hungary and Poland grappled with large foreign debts, growing budget deficits, high inflation, and contentious policy fights, Czechoslovakia's new political leaders took advantage of the country's relative macroeconomic stability and lack of organized resistance to market reforms to create a powerful central policy-making apparatus for the execution of rapid, wholesale transformation of economic governance institutions. By the early 1990s, the Western business press, academics, and the multilateral lending institutions would crown the Czech government's cohesion and mass privatization policies as the models of transformation strategy, often overlooking or brushing aside the drastic fall in GDP and industrial output, the alarming growth in insolvency, the slowness of firm and bank restructuring, and relative lack of FDI.[1]

But why wouldn't they? A strong, autonomous change team committed to the rapid establishment of hard budget constraints, a new private property rights regime, and prudent, rule-based financial assistance to domestic banks were necessary and sufficient for the standard approaches to transformation. Whether the rapid collapse of Czechoslovak communism had left behind atomized economic actors or networks of stakeholders mattered little. For some, a government cut off from the rent-seeking special interest groups as well as the rapid creation clear ownership and creditor rights would allow economic actors to resolve restructuring disputes through contracts, buyouts, and closures. For others, a coherent state apparatus that used clear rules for debt relief would allow members of industrial networks to convert past ties into a new, stable form of governance based on cross-ownership.

This chapter begins a three-part examination of Czech transformation that attempts to make sense of the unexpected successes and failures in restructuring by employing my embedded politics approach. This chapter in particular gives an overview of the macropolitics of government institutional designs and their initial impacts on industrial and financial restructuring. Initial praise for the Czech model turned to criticism of a faulty capital-markets regulatory structure—but only after the Czech market collapsed under the weight of the 1998 Russian crisis.[2] It was as if the Czechs, like the Russians, forgot to read the last chapter of the technocratic handbook. No one could imagine that the depoliticization strategy itself, with its dismissal of the sociopolitical embeddedness of economic activity and institution building, was flawed at its roots. In contrast, in this chapter I argue that the apparently prudent adherence by the Czechoslovak and then Czech governments to the depoliticization strategy actually exacerbated a growing restructuring and investment stalemate among domestic banks, investment funds, firms, and foreign investors.

In the first section, I analyze how initial disputes within the dominant Czech coalition led the government to create a centralized, insulated policy-making apparatus and to address the transfer of ownership and the maintenance of asset value as separate issues. The expectation was that the main domestic banks, equity investment companies, and foreign investors would become the principal agents of restructuring.

Through the rest of the chapter, I examine why these actors failed to fulfill this expectation. I first analyze the government's attempt to strengthen creditor rights, budget constraints, and the capital base of banks. These policies reinforced the financial interdependencies between the main Czech banks and industrial firms and left the banks with little means and interest in leading the bankruptcy or restructuring of firms. I then examine why the famous Czech voucher privatization not only failed to create governance institutions to help limit these risks but also probably worsened them. In creating incentives for the main Czech banks and insurance company to control the principal investment companies (IPCs), voucher privatization left the banks virtually alone to bear all the risks and responsibilities of firm restructuring. In turn, the main Czech banks had their IPCs, at best, protect firms from hostile takeovers and invest in arbitrage activities rather than in active corporate governance.

In the final section of the chapter, I bring the growing financial crisis in the Czech Republic (CR) full circle by briefly analyzing the failure of FDI to play an active role in industrial restructuring. Foreign direct investors aimed to invest in only parts of interlinked firms and plants through joint ventures and not complete buyouts of assets. In turn, they sought contractual commitments from both Czech managers and the Czech government to limit their risk of financing the inherited debt burdens of industrial firms. Since these commitments were tantamount to a major revision of Czech privatization policy, the Czechs rejected the demands of prospective foreign investors. (A more detailed analysis of the problems surrounding the entry of FDI will be given in chapter 4.)

Constructing a State and Institutional System in the Post-1989 Czech Republic

The November 1989 "velvet revolution" in Czechoslovakia (CSFR)[3] ushered in a liberally oriented transitional government, whose main aims were to prepare the country for massive economic transformation and free parliamentary elections in June 1990.[4] In their efforts to consolidate government power and rally public support, the new federal, and particularly Czech, politicians would take advantage of three critical legacies of the former regime that their Hungarian and Polish neighbors lacked.

First, the communists had left the country with a relatively equal distribution of income, the second highest GDP per capita in the CMEA, and relatively favorable macroeconomic conditions.[5] For instance, by 1989, consumer price inflation was about 1.4 percent, with most basic goods available. The savings rate was 3.6 percent. Unemployment was nonexistent and reached about 1 percent in 1990. The federal budget had a deficit of 5.5 billion Kcs, less than 2 percent of expenditures, and was in a slight surplus of .8 billion Kcs in 1990. By 1989, Czechoslovakia was a net creditor within the CMEA, and its foreign debt stood at a modest $7.9 billion, rising to only $9.8 billion by the end of 1992. (See tables 3.1–3.5.)

This stability and low debt allowed the government officials to use privatization mainly as a vehicle for institution building rather than as a way to achieve other objectives, such as improving revenues, employment, and regional development.[6] In contrast, problems in the stop-and-go policies in Hungary and Poland were partially attributed to their governments trying to fulfill too many (and often conflicting) objectives through privatization.[7]

Second, the lack of partial reform experiments with market socialism in Czechoslovakia had left virtually all productive assets under formal state control. By the late 1980s, the state sector accounted for 97 percent of output and about 95 percent of employment, significantly higher than those for Hungary and Poland.[8] The lack of reforms avoided a partial distribution of property rights that could be used to thwart privatization. For instance, in Poland worker councils had obtained veto powers on ownership changes and used

TABLE 3.1. Annual Percent Change in Real Gross Domestic Product (GDP)

	1989	1990	1991	1992	1993	1994	1995	1996	1997
Czechoslovakia	—	0.5	—	—	—	—	—	—	—
Czech Republic	4.5	−1.2	−11.5	−3.3	0.6	2.2	5.9	4.8	−1.0
Slovak Republic	−0.6	−3.4	−14.5	−7.0	−4.1	4.9	6.8	6.6	6.5
Hungary	0.4	−3.5	−11.9	−3.3	−0.6	2.9	1.5	1.3	4.6
Poland	0.2	−11.6	−7.0	2.6	3.8	5.2	7.0	6.0	6.8

Source: Business Central Europe (2001), Slovak Statistical Yearbook (Relevant Years), World Bank (1999b).

TABLE 3.2. Annual Percent Change in Consumer Price Index (CPI)

	1989	1990	1991	1992	1993	1994	1995	1996	1997
Czechoslovakia	1.4	10.0	57.9	10.9	—	—	—	—	—
Czech Republic	1.4	9.7	56.6	11.1	20.8	10.0	9.1	8.8	8.5
Slovak Republic	1.3	10.4	61.2	10.0	23.2	13.5	9.9	5.8	6.1
Hungary	17.1	28.4	35.0	23.0	22.5	18.8	28.2	23.6	18.3
Poland	0.0	585.8	70.3	43.0	35.3	32.2	27.8	19.9	14.9

Source: Business Central Europe (2001), Slovak Statistical Yearbook (Relevant Years), World Bank (1999b).

TABLE 3.3. Unemployment Rate

	1990	1991	1992	1993	1994	1995	1996	1997
Czech Republic	0.8	4.1	2.6	3.5	3.2	2.9	3.5	5.2
Slovak Republic	1.6	11.8	10.4	14.4	14.8	13.1	12.8	12.5
Hungary	1.9	7.4	12.3	12.1	10.4	11.7	11.4	11.0
Poland	6.3	11.8	13.6	16.4	16.0	14.9	13.2	10.3

Source: Business Central Europe (2001), Slovak Statistical Yearbook (Relevant Years), World Bank (1999b).

TABLE 3.4. Fiscal Budget Surplus (+) or Deficit (−) as a Percent of GDP

	1989	1990	1991	1992	1993	1994	1995
Czechoslovakia	−0.007	—	−2.7	−2.6	—	—	—
Czech Republic	—	—	−1.9	−3.1	0.5	−1.3	−1.2
Slovak Republic	—	—	−3.2	−2.4	−6.2	−5.2	−1.6
Hungary	−1.5	0.5	−2.9	−6.8	−5.5	−9.2	−5.5
Poland	−7	−3.1	−6.7	−6.7	−3.1	−2.4	−2.4

Source: Business Central Europe (2001), Slovak Statistical Yearbook (Relevant Years), World Bank (1999b).

them to block mass privatization. In Hungary reforms that spurred the growth in the second economy, the dispersion of property rights among managers, and the emergence of certain forms of cross-ownership among banks and firms created obstacles for the rapid reorganization and sale of assets.[9] In short, the CSFR could avoid the arduous and politically explosive

TABLE 3.5. External Debt in Dollars and Its Ratio to Exports

	1989	1990	1991		1992		1993	1994	1995	1996	1997
	Billions of U.S. Dollars	Billions of U.S. Dollars	Billions of U.S. Dollars	Debt/ Exports	Billions of U.S. Dollars	Debt/ Exports	Debt/ Exports	Debt/ Exports	Debt/ Exports	Debt/ Exports	Debt/ Exports
Czechoslovakia	7.9	8.1	9.4	0.8	9.7	0.9	—	—	—	—	—
Czech Republic	—	—	—	—	—	—	0.5	0.5	0.6	0.6	0.7
Slovak Republic	—	—	—	—	—	—	0.4	0.4	0.5	0.7	0.9
Hungary	—	21.3	22.6	1.8	22.6	2.2	2.1	2.1	1.8	1.3	0.9
Poland	—	49.4	53.4	2.9	53.4	4.1	2.5	2.5	1.2	1.1	1.0

Source: Svejnar and Dyba (1994), Budina, Hanousek, and Tuma (1994), World Bank (1999b).

tasks of renationalizing firms and reasserting state control over them, which hindered Polish and Hungarian attempts to form governance institutions and privatize firms quickly.[10]

Third, the lack of reforms and the sudden collapse of communist power had left the new governing politicians with little organized resistance to reform and the opportunity to create broad catchall political parties and movements.[11] The only strong political organizations in the CSFR were the revolutionary umbrella movements of Civic Forum (OF) in the Czech Republic and Public Against Violence (VPN) in Slovakia. The Czechoslovak Communist Party became quickly discredited, and the only other parties with a potentially significant following, the Czech and Slovak Christian Democrats, had pledged their support to radical reforms. Moreover, even after OF split, the largest political party, the Civic Democratic Party, had the strong support of a wide range of social groups. In contrast, the partial reforms and negotiated revolutions in Hungary and Poland had allowed for several parties to emerge and fight vigorously for control over transformation policies.[12]

The lack of reforms in Czechoslovakia also left poorly organized social groups to lobby and fight the new government over policies.[13] The potentially strongest group, the former communist trade union, had become fragmented as it struggled to reorganize itself and establish public credibility. For instance, the transition government easily dissolved in March 1990 the right by workers' councils to elect management, while the union fought an uphill battle to obtain the right to exist and to strike (eventually with the aid of the International Labor Organization).[14] In contrast, Polish politics in the 1980s provided solid legacies for the Solidarity and communist trade unions that would actively contest transformation policies. In turn, such organized social groups would create havoc for the Hungarian and Polish transformation designs.[15]

To sum up, in contrast to those of their neighbors, the ČSSR legacies of macroeconomic stability, state retention of virtually all property rights, and poorly organized interest groups gave the Czechs the social, economic, and political preconditions often cited as optimal by advocates of the depoliticization strategy and by path dependent analyses of Czech economic reform.[16] Moreover, the CSFR, and particularly the Czechs, were blessed with high standards of education, especially in literacy, mathematics, and the sciences, as well as strong traditions of moderation and tolerance.[17]

Policy Formation and the Centralization of Power

In the June 1990 parliamentary elections, OF and VPN won resounding victories for control of the federal parliament as well as of their respective republic parliaments. Together, they had planned to use the electoral momentum to pass quickly the Scenario for Economic Reform, which outlined the basic terms of standard liberalization and stabilization packages and microeconomic policies, including tax reform, de-etatization and privatization of property, and increased transparency and central control of budget allocation.[18] The legislation also outlined the reorganization of ministries, with the continuance of a single central bank and Ministry of Finance (MF), the dissolution of the planning commission and most subsidies by the end of 1990, the consolidation of branch and trade ministries into strengthened republic-level Ministries of Industry, and the creation at the republic levels of ministries of privatization and state administrators of property (Funds for National Property, or FNMs).[19]

It took, however, over three months to pass the legislation, with the delays revealing a growing rift between the republics and particularly within OF. Citing a need to quell infighting, OF leaders called for internal elections of an OF chairman. The clear winner was Finance Minister and "reform czar" Vaclav Klaus, who vowed to keep the country on the fast track of economic reform and convert OF into a properly organized center-right party.[20] By early 1991, OF formally split into three parties: Klaus's Civic Democratic Party (ODS), the largest party; the center-left Civic Movement (OH); and the liberal, small Civic Democratic Alliance (ODA), whose members were long associates of Klaus but refused to succumb to his autocratic style. ODS and ODA controlled most of the key economic and privatization agencies, while OH maintained some influence through its control of the Federal Ministry of Labor (ML), and the Czech Ministry of Industry (MPO).[21]

The divisions between the parties reflected conflicts not so much over the general aims of reform but rather over two key issues about how policy was to be created: whether policies should include a variety of methods and whether they should include participation from different ministries and social groups. In the three most contested policy areas, the trend was to centralize policy-making powers and to create clear rules and procedures that favored rapid execution of policies.

The first confrontation concerned labor market policy.[22] Fearing inflationary effects of the devaluation and price liberalization, Klaus aimed to control wage growth through minimum wage controls, restrictive unemployment compensation, and tax penalties on firms (over twenty-five employees) that exceeded specified limits to the average nominal wage rate. At the same time OH Labor Minister Petr Miller advocated strengthening organized labor and an active labor market policy. The result was the creation of a tripartite bargaining structure between the government, the newly converted communist labor union (Czech and Slovak Confederation of Trade Unions, or

ČMKOS), and the nascent employers association. Klaus, however, positioned his ministry to have substantial influence on the terms and substance of discussions in the tripartite council. In turn, the council was used mainly to inform labor and management about labor market policies and allow the government to impose restrictions on wage growth.[23] Given its weak public standing, fragmented organization, and its determination to distance itself from the communist past, ČMKOS viewed this as the best possible deal, declaring "unceasing dialogue" was the best way to ensure speedy reform.[24] In 1991 and 1992, real wages and income declined substantially and at rates faster than the declines in productivity.

The second issue was the reorganization of local government.[25] All sides had agreed to the dismantling of *narodni vybory* system. Viewed as strongholds of communist aparatchiks, the eight regional councils were dissolved and the finances of district councils were brought under immediate control of the central government. Disagreement came over the future decentralization of governmental powers. OH supported the rapid creation of new regional councils with popular elections and increased financial autonomy for subnational governments, as well as a new constitution that would grant republics greater policy-making powers and weaken the federal government. ODS and ODA saw both actions as a direct assault on the tight control needed to implement restrictive fiscal and monetary policies and rapid mass privatization. ODS and ODA, in turn, outmaneuvered OH in parliament to delay reforms for councils until 1993 and block discussions of a new constitution until the June 1992 parliamentary elections. The result was a fragmentation and weakening of local governments, which lacked any autonomous coordinating powers. For instance, in the CR the number of municipalities increased by 50 percent to over 6,200, and they remained dependent on the central government for over 60 percent of their revenues. Moreover, although the constituent municipal councils elected the councils of the seventy-five districts in the CR, the republic governments appointed district chairmen, and their revenues came essentially through various ministry grants for specific programs. Subsequently, several leading Czech scholars of local politics have argued that local governments were beholden to a distant center and unable to play a serious role in privatization and regional development.

The third issue, on the potential conflict between rapid privatization and industrial restructuring, was personified by Jan Vrba (OH), the Czech Minister of Industry (MPO), and Vaclav Klaus with his allies in the Czech Ministry of Privatization and FNM.[26] Both sides were in agreement on the main points of privatization: that low levels of domestic capital limited the use of standard sales of assets; that fire sales and asset stripping had to be prevented; that bureaucracy had to be minimized; and that the implementation of government policy had to be protected from debilitating rent seekers. The main differences concerned the speed and methods of Large Privatization. The Klausians believed that government intervention into industries could lead to prolonged state ownership, managerial manipulations of assets and state policy, and, ultimately, a breakdown of popular support for market reforms. The Klausians advocated rapid privatization through vouchers—a give-away scheme whereby each adult citizen would receive vouchers to be redeemed in a "stock market" to acquire actual shares in companies. Voucher privatization could end-run attempts by managers to block the process and could quickly install private owners to discipline managers. Vrba shared the Klausians' suspicions of managers but was equally skeptical about the ability of new voucher owners to provide the needed capital and know-how to upgrade antiquated Czech industries for competing in world markets. Citing an MPO-sponsored study that Czechoslovak industry would need $2 to $3 billion of direct investment per year from 1991–2000, Vrba advocated a government strategy for attracting foreign investment, namely through asset purchases.[27] The Klausians saw this as a recipe for unconstrained government intervention.

The resulting compromise combined vouchers and foreign purchases for privatization of industrial firms but limited the risk of delays and government intervention. The compromise had two main parts: the rules of privatization and the organization of a state apparatus to implement the process. Privatization proposals for whole or parts of firms would be accepted from both management and outsiders, who could combine such methods as vouchers, direct sales, public tenders, and management buyouts (MBOs).[28] With vouchers as the default method, priority using other methods would be given to projects that exhibited transparency, speed, and well-defined business plans with certified capital injection schedules. Vrba was satisfied because a significant share of firm equity could be reserved for purchase, the rules for purchases of large assets favored foreign strategic buyers, and privatization of such sectors as utilities, raw materials, and chemo-petrols would be put off until the second wave in 1992–93. The Klausians were satisfied because the majority of assets would be privatized through vouchers, and the government would be restricted from directly restructuring industrial assets before, during, or after privatization.[29]

The formation of a state apparatus for privatization focused on establishing clear state boundaries, a system of internal checks, and certain decree powers.[30] The founding ministry (e.g., MPO) reviewed and approved privatization proposals for firms under its jurisdiction, which were sent for final approval to the Ministry of Privatization. Firms marked for privatization were corporatized and their assets/liabilities transferred to the FNM, which then had to implement the approved privatization projects. As an independent legal entity representing the state, the FNM had strict rules that cut off ministries and parliament from direct access to firms and to privatization revenues. Revenues were earmarked for specific programs (such as health services) and the rest could be used only with the agreement of the council of economic ministers, which included the ministers of finance, industry, privatization, economy, and agriculture, the chairman of the state bank, and the prime minister.[31] The council of economic ministers also held decree powers to amend parts of the existing privatization law and to review any alterations in already approved privatization projects. The whole process was held by law to a strict timetable for the approval and implementation of projects, and the commencement of voucher trading.

These compromises, particularly on privatization, allowed policymakers to depoliticize institution building and restructuring in two ways. First, they appeared to create a state structure with the traits that the standard approaches view as vital for a group of technocrats to define and implement on its own the new policies and institutional foundations of the economy. These often-cited traits boil down to a system of executive dominance and rules that create space for an elite team or apparatus of technocrats with a unity of purpose, a high degree of insulation from social groups, and a virtual monopoly over legal and financial resources.[32] Through the tripartite council, the weakening of local government, and confining of financial and privatization policy to a small group with decree powers, the new state apparatus could maintain the unity of purpose of rapid institution building and tight fiscal and monetary policies. The use of vouchers and the rules guiding privatization further limited the influence of social and interest groups. Moreover, the new apparatus controlled critical resources, from tax and privatization revenues to wage controls and property rights.

Second, the compromises created a policy framework that could facilitate the depoliticization of restructuring conflicts by addressing the delineation of ownership and the preservation of asset value as separate matters. Voucher privatization would quickly create new owners, who could reward and punish managers and resolve restructuring conflicts by the use of contracts, foreclosures, and buyouts. The procedures on foreign purchases would ensure rapid sales and the potential renovation of industries by foreigners without protracted state involvement. In the meantime, reform of the bankruptcy law and a well-defined partial write-off of bank debt would prevent asset stripping and strengthen the main banks to become active senior creditors.

The Duality of Privatization and Bank Restructuring in the Czech Republic

The main banks in the Czech Republic faced the dual challenge of cleaning their portfolios and maintaining a client base. In accordance with the de-politicization approaches,[33] the government aimed to help banks overcome this challenge by establishing a proper legal framework for universal banking and creditor rights, rapidly transferring majority ownership stakes into private hands through vouchers, and implementing strict supervisory rules, competition, and limited, rule-based recapitalization and debt-relief measures. This policy approach had the advantages of hardening budget constraints and preserving asset value while maintaining state autonomy. The view was that once given space to improve their capital adequacy and armed with senior creditor rights, the main banks would cut off problem firms and channel resources to more fruitful clients.

These policies, however, reinforced the interdependence between the main banks and industrial firms, and led the banks to view value preservation and use of their new rights as conflicting aims. The preexistence of tight financial links between banks and firms implies that the reorganization of one is closely tied with the reorganization of the other. But the new incentives and the absence of a public actor to support workouts reduced financial restructuring to the banks becoming the sole risk bearers of both their own and firm reorganization. The banks could not support this role, as cutting off insolvent clients or leading firm reorganization threatened their weak financial base given the current uncertainties and lack of experienced personnel. In turn, the defensive strategy of banks to protect their position vis-à-vis industrial firms but limit new loan exposure was an effort to buy time for the arrival of new firm owners who could alleviate some of the risk of resuscitating clients.

The Deepening of Financial Interdependencies

In chapter 2, I discussed how the financial experiments during the 1970s and 1980s had allowed the main sources of finance for Czechoslovak industrial firms to become retained earnings and bank loans. Indeed, by 1989 Czechoslovakia stood out among its comrades with domestic bank debt at 70 percent of GDP; for Hungary and Poland it was 46 percent and 30 percent, respectively.[34] Thus, if earnings became scarce, where could firms turn to cover operating costs? In light of the restrictive monetary and fiscal policies of the post-1989 government, the answer would be to one another, for partial finance through interfirm debt, but ultimately to the main domestic banks.

TABLE 3.6. Annual Rate of Change in Inflation, GDP, Investment, Industrial Production, and Exports, Czech Republic, 1989–93 (real indicators)

Indicator (%)	1989	1990	1991	1992	1993
Consumer Price Index	1.4	9.7	56.7	11.1	20.8
Producers Price Index	0.1	4.3	70.4	9.9	13.4
Gross Domestic Product	4.5	−1.2	−11.5	−3.3	0.57
Gross[a] investment	1.7	6.5	−26.7	10.2	8
Machinery and equipment[a]	0.9	12.7	−31	9.8	17.3
Industrial output	1.6	−3.3	−22.3	−7.7	−5.5
Export (nominal)[b]	162.1	162.5	233.6	248.1	338.4

Source: Statistical Yearbook (1993, 1994); Czech Statistical Office (1994); own calculations.
[a]Gross investment includes total work and deliveries; figures based on 1989 prices.
[b]Calculated in billions of Kcs/Kc FOB.

TABLE 3.7. Change in Territorial Structure of Czechoslovak Exports, 1989–92 (percent of total)

	1989	1990	1991	1992
Former CMEA	60.8[a]	49.4[a]	39.4	25.7
Former USSR	3.5	25.2	19.6	10.9

Source: Kolanda (1993, 21), Czech Statistical Office (1993).
[a] Includes GDR; for 1990, exports to former CMEA, excluding the GDR was 44.7 percent of total exports.

The collapse of the CMEA and the stabilization policies had the immediate effects of sharply reducing industrial firm liquidity and increasing firm leverage. Tables 3.6–3.8 show the large and persistent decline in GDP, industrial production, investment, and exports. Industrial sectors were hit the hardest. With their export orientation toward the CMEA and USSR, key Czech value-added sectors, such as machinery, were unable to find new markets quickly and watched their exports (measured in constant prices) drop by almost 25 percent in 1991 and 35 percent in 1992.[35] Second, real industrial output of manufacturing sectors declined even more rapidly than the national average. Between 1989 and 1992, real output for Czech mechanical machinery, electrical machinery, chemicals, and transport equipment fell by 50 percent, 66 percent, 35 percent, and 33 percent, respectively.[36] Although reliable sectoral financial data was not available for the early years, various estimates do show a consistent and significant decline in the cash flow and liquidity of manufacturing firms.[37] (See tables 3.9 and 3.10 for examples.)

The impact on the economy as a whole, and industrial firms in particular, was a drastic rise in indebtedness and insolvency, as firms turned to one another and to banks for credits to cover operating costs. The various government

TABLE 3.8. Comparison of Output (in constant prices), Average Profitability (current prices), and Exports (in constant prices) for Selected Branches, Czech Republic, 1989–92

Manufactured Branch	Real Output			Average Profitability			Real Export[b]		
(NACE)[a]	1990/1989	1991/1989	1992/1989	1990/1989	1991/1989	1992/1989	1991/1990	1992/1991
Coke, refined petroleum	78.35	68.61	63.81	124.17	92.05	176.27	61.44	116.72
Basic metals	97.48	70.05	58.07	126.05	152.79	161.4	123.07	99.99
Chemicals and chemical products	85.77	61.34	65.68	99.63	182.19	160.67	109.53	112.76
Rubber and plastic	91.12	64.33	73.58	140.09	167.93	193.19	100.46	118.34
Electrical machinery	94.92	69.8	44.08	91.5	198.75	165.6	78.4	96.65
Medical, precision instruments	84.16	42.12	51.62	45.07	45.14	−73.19	67.49	62.96
Motor vehicles, trailers	99.41	71.04	67.23	113.85	68.03	164.12	110	74.2
Other transport equipment	96.78	79.54	30.25	108.16	59.58	6.06	96.07	21.93
Textiles	99.42	65.53	61.06	103.65	93.66	41.36	104.55	93.57
Fabricated metal products	99.61	66.52	66.42	160.19	200.94	97.72	91.74	138.94
Machinery	94.48	64.7	50.95	106.55	109.38	36.64	75.47	65.08
Total industry	94.41	71.46	63.66	110.06	180.91	188.23	98.57	88.05

Source: Buchtikova and Flek (1993, 19, 23).
[a] NACE = Branch Classification of Economic Activities.
[b] Base periods are 1990 and 1991, respectively.

TABLE 3.9.   Liquidity and Debt Indicators by Manufacturing Sector

Manufacturing Sector	Current Assets/Total Payables[a]			Equity/Payables (current liabilities)[a]		
	1990	1991	1992	1990	1991	1992
Machines and Equipment of which:	4.53	2.98	2.37	5.96	2.6	2.44
Machines for production and mechanical energy	17.75	2.13	2.15	27.05	1.86	2.12
Motors (combustion, hydraulic)	25.98	2.39	2.04	40.06	2.01	2.12
Lifting and transport equipment	4.99	2.26	2.42	6.71	2.07	2.63
Industrial refrigeration equipment	6.48	4.65	2.74	4.34	1.79	1.86
Other equipment for general engineering	12.63	5.79	3.26	15.17	5.71	2.51
Machine tools, forming machines	3.82	2.79	2.16	4.88	2.09	2.01

Source: Spring (1993).
[a] Ratios are medians of selected branches.

TABLE 3.10.   Liquidity and Debt Indicators by Industry

Industry (selected)	Cash/Current Liabilities[a]		Equity/Cash (years of reproduction)	
	1991	1992	1991	1992
Iron and Steel	0.07	0.08	7.1	8.5
Nonferrous metals	0.08	0.1	11.1	11.5
Chemicals	0.15	0.15	5.9	6.5
Engineering	0.22	0.24	5.9	6.5
Electronics	0.1	0.1	9.5	9.5
Industry total average	0.17	0.19	6.3	7.8

Source: Hlavacek and Tuma (1993); MPOCR (1993).
[a] Healthy industrial firms commonly have a ratio of 0.4 or more. See Davidson et al. (1988); Casey and Bartczak (1995).

TABLE 3.11.   Interest Coverage Ratios (times interest earned), Part 1

Industrial Sector (number of firms)	1992	1993
Metallurgy (31)	3.85	1.97
Metal products (36)	2.88	1.86
Machines and equipment (88)	1.53	0.75
Electronic machinery and equipment (23)	3.19	2.12
Total Industry Average (424)	3.24	1.22

Source: Czech Union of Industry (internal documents).
Note: Computed as: (pretax profits + interest rate costs)/(interest rate costs).

estimates showed that total payment arrears (i.e., inability of payments between firms and to banks) were more than doubling annually and reached as high as 102.6 percent of GDP by 1992.[38] Industrial firms took the lion's share. Government estimates, for instance, showed that industry accounted for about 70 percent of total arrears by late 1991. Of this, engineering accounted for 37.5 percent, steel for 14.4 percent, and electronics for 12.1 percent.[39] The Czech Union of Industry estimated that 60 to 70 percent of its members were delinquent in payments, with engineering firms accounting for over 40 percent of industrial arrears in 1992 and 1993.[40]

Not surprisingly, industrial firms became highly leveraged and increasingly dependent on bank loans. For instance, when firm financial data was more unified, the Czech MPO estimated that in 1993 the debt–equity ratios for such sectors as general and capital goods engineering were 85.8 percent and 99.1 percent, respectively, three times greater than their 1990 averages.[41] Tables 3.11 and 3.12 show the corresponding significant decline in the ability of industrial firms to cover their interest rate costs. MPO estimates showed that the average interest rate coverage ratio for the engineering industry fell to .71 by late 1993.[42] If Czech industrial firms were becoming so tied to debt, and, in turn, to the banks, the question remained as to what the main banks and the government would do about these firms and systemwide default.

TABLE 3.12. Interest Coverage Ratios (times interest earned), Part 2

Industrial Sector	1992	1993
Chemicals	5.37	2.89
Rubber products	4.19	2.65
Metalworking products	3.51	1.58
Machines and equipment	1.56	0.6
Electrical and optical equipment	1.69	0.84
Transportation vehicles and equipment	2.74	−0.08
Total manufacturing average	5.34	2.52

Source: Analýza ekonomiky CR a odvětví působnosti MPO v roce 1993, Ministry of Industry and Trade, Czech Republic (1993, 1994). Author's own calculations.

The New Rules for Financial Stalemate

Five universal Czech banks were carved out of the former Czechoslovak State Bank in late 1989. Komercni Banka (KB) and Investicni Banka (IB) were the leading commercial banks, and the Czech Savings Bank (CSB) held 68 percent of houschold savings. Along with the KOB, the state clearinghouse for certain old, nonperforming loans, the five banks accounted for 82 percent of total loans and 85 percent of total deposits in 1992.[43] Although the government allowed foreign banks to operate in the CR and new domestic banks to be established, the banking sector remained highly concentrated. As of November 1994, the five banks plus KOB accounted for 79.1 percent of loans and 83.6 percent of deposits.[44] Over 50 percent of equity for each of these banks was privatized in the first wave of voucher privatization, quickly allowing the Czechs to become the regional leaders of bank privatization. By 1993, only 20.6 percent of total bank assets were under state control in the CR, while the comparable figures for Hungary and Poland were, respectively, 74.4 percent and 86.2 percent.[45]

As the ownership and creditor rights of banks were delineated, the government used a three-pronged strategy to harden budget constraints and strengthen the financial position of the banks. The banks first were under pressure to increase their capital base and cleanup their balance sheets.[46] The Ministry of Finance (MF) and the newly independent Central Bank (CNB) moved quickly to use the opportunities of a relatively stable macroeconomy to set strict operating conditions for the newly formed banks.[47] The aim was to strengthen their capital base and shut down the easy access of transforming state firms to cheap money, a growing problem in Poland and Hungary.[48] The main Czech banks, notably IB and KB, started with meager capital adequacy ratios between 1.25 and 1.5 percent. The CNB and international audits monitored the banks in meeting legal standards based on the Basle Banking Accords—6.25 percent by the end of 1993 and 8 percent by the end of 1996.[49]

As corporate debt rose, the government became increasingly concerned about transferring worthless bank and firm equity to the public. The
Klausians recognized the immediate need of protecting asset value, but they
also sought to strengthen creditor rights, limit public actors engaging in arduous financial negotiations, and maintain the centralization of power.[50]
On the one hand, the government suspended and reformed the bankruptcy
law between September 1992 and April 1993 to protect the assets for privatization and limit mass liquidations due to dubious bankruptcy schemes
initiated by insiders and trade creditors that were becoming prominent in
Hungary and Poland at the time.[51] The new legal provisions—a three-
month protection period for debtors, a special regime for firms involved in
large privatization, and a conflict of interest clause—were to prevent both
theft and the likelihood that the new shareholders would receive assets
about to be liquidated. In doing so, the law effectively strengthened the position of senior creditors (i.e., banks) and kept the focus of bankruptcy as a
liquidation process rather than a protracted workout negotiation. On the
other hand, to avoid an impact on the state budget, the FNM, the administrator for property to be privatized, financed a limited write-off from its ac-
cumulated and expected privatization receipts. In early 1992, the FNM
transferred to the main Czech banks 22.2 billion Kcs for loan write-offs and
7.8 billion Kcs in bonds for bank recapitalization. In the autumn of 1992,
the KOB purchased 15 billion Kcs of loans from KB and IB at 80 percent of
the nominal value.[52] As the write-offs were rule based and KOB purchased
only loans made before 1990, the government did not create the impression
of more bailouts to come. Moreover, the FNM resources were virtually ex-
hausted.[53] Klaus blocked an alternative and more extensive write-off program, which would have been directed by the Czech and Slovak MPOs, for
fear of jeopardizing the stabilization program and delaying privatization.
The republic ministries of privatization had already shown their willingness
to use their authority to delay the review of privatization projects by three
months.[54]

From the viewpoint of the standard approaches, these measures had the
attractions of not only keeping rapid privatization on track and maintaining
state autonomy but also giving the main banks the means and incentives to
rid themselves of the few most problem debtors and become active agents of
corporate restructuring.[55] In this view, banks and firms are autonomous actors, with unitary and independent preferences or goals. Banks, for instance,
have a primary interest to recover loans as soon as possible and improve their
capital base. Debts are viewed as stocks: they not only connote a net value of
a firm but they can also aid banks to discipline firms with the threat of liqui-

dation and lead performing clients with long-term financing. The main banks could drop troubled industrial firms and attempt to retain the custom of good firms in the face of increased competition from the foreign banks. To the extent that the main banks retained some financially distressed firms, they could use their improved capital base and creditor rights to manage directly corporate restructuring. These powers could be all the more enhanced for the main banks with their dominant equity investment companies potentially controlling corporate boards of clients (to be discussed).[56] For the government, policy is reduced to single legislative acts about property rights and debt relief, restructuring conflicts are resolved, and cohesion and autonomy are retained.

Yet, from a network point of view, the interests of economic actors are more ambiguous, allowing the assertion of new independent property rights and leverage powers on the one hand, and the preservation of asset value on the other, to come into conflict.[57] The tight financial links between the banks and industrial firms create interdependencies that constrain bank discretion. Because value depends on future income flows—the interest income banks generate from a limited number of clients and the cash flows generated by new production experiments of closely connected firms—the potential governance power of creditor rights and leverage is diluted. If the links have potential value, then one would not want to cut them. But maintaining them by asserting exclusive control could be extremely risky for a single actor under present conditions.

For instance, estimations of risky loans in 1991 ranged between 25 percent and 40 percent of total loans.[58] Although total growth of loans to manufacturing firms was minimal, these firms still represented the bulk of loans classified as risky and doubtful (see table 3.13). Perhaps more problematic, classified loans continued to increase as a percentage of total outstanding loans, with the percentages in the manufacturing sectors, especially metallurgy, engineering, and electronics outpacing most other sectors to reach alarming levels (see fig. 3.1). Yet, the main banks were highly dependent on interest income rather than fee income, and industrial firms formed the base of their clientele. Cutting them off could seriously harm bank stability. As of December 1992, IB's and KB's interest income accounted for 96 percent and 93 percent of total income, respectively, and industrial manufacturing firms continued to account for about 35 percent of KB's and over 40 percent of IB's loan portfolio.[59] Indeed, in a 1992–93 analysis of the investment engineering sector, KB noted that although thirty-nine of the fifty firms had stagnating or declining financial accounts, it regarded forty of the fifty firms as favorable long-term clients.[60]

TABLE 3.13. Stratification by Sector of Total and Classified (doubtful) Outstanding Loans for Nonfinancial Institutions (firms), Czech Republic, 1992–94 (in millions of Kcs)

	31 December 1992		31 December 1993		30 September 1994	
	Total Loans (nominal)	Share of Total Loans to Nonfinancial Institutions	Total Loans (nominal)	Share of Total Loans to Nonfinancial Institutions	Total Loans (nominal)	Share of Total Loans to Nonfinancial Institutions
Nonfinancial institutions	484,085	100	520,563	100	567,609	100
— of which:						
Manufacturing	186,741	38.6	198,033	38.0	215,748	38.0
Chemicals	18,668	3.9	20,812	4.0	20,278	3.6
Metallurgy and engineering	82,556	17.1	84,064	16.2	85,659	15.1
Electrical	16,615	3.4	15,119	2.9	15,743	2.8

	Total Classified Loans (nominal)	Share of Total Classified Loans to Nonfinancial Institutions	Total Classified Loans (nominal)	Share of Total Classified Loans to Nonfinancial Institutions	Total Classified Loans (nominal)	Share of Total Classified Loans to Nonfinancial Institutions
Nonfinancial institutions	103,942	100.0	142,117	100.0	222,404	100.0
— of which:						
Manufacturing	52,238	50.3	61,523	43.3	81,839	36.8
Chemicals	3,281	3.2	2,315	1.6	2,985	1.3
Metallurgy and engineering	28,880	27.8	35,123	24.7	41,424	18.6
Electrical	7,799	7.5	8,386	5.9	8,832	4.0

Source: Czech National Bank (relevant months, 1992, 1993, 1994).

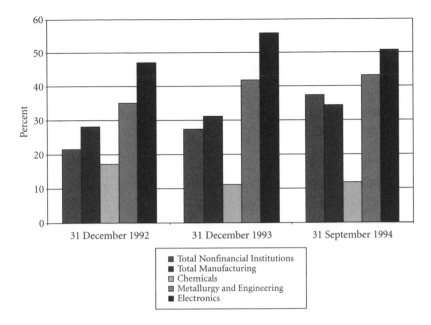

Figure 3.1.   Classified Loans as a Percentage of Total Loans to Given Sector

Source: Czech National Bank (relevant months)

Moreover, as sociopolitical creations, network relations were maintained with the aid of public organs like the former councils. Once councils were removed and new uncertainties arose, not only did banks lose a critical managing partner but also interfirm financial relations became undone. Thus, for example, a one-time state subsidy to net-out interfirm debt would have minimal affect since network relations would not be stable or self-repairing. Financial links both between members of a distinct production network and, perhaps more importantly, between network members and external actors (i.e., other former VHJ networks and exporters) were maintained by former VHJ directorates and allied councils, which no longer existed. If interlinked firms were not able to reconstitute mechanisms that govern their relationships on their own, then they would be unwilling to provide the information needed to pursue effective factoring operations.[61]

The banks themselves recognized that the complex production linkages among firms and plants within former industrial VHJs had been reproduced in such ways that seriously constrained active bank intervention. As noted in the aforementioned KB analysis, one way was the conversion of the VHJ into a holding company, which protected critical upstream and downstream units, despite their increasing insolvency. The other concerned tightly linked former VHJ units, which were now independent, medium-sized firms.[62] Their interdependencies were evident in the continued narrow segmentation of suppliers and users of particular components and the expansion of secondary insolvency through interfirm debt.[63] But the interfirm links did not appear stable or closed-ended. Firms refused to fully divulge critical information on payables and the Czech government's rule-based program to net-out interfirm debt removed less than 10 percent of interfirm debt.[64]

The reproduction of interfirm linkages, therefore, cut two ways into bank stability. On the one hand, the links were still strong enough that liquidations or a halt to lending could bring huge, immediate losses by setting off a string of failures within holding companies or among the groups of independent firms. The risk was compounded by the lack of proper securitization on inherited loans and the low loan-loss reserves. On the other hand, active management and financing of industrial restructuring would demand taking over large groups of producers, for which the banks alone had neither the financial or human resources, at least under current conditions. Moreover, the failure of the targeted financial incentive to reduce interfirm debt suggested there was a missing link to interfirm relations and serious problems in getting firms to cooperate.[65] Either case represented potentially high organizational and governance costs for bank-led management of firms.

The Optimal Strategy: Protect Your Position and Wait for a Partner

Rather than use their new rights and debt relief to lead bankruptcies and restructuring, the Czech banks chose to clean their portfolios gradually, while making sure that industrial firms did not perish in the process. They demonstrated this strategy by replenishing their capital with increased interest rates, reducing lending, and protecting their links to firms. First, in commercializing inherited loans, banks increased interest rates from a 1989 average of 4–6 percent to 18 percent and then to 24 percent. Margins between deposit and credit rates stayed at about 6.7 to 7 percent between 1990 and 1997.[66] Collateralization of existing loans and an interest rate increases on them were preconditions for firms to receive new, short-term loans. In 1992, KB and IB set aside, respectively, 30 percent and 18 percent of their income for loan-loss reserves alone.[67]

Second, the main banks severely restricted lending. As lending grew well below the rate of inflation, notably toward industrial sectors, the share of short-term loans grew dramatically and long-term loans declined. Total loans grew in 1991 by only 9 percent and in 1992 by 15 percent. But loans by IB, KB, and the Čzechoslovenská Obchodní Banka (for foreign trade), the primary lenders to the industrial sectors, grew in 1992 by only 4 percent, −5 percent, and −1 percent, respectively.[68] Recognizing the lack of lending, the FNM issued 23.2 billion Kcs of bonds to KB and IB in late 1992 to increase their lending capital. But by the end of 1993, all but 2 billion Kcs of these bonds were transferred back to the FNM because there were no significant increases in bank lending.[69] Total loans to manufacturing sectors grew by only 4.5 percent and to engineering and steel only 6.3 percent in 1992–93 (see table 3.13).[70]

Third, the government recapitalization schemes and amendments in the bankruptcy law gave the banks the opportunity to cut off insolvent industrial firms, but they chose not to do so.[71] Rather than writing off significantly risky loans of the largest firms, which would be tantamount to a speedy bankruptcy from the banks' point of view, the banks spread the write-offs broadly over their portfolios.[72] This was a clear indication that they did not want to sever their ties with the troubled industrial firms.

Evident in the virtual absence of bankruptcies through most of the 1990s,[73] the main banks refrained from initiating bankruptcies, even after the FNM provided the KOB with added funds to cover some of the costs borne by the banks and even as classified loans grew to an alarming level.[74] Without credible workout procedures, bankruptcy meant liquidation. The banks viewed this as unviable, since any financial gains could not overcome the cost of destroying their future client base. Not only would the sale of collateralized assets, like real estate and old equipment, bring a fraction of the value of the outstanding loans but also the banks lacked the experience and risk-bearing capabilities to undertake restructuring.

To sum up, the deepening financial interdependence among firms and the few main banks brought the dual aims of cleaning up balance sheets and building a client base into conflict. Government policy had shifted much of the risks of foreclosing manufacturing firms and financing their restructuring onto the banks, which, like their counterparts in neighboring countries, viewed such risks as unbearable.[75] The main banks kept their links to manufacturing firms, marginally increasing loans to them and increasing spreads. At the same time, collateralization and the use of some short-term lending allowed the banks to stabilize their lock on clients as the senior creditors and thus dilute the incentives of other creditors to intervene into the firms.[76] Thus, while the main banks positioned themselves as the principal arbitrators of industrial restructuring, the structure of firm finance changed little for the better. Indeed, by the mid-1990s, domestic debt continued to amount to more than 70 percent of GDP, with the average Czech company carrying twice as much debt as enterprises in elsewhere in East Central Europe.[77]

The Limits of Equity Investment Companies

If the main banks were hesitant to intervene actively in industrial firms, then the newly created private owners and equity market could very well provide the risk sharing and monitoring mechanisms necessary to discipline and reorganize industries. Indeed, the extensive literature on the CR's use of vouchers for mass privatization and the subsequent emergence of voucher investment companies (IPCs), especially bank-sponsored IPCs,[78] has focused on the ability of the voucher method to establish private corporate control virtually overnight.[79] Yet evident in the utter lack of public issues for raising capital for new or existing companies, both the IPCs and the Czech stock market have not been useful in restructuring or monitoring.[80] As a result of trying to protect their already weak financial structure and their new equity links, the main banks and their IPCs effectively created a thin, intransparent stock market. IPCs, in turn, had greater incentives to remain passive owners than to build new mechanisms of active corporate governance.

Dušan Tříska, the architect of voucher privatization, succinctly clarified the dual political-economic aims of the voucher privatization.[81] First, vouchers would transfer ownership from state to private hands more rapidly than any other method. By giving away ownership rights to the populace and avoiding negotiations about restructuring or the division of ownership, the state could avoid getting captured by particularistic interests, such as management or labor. Second, vouchers would quickly create a large group of individual and institutional owners, which would have a direct interest to build governance structures and restructure firms.

Mass privatization included over 1,800 companies and was divided into two waves, the larger of which was the first wave.[82] The first wave of voucher trading commenced in mid-May 1992 and, after five rounds, ended in December 1992. Shares were distributed by mid-1993.[83] The total value of the 988 Czech companies participating in the first wave of voucher privatization was 345 billion Kcs (approximately $12 billion). About 61.6 percent of these assets were offered for vouchers; 23 to 28 percent was to be held in the FNM, mostly for future sale to a foreign investor.[84] (See table 3.14.) About 80 percent of the adult population participated in the program.

The most immediate consequence of voucher privatization was the rapid rise of private IPCs, which could concentrate shareholdings and presumably perform the corporate governance and restructuring tasks that dispersed shareholding would undermine. This view was all the more encouraged since most of the largest IPCs were owned or sponsored by the main domestic financial institutions.[85] IPCs were investment companies that managed the equivalent of mutual funds. Diversification laws prohibited IPCs

TABLE 3.14.   First Wave Data for Voucher Privatization (Sept. 1993)

Type of Share	Average (percent)	Share Value (billion Kcs)	Standard deviation (percent)	Minimum (percent)	Maximum (percent)
Vouchers	61.44	203.25	20.44	7.98	98.76
Direct sale to foreign investor	1.64	5.43	10.27	0	79.32
Direct sale to domestic investor	1.4	4.64	8.63	0	77
Employee shares	0.85	2.79	2.27	0	10
Intermediary	1.81	5.6	6.85	0	72
Municipality	2.75	9.09	4.22	0	86.55
Temporary holdings of FNM	9.96	32.96	12.39	0	82
Permanent holdings of FNM	13.34	44.12	4.71	0	85.34
Restitution	3	9.93	0.91	0	27.52
Personal restitution	0.29	0.96	2.15	0	53.08
Additional restitution	1.84	6.09	4.26	0	72
Differentiation fund	1.68	5.55	3.12	0	25.25
KAD	—	1.05	7.9[a]	0	139.7[a]
Foundation fund	0	0.005	0.03	0	1
Total shares	100	330.895	1.856[a]	2.2[a]	53.521[a]

Source: Mejstrik, Marcincin, and Lastovicka (1997, table 4.7)
Note: Numbers may not add up to 100 due to rounding.
[a]Values in billions of Kcs.

from holding more than 20 percent of the equity in any one firm and from investing more than 10 percent of their assets in any single security. Individuals could invest their points alone or give a portion of them to a fund. Indeed, most adults invested their points in a fund.[86] The 343 IPCs collected about 72 percent of all voucher points and 63 percent of all shares in the first wave. As can be seen in table 3.15, the largest 13 IPCs controlled over 77 percent of voucher points and 67 percent of shares obtained by all IPCs. When one adjusts for the minimal control that individual shareholders have in firms, IPC control on corporate boards is even greater. Estimates indicated that the 3 to 5 largest shareholders of a firm (usually IPCs and the FNM) could control virtually all corporate boards and that the 3 to 5 largest IPCs of a firm could control almost 75 percent of corporate boards.[87]

In turn, voucher privatization appeared to create rapidly two related mechanisms for shareholders to play an active role in disciplining management and restructuring firms.[88] With a market capitalization on par with advance industrialized economies and the increasing presence of foreign institutional investors, the Czech stock market could play a vital role in evaluating IPC and firm performance and providing needed capital.[89] With one of the

TABLE 3.15.   Voucher Points and Equity Shares Held by the Thirteen Largest IPCs after First Wave

IPC	Points acquired (in millions)	Percent TPC[a]	Percent TP[b]	Shares held[c] (in millions)	Percent TSC[d]	Percent TS[e]
SIS CSP	950.432	15.6	11.1	21.375	12.2	7.7
PIAS IB	724.123	11.9	8.45	13.594	7.27	4.9
HCC	638.548	10.5	7.45	15.225	8.65	5.5
VUB	500.587	8.19	5.84	11.985	6.81	4.3
IKS KB	465.53	7.62	5.43	11.932	6.78	4.3
KIS CP	334.04	5.47	3.9	7.623	4.33	2.7
SIB	333.045	5.45	3.89	10.986	6.24	4
SSK	168.864	2.76	1.97	7.707	4.38	2.8
CA	166.256	2.72	1.94	3.61	2.05	1.3
PPF	117.541	1.92	1.37	4.92	2.8	1.8
ZB	117.541	1.92	1.37	1.885	1.07	0.7
SLP	116.682	1.91	1.36	4.362	2.48	1.6
AG	111.088	1.82	1.3	3.941	2.24	1.4
Total	4744.365	77.63	55.39	119.15	67.71	43

Source: Mejstřík (1997, table 6.6).
[a]TFP = Percentage of investment points acquired by all IPCs (100% = 6,111.812 million points).
[b] TP = Percentage of all investment points (100% = 8,565.642 million points).
[c]Number of shares in the portfolio of an IPC or IPF. Nominal value = Shares held × 1,000 Kcs.
[d]TSC = Percentage of the shares held by all funds (100% = 175, 975, 880 shares).
[e]TS = Percentage of total shares offered in voucher privatization (100% = 277,711,577 shares).

most concentrated equity markets in the world, the Czechs appeared to avoid the problems of dispersed shareholding and effectively merged ownership and control as well as equity and creditor rights. That is, IPCs gave banks the opportunity to prevent managers from gambling away debt through overly risky projects or to control corporate boards and provide insider information to aid the lending of restructuring finance.[90]

Recent research shows, however, that both the stock market and the dominant IPCs did not play active roles in the governance and restructuring of firms and, indeed, that no firm, new or established, used the Czech bourse to raise capital.[91] Although many researchers speculate whether refinements in capital market regulation could have proven otherwise, they fail to appreciate the way in which the interdependencies between the few main banks and industrial firms debilitated conventional means of risk sharing. The initial resource advantages of the main banks and their ability to protect themselves and client firms from corporate raiders, such as nonbank IPCs and foreign mutual funds, restricted capital market entry and put the financial burdens further on the shoulders of the main Czech banks.

On the one hand, the main banks, through their IPCs, obtained significant cross-holding equity stakes in one another. This maneuver allowed the main IPCs and the FNM to be the principal shareholders in such financial institutions as KB, IB, Československá Obchodní Banka, Česká Spořitelna, and Česká Pojišťovna, the main insurance company.[92] On the other hand, IPCs organized their funds as unit trusts or close-ended joint-stock companies with long-term, unbreakable management contracts for the IPCs.[93] These actions effectively blocked any attempts by existing or predatory shareholders from using voice or exit to change the management strategy of IPCs. In turn, outsiders interested in taking over IPCs or the main banks were clearly hindered.[94] This intransparency led to an extremely thin equity market and a precipitous fall in the Prague Stock Exchange (PSE) by 60 percent between March and December 1994, from which the market barely recovered.[95] Such a decline made the main IPCs even more reluctant to sell significant equity stakes for fear of devaluing their net asset value and thus their financial stability.[96]

The lack of transparency weakened the equity market's capacity to monitor and discipline IPCs, and thus firms (i.e., through valid threats of takeover, portfolio devaluation, or management change), as well as to provide restructuring capital to firms. In such market conditions, the main banks and insurance company could have hypothetically used their IPCs to gather additional information to limit their risks of financing restructuring, yet the main IPCs were used to become active monitoring or restructuring agents.[97] While there is much debate as to whether the main banks ever had any initial intentions of using their IPCs as active monitoring agents, it became clear that to do so would have demanded significant investments by the main banks into their IPCs and cooperation between the main IPCs.[98]

The large bank-owned IPCs were organized to amass broad and diversified portfolios. For instance, the largest 20 funds held on average over 200 firms each, across 28 industries.[99] This created two interrelated hurdles for IPCs to become active owners and agents of the banks. On the one hand, there were weak incentives to focus on any one or group of firms, as each firm represented a relatively small share of an IPC portfolio. On the other hand, although the main IPCs were often the biggest shareholders of a firm, several would have had to cooperate to build a large enough coalition to enact substantial restructuring plans. The evidence shows that IPCs were more willing to create smaller blocking coalitions to avoid any risks.[100]

Why, then, were the banks so reluctant to have IPCs focus on share value and increase productive cooperation among one another? The simple answer has been the perceived relative risks and costs in doing so. First, research on IPC strategy has shown that apart from ensuring that managers did not further trouble the financial burdens of the firm or that any other bank/IPC did not gain an upper hand in the firm, IPCs could gradually generate revenues at relatively low cost through finding arbitrage opportunities between the

Prague Stock Exchange and the over-the-counter market (RM-System).[101] That is, IPCs viewed returns on passive corporate governance as much more secure and less costly than investments into active corporate governance focusing on some uncertain increases in the asset value of the firm. This view was reinforced by the limited opportunities to sell large blocks of shares in such a thin market.

Second, bank managers believed that building on their existing lending ties with firms was sufficient and less costly than building any new informational links via IPCs.[102] For instance, loan officers did not view the IPCs as particularly useful in offering any new information about firm operations, since the main banks, with their lock on the accounts of virtually all firms, already monitored the financial activities of clients. Moreover, as the only few senior creditors, such banks as IB and KB, believed they could protect against any unfortunate surprises. To the extent that bank and fund managers interacted, it was usually the fund managers who sought better information to aid their arbitrage activities.

The Failed Entry of Foreign Direct Investment

If the main banks and IPCs were reluctant to initiate industrial restructuring, foreign direct investors were the fail-safe alternative to lead investment and share the risks. As discussed earlier in this chapter, stabilization policies and relatively low wages created an amenable macroeconomic environment for investment, and the rules of privatization had apparently created the conduits to channel the investment directly into firms. Recall that government policy allowed firms to combine methods of privatization, namely vouchers and asset sales. The rules for the latter favored foreign investors. Foreign direct investment, however, has largely failed to enter into Czech industries and initiate restructuring. Part of the explanation for this failure lies in the preceding sections. The very policies that were to create active banks and relieve inherited debts allowed banks to form a defensive strategy that left industrial firms heavily indebted. If foreign investors were to take over both debt and production restructuring of firms, then they demanded either concessions from managers, which were refused, or changes in government policy, which ran against the political plank of an increasingly powerful Vaclav Klaus. A fuller explanation demands a detailed analysis of the reproduction and conflicts within production networks and will therefore come in the following chapter.

Fulfilling the initial expectations of privatization policy, Czech industrial firms chose largely to combine the methods of vouchers and FDI. About 22 percent and 46 percent of equity in the steel and chemical sectors, respectively, was privatized through vouchers. Over 57 percent of the 88 percent of engineering equity privatized in the first wave was entered the voucher method. For each of these sectors, virtually all of the remaining shares were left in the FNM for future sale. Half of the engineering firms had at least 25 percent of equity in the FNM for future sale.[103]

How firms would prepare themselves and attract foreign investment, however, was mainly left to the firms themselves.[104] Privatization policy had two important rules to protect the government from getting caught in protracted interventions. One was that breakups, mergers, and restructuring steps were to take place during or after privatization, namely through the privatization proposals submitted by management and prospective investors. The other was that the team of foreign investment bankers advising the Ministries of Privatization and Industry could only participate in negotiations if assets of the registered firm were actually to be sold to investors. These rules had two major consequences.[105]

First, privatization policy did little to diminish the inherited high industrial product concentration and allowed firms to recombine and legally define themselves largely as they wished.[106] As mentioned previously, former VHJs reproduced themselves in two principal ways: as large decentralized holding companies that comprised and protected upstream and downstream producers (subsidiary firms); and as voluntary associations of independent, medium-sized firms. In either case, production and financial interdependencies between firms remained. When prospective foreign investors arrived, they found firms with broad production capabilities, with tight financial and technical interdependencies, and, as a consequence of financial and banking policies, with large debts and little cash flow. Indeed, the majority of assets marked for privatization through sale were in the large holding companies, which only made the critical issues of identifying quality production units and dividing assets and liabilities even more complicated. Among the most noted candidates for FDI were the holdings Škoda Plzeň and ČKD Praha in engineering, Tatra and Liaz in trucks, Aero in aircrafts, Chemapol in chemopetrols, Poldi in high-end steel, and Vitkovice, Třinecké Železarny, and Nová Hut' in medium- and low-end steel.[107]

Second, the combination of the privatization rules, industrial structure, and high debt created incentives for both management and foreign direct investors to utilize joint ventures (JVs) and not direct sales as the primary conduit for FDI. For foreign investors, beginning with a partial stake in a JV was less risky than immediate takeover of whole groups of firms, plants, or divisions, since foreign investors were usually interested in the products of only a part of a holding or collection of linked firms. For Czech managers, a JV allowed them to acquire markets, know-how, and finance without dismantling their current production and organizational experiments. For both, a JV allowed capital to stay within the Czech firm or plants instead of going directly into the coffers of the FNM, as would be the case of a purchase during privatization.[108]

JVs were not, however, contracts for a specific project, but rather fragile agreements about the future control and use of assets. As the foreign partner invested money into the operations over time, Czech managers would have to agree to certain restructuring steps and the relinquishment of majority control over the assets in question. But because foreigners feared their investment would be used to finance the debt and restructuring of non-JV units, they sought independent commitments to isolate the JV units from the other units.[109] With their inherited production and financial interdependencies, Czech managers saw such commitments as a threat to non-JV units and the former VHJ network itself. Unable to reach an accord, both sides turned to the government for mediation and assistance with certain financial and environmental liabilities. With Czech privatization rules already restricting government intervention into deals that did not contain outright sales by and revenues to the state, such participation was tantamount to revising Czech privatization policy and the clear roles of government organs.[110] The Klausians saw this as an invitation for protracted government intervention and capture by private interests, and thus antithetical to their designs. As they gained increasing political power and control over policy from late 1991 through their victory in the June 1992 parliamentary elections, the Klausians blocked efforts by Vrba, then the minister of industry, to allow the government to become a financial and negotiating partner.

The consequence of these events was the collapse of major industrial JVs and virtually all JVs concerning industrial holding companies during 1992–93.[111] As late as December 1994, only a relatively small share of FDI entered the Czech industrial sectors.[112]

Concluding Remarks

More than any other government in the region, the Czechs took advantage of their relatively optimal starting conditions by following the standard approaches of constructing a government structure and a set of policies that would eschew negotiations between public and private actors about policymaking, implementation, and restructuring. Led by Vaclav Klaus, they formed a state-policy apparatus of elite, like-minded technocrats, which were insulated from particularistic interests through a centralization of powers, clear procedural rules, and legal limitations to protracted government intervention in industrial restructuring. They also implemented policies that addressed the delineation of private property rights and the preservation of asset value as separate and distinct matters, thus relying on complete contract methods to resolve restructuring conflict. These policies were to provide the necessary and sufficient financial and legal incentives for the main banks, newly created owners (namely IPCs), and foreign investors to become the principal agents of restructuring.

In this chapter, I have argued that this vision failed since the reform strategy of depoliticization undermined the ability of economic actors to share the risks of restructuring inherited financial ties and constructing new methods of governance. The policies allowed for the reproduction of tight financial links between the few main banks and industrial firms, but they forced the banks to view asserting their new rights and strengthening their long-term capital base as conflicting aims. At the same time, the centralization of powers virtually eliminated the ability of traditional partners to the banks and former VHJ production networks, namely regional and district councils, from aiding in the management of financial restructuring. As a result, the main banks repositioned themselves as the only senior creditors but refrained from either cutting off industrial firms or leading their restructuring.

The defensive strategies by the banks and their IPCs to protect their own financial stability and their links to firms had the initial effect of creating a weak, thin stock market. With restructuring responsibilities still weighing solely on their shoulders, the main CR banks appeared to view the risks of investing into active IPC corporate governance and inter-IPC cooperation as too great to bear alone. Rather, they preferred that their IPCs gain arbitrage revenues and block any projects that might further distress the stability of industrial firms.

Moreover, despite the clear rules favoring asset sales to foreign investors, FDI largely failed to enter into the Czech industrial sectors. The combination of these rules and the inherited tight financial and technical links between firms created conditions for Czech managers and potential foreign partners to use joint ventures as the primary conduit for FDI. But since foreign partners were interested in only a subset of the interlinked assets and were fearful losing their investments to the existing debt burdens of Czech firms, foreigners demanded commitments from Czech managers and the government that neither was willing to provide. As a result, JVs collapsed.

The subsequent financial and restructuring stalemate surrounding Czech industrial firms led to two distinct crises in the Czech Republic. In 1992–93, the failure of JVs brought the industrial holding companies to the brink of collapse, as they remained highly leveraged and lacked sufficient new sales and exports for cash flow. In 1995–96, a string of insolvencies in new medium-sized banks and attempts by nonbank IPCs to take control the funds of the leading Czech financial institutions, threatened the solvency of the former state insurance monopoly and the main banks themselves. In both cases, the Czech government was forced to reengage domestic firms and banks and create contrasting governance orders. At the heart of both crises and negotiated solutions were the two ideal types of former VHJ networks. In the following chapters, I will examine how the reproduction of these networks interacted with Czech government policies and created distinctly different patterns of restructuring conflicts and government-backed institutions for economic governance.

Hierarchical Networks and the Negotiated Restructuring of Czech Holding Companies: The Case of Škoda Plzeň

The last chapter noted that industrial firms privatized themselves often by using the voucher method and reserving an equity stake in the Fund for National Property (FNM) for future sale. By early 1995, however, the share of industrial firm equity held in the FNM was largely unchanged, and the Czech government was actively engaged in corporate restructuring.[1] In June 1993, it had amended legislation to allow the Ministry of Privatization to rewrite already approved privatization projects of firms, and to allow the Council of Economic Ministers to earmark equity in the FNM to guarantee new loans to industrial firms. In June 1994, the government even transferred the administration of forty-four large manufacturing firms from the FNM back to the Ministry of Industry (MPO). These firms still had an average 50 percent of equity remaining in state hands.[2] This pattern of privatization failures and policy reversals was most visible in industrial companies called *holdings*, which emerged from the hierarchical form of VHJ network discussed in chapter 2. The most notable were: Škoda Plzeň and ČKD Praha in engineering; Poldi Kladno in high-end steel; Vitkovice, Nová Huť, and Třinecké Železarny in low-end steel; Aero in aircraft manufacturing; the Chemapol Group in chemo-petrols; and Avia, Liaz, and Tatra in truck manufacturing. The new state intervention into firms became so marked that by 1994 even Tatra, with 97 percent of its shares already privatized by vouchers, was effectively managed by a department in the MPO.

This chapter examines how the interaction between the state's efforts to depoliticize economic transformation and the emergence of holding companies contributed to a stalemate in industrial privatization, and then led to the formation of a particular structure for state backed, negotiated solutions for restructuring and corporate governance. In viewing holdings as products of sociopolitical networks, one can gain two critical insights into institutional change and the role of government during transformation. First, the hierarchical form of former VHJ networks defined a particular form of business organization, a distinct pattern of restructuring strategies and conflicts and, in turn, particular attributes of the negotiated solutions—that is, the selection of private and public participants, their relative bargaining powers, and the new roles to be played by government agencies, banks, and producers. The subsequent governance order is what I call *DDR,* or *delegated deliberative restructuring*[3]—where the government became both a mediator and financial partner to the particular banks and producers connected to the holding company.

Second, an examination of the inability of holding members to resolve hold up problems on their own or with the aid of outside private investors reveals the political roots of industrial networks and the construction of new rules for economic governance. Inherited financial and technical links constrained the discretion of members and made outsiders view investment as too risky. But the depoliticization strategy planted the seeds of its own demise in hindering the ability of insiders and outsiders to cooperate: the elimination of regional councils undermined the authority structure and risk-sharing capabilities of the former hierarchical networks; the Klausians blocked public agencies from providing third-party commitments to investors; and bankruptcy lacked any mechanisms to facilitate extended negotiated workouts between creditors and debtors. DDR emerged as an attempt by the government to avoid economic collapse and fulfill its political commitment to privatization by resolving the cooperation problems inherent in the restructuring of networks. DDR allowed holding members, the main banks, and certain government agencies to collectively define rules to govern organizational and production experiments through the dual processes of delegation and deliberation. The identification of the political roots of the impediments and solutions to the investment-workout dilemma of holding helps one understand not only *the need for* public intervention in the restructuring but also *the conditions* under which public and private actors can jointly learn how to monitor one another and prudently share risk.

First, I analyze how the legacies of the hierarchical network shaped the initial strategy of members—to form a decentralized holding company and create JVs with foreign partners. This strategy made vital decisions about the reorganization of production and definition of new boundaries ones of high conflict. Then I discuss why network members could not easily resolve these conflicts, that is, why the reproduced network was not self-organizing or self-governing. Decentralized organizational and production experiments broke up former contracting relationship and create risks that neither members nor outside investors were willing to bear. At the same time, the elimination of regional councils removed a key part of the sociopolitical structure that traditionally repaired such disruptions. And no public actor was available to take on such a role.

These sections provide supporting evidence from other holdings to show that Škoda Plzeň is representative of the hierarchical network and back my argument that this type of network had a determining impact on the formation of holdings and DDR. Although Škoda Plzeň and other industrial holding companies were in separate industrial sectors with different technologies, end-markets, and regions, they shared similar network legacies and patterns of restructuring strategies, conflicts, and state backed negotiated solutions. Škoda Plzeň is distinctive as it was the first case to force the Klaus government to experiment with alternative arrangements of corporate governance and restructuring.[4]

Next, I examine the rise and fall of JVs as main conduit for FDI into holdings. Both privatization policy and managers themselves viewed foreign investors as new, crucial external partners for holdings. The failure of JVs was the first clear sign of the limitations to restructuring holdings through solely private actors. They also revealed the potential need for government support of organizational forms governed by shared property rights. I then discuss the resolution of the existing stalemates in the eventual privatization and restructuring of holdings, particularly Škoda Plzeň. I examine how the internal and external holdup problems were resolved not through state imposed or pure ownership solutions. Rather the Czech government delegated restructuring authority to Škoda management and the main banks and helped create a structure for public and private actors to resolve conflicts through deliberation. This process lasted over two years, from late 1992 to early 1995. What emerged was a framework (DDR) that balanced the interests of the central management of the holding and its subsidiaries through mutual monitoring between the holding center, subsidiaries, banks, and the government. With such a balance, the parties were able to create and revise new governance rules and production strategies simultaneously.

Inherited Networks and the Emergence of Industrial Holding Companies

As discussed in chapter 2, Czechoslovak industrialization and central planning experiments had produced two main patterns of VHJ networks that varied in terms of their distribution of authority, associationalism, and organization of production. One ideal type, a hierarchical network, was examined in the evolution of the Škoda VHJ. By the end of the 1980s, the VHJ as a whole as well as individual firms and plants produced a broad assortment of end products and inputs, allowing most units to be both end producers and mutual suppliers. Yet with the dissolution of the VHJ system in 1987–88, centralized legal and financial powers, combined with close cooperation of the regional council, allowed the head office to transform the group into a single state firm, rather than a break up into individual producers. The head office kept control of, among other things, foreign trade relations, R&D, and credit links to the new state commercial banks. In turn, such VHJs as Škoda Plzeň, ČKD Praha, Tatra, Aero, and Poldi, all became unified firms in their own right.

The post-1989 privatization and economic policies were to break up this old order.[5] Subjected to open market forces and new ownership opportunities, firms were to close loss-making units, spin-off plants and divisions, and seek new customers and suppliers. These same policies, however, offered strong incentives for existing industrial networks to reproduce and protect themselves from outside intervention. The combination of new financial constraints, a collapse of stable markets, and government avoidance of directly restructuring or breaking up firms allowed for the continuation of a rigid and segmented industrial structure.[6] Surveys showed that the lack of new sources of sales, inputs, and financing led firms and plants to work with their few existing suppliers and customers to gain resources and reorganize production.[7]

The priority of rapid privatization with limited government intervention provided also an opportunity for managers to try to maintain control over the firm.[8] Since the program depended on the submission of projects by management and a limited time frame for government review, managers could gain autonomy by becoming joint-stock companies to be privatized partially or wholly through vouchers. Surveys revealed that managers expected that the broad dispersion of voucher owners, in the midterm at least, would help them to increase their own decision-making powers but provide little aid to improve the health of the firm and gain investment. In the meantime, managers sought direct foreign investment through JVs, the legal decision-making powers for which rested with the company and not the state.[9] Aggregate analyses of approved projects, voucher bidding, and ownership data all confirm the preference of the Ministry of Privatization to approve projects from incumbent management, the lack of information by external actors, and the broad use of vouchers and JVs by Czech managers.[10]

For members of a hierarchical network, like Škoda Plzeň, the tight internal economic links and turbulent financial conditions offered good reasons to remain unified. But for many units privatization also meant an opportunity for independent control over sales, production and revenues. During the dissolution of VHJs in 1987–88, a similar debate about fundamental organizational changes arose within the aforementioned former VHJs,[11] but top managers quickly consolidated the VHJs into single unified firms with the aid of conservative regional councils and their control of channels to ministerial subsidies and state bank credits. In 1990, the legal and political environment changed. Top management could no longer monopolize external channels and thus lost much of its authority. Regional councils were dissolved with no replacement, the planning system was disassembled, ministries were diluted of resources, and the state-owned banks were reluctant to lend. Plants and units also had the right to submit their own privatization projects to the government.

Members within the hierarchical network appeared to strike an initial compromise: to privatize the group as a whole in the form of holding, combining the use of voucher and foreign partners.[12] (See table 4.1.[13]) The holding structure allowed a diffusion of authority and a sharing of common resources, while mangers would explore further legal, organizational, and production changes. Units would become subsidiaries or divisions, with decision-making power over production changes and new independent financial accounts. The holding would become an internal, regulated market, providing critical resources each lack on its own: financing and mutual subsidization through internal credit, strategic management for common production programs, foreign trade and partnership contacts, and shared labor and production facilities. As the holding provided short-term financial protection, members, collectively or individually, would formulate restructuring strategies and find foreign partners to gain needed investment, market niches, and know-how. The central idea was that while managers used new sales revenue and investment to pay off existing debts, they would decide over the future role of the holding, including spin-offs, breakups, and closures.

These decisions, however, demanded choices about how new asset boundaries would be drawn, new rights distributed, liabilities divided, and investment directed. The joint control over assets, implicit in the existing network structure, had already complicated such choices. The holding structure was to be transitional, providing the protection for managers to learn about their possibilities and the way to make these choices. The following subsections examine in detail how this apparently yet-to-be-defined structure actually reinforced existing economic links and fostered conflicting restructuring strategies among holding members.

TABLE 4.1. Sample of Czech Holdings and Their Privatization Strategies

Firm/Sector	Employment, Organization, 1991[a]	Original Privatization Project and Strategy[b]	Main Foreign Partnerships	Government Action Taken as of 1995
Škoda / Engineering	34,231 employees (2.3%); 25 plants to be subsidiaries.	48.5%—First wave vouchers; 42.1%—in FNM for FI; 5%—City of Plzeň. Create JVs with FIs for different production groups or divisions.	Plan double JV with Siemens. Fails in 1992.	1992 equity tenders with Czech firm and banks lead to negotiated restructuring model. MPO sits on board. Process lasts over 2½ years before equity transferred to Czech firm and banks.
ČKD / Engineering	21,776 employees (1.5%). Holding of 18 subsidiaries (a.s.).[c]	49.2%—First wave vouchers; 41.6%—in FNM for FI. Create divisons from subsidiaries. Pursue JVs with FIs.	Plan JV with AEG for transport division. Fails in 1993. Plan JV for Kompresory with DBB. Fails in 1993–94.	1994 equity tender with Czech firm leads to negotiated restructuring model. Czech banks to finance, with state loan guarantees. MPO sits on board. 1½ years before equity transferred.
Aero / Aircraft	19,820 employees (1.4%); Holding of 11 subsidiaries (a.s.).[c]	49%—First wave, vouchers; 48%—in FNM for FI and second wave vouchers. Create recreational and military divisions and pursue JVs or partial buyouts of subsidiaries or divisions.	Plan JVs with Fairchild, Pratt &Whitney and Hamilton Std. All Fail by 1993.	By December 1993, three failed attempts at financial restructuring and debt-equity swaps. 1994 plan: Government and Czech banks share ownership of holding and certain subsidiaries, while seeking FIs. MPO and banks manage holding and subsidiaries.
Poldi Kladno/ High-grade steel	16,471 employees (1.2%); Holding of 19 subsidiaries (a.s.).[c] Creates two main steel subsidiaries: Poldi I & II.	97%—in FNM for FIs. Plan a JV for Poldi I & II and partial equity sales or JVs of other subsidiaries with different FIs.	Plan JV for Poldi I & II with consortium led by Maison Lazard. Fails by May 1993.	1993 equity tender of Poldi I & II to Czech firm, while FNM and Czech bank retain control of Poldi Holding. 1995–96 FNM and bank sue Czech firm for embezzlement. Poldi Holding reclaims Poldi I & II.

(continued)

TABLE 4.1.—Continued

Firm/Sector	Employment, Organization, 1991[a]	Original Privatization Project and Strategy[b]	Main Foreign Partnerships	Government Action Taken as of 1995
Tatra Kopřivnice / Heavy trucks	14,685 (1.0%); Holding of 7 subsidiaries.	97%—First wave vouchers. Create JVs in assembly and parts.	Plan JVs with IVECO for assembly and Detroit Diesel for engines. Both fail by 1993.	1993–94 failed attempt to create new foreign manager-owner. MPO creates new department to help run Tatra. Orchestrates sale of Tatra to Škoda Plzeň in 1995–96. Czech banks finance.
Liaz / Medium trucks	8,606 employees (0.6%); 9 plants to become subsidiaries (a.s.)[c] of new Holding.	42.9%—First wave vouchers; 51.1%—in FNM for FI. Create JVs for subsidiaries. Focus on engine upgrades and modular vehicle design.	Plan simultaneous JVs for assembly and parts with Mercedes consortium. Fails by December 1993.	MPO runs restructuring of Liaz along with Tatra. Orchestrates sale of Tatra to Škoda Plzeň in 1995–96. Czech banks finance.

Note: [a]Percentages in parentheses are firm employment as a share of total Czech industrial employment in 1991.
[b]Shares left in FNM to attract a direct foreign investor (FI) via a future sale or JV. Percentage of shares not noted are those left by law in a fund for restitution compensation.
[c]a.s. = Czech equivalent of joint-stock company; s.r.o. = Czech equivalent of limited liability company.

The Binding Force of Production Linkages

If the inherent scope and flexibilities were clear sources for unit autonomy, the overlapping supply links with relatively narrow technical specifications constrained individual discretion. Intraholding subcontracting links remained vital for the flow of production across different common programs as well as those of individual units. The importance of these internal links, however, varied according to one's place in the network. In turn, managers held different views over production interdependencies, which provoked clashes over such critical restructuring issues as asset control, spin-offs, new subgroups, and plant closings.

By 1989, the production profile of Škoda Plzeň accounted for ninety-one different product groups across more than twenty plants.[14] While the main final production programs included transport (electric locomotives and trolleybuses), energy equipment and systems (nuclear and steam turbines), and heavy industrial machinery, upstream production included gearboxes, transmissions, engines, generators, transformers, electrical control systems, forgings and presses, and rolled steel and castings. An aggregate analysis of its output and supply structure indicates that units were already less dependent on the group for sales but were highly dependent on one another for inputs and parts.[15] Between 1986 and 1993, average production for customers outside the group accounted consistently for over 70 percent of total output. Between 1986 and 1990 inputs from outside the group, however, accounted consistently for only 21 percent of production value. From 1991 through 1993 this share dropped to about 12 percent, suggesting an even greater tendency for Škoda units to turn toward one another for inputs when hit by the new uncertainties. These trends created three essential problems in the reorganization of production and decision-making rights.[16]

First, although many units faced strong incentives to increase their independence from the group, such actions threatened their own and joint production programs. Critical upstream suppliers, such as OK for gearboxes and transmissions, Kovarna for large forged metal parts, ETD for industrial transformers and generators, and Controls for automated injection, rectifier, and traction control systems, all had sales to customers outside the group accounting for 40 to 65 percent of their total output by 1990. Also, over 50 percent of inputs and parts were produced within their plants. In turn, these units had both the experience and capability to increase their focus on external sales and split from the group. Yet these plants still supplied unique parts for both the previously mentioned main production programs and smaller programs of other plants. Greater independence could seriously impede the flow of production and product development. Moreover, these plants still depended on

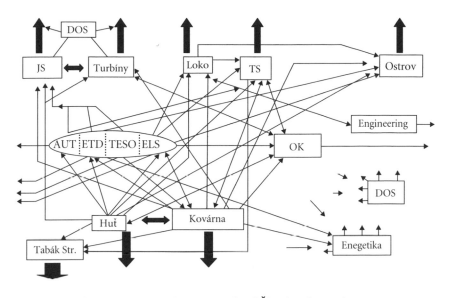

Figure 4.1.   Main Network of Škoda Plzeň Plants

Based on sales, receivable, payables data, 1990–92.
Source: Internal Škoda Documents on file with author.

members of the holding for the supply of 20 to 45 percent of needed inputs as well as services, such as energy, marketing, procurement, and maintenance.

Second, the scope of plant level production and density of multiple production links impeded the clear definition of new divisions for the main programs. (See fig. 4.1.) Such divisions would incorporate upstream units into specific joint programs and aid in streamlining production and R&D. Yet upstream suppliers like OK, Kovarna, ETD, and Controls produced different parts for all of the main programs as well as other plants. Splitting up a unit was constrained by the fact that these different parts were manufactured, developed, and tested using largely the same facilities and personnel. Given the uncertainties of each program and the limited finances, there was no clear reason why one program should be given priority over the other.

The third source of conflict came in closing certain plants or workshops and replacing internal suppliers with external ones. This might be expected in specialty component manufacturing, such as in the two problems just discussed. But the same problem came even with more basic inputs, such as steel. Many of the largest upstream and downstream units purchased much of their rolled steel, ingots, castings and molds from the unit, Huť. At the same time, every manager branded Huť the "loser" of Škoda, in terms of financial losses and quality of service. With numerous steel plants and firms throughout the

CR, there were clear opportunities and advantages for Huť's internal customers to find other suppliers and Škoda to close Huť.[17] Yet Škoda managers resisted any bold moves, arguing that the years of collaboration afforded flexible payments as well as Huť's detailed knowledge of the specific technical needs of each Škoda customer, neither of which could easily be found with other steel producers.

The continued use of intragroup production links constrained the initial ambitions of Škoda units for autonomy and was a source of ongoing tension about reorganization and cost cutting. A brief examination other holding companies will show how these production legacies were not unique to Škoda's locality or its production profile but more a product of the former hierarchical network.

ČKD Praha was a general engineering *koncern*-VHJ under communism, with a production profile of eighty-one product groups by 1989.[18] In anticipation of privatization, its management transformed the company into a joint-stock holding in 1990 with eighteen subsidiaries.[19] Management attempted both to create four divisions according to the major joint programs and to encourage subsidiaries to increase their direct sales outside the holding. The inherited production links and scopes caused this dual strategy to provoke two main conflicts. First, the demands by upstream units for increased autonomy clashed with the designs of top management. For instance, such units as Kompressory, Elektrotechnika, Chocen, and DIZ already sold 40 to 70 percent of their output to outside customers. They planned to orient their production more to these areas but demanded certain guarantees from the holding on continued internal supplies, sales, and services. These units, however, held virtual monopolies in supplying specific parts for such areas as diesel engines, transport, industrial refrigeration, and large hydraulics. In turn, holding management argued that guarantees could be given only if the units gave priority in their production changes to the standards set by the new divisions. Second, ČKD's attempt at consolidation through divisions conflicted with the high degree of technical synergies across the main programs. (See fig. 4.2.) Often a subsidiary supplied several divisions, which increased tensions about internal boundaries for future foreign partnerships and production priorities. For instance, final producers for the rail program (Lokomotivka and Tatra) as well as the finalist for complete plant equipment (DIZ) depended on semi-finished goods from members in all divisions; motor and compressor production shared components; metal-working units in Hradec Kralové, Slevarny, Žandov, and Hořovice supplied all programs.[20]

Aero created eleven subsidiaries from its plants and had two main final production programs: military and civilian aircraft.[21] Despite its narrow final production profile, relative to Škoda and ČKD, Aero adapted to shortage

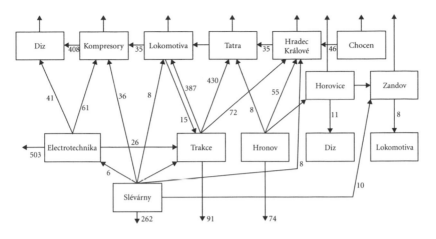

Figure 4.2.   Internal Contracting Network, ČKD, 1990

Internal production and supply links among subsidiaries of ČKD Praha, 1990 (sales data in million Kcs). Arrows between subsidiaries connote intersubsidiary sales; arrows pointing to outside of large box connote sales to external customers.
Source: Internal analysis of ČKD Praha by AT Kearney, 1992.

through a similar pattern of centralized autarky: many plants with large in-house production capabilities and extensive subcontracting arrangements between them. On average, 70 percent of subsidiary output and 80 percent of needed inputs and parts were intraholding. This pattern continually blocked internal agreement about grouping units into the two main programs in preparation for JVs and a breakup into two or three large firms. Upstream units of different programs continued to develop component and engine production jointly. They also would out source to one another to utilize idle capacity since production and development cycles of each program would alternate. Moreover, four subsidiaries with diversified activities provided R&D, electronic components, seats, and hydraulics to both programs. These subsidiaries became the center of a bitter tug-of-war between members of the two programs.[22]

Both Tatra (off-road trucks) and Liaz (on-road trucks) had long histories of producing unique, high-performance heavy trucks, winning awards in top international rallies for their respective classes and receiving honors for their endurance in the Gulf War.[23] These trucks were able to perform in extreme conditions largely because of their highly specialized engine, gearbox and axle designs, such as Tatra's air-cooled engines and their respective flexible swing half-axles. But these specializations and modular vehicle designs brought constraints to the reorganization of Tatra and Liaz. Among Tatra's seven subsidiaries and Liaz's nine, both firms maintained their own foundries as well as engine, gearbox, cabin, frame, and testing factories. Because of their specializations, both firms were reluctant to spin-off subsidiaries and plants, despite falling sales and cash flow. At the same time, since foreign firms were interested in joint ventures with only a one or two plants or subsidiaries, Tatra and Liaz faced the daunting task making multiple, simultaneous joint ventures compatible with one another. Management's preoccupation with maintaining production synergies had already been reinforced with the insolvencies of Czech producers of fuel injection systems, chargers, and anti-brake systems (Motorpal, CZM, and Meotopa, respectively).[24] Unable to coordinate interfirm relations, Tatra and Liaz management preferred to cling to their subsidiaries and wrestle with the ensuing restructuring conflicts and financial burdens than allow full independence of their member subsidiaries and plants.

The high-end steel producer, Poldi, contained thirteen subsidiaries.[25] The two largest subsidiaries were Poldi I and II, producers of large industrial specialty steel products and rolled steel, respectively. Critical supporting subsidiaries were Strojírny (specialized machinery for steel production), Energetické Centrum (power supplier for both Poldi and the city of Kladno), Anticorro (stainless steel medical products), KND and SID (transportation for large steel products), and Termosondy and Autech (electronic guidance and measuring systems). With a drastic reduction in sales by almost 80 percent between 1989 and 1992, Poldi faced the conflicting aims of spinning off assets and maintaining production through internal subcontracting. The combination of rising costs, decreasing cash flow, and constraints of specialty steel production increased production interdependencies between Poldi I and II and the other subsidiaries. For instance, development of new large steel products depended on the services and development of Strojírny, Termosondy, and Autech. Although KND, SID, and Energetické Centrum were loss makers, limited cash flow made Poldi managers reluctant dispel these subsidiaries and to buy these services from other providers. Even one of the most profitable and easily sellable subsidiaries, Anticorro, was reluctant to break full ties with Poldi, since Poldi II was the principle supplier of its rolled steel inputs. To maintain holding integrity but increase unit independence, Poldi management attempted a number of strategies, including sales of strategic equity stakes of subsidiaries, the permission for skilled workers to create semi-autonomous firms with spare Poldi facilities, and the transfer of 5 percent of Poldi equity to the Kladno municipal council.[26] Yet with investors interested in complete control of subsidiaries and the council lacking political and financial resources, maintenance of production links, skilled work groups, and vital services grew increasingly costly for Poldi.

Liquidity Constraints and Overlapping Debts

As examined in chapter 3, undercapitalized Czech industrial firms generally reacted to the sudden and persistent drop in liquidity by sharply increasing interfirm debt through existing networks and acquiring short-term bank loans.[27] For holdings, the collapse of payments for in-process production to the CMEA filtered from end producers to internal suppliers, and the groups became dependent on the banks for operating capital. But the inherited economic links and the choice to privatize the group as a whole shaped the growth in commercial and bank debt of holdings in two distinctive ways. First, units utilized their inherited ties and the umbrella of the holding to hold down costs and to negotiate more flexible terms of interunit payment. In turn, continued intraholding subcontracting also deepened the financial interdependence among members. Second, the practice of cross-collateralization within holdings tied the financial problems of one unit directly to more prosperous units. Given their weak capital base and limited legal position, members depended on the holding center to acquire loans for working capital. In doing so, the holding securitized old and new loans by using valuable assets of a certain unit as collateral for loans used by other units.[28] In turn, the autonomy of a potentially strong unit to reorganize production, spin off, or create its own JV was severely constrained. Any attempt at gaining independent financing or regaining control over its assets was now intimately connected to the solvency and reorganization of other, usually more distressed, members.

We can see these patterns of interlocking commercial and bank debt in Škoda and the others. Tables 4.2 and 4.3 show their unattractive financial development. During 1990 and early 1991, when it was still unable to define subsidiaries, Škoda used the property of more physically independent plants like Ostrov, Ejpovice, and ETD, as collateral for various loans.[29] By mid-1992, Škoda's payables in arrear reached 2.8 billion Kcs (about 85 percent of total payables), exceeding overdue receivables. The majority of arrears were internal. The 16 main production units had 55 to 95 percent of their arrears within Škoda, 50 to 89 percent of which was overdue. In general, end producers of the main programs were net internal debtors, while upstream units mainly oriented to intra-Škoda sales were net internal creditors. But even upstream units that sold most of their total output outside Škoda, such as OK and Kovarna, had become net internal debtors. Thus, cross-collateralization and the extensive use of internal suppliers caused potentially independent units to depend on the financial protection of the holding. At the same time interlocking debts cut across production programs, hindering the definition of new subgroups or divisions.

The other holdings developed similar debt entanglements. ČKD's financial difficulties grew out of its large overdue receivables for locomotives in Russia and the precipitous decline in sales in transport, compressors, and metallurgy.[30] Arrears within the holding accounted for about half of all ČKD nonbank liabilities. By 1992–93, five subsidiaries were legally insolvent and accounted for almost half of the overdue payables for all of ČKD. Eight had

TABLE 4.2.　Financial Status of Selected Czech Holding Companies, 1992, Part 1

Firm	Change in Sales (current prices)		Change in Exports (current prices)		Pretax Profits (current prices)	
	92/89	92/91	92/89	92/91	92/89	92/91
Škoda Plzeň	1.01	0.78	0.64	0.56	0.88	1.04
ČKD Praha	1.13	0.56	0.3	0.17	0.49	0.38
Aero	.93[a]	0.75	—	—	—	−8.53
Poldi Kladno	0.35	0.41	—	—	−2.5	−0.86
Tatra Kopřivnice	0.53	0.26	—	—	−1.81	−1.4

Source: Annual Reports, internal documents, and government documents on respective companies, as cited in the footnotes and listed in the tables for references. Author's calculations.
Note: PPI of CR: 1990—2.5%, 1991—72.2%, 1992—17.3%
[a] Sales ratio for Aero is for 1992/1990.

defaulted on their payments for the principle of their loans, and six defaulted on their interest rate payments. Similar to Škoda, the internal arrears and the most financially distressed units cut across production programs and various stages of production. Unable to isolate and resolve these financial burdens, ČKD threatened to shut down in late 1992.[31]

By mid-1991, six of the eleven subsidiaries of Aero were already in default of their loans and all were legally insolvent to their suppliers.[32] The main final assemblers, Vodochody and Let, had debt-equity ratios of 367 percent and 130 percent, respectively, and the other subsidiaries had ratios ranging from 45 percent-80 percent by 1993. For all members and the holding center financial costs accounted for over half of total costs. A key problem was Aero's practice of taking loans for its two final assemblers, and securitizing them with assets of other subsidiaries. As the main programs failed to generate new export revenues and service their debts, promising upstream members were then unable to receive sufficient loans to counter the loss of cash flow. In turn, commercial arrears rose by over 400 percent in 1991 and 200 percent in 1992. The majority of these arrears was from debts between Aero subsidiaries. The weight of these overlapping debts grew so severe that by mid-1993 Aero and the MPO had already failed with three different debt restructuring and JV arrangements.[33]

The truck producers, Tatra and Liaz, had taken loans to support the development of existing and new trucks and cars by using the engine, foundry, and cabin subsidiaries as security.[34] Yet when exports failed to rebound (sales fell for both by over 60 percent between 1989 and 1992), Tatra and Liaz faced mounting interest rate payments, and their subsidiaries were unable to receive additional loans for ongoing product development. In June 1992, Tatra had to shut down for four months and cancel development of their new luxury T 93 car and new engine system. Liaz shut down for two months at the

TABLE 4.3. Financial Status of Selected Czech Holding Companies, 1992, Part 2

| | Leverage and Liquidity | | | | | | | | | |
| Firm | Total Debt / Equity | | Bank Debt / Equity | | Interest-Rate Burden | | Cash Ratio | | Current Liabilities/ Gross Earnings | |
	1991	1992	1991	1992	1991	1992	1991	1992	1991	1992
Škoda Plzeň	1.62	1.59	0.66	0.5	0.015	0.019[a]	0.098	0.087	0.78	1.146
ČKD Praha	2.4	2.64	0.88	0.95	—	0.36[b]	0.005	0.066	0.85	0.99
Aero	1.42	1.89	0.58	0.95	—	0.019	0.14	0.07	1.37	2.3
Poldi Kladno	—	0.8	0.34	0.29	—	—	—	0.002	0.63	1.57
Tatra Kopřivnice	—	1.22	—	0.75	—	−0.54	—	0.03	—	1.75

Source: Annual Reports, internal documents, and government documents on respective companies, as cited in the footnotes and listed in the table of references. Author's calculations.

[a]As of 9/92, when Škoda faced a shutdown, and government initiated intervention.

[b]1993

Total Debt/Equity = (bank debt+trade debt) / equity

Interest Rate Burden = (pretax profit+current interest payments)/current interest payments

Cash Ratio = cash and cash equivalents / current liabilities end of 1992. In both cases, prospective JV partners declined to finalize any deals due in part to the debt burdens of interested subsidiaries.

Poldi's attempts to maintain internal production and service links would meet a similar fate.[35] In 1992, its steel output reached only 20 percent of 1989 figures, and it produced substantial losses in 1991 and 1992. As Energetické Centrum, Strojírny, KND, and SID all became insolvent in 1991–92, Poldi was reluctant to close them or simply sell them for a nominal price. Poldi's financial entanglements even hindered the sale of Anticorro, which started to turn a profit and court several prospective buyers. Poldi management refused to give up its demand for a 34 percent stake in Anticorro, since Anticorro supplied consistent cash flow and was critical for Poldi gaining ISO 9002 certification.[36] In February 1993, Poldi began a series of forced shut downs. Electricity and raw-steel providers refused delivery because of Poldi's inability to pay them.[37]

With growing financial entanglements, holding members were increasingly constrained in their decisions to downsize and spin off. On the one hand, many critical upstream units in holdings had become legally insolvent but were not easily replaceable with external contractors.[38] In turn, holding management continued to cross-subsidize them. On the other hand, the negative experiences of several self-liberated and previously profitable plants restrained the ambitions of holding units to spin-off.[39] The new firms quickly lost production and financial aid of their former cohorts, failed to connect with expected foreign partners, and languished alone in insolvency. By early 1992, several even requested to be reabsorbed in the holdings.[40] Their failures were stark reminders to holding members that production and financial conflicts could easily end by one of the partners walking away, leaving the other to bear the new economic uncertainties alone. Indeed, statistical analysis of privatization shows a very small number of industrial spin-offs, which also performed significantly worse than their former parents.[41]

Probing: Innovation and the Barriers to Internal Cooperation

Much of the recent research on economic networks, institutional change, and common resource management would lead one to believe that the reinforcement of production and financial linkages within holdings would not present insurmountable barriers to restructuring, particularly in light of strong market based policies and the long history among members. The research suggests that networks are self-governing and, thus, that holding members would still be able to use contractual methods or past power structures and norms to resolve restructuring conflicts on their own.[42] However, restructuring conflicts actually worsened.

My embedded politics approach makes sense of this problem by accounting for how the authority structure of networks is closely linked to the broader sociopolitical environment. Reproduction of the hierarchical network in the form of a holding company was as much a product of the past socioeconomic constraints as it was a product of the undermining of the past authority structure by the Czech policies. The latter created space for members to pursue decentralized restructuring experiments, which in turn produced conflicts for redistributing power and asset control within the network. By highlighting how these experiments nullify the use of contracts and past norms, my approach points to the need for risk- and power-sharing arrangements that private actors—inside or outside the network—are unable to produce voluntarily or by force. In turn, this analytical lens clarifies the limits of depoliticization and the conditions for intervention by government agencies. To begin, consider the way experimentation can reshape the goals and power of network members even with the existence of strong economic and social constraints.

With the collapse of sales in the main joint-production programs and no immediate sources of investment, holding units were forced to explore new market niches and generate cash flow on their own or in small groups. That is, units tried to adapt their inherited broad production capabilities to innovate in a number of production areas, in small batches, and simultaneously. I call this cumulative process of production and organizational experimentation *probing*. Probing, however, causes units to reconfigure their subcontracting, sales, product development, and financial relations with one another.[43] Consequently, units begin to alter their views on the relative importance and role of individual members as well as the group as a whole. This ongoing alteration in views can clash with the existing network interdependencies. As units create multiple visions and strategies of their future opportunities and needs, they can be all too unwilling to commit themselves to another's designs. The preference is to improve one's relative position and bargaining power in the network, eroding the inherited sociopolitical fabric.

While partial evidence was already given earlier in the chapter, additional evidence of probing taking root in holdings by 1991–92 can be found in the product areas of increased output and the numerous foreign partnerships that units pursued independently. For instance, in Škoda Plzeň, sales and output for main common programs, such as locomotives, trolleybuses, heavy machinery, complete manufacturing systems, and power plant systems, all declined in 1990–92. But significant increases came in product lines of individual or small groups of units—machine parts, gearboxes and transmissions, small steam turbines, aluminum forgings, crank shafts, steel castings, nuclear plant equipment, ceramic casings, and electric motors.[44] Even traditional final producers, such as Loco for locomotives and TS for milling and food-processing machinery began to utilize side-production for new sales, devoting 10 percent of output to supplying other Škoda units with machine and electrical parts. Besides two large JVs for the transport and energy programs, units pursued partnerships and JVs in smaller, more specialized areas, such as heavy machine tool components, traction systems, low temperature fuel injection and engine parts, ecological equipment, and CAD/CAM systems. Units in ČKD Praha were similarly increasing their production in new motor, and machinery parts, small compressors, low-temperature electrical guidance systems, and castings.[45] Besides a major JV for the transport program, each unit was pursuing at least one (in some cases five) JV and partnerships in previously underutilized areas. Aero units were increasing production not just for aircraft parts but particularly new engine parts, fuel injection systems, seats and seatbelts, axles, and shafts for the automotive industry.[46] A similar development took place in Tatra, Liaz, and Poldi.[47]

As units probed new markets and generated cash flow, they began experimenting with different organizational, investment, and product development strategies.[48] Yet because they were not exactly sure which particular product line(s) would become their future specialization, they were reluctant to fully commit resources to or eliminate any one area. This created two major restructuring problems for holdings: under investment and over employment. Simultaneous probing among many units and across production programs led managers to put increasingly different demands on one another to commit to altering or maintaining existing inputs, end products, and production methods. At the same time, assets were jointly controlled, which demanded units cooperate with one another to develop new products and so forth. The vast literature on product development and common resources already informs us that under conditions like probing, it is virtually impossible for parties to write ex ante contracts to determine the effort-reward allocation for all contingencies—hence the use of incomplete contracts.[49] Incomplete contracts, however, are well known for leading to underinvestment.[50] Each unit participating in a probe must undertake some irreversible and specific investment to carry it one step ahead. In the absence of explicit contractual guarantees, other units may take advantage of the one that sinks its money into a specific investment. In other words, because of current economic uncertainties and financial constraints, no one, neither individual units nor top management, could guarantee the success of their strategy or force another to follow a proposed strategy. In turn, the members were noncommittal to avoid possible holdups.

Probing then impedes downsizing, as it is essentially a slow process of multiple experiments about what combination of facilities and personnel can penetrate new markets. Lacking any immediately credible guarantees of one's own or another's experiments, managers were reluctant to cut production lines and workers involved in probing, as it could be premature. Managers came to see redundancy in facilities and work groups and financial slack as a necessary part of probing.[51] A vicious circle emerged as holdings were already financially distressed. On the one hand, holdings continually suffered from overemployment in the face of falling output and sales during 1990–93. Interviews at all the previously mentioned holdings revealed that managers were extremely concerned about losing experienced, skilled production and design workers, since they were the principal value of the companies and potentially vital as new or old areas developed. This could be seen in the personnel policy and employment data of holdings as well as their creation of so-called conversion and new design units.[52] On the other hand, these practices increased the financial uncertainty of holdings, causing skilled employees to flee. Both the employment data and MPO white papers show that the large majority of decreases in holding employment was due to skilled employees finding higher wages in new private firms or abroad.[53] In turn, holdings began to suffer a brain drain that threatened to destroy key production programs.

The tight economic links and probing became both aids and barriers to the survival and restructuring of holdings. Yet, the Czech government's depoliticization strategy that relied on complete contracts and autonomous, centralized power undermined the ability of holding members to resolve their internal collective action problems.

In creating new production and organizational possibilities, probing breaks up existing product niches and social relations. As discussed in previous chapters, the standard approaches argue that policymakers can depoliticize restructuring by addressing the delineation of property rights and the maintenance of asset value as separable issues, since restructuring conflicts can be resolved through complete contracts. This view of complete contracts stems from the idea that a group of economic actors is self-governing, with an unchanged set of internal interests and power structures.[54] For instance, the statist approach argues that the underinvestment problem can be resolved by the state constructing a complete contract with an industrial sector—an industrial policy in the form of technology standards and clear incentives for investment into a new technology. This view assumes that the firm already knows which products to pursue and how best to pursue them.[55] In contrast, each product in a holding involves several units, and each unit is involved in several products. For each unit there is then no single product it can focus on and develop independently of others. The choice of the new technology must optimize over all the products the unit could generate. But each unit would tend to hold back technological modifications until its role in each product line is cleared.

The more sophisticated variants of the economistic approach take into account past social relations.[56] They argue that preexisting power asymmetries, contracting relationships, and rules of coordination are carried directly into a new period and enable parties to common assets to agree to a new set of rules or strategies through consensus or force. With this new comprehensive contract for the group, all that is needed is a clear legal system to enforce the new contract. In contrast, probing is as much about reconfiguring old relationships as it is about exploiting them. As units probe, they experiment not only with new products but also new perceptions of contracting norms and control over resources. For instance, new production experiments can alter a unit's position in the network, as a subcontractor or end producer. Both options bring potentially high risks since one is ultimately dependent on or liable for a project with uncertain returns.

The combination of tight economic links with probing thus causes the two components of privatization—reordering the property rights and preserving value—to be simultaneous and subject to frequent revision. The Czech policy of addressing the two components separately forced members to view individual needs and collective needs as mutually exclusive. If a unit were to preserve the value of the holding, then it had to subsume its interests to the production strategy of another. If a unit were to assert its independent control rights, then it had to break off from the group or buy out the others. Either way the risks were prohibitively high, as the consequence was a complete relinquishment of control or a complete assumption of control, albeit for a project with uncertain returns. Indeed, an apparent reason for creating the holdings in the first place was to avoid these extreme decisions and find a way to share both risk and control.

Perhaps more importantly, holdings emerged from networks that had an authority structure politically constructed by managers and public actors. Czech policy efforts to centralize power effectively had eliminated a critical source of sociopolitical power and order. As probing began to foster potentially conflicting strategies and altered the position of units within the group, the authority structure of the group was thrown into question: how should new boundaries around assets be drawn and who had the authority to decide them? Under the former hierarchical network, such debates may have emerged from adapting to the shortage environment and new export demands of the government, but the regional councils possessed the political and social resources to aid a resolution to conflicts—be it by force or compromise. After 1989, no such actor was around. The dissolution of regional councils and the weakening of district and municipal councils eliminated a source of power for some members and a source of external resources and mediation for the group as a whole. Indeed, the aggregate and holdings data on privatization show that firms solicited the aid of local municipalities by offering them free transfers of significant equity stakes.[57] Yet as discussed in chapter 3, the changes in the systems of territorial administration and taxes effectively left municipalities with little control over political and financial resources.[58]

Joint Ventures: The Rise and Fall of a Possible Framework

If the Czech depoliticization strategy had eliminated a traditional external partner for the holding companies, it also held out the promise of providing a new one, albeit in the form of a private actor—a foreign direct investor.[59] Privatization policy created a clear incentive structure for foreign investors to purchase whole or parts of assets and inject needed resources into firms. A foreign partner may not have held the local sociopolitical capital that former councils once did, but it surely held an international reputation and financial capital, which were in short supply among domestic actors. Indeed, the compromise that created the holding structure also produced privatization strategies based heavily on gaining foreign direct investors. However, as mentioned in chapter 3 and evident in table 4.1, virtually all proposed JVs fell apart in 1992–93, and FDI played a relatively small role in Czech industry.[60] A closer look at the rise and fall of Škoda Plzeň's JVs throws into sharper relief how the interaction between the macropolitics of state designs and the micropolitics of intranetwork conflicts shaped the possibilities for holdings to obtain even a strong private, external partner. While the combination of tight economic links and probing among network members forced foreign investors to adopt an incomplete contract as the basis for entry, macro-level fights over political control conditioned the ability of the government to become a needed third party to share risk and mediate differences.

According to its original 1991 privatization project, Škoda Plzeň put 48.5 percent of its equity into voucher privatization and left 42.1 percent in the FNM for future sale to foreign partners.[61] Škoda set out to create JVs with Western firms, notably a double JV between Siemens and the units in its Energo and Transport programs, which represented almost half of Škoda's output and sales. The selection of Siemens as the finalist had already created internal conflicts, as different groups of plant managers had supported proposals with Westinghouse and ABB. They viewed top management's designs for JVs with Siemens as "making decisions about us but without us"—a clear violation of the compromise that had forged the holding in the first place. As a price for gaining the acceptance of Siemens, plant managers demanded that their restructuring concerns be addressed in the negotiations.[62]

Similar to the JVs proposed for other holdings, Škoda's potential JV would include only selected units.[63] As Siemens invested new capital into the JV, Škoda would cede majority control of the relevant units over time. Due to the financial and production links between the chosen units and the others in Škoda, the partnership assumed the form of a JV rather than a takeover: a framework in which both parties would observe and learn about how to use and invest into their mutual capabilities to develop new products. On the one hand, Škoda managers wanted assurances that JV units would continue to contribute to certain debt-reduction and product development plans, which were vital to the restructuring of non-JV units. On the other hand, Siemens refused to commit to open-ended production and financial commitments and wanted clearer boundaries drawn around the JV units.

A typical example of this cooperation problem was the reorganization of the large electro-technical complex that produced various components, motors, and transformers for the Energo and Transport programs as well as others.[64] The complex would have to be divided into five units, two of which would be in the Energo JV. Yet many other units outside the two programs still depended on the complex as a key supplier. Also, two units of the complex not in the JV had always been partial subcontractors for and shared facilities and product development with the units included in the JV. If Siemens wanted a majority share in a JV with Energo, it had then to ensure continued cooperation and take over many of Energo's old production and financial obligations toward other units.[65] Siemens refused this and the absorption of other existing debts, assuming that the government or Škoda would cover the obligations the firm had incurred while it was state owned. This disagreement led Škoda management to declare its reservations about ceding significant control to any foreign partner. If Siemens had the discretion to disregard the continued obligations between units, it could harm the product development and liquidity of non-JV units and the holding itself.

A related conflict grew out of differences over the future development strategies of core projects within Energo and Transport—nuclear plant production and locomotive production. In both areas, Škoda managers saw the modernization, servicing, and component production for existing products already in use throughout the former CMEA countries as critical for the development of existing production capabilities and cash flow. The units of the Energo program had begun to focus on the production of improved turbines, fuel containers, and parts for plants in Eastern Europe. Yet Siemens appeared intent on replacing much of Škoda's nuclear turbine production with its own. In Transport, Škoda had begun to renew relations in Russia and Ukraine, where it already had 3,000 locomotives in operation, for sales of locomotives through third-party financing and barter deals. Škoda planned JVs in these countries to produce engine components and to recoup large uncollected receivables. Siemens however wanted to shift more of its own production into Transport and orient Škoda's units toward simple wagon production.

To mitigate these differences, Škoda and Siemens turned the JV into an incomplete contract, in which the relations between the JV and non-JV units would be specified over time. They then sought the aid of a third party to ensure one another's interests. The main banks were unhelpful, since they had no ownership authority over assets and were already reluctant to make long-term financial commitments.[66] The Czech government, however, continued to possess, at least partially, the authority and resources to fulfill Škoda's privatization. In turn, the JV hinged on the government's willingness to absorb some of the liabilities and act as a guarantor of mutual commitments.

To alleviate these tensions, Minister of Industry Vrba began to revise his arm's-length policies. Using the successful model for the JV between Volkswagon and Škoda Mlada Boleslav,[67] he positioned his ministry in the Siemens-Škoda negotiations to coax compromises from each side and provide guarantees for liabilities and technology development. In January 1992, he managed to have letters of intent signed by all parties. Both Siemens and Škoda argued that the government's participation in the resolution of inherited liabilities was essential for signing the final agreement expected in March. When the government's commitment to the JV parties was tested, it wavered, notably in assistance with a 1.2 billion Kcs receivable from the state railway company and a 1.9 billion Kcs debt in Energo's nuclear program.[68] The Klausians had increased their political strength, and rejected any protracted government involvement in the JV. Following their victory in the June 1992 elections, the Klausians took control of the government and Vrba was ousted. They continued to refuse to pay for the locomotives and relieve any debts. A restructuring vehicle supported by government guarantees and medium-term participation could set a precedent and lead to a major change in both policy and Klausian control of it.

With the collapse of JV talks, Škoda managers grew openly hostile to the government during the summer of 1992. They created a smaller managing board without any government members (representatives of the FNM). Then on 17 September they shut down three major units for a week and defaulted on loans. Two weeks later, the government announced that it would appoint a new, bigger managing board to Škoda and would sell 37 percent of Škoda in a public tender. The existing board members walked out in protest of the government's intervention. On 16 October, the tender was announced, and it was closed four days later. This move was an attempt to use a pure ownership solution to maintain government insulation. Its failings, however, would give rise to DDR, a public-private restructuring vehicle that attempted to resolve internal and external hold-up problems of holdings through deliberative governance mechanisms.

Delegation and Deliberation:
Toward a Negotiated Restructuring

Creating unitary owners with incentive contracts would, in theory, force the new owners and the units to settle restructuring disputes on their own and cut the remaining links between the government and the firm.[69] In analyzing the failure and aftermath of this strategy, this section pulls together the two critical strands of my argument previously laid out: (1) how the politics of reproducing the hierarchical network set the basic background conditions for the way certain government agencies, Czech banks, and Škoda members would seek a negotiated solution; (2) how the principles of delegation and deliberation allowed the new public-private governance institution, DDR, to be a sustainable restructuring governance model, though violating the basic tenets of depoliticization.

As interest in the tender was rather limited and the IPCs were passive, the main candidates were: Lubomír Soudek, a former Škoda manager without additional funds; and the KB-IB consortium, the principal Škoda creditors with whom government had been holding discussions.[70] Through the tender, the government aimed to maintain the depoliticization of restructuring by assigning certain tasks to the candidates, setting strong ownership and financial incentives, and walking away. Soudek's main tasks were to increase the legal independents of units and the financial transparency of Škoda. The banks were to grant a moratorium on debt service and restructure the debts of both the holding and individual units.[71] As incentives, the government would allocate 20 percent of equity to Soudek and 14 to 17 percent to the consortium, help finance the locomotive and nuclear debts (via the FNM and Ministry of Finance), and deduct some of the banks' expenses from their share price. The banks and Soudek would receive seats on the board, with Soudek as the director and chairman.

Soon after the agreement was concluded, three points of conflict emerged, reflecting again the incompatibility between network restructuring and contractual or state imposed methods. First, the JV talks resumed and immediately collapsed, as there were no new provisions to mitigate the aforementioned conflicts between Škoda and Siemens. In need of new funds to start restructuring, Soudek turned to the government and banks, which initially rejected his plea.

Only after the Ministry of Finance's persuasion did the banks agree to underwrite and purchase 1 billion Kcs of Škoda bonds at a relatively low interest rate in December 1992.[72] Second, the banks and Soudek rejected the government's ultimatum to atomize Škoda.[73]

Third, and most serious, was the refusal by the Ministry of Finance and FNM in December 1992 and again in January 1993 to finance the nuclear and locomotive debts. The key reason was Soudek's reorganization plan, according to which each unit would be a limited liability company (subsidiary), with the center of the holding company owning 100 percent of their equity, buildings, and property. In addition to dividends and a fee for the use of the Škoda trademark, the subsidiaries would also have to pay rent to the center. The government argued that without an imminent JV or atomization, Škoda's center would have unwarranted control over the subsidiaries: the rents would help preserve the old hierarchy; the subsidiaries could not easily receive outside funding without owning their own property; cross-collateralization of assets among subsidiaries would continue and block a future breakup of Škoda.

As all parties accused each other of reneging, no one, however, left the table. The agreement (and, note, not an official contract) was again revised[74]: two MPO officials, legally representing the FNM, would sit on the Škoda board of directors for at least twelve months; the Council of Economic Ministers ordered a review of Škoda for June 1993, at which point heads of the FNM and MPO would officially name the recipients and size of the equity stakes in Škoda. In the meantime, the parties would negotiate the price of shares and debt relief, as the banks demonstrated their debt restructuring and Soudek demonstrated adequate decentralization within Škoda. From June until the end of 1994, the parties continued negotiations over the ongoing restructuring and lending actions as well as about the terms of payment, share transfer, and government debt contributions. The Czech government eventually guaranteed the debts from the nuclear program in early 1994 and partially paid for the locomotives in mid-1994. The banks and Soudek finally received their shares in early 1995, with moratoriums on the resale of the shares and the bankruptcy of Škoda.[75]

As it would with other holdings, the Czech government was forced to retreat from its depoliticization agenda and negotiate the privatization-cum-workout of Škoda directly with the banks and firm but on new terms. The reasons for both the reversal and the new terms can be found in the intertwined internal and external holdup problems of holding that had emerged from the way the former VHJ network had shaped strategic choices in the face of the initial privatization designs. The financial interdependencies between the main banks and the holdings had led KB and IB to become the sole senior creditors and to wait for a partner to share the costs of restructuring. As Soudek had no independent financial resources, these banks would have to bear the brunt of Škoda's borrowing needs. Soudek was, however, a monitoring partner with specific knowledge of Škoda. Thus, KB and IB's future risk depended on how well they could observe Soudek and the subsidiaries.

But because Škoda's network assets prevented an immediate division of assets or the definition of a particular production project, the regime of incomplete contracts within the holding extended to the banks themselves. Since the ability of the banks (or any external partner) to define their own goals and lending strategies depended on how Soudek and the subsidiaries would cooperate and define their production goals, KB and IB could not rely on the terms of some prior contract.[76] That is, the banks were unable to assess both the ex ante risks of lending requirements and the actions of holding members, and thus feared being pulled into long-term lending obligations with little recourse. Without clear financial support, Soudek and Škoda management then had no reason to submit to the constraints of the tender. This put the banks and Škoda right back where they began—uncertain of either's intentions. Similar to the collapse of the JVs, the stalemate reappeared without clear government commitment to sharing both the financial risks and monitoring.

Ironically, the Czech government's attempt to depoliticize the formation of new governance institutions and its commitment to privatization had planted the seeds for it to become a bargaining partner with the banks and Škoda. On the one hand, its policy of rapid privatization had allowed the former hierarchical network to be reproduced in such a way that prevented complete contract solutions to restructuring conflicts and necessitated third-party mediation and financial commitments. But the policy also demanded a centralization of power, which left the government, in particular the MPO and FNM, as the main candidates for this role. On the other hand, the government's public commitment to privatization had tied its political health to ensuring both the reassignment of property rights and the value of the assets. Any further actions of force against the banks and Škoda or inattention to the conflicts, would have threatened these basic components of privatization. In turn, the government gradually reengaged the banks and Škoda to resolve their disputes, and the failed tender became the basis of a new structure to govern the transfer of ownership and the workout of distressed assets.

Delegation and Deliberation as Founding Principles

The tender turned into an informal, implicit contract, whereby: (1) the government delegated to Soudek's central management team the authority to

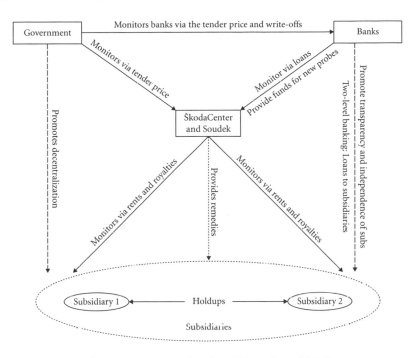

Figure 4.3.   Monitoring Triangles of DDR

Broken and dotted lines denote noncontractual and often indirect means of enabling subsidiary-level governance.

rebuild the internal organization of the firm and to the banks the authority to finance this reorganization on the behalf of the government; and (2) it used the debts and the vague pricing of shares to provoke the parties to reveal information about their actions and monitor one another's progress in meeting their restructuring obligations. The ensuing pattern of negotiations set the foundations for forums to administer the incomplete contracts, what I call delegated deliberative restructuring, or DDR. The core traits are the dual processes of the delegation of authority and of the creation of structured deliberations. The forums for deliberation comprise two overlapping monitoring triangles. (See fig. 4.3.) In the external triangle, the government, the banks, and the central management team exchanged information and control rights in deliberating each other's contribution to debt restructuring, decentralization, and financial transparency. In the internal triangle, Škoda's Center, the banks and the subsidiaries similarly exchanged information and control rights in negotiating debts, transfer prices, and project finance.

Delegation is distinct from both pure ownership and state imposed solutions since (1) the parties receive partial control rights, and (2) the government, as the existing owner and seller, holds them accountable for their actions.[77] For instance, as the center increased the autonomy of subsidiaries and internal transparency of the holding, the government would compensate through resolving the train and nuclear debts. The center, however, still had the discretion to determine how the new investments and subsidies would be absorbed within the firm. The banks had a more peculiar place in this delegation: as owner creditors, they ended up providing most of the outside funding, but they were partially reimbursed by the government. As such, the government was monitoring the banks, which were also affecting changes in the holding.

As pointed out in the literature, delegation allows the government to make use of private knowledge more efficiently than pure private ownership and state directed methods, since it can avoid commitment and adverse selection problems.[78] But to do so, the government goes beyond typical incentive contracts and develops mechanisms of iterative deliberations to monitor actions. Linking the delegation of authority with general agreements on compensation and risk sharing forces the parties to demonstrate concrete results and difficulties in meeting them. In doing so, the parties reveal information to one another about their intentions and points of further negotiation and problem solving. They monitor one another as well as trade control rights and responsibilities.[79] For instance, as Škoda's Center allowed the subsidiaries greater decision-making rights and direct access to material and financial resources, the government clarified the share prices and debt relief. As the banks provided alternative forms of refinancing and operating credits, the government clarified the banks' compensation and the Center ceded valuable assets as debt collateral.

In facilitating such gradual sharing of rights and risks, delegation and deliberation facilitates a multilevel experiment in which participants learn how to monitor and cooperate with one another. Just as the government, banks, and Škoda's Center had to learn to reveal their vulnerabilities and create new common goals and strategies, so too must Škoda's Center, the banks, and the subsidiaries learn to share risks and asset control to devise new production possibilities. The rest of the chapter illustrates in more detail how DDR allowed these principles to resolve the internal and external hold up problems that had plagued holdings from the beginning.

Probing Holdups and Their Resolution within Škoda

As examined earlier, the viability of holdings, such as Škoda Plzeň, depended on the ability of its members to cooperate on the generation and development of probes. But as probes were regulated by incomplete contracts, they were prone to holdup problems. Interviews with ten major subsidiaries of Škoda revealed that nine of them were involved in at least one probing activity.[80] Two-thirds of all reported probes involved more than one unit. Six of them gave specific examples of product quality and R&D disputes that, they claim, jeopardized further cooperation. Three subsidiaries cited instances of attempts by their suppliers to charge monopoly prices. Seven subsidiaries reported that the recently introduced last-call principle, which liberalized procurement from outside, had at least brought monopoly pricing problems out into the open. Only two subsidiaries reported the long-term relations with other units as a main factor in conflict resolution. Most of them reported that due to narrow technical specifications, it was not practical to go to outside suppliers. The interviews also revealed that these problems were more pronounced in the subsidiaries that are engaged in large scale probing activities. Thus, the subsidiaries had strong fears about monopoly pricing and deficient components disrupting their production experiments. Two examples of how DDR and Škoda's center helped the subsidiaries to resolve such holdups follow.

TS and OK
Two subsidiaries of Škoda, TS and OK, were merged in 1983 and then separated in 1990. Despite their shared past, they could not agree to develop a common project for over three years. TS produced rolling mills, heavy presses, and sugarcane mills, and OK produced a wide range of industrial gearboxes. After separation, TS ran aground with the collapse of the CMEA. OK focused on its universal gearboxes, rather than the specialized designs TS required, and started its own probe into the gearboxes for textile machines. In 1991, TS was a finalist in a lucrative contract for sugar cane mills in Uzbekistan and asked OK to come up with a new design for gearboxes of these mills. OK refused. Since OK was about to decide whether to upgrade its existing machinery or move toward a line for the textile machines, it demanded assurances that the developed designs would not be thrown away after a few production cycles. Due to fluctuating orders from TS, OK viewed TS as unreliable and would not commit to TS. Also, TS tried to buy gears from outside contractors, but found it costly because of its specific designs and small volume orders for development runs.

Progress towards the resolution of the long running dispute between OK and TS came through "moral" and financial backing of the holding center and the aid of IB and KB. The center would guarantee an export loan and contribute to export insurance for the sugar mill project, if OK and TS could agree to a financial and production plan that involved revenue sharing among TS, OK, and the center. IB and KB, however, declined to finance the whole project up front. Rather, they demanded more progress in product development, which they would finance only with direct short-term loans to TS and OK and liens directly on their other in-process receivables. The center ceded to these demands, and the banks began directly monitoring the project. With this encouragement and active involvement of the banks and center, TS and OK started negotiating again, aiming to modify both the gearbox designs and the specifications of the new machine to make both of them more compatible with OK's other probes. As the modifications progressed, the banks and the center's marketing and finance departments met with TS and OK to negotiate the terms of the export financing and target other potential export markets where the banks and Škoda had trade affiliates. To relieve the insurance costs, the parties then turned to their monitoring partner at the MPO to facilitate a partial state guarantee on the export insurance via the government's new export promotion agency, EGAP.

Locomotives

Loco, the locomotive assembly subsidiary, procured electric motors, transformers, and pneumatics from other subsidiaries. Riddled by old debts and the loss of its main customer (USSR), Loco needed to commence a three-to-five-year project to improve the performance and production time of its suburban and long-haul locomotives for new market niches. But while Loco was in a slump, its suppliers were generating cash flow and developing other products, particularly for trolleybuses, generators, and power plants. When Loco asked them to reduce their side activities and focus, once again, on developing parts for it, they refused. Loco was too weak to provide upfront payments or other financial assurances to win over its suppliers.

To resolve this holdup, the center's development and finance departments initiated regular joint meetings with Loco and the other subsidiaries to generate a medium-term strategy. The team estimated financing of 150 million Kcs for 3–5 years. Since no bank would lend to Loco, the center would obtain a loan for it, adding a small surcharge. When the center turned to KB and IB for the loan, the banks declined since there was still no payment on Škoda's old receivable from the state railway company. The government had delayed, saying that the MPO and Škoda had still not found a buyer or lessee for the locomotives and that KB and IB had padded their loan restructuring costs. Soudek then started to go public about the government not fulfilling its commitments (August 1993).[81] Negotiations between the banks, Škoda's Center, and the government resumed in late September only after all agreed not to go to the press on these issues. The resulting compromise was that the government would make an immediate down payment on the locomotives through the KOB, the price of locomotives would be renegotiated, and KB and IB would negotiate with the team of foreign investment bankers at the Ministry of Privatization about their restructuring costs. KB and IB then released the loan to Škoda, with the valuable subsidiary of Ostrov as the security. Loco's supplier subsidiaries took on short-term development loans for the project from KB. The center and the subsidiaries set annual and semi-annual progress indicators for each party to reveal bottlenecks, while the subsidiaries were largely responsible to resolve glitches and take new approaches among themselves.

These examples show that probing required experimental runs and frequent specification changes that could only be delivered by the existing suppliers.[82] The parties failed to provide one another with explicit guarantees, a sign of incomplete contracts. Past relations, even among the subsidiaries that have worked together for years and still shared facilities, were not strong enough to overcome holdup fears. These fears were so significant that in both cases potentially profitable probes were about to be abolished without starting a meaningful conversation between the parties. These impasses were broken in three ways. First, the center managed to lure parties back into negotiations by backing the projects. Such actions moved the parties to exchange control rights on the production plans and agree on the parameters of their joint development efforts. Second, KB and IB provided two-level debt financing, which allowed them to build closer direct relations to the subsidiaries and exchange monitoring responsibilities and asset control with the center. Third, financial difficulties with the new projects helped clarify the parties' negotiations with government on both the general prior commitments and the future development of Škoda.

Conflict Resolution and the Generation of New Governance Rules: DDR

I now present how the two monitoring triangles work together to form DDR. There are three main components for the resolution of possible holdups: Škoda's internal market regulation, two-level debt financing, and the government's new role as a direct and indirect mediator.

Škoda's holding center created 36 wholly owned subsidiaries as limited liability companies. While the center managed general production, financial, and marketing strategy, subsidiaries had broad decision-making powers over their own operations, including assessment of penalties against internal and external parties. Horizontal links were liberated. Subsidiaries could pursue sales and suppliers directly outside the boundaries of Škoda, but first had to see if an internal supplier could match or beat the offer (so-called last-call principle). The background mechanisms for coordination and conflict resolution were negotiating forums and the center's discretionary powers of coercion.

First, the center and subsidiaries annually formulated a new set of rules for internal contracting, product development, and finances.[83] The rules on their own did not necessarily govern relations, but triggered collective deliberations over specific issues. For instance, all ten subsidiaries interviewed regarded the use of penalties for overdue payables or deliveries as minimally effective to improve internal subcontracting. Yet they did note that the rules and monthly meetings among subsidiary financial officers exposed financial and production problems and generated collective solutions. In addition, the center convened regular strategy meetings for related subsidiaries to resolve production breakdowns and share information on new technologies and markets. The information and preliminary objections or assurances allowed the subsidiaries to monitor and resolve conflicts directly among themselves. The center also used information to set indicative benchmarks for debt ratios, cash flow, employment, productivity and energy use.

Second, in many stalled initiatives, the center managed to bring everyone back to the negotiating table, using, if necessary, its coercive powers. The power of the center came from its leeway to determine rents and royalties, which were subject to annual negotiation. The center used these for cross-subsidiary subsidization and monitoring—to solicit information and discipline the units. Yet credible use of this authority was checked. Managers judged abuses of the center and one another through the previously mentioned forums. An alternative check came through the two-level debt financing, which brings us to the second component of DDR.

Since Škoda was heavily indebted, the subsidiaries were chronically short of funds and unable to finance the probes on their own. This made it difficult for the subsidiaries to cooperate with one another. The banks, however, were unwilling to provide long-term loans or support atomization, despite the offer of partial compensation for partial write-offs. Rather, the banks pushed for greater information about the subsidiaries and guarantees from the center for existing and future loans. The result of this bargaining between Soudek, the banks, and the government was a new lending structure that combined increased monitoring with the sharing of risk and control rights. IB and KB created a two-level debt financing system for Škoda: they kept large investment loans on the accounts of the holding and delimited the rest among the subsidiaries in October 1993.

Two-level debt financing reconfigured internal and external monitoring in two ways.[84] First, bank lending for development of the major programs, export contracts, and operations in the most distressed subsidiaries occurred via Škoda's center, as it owned all the real estate. Recall that one of the center's main contributions for probing was to offer project financing to coax subsidiaries into making compromises. In re-issuing loans to the subsidiaries, the center acted as a screen for the banks—by engaging in re-intermediation and ensuring projects. Second, with direct lending to the subsidiaries, the banks enhanced their monitoring of the whole group and the subsidiaries increase their autonomy.[85] As short-term lending increased the cash flow of subsidiaries, it offered the banks a low risk evaluation period of subsidiary operations and an avenue to observe any abuses by the center of its internal taxing and cross-subsidizing powers. With increased financial autonomy, the subsidiaries were in a stronger position to bargain with the center and with one another.

The government originally planned to act as first-mover to get the parties to restructure the assets and walk away.[86] The failure of this plan, however, created the basis for the government to become a credible financial and monitoring partner with the banks and Škoda. It did so by delegating public authority to the parties and formulating an incomplete contract (i.e., the vague pricing of shares, amendable restructuring criteria), backed by its financial and monitoring commitments. These steps allowed the government to directly and indirectly ensure cooperation and restructuring progress. The government directly monitored and pressured the parties via negotiations about debt relief, share prices, Škoda's internal structure, and debt restructuring. Additionally, by having two representatives from the MPO on the board of Škoda for over a year, the government enhanced its abilities to monitor the progress with decentralization and prevent abuses by the center. As it established itself as a credible mediator of last resort, the government allowed the banks and Škoda breathing room to improvise and learn to resolve their disputes directly with one another.[87] The government's credibility to play this role was initially established by its financial commitment (via the FNM) but was continually tested by the way it treated each party in altering or relaxing the restructuring criteria.

Note, however, that to become this credible partner, the government had to change its role in two significant ways. First, to ensure that the delegated authority had meaning, the government had to allow the banks and Škoda to improvise their restructuring actions and perhaps alter the original agreement.[88] The government was then forced to change its own designs and treat their suggestions seriously. It was not simply enforcing a contract created by itself or by the holding members and the banks. Rather, as a partner to the extended incomplete contract, the government was developing the new governance rules and the restructuring criteria simultaneously with the banks and Škoda. Second, to maintain its own public and bargaining credibility, the government made itself more accountable.[89] As a partner and mediator, the government was subject to continual scrutiny by both the banks and Škoda, who were trying to ensure that they were treated fairly—together and separately.[90] As a public entity altering the use of budget revenues (e.g., for the locomotive debt) and the disposal of state property (e.g., in the change of a highly visible privatization project), the government incited parliamentary review by the oversight committees for the budget and the FNM.[91]

Within DDR, both control rights and risk were frequently being reassigned to facilitate the flow of information and coordination on multiple probing experiments. The dual monitoring triangles with delegation of partial authority helped maintain flexibility as well as created channels of deliberation in which the parties could head-off major showdowns. Just as the government traded control rights and risk with Soudek and the banks, the center was doing the same with the banks and the subsidiaries on more detailed restructuring issues. Moreover, the shared responsibilities and vagueness of the initial agreement forced the parties at both levels to reveal information and thus monitor one another. In turn, abuses of discretionary powers, such as those of Soudek and his center, were held in check by both Škoda's internal forum and the scrutiny of the government and the banks. This allowed the parties to learn to cooperate without the fear that they would simply be taken advantage of. A short-term concession would likely be compensated over time, perhaps into a long-term gain.

Concluding Remarks

In this chapter, I have attempted to show how the sociopolitical characteristics of former hierarchical VHJ networks shaped both the strategic choices of constituent economic actors and the conditions under which the Czech government eventually reengaged these actors to forge DDR—a structure that resolves restructuring conflicts through the delegation and deliberation. Members of this ideal-typical network elected to create a decentralized holding company as a way to reorganize their inherited economic linkages in the face of new privatization policies, economic uncertainties, and the dissolution of allied regional councils. The subsequent combination of reinforced intermember linkages and the proliferation of decentralized restructuring experiments (probing) created holdup problems since no member alone had the sociopolitical or financial capital to force or coax cooperation. Czech policy held out strong incentives for private actors, such as FDI, to become the new partners to holdings. Yet since the network properties of holdings prohibited a clear division of asset control and risk, relations with an external partner would also have to be regulated by an incomplete contract with third-party guarantees—principally the government. As demonstrated in the Škoda case, the Klausians saw any such role as threat to their power, and the prospective JVs collapsed.

Unable to use pure private ownership or state imposed solutions, the Klausians were forced to re-engage the holdings and banks (with Škoda being the first) and become both a financial partner and conflict mediator. This new role grew not simply from the restructuring needs of holdings but also from the Klausians own efforts to centralize power in their hands and publicly commit themselves to fulfilling the dual components of privatization. The resulting structure that I have called DDR helped the Klausians fulfill the components simultaneous and through incomplete contracts because collective disciplined governance emerged through the use of delegation and deliberation. Through their iterative deliberations the relevant private and public actors were able to learn how to monitor one another, share risk and information, and gradually create and revise new governance rules to facilitate experiments. As such DDR helped these actors learn new roles for themselves—in constructing both corporate governance and a definition prudent government support for restructuring.

DDR appeared to revive a company whose obituary had been written long ago. By 1995, Škoda's debt had fallen to 50 percent of its 1992 level, revenues had increased over 50 percent, and employment was increasing. Škoda's rebound was even recognized by independent observers such as the stock market, the *Economist,* the *Wall Street Journal,* and *Balkan News International.*[92] By mid-1995, its share price had increased threefold and it had a market capitalization of 55 billion Czech Korunas (U.S. $2.2 billion). By 1996 two-thirds of Škoda's subsidiaries had obtained ISO 9001 or 9002 certification. During 1994–95 it initiated new ventures for locomotives in Russia and Germany; trolleybuses, electric car engines, and turbines in the United States; and power plant technology in China. Škoda's acquisition of an Eastern German pressed-steel maker solidified its growing involvement in European and Asian markets as a supplier of heavy machinery and automotive crankshafts and chassis.

But what would the future spell for DDR? DDR for Škoda appeared not as a design but through conflict and negotiations. Upon observing its relative success, the Czech government has attempted to replicate DDR with troubled holdings in various industries. ČKD followed a remarkably similar pattern of government backed negotiated restructuring as in Škoda. After the failure of the JV between Dow Chemicals and the Chemapol Group, the government created a partnership between itself (represented by the MPO), a foreign chemical consortium, and Chemapol member firms. A similar structure emerged for Vitkovice, Nová Huť, and Třinecké Železarny, but with a U.S. consortium of mini-mills. Each had an ownership stake, with the clarification of the size and payment terms of the equity occurring over time; the main Czech banks provided some financing. In the aircraft manufacturer, Aero, the joint owners and partners in both the holding and various subsidiaries were the three main Czech banks and the state's clearing house bank, KOB. As these parties resolve Aero's debt problems, the MPO on behalf of the KOB negotiated with Aero management and the banks on the reorganization of production. Rockwell and Pratt and Whitney soon became 50 percent partners in two subsidiaries, while Boeing became a controlling partner of the holding in 1997.

But the recent troubles and allegations of fraud at Poldi, the high-end steel producer, revealed that DDR was not a simple mechanical structure and was susceptible to intragovernment turf battles. At Poldi, the state administrator of property, FNM, took control of the project and simply put the actors in place, wrote some incentive-based ownership contracts, and walked away. Unwilling to provide room for continued negotiations and changes in the original contract, the FNM allowed initial conflicts to turn into a public war of words. The FNM and KB eventually forced the ouster of their owner-manager in the courts. It appears, then, that the government's vigilant tending to the mechanisms that force deliberation are critical to the sharing of information and risk, and, in turn, to conflict resolution and probing. The recent work on Japanese and Chinese industrialization support this.[93]

This view is only reinforced by the troubles Škoda ran into in the wake of the Asian and Russian crises. Bolstered initially by the financial support of international banks and the EBRD, Škoda expanded rapidly, even acquiring the truck producers Tatra and Liaz in 1995–96. As sales in Asia and East Europe dropped in 1997 and 1998, Škoda defaulted on its loans, Soudek was removed, but the old bankruptcy laws still hindered the ability of creditors to cooperate and reorganize the firm. In 1999, Škoda and other holdings were forced to enter into a special government workout vehicle. Although the Czech government nurtured DDR at Škoda much more than in Poldi, by the mid-1990s it had left Škoda to be governed by the banks and ultimately the dysfunctional system of investment funds. The Czech government failed to build on the experience it gained in the initial successes and failures of DDR for holdings and further institutional reforms, such as in strengthening export banking and insurance programs, improving the regulation of banks and investment funds, and changing the bankruptcy regime to facilitate workouts. The apparent reason for the failure was forecasted in the debacle with Poldi: a growing rift within the Klausian coalition over revisions to the original depoliticization agenda had stalled the ability of the government to take these DDR experiments one step further and formalize the general lessons into public policies. In short, further experiments meant empowerment of new institutional actors, an issue that was antithetical to depolitization and split the coalition deeply. This may not be so surprising. The work on public-private partnerships in places as diverse as

Brazil and Ireland argues that a key aspect of such partnerships and deliberative governance—the blurring of and potential encroachment across jurisdictions of public agencies—becomes a key source of political instability for sustaining and learning from experiments like DDR.[94]

The problems of duplication and durability suggest that deliberation is vital to the continued restructuring of assets and that politics—both at the micro and macro levels—is central to the evolution of the multilevel governance orders that aid deliberative mechanisms for cooperation. These issues will be discussed in greater detail—both for the Czech Republic and approaches to comparative political economy—in the concluding chapter. But for now, let us turn to an examination of how former polycentric networks interacted with Czech policy after 1989 and led to an alternative governance order within the Czech engineering industry.

CHAPTER 5

Polycentric Networks and Fragmented Restructuring: The Case of SST

As the Czech government became both a partner and mediator to holding companies and the big banks, another pattern of restructuring conflicts emerged in the CR.[1] Groups of medium-sized firms attached themselves to new private banks and smaller, non-big bank investment companies (IPCs). Given the concentration of capital and the lack of risk-sharing incentives, these funds and banks often took advantage of weak capital market regulations to acquire assets of the major Czech financial institutions, namely the five main Czech banks, their investment funds, and the former state monopoly for insurance, Česká Pojišťovna. In the wake of the sudden insolvency of several of these smaller banks and successful raids by smaller IPCs into several of these institutions, the government took steps to protect the financial system. It began to use the main banks to help restructure and monitor the teetering new banks. This new development in government intervention culminated in mid-1996 as a coalition of government agencies, main banks, and one of the nonbank IPCs began to reorganize Pojišťovna and its subsidiaries.[2] At the heart of these events were two banks and IPCs that were closely allied to the member firms of the former machine tool VHJ, TST.

In this chapter, I analyze the privatization and restructuring of the former machine tool VHJ, TST. This analysis shows not only how a different network structure shaped a distinct pattern of restructuring conflicts and economic governance order for economic governance but also how my embedded politics approach can clarify the cooperation problems within industrial networks that can often lead to destabilizing strategies of resource acquisition.

First, as a matched pair with Škoda, TST's contrasting pattern of privatization strategies, restructuring conflicts, and institution-building shows how distinct, inherited sociopolitical networks mediate in different ways the interaction between government policy and firm restructuring and produce different conditions under which public and private actors negotiate governance rules. Škoda and TST shared similar technologies, end-markets, and unit labor costs; they were beholden to the same state banking institutions (KB, IB); their workforces were organized by the same union (KOVO); their former VHJs had the same legal structure *(koncern)*; they operated within the same national setting and reform policies; and both had roughly the same number of employees both at the unit and VHJ level.[3] Yet their stories are very different. As discussed in the previous chapter, the authority structure and organization of production constitutive of the *hierarchical network* led Škoda's members to develop privatization and restructuring strategies based on their organization of a holding company. Consequently, Škoda's position in the economy and its pattern of conflicts led to the formation of DDR that facilitated government-backed negotiated restructuring for stakeholders. The characteristics of the *polycentric network* would, in contrast, lead TST's members to privatize themselves as individual firms and create a new industry association, SST, both to coordinate common needs and to convert TST's ties to Czech import-export organizations into an alliance with new banks and investment funds. This strategy of network reproduction was, however, unstable. As relationships between SST members fragmented, one SST member, the firm ZPS, attempted to impose its own production and governance order over the branch. But it could do so only by manipulating weak capital market regulations to control financial resources from the state insurance company Česká Pojišťovna. As a result, a new and alternative governance order emerged within the mechanical engineering sector. The forum of conflict resolution as well as critical production, financial, and training resources lay largely outside the confines of a single firm, while the government became only indirectly involved in the restructuring of SST firms.

Second, the failure of the strategy to replace sociopolitical external partners (i.e., the regional and district councils) with private ones reinforces my argument that industrial networks and governance institutions are politically constructed. Despite constituting an economic network with attributes conducive for restructuring through typical contractual and social capital approaches, former TST firms failed to cooperate and restructuring stalled. The resulting fragmentation of the network allowed ZPS to use its own local social network for a strategy of imposing order that would threaten the stability of the Czech financial system and force the government into a belated, negotiated restructuring solution. These outcomes show how periods of transformation can alter the authority structure and individual interests within networks to create restructuring conflicts that cannot be resolved through contractual means or historical social bonds.

Moreover, they highlight how the demands of sociopolitical networks for external political and financial risk sharing cause the resolution of these conflicts to extend into the heart of financial and public institutions. The analysis of holdings showed how the intranetwork cooperation demanded an incomplete contract structure that extended to private external partners and required third-party mediation and financing by public agencies. Conversely, the analysis of TST/SST will show that when this public intervention is not forthcoming to facilitate workouts, network actors will have strong incentives to pursue a strategy of asset control that forces the needed risk sharing upon public institutions. The upshot is that a policy of depoliticization can easily create conditions for actors to use a potentially productive network for self-dealing and financial instability.

The chapter is organized as follows. First, I analyze how the inherited TST network shaped the initial restructuring and privatization strategies as well as the governance of the network in the face of the depoliticization policies of the Czech government. I then examine the subsequent internal conflicts and fragmentation of SST. In the midst of these problems, one SST member, ZPS, was able to transform local social-political capital into a powerful export and financial network. Finally, I show how ZPS then came to control SST. To solidify their hold, ZPS and its allied IPC attempted to takeover SST firms and increase control over Česká Pojišťovna, which forced the government and the main banks into negotiations.

The Polycentric Network's Initial Impact on Privatization Strategies

As discussed in chapter 2, TST represented the second ideal type of VHJ network—a *polycentric network*—that differed significantly from Škoda's. TST's polycentric network possessed many of the qualities associated with potentially dynamic entrepreneurial networks—a combination of rich social ties and so-called brokerage opportunities for members that could facilitate the transfer of tacit knowledge, flexibility, and access to new information and resources.[4] Structurally, several central TST firms worked on a relatively consensual basis with the directorate in its bargaining with the headquarters of the state bank and the ministries; its intervention in disputes with other VHJs, such as in the supply of electronic components; and its coordination of certain intra-TST inputs. Members had also retained considerable decision-making powers and independent financial accounts. Relationally, although members had a deep history of overlapping, direct social and professional ties, they were usually horizontally associated with limited direct operational links and had often generated their own links outside of TST. For instance, a TST firm typically focused on a certain class of machines, had several plants, and produced about 80 percent of its inputs in-house.[5] As shown in table 5.1, intra-TST supply links were relegated to a set of specific inputs, including certain hydraulics, pneumatics, ball-bearing screws, gears, shafts, casings palettes, spindles, and chucks.[6] Nine TST units had their own forges or foundries, which supplied up to 60 percent of TST's needs but still sold almost half of their output outside of the VHJ.

This relatively multipolar and decentralized production and authority structure came not only from the geographic dispersion of units (relative to many units in the Škoda VHJ) but particularly from the close relationships that members developed with their district and regional party councils and bank branches. These linkages aided firms in managing interfirm debts, mediated delivery disputes with non-TST firms in the region, and became sources of countervailing bargaining power vis-à-vis one another, the TST directorate, and the central state ministries.

TST's polycentric network had a clear impact on the transformation of group during two critical reforms—the dissolution of VHJs in 1987–88 and privatization in 1991–92. With the aid of their local councils, TST members pushed to become legally independent state firms in 1987–88, while forming a branch association, "the Union of Manufacturers and Suppliers of Engineering Technique," or SST, in which each firm held equity shares. The TST headquarters in Prague was converted into the SST directorate. The directors of member firms composed the SST board, and former employees of the TST headquarters became the staff of the SST directorate. SST aimed to help members share product and market information and to provide members with services and resources each lacked on its own. The SST directorate was to help coordinate key areas of procurement,[7] investment, R&D, training, and relations with the Ministry of Industry and main commercial banks.[8] The managing director of SST would also represent its members' 40 percent ownership in the former state monopoly of the sector's import-export firm, Strojimport, as chairman of the board.[9]

Privatization brought forth a similar set of strategies to balance firm autonomy and group cohesion.[10] SST firms were intent on furthering decentralization and breeding new firms. Between 1988 and 1991, former TST firms had already broken themselves up from twenty to forty firms, while the six largest firms allowed many of their plants to operate as autonomous profit-centers and to prepare themselves for eventual spin-offs. At the same time, SST firms elected to privatize themselves individually. The large majority of SST firms chose to privatize virtually all their equity through vouchers and build joint ventures with foreign partners. A few smaller firms attempted full or partial MBOs.

With the dissolution of regional councils and the weakening of district and municipal councils, however, firms often lacked the power to control on

TABLE 5.1. Production Profiles of Leading SST Firms (break-away plants in italics), 1990

Firm	Employment (1991)	Final Products (number of models in parenthesis)[a]	Parts and Inputs Supplied to TST Firms
ZPS Zlín	5,393	Single spindle semiautomatic lathe (4); Multispindle semiautomatic lathe (1); turret lathe (1); turret automatic—single spin (1); multispin (5); machine centers—horizontal (5), vertical (1); shoe making machines	Milling tools of high-speed steel; iron castings; foundry
Kovosvit *Dobříš*	4,775	Universal center lathe (1); single spindle semiautomatic lathe (5); radial (7) and coordinate (5) drilling machine; jig boring machine (2); vertical surface grinder (2); machining canter (1)	Iron castings and molds
Čelákovice	2,133	Universal center lathe (6); gear hobbing (6) and boring (4) machines; cutting conveyors.	Iron castings; gear tooling; chroming
Aš *Žebrak*	587	Universal center lathe (1); universal milling machine (5)	
Hostivař	1,435	Cylindrical grinder—universal (5), infeed (5); tool grinding machine (3); crankshaft grinding machine (1).	Hydraulic aggregates for grinding machines (Čtyřkoly); chucks
Mělník	257	Universal cylindrical grinder (1); tool grinding machines (1).	
Středokluky	118		
Čtyřkoly	106		
Holice	708	Universal cylindrical grinder (4); surface (2), centerless (2), vertical (1) grinding machine	

			Ball-bearing screws; variators; electro-distributors; shafts; iron castings and moldings; forgings automatic lines.
Kuřim	6,300	Knee-type milling machine (6); table-type milling machine (6); machining center (1); multipurpose machine tool (1); single purpose machine tool (1);	
Jasová *Lipník* *Znojmo* *Slevárna*		Universal center lathe (1)	
Hulín	1,259	Vertical lathe (7); copy milling machine (3)	Forgings; chroming
OSO	969	Knee-type milling machine (6)	Bevel gears; gearboxes; palettes
Svitavy	1,150	Woodworking machine (saws, milling, molding, grinder)	Lathe chucks and spindles; castings
Rakovník	1,059	Hydraulics (distributors, pressure and current control valves, axial piston hydromotors, electrohydraulic servodrives, etc.)	Hydraulics; aggregates
Vrchlabí	800	Horizontal boring machine (9); circular saw (1)	Iron castings; trapezium screws; coatings
Varnsdorf	1,980		
Šmeral	1,678	Eccentric press (1); crank and toggle presses (13); forging press (10); pneumatic-hydraulic hammer (3); Cross-wedge rolling machine (2); automatic forming machine (7); powder metallurgy press (2)	Forgings; chroming
Zastávka	517		

Source: SST (1991, 1992).

[a]Although two firms may have same general final product category, the products differed by size, weight, target materials, turning dimensions, and add-ons. Different models of same type of machine also varied according to these classifications.

TABLE 5.2. Privatization Methods of Leading TST/SST Firms (break-away plants in italics), 1991

Firm	Employment (1991)	Privatization Method
ZPS Zlin	5,393	Vouchers—88.7%, Employment—8.25%
Kovosvit	4,775	Vouchers—79%, Employment—9.5%, FNM (for sale)[a]—6.2%
Čelákovice	2,133	Vouchers—90.3%, Municipal[a]—5%
Aš	230	Direct sale[a]—97%
Žebrak	587	Direct sale[a]—97%
Hostivař	1,435	FNM (for FDI/JV)[a]—97% (moved to second wave)
Mělník	257	Buyout FDI
Středokluky	118	Buyout FDI
Čtyřkoly	106	Direct sale[a]—97%
Holice	708	Vouchers—97%
Kuřim	6,300	Vouchers—48.5%, FNM (FDI/JV)—48.5%
Jasová		Vouchers—29%, MBO (pending)—51%, Employment—7%, FNM (FDI/JV, pending)—10%
Lipník		Vouchers—95%
Znojmo		Tender[a]—97%
Slevárna		Vouchers—46%, MBO[a]—51%
Hulín	1,259	
OSO	969	MBO[a]—97%
Svitavy	1,150	Vouchers—92%, Municipal—5%
Rakovnik	1,059	Vouchers—97%
Vrchlabí	800	Vouchers—96% (main assets put in JV, FI owns 67%)
Varnsdorf	1,980	Direct sale and MBO[a]—97%
Šmeral Brno	1,678	Vouchers—45%, FNM (MBO) — 52% (MBO failed, 52% in second wave of vouchers.)
Zastávka	517	MBO[a]—97%
LADA Sobeslav	1,974	Vouchers—86%, FNM (FDI)[a]—6.5%, Employment—2%

Source: Summaries of privatization projects provided by the Ministry of Privatization CR.
[a]Signifies method of sale still pending as of December 1994.

their own the liberation movement by many leading plants, which equally had the right to submit privatization projects. Table 5.2 shows the privatization strategies of respective members as well as the extent to which SST firms lost control of critical plants. The message was clear: decentralization and independent privatization had their benefits, but without the supporting political buttressing of the respective local councils, it hindered the group from restraining a spiral of fragmentation and the possible loss of key producers.

To counter this trend, leading members authorized the SST directorate to seek an alliance with a bank and investment company in 1991 through past socioeconomic ties.[11] This was essentially an attempt to replace decentralized public external partners with a centralized set of private ones, effec-

tively turning their individual brokerage links outside the group into a unified, collective one. TST had strong external contacts through Strojimport
and FINOP, a state-created holding company that held shares in the main industrial trade houses and that had direct links to the main communist-era
trade bank, ČSOB (one of the big-five Czech banks).[12] A group from FINOP
created a new private bank, Banka Bohemia, to which SST turned for help.
Though small compared to the big CR banks, Banka Bohemia was the second-largest new private bank at the time and brought with it links to foreign
trade and ČSOB. In 1992, the ČSOB owned 30 percent of FINOP, which, in
turn, owned almost 20 percent of Strojimport and 30 to 40 percent of Banka
Bohemia.[13] SST bought into an investment company, ISB, which Banka Bohemia had established.[14] ISB had four voucher investment funds, each of
which focused on a specific sector (i.e., engineering, transport, utilities and
chemicals, agriculture).[15] SST chaired and had a direct ownership stake in
the engineering fund, which bought shares in 150 firms. ISB and the engineering fund together acquired 3 to 20 percent of equity in all SST firms and
key supplier and customer firms for SST members. Given the shareholding
regulations and the dispersion of ownership, these stakes enabled SST, on
behalf of ISB and the engineering fund, to gain a seat on the board of directors or supervisory board of the respective firm.[16]

Figure 5.1 shows the resulting equity links between SST and its new potential private allies. As SST firms developed their own restructuring strategies, SST's alliances were to aid the directorate in strengthening group cohesion. Through FINOP and ISB, SST was to build relationships with the big
bank investment companies and could increase its control over Strojimport,
which had facilities for trade finance and affiliates throughout the world.
Through its direct relationship with Banka Bohemia and indirect relationship with ČSOB, SST could potentially tap into much needed loans. Strategic
stakes via ISB in member firms and in important consumers/suppliers of
member firms were to help SST gain strategic information for its members,
influence the restructuring of the industry, and protect firms from new,
overly zealous owners.

The Fragmentation of SST

From the viewpoint of transformation approaches that emphasize private
property rights as well as those that emphasize the continuity of past social ties
and structures, this strategy of network reproduction would appear conducive
for the former TST firms to settle restructuring disputes on their own.[17] In contrast to the strategies of holding companies like Škoda, the rapid privatization

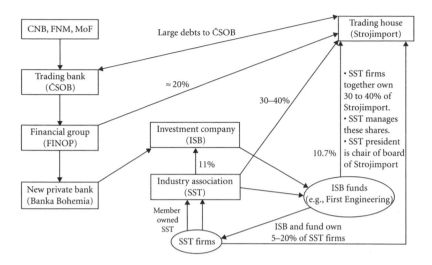

Figure 5.1.   New Ownership and Financial Network for TST/ SST, 1992–93

Note: Direction of arrows denotes direction of ownership. Percentages denote ownership share.

of smaller individual firms created relative financial and legal transparency, conducive for profit maximization and the resolution of restructuring conflicts through contracts and buyouts. Former TST firms also used their past social ties to build an association and links to new private financial organizations that could help coordinate interfirm activities, information flows, and investment. Restructuring, however, stagnated as members became increasingly distrustful of and isolated from one another. Individual members began to probe new market niches and methods of production, in turn creating conflicting strategies that were too risky to promote either compromise or buyouts. At the same time, the alliances created by SST via social and equity links lacked the political and economic resources to mediate these conflicts and risks.

The Conflict between Probing and Inherited Economic Ties within SST

Similar to other Czech industrial firms, the members of SST were hit hard by the collapse of the CMEA, the domestic recession, and tight monetary policy. By the end of 1992, the average output of SST members had fallen by 30 to 40 percent. By 1994, seven of the top nine posted losses and all were becoming increasingly leveraged.[18] Facing a serious decline in sales and liquidity, SST firms followed a strategy of probing. Recall from chapter 4 that *probing* is the term I give to the comprehensive set of organizational and product development experiments, in which firms utilize their inherited broad production capabilities to penetrate new market niches, form partnerships with foreign firms, and generate cash flow.

Probing altered production profiles in two ways. First, SST firms allowed such upstream units as machining, parts, and forging to utilize excess capacity and expand sales directly outside of the firm. Thus, whereas inputs and semi-finished goods accounted for approximately 10 percent of total sales of the top nine firms in the 1980s, they accounted for 30 to 40 percent of total sales by 1993.[19] In one firm, this share reached almost 60 percent, even with steady increases in sales of its main final product between 1992 and 1994. Second, individual firms attempted to broaden their assortment of final goods. Freed from production segmentation rules under TST, such firms as Šmeral Brno updated designs of a middle-sized metal press, which TST had dropped in the 1960s, to produce a prototype by 1993 for a potential market in Germany. Other firms, such as ZPS and Kovosvit, began to develop completely new vertical and universal machining centers and automatic lathes. Čelákovice and Hostivař attempted to alter the size and use of their grinding machines (e.g., for transmissions and ceramics). Kuřim and OSO attempted to revive previous production in different types of milling machines (e.g., knee-type, universal, console, and rotating machines). ZPS and OSO also created new pallets.

Although probing opened up new production possibilities for each firm, its experimental nature undermined the ability of a firm to pursue probes alone or in concert with other members. In the face of a rigid industrial structure and cash constraints, it was costly for each firm to internalize all facets of probing that were previously done jointly, that is, development of specific components, import-export, and training. But because probing entailed short production runs with uncertain returns, SST firms could not offer credible guarantees to one another to nurture cooperation in these key joint operations.

Intra-SST subcontracting and development of critical components suffered for obvious reasons. While probing made second sourcing unlikely, members preferred to sell parts for immediate hard currency and potentially gain a new contact than commit scarce resources for a project based on a vaguely defined, deferred profit-sharing or payment contract.[20] For instance, OSO's attempt to supply gearboxes to the automotive industry and to change its assortment of milling machines undercut its development of certain transmission cases and gearboxes that it had previously supplied to former TST firms. By 1993, Svitavy had focused virtually all its spindle production for cheap but cash-rich exports and wood milling machines, cutting off its traditional supplies of other spindles for producers of lathes and boring machines. After Volkswagen demanded that Kuřim alter the prototypes of its single-purpose machines, Kuřim turned to its former plant and now independent firm, Lipník, to collaborate on new designs of certain components. Lipník refused without upfront financing, which Kuřim lacked. Kuřim also began to refuse orders for its vital ball-bearing screws, as it prioritized short-term exports of the screws over deferred payment contracts to other SST firms. Such stories of longtime common suppliers refusing collaboration on new or modified parts or cutting back production of critical existing components, such as hydraulics, became widespread among SST members.[21] Even iron castings, previously in ample supply within TST, became an area of subcontracting conflict, as some of the largest SST foundries focused on specific castings to German and Austrian companies at the expense of orders from other SST firms and often from fellow subsidiaries.[22]

Probing also inhibited collaboration among SST firms for procurement of critical inputs, like certain grades of cast iron and CNC (computer numerically controlled) control systems. The domestic monopoly for the distribution of iron castings, Ferrona, remained intact. But SST firms each needed different specifications in small volumes, thus impeding joint, bulk purchases. All twelve SST firms interviewed reported that by 1993–94 Ferrona was charging monopolistic prices. The domestic electronics VHJ, Tesla, had fragmented into fifteen firms, most of which bordered on insolvency and lacked the capital and know-how to make the needed leaps in quality. SST firms, in turn, grew reliant on relatively expensive imported CNC components. Yet, none of the twelve members interviewed reported taking part in joint purchases with one another because of increasingly different needs and batch sizes. In turn, production costs rose and, lacking cash flow and large batches, firms often had to delay production of new machines. For instance, interest from a potential British customer led Kovosvit, the second largest member of SST, to develop a new drilling and milling center financed through retained earnings and short-term operating loans. Kovosvit could produce virtually all components in-house, with the exception of the CNC guidance system, which had to be imported from Japan (Fanuc). To capture any sort of returns to scale, Kovosvit would have to produce a minimum of sixty units, for which it still had not secured orders. Fanuc would sell the CNC controls in a volume of no less than one hundred units. Already strapped for cash, Kovosvit was unable to make such an investment and the banks were unwilling to lend for it. Kovosvit then solicited other SST members to purchase the controls jointly and divide them among themselves. However, of those interested in the controls, none were willing to purchase the needed quantities. Consequently, Kovosvit had to delayed production for over a year and the British customer chose another supplier.

Joint export development similarly suffered, despite potential savings in marketing, financing, and transport costs. On the one hand, probing often increased product differentiation to the extent that SST members felt that collaboration was not worth the effort. For instance, Šmeral was developing a JV with a former Strojimport affiliate in Spain. Despite strong market surveys, other SST firms refused to participate, as they felt that Šmeral's interests in its forming machines would over-ride their interests in lathes, machining centers, and grinding machines. On the other hand, freed from TST rules restricting competition in end products, producers of similar machines attempted to expand their product assortment, encroaching into one another's traditional market niches.[23] Already under pressure from the recession, producers of lathes, machining centers, and drilling, boring, and grinding machines viewed one another as competitors for ever smaller niches and export opportunities. All twelve members interviewed stated that they were not developing export networks with other members because of these fears. Five members noted that they had solicited cooperation within SST (e.g., for Asia and the United States), but that the other members declined the offers. The clearest example was with the largest SST firm, ZPS, which had begun developing its own export network in the United States, China, and Japan through its former employees for sales of its vertical and universal machining centers and automatic lathes. But ZPS refused to share these contacts with other SST producers in these product groups, such as Kovosvit, Hostivař, Hulín, and OSO, for fear of undercutting its own nascent growth in exports. When these firms tried to negotiate profit-sharing agreements with ZPS for direct exports of such parts as gearboxes, pallets, spindles, and castings, ZPS also refused. ZPS preferred to develop export sales for these areas on its own to utilize its own plants and then, if necessary, subcontract the jobs to the others. ZPS could then control access to new markets.

The more indirect joint-investment areas, such as basic R&D and vocational training, suffered to an even greater degree. As SST firms probed in-house, their increasingly different priorities for product development and liquidity constraints hindered their ability to agree on joint R&D. By late 1993, the two former TST R&D firms were insolvent, with virtually no projects from SST members. The regional councils and the relevant TST firms had jointly managed regional vocational training centers.[24] These two parties then collaborated with the TST directorate to set program standards and to bargain with government ministries over funding. After 1990, the centers became self-financing, with only partial state subsidies for theoretical training. With the dissolution of regional councils, SST firms were left to influence and

pay training centers on their own. But as SST firms faced increasing cash constraints and unclear production development, they were unable to provide
the funds and employment guarantees that the centers demanded. In turn,
the centers began to focus their programs on ever broader, nonproduction
careers. Both SST and independent analyses of vocational training for the
machine tool industry show the negative impact this process has had on
member firms.[25] By the end of 1993, SST employment had dropped by 40
percent, with many skilled, experienced employees leaving for the new service
sector.[26] By 1995, enrollment for classic machine tool trades had fallen to
about 5 to 10 percent of 1991 enrollment.[27] SST firms were in great need of
skilled craftsman to maintain probing but could not support the centers to
provide the needed training nor new recruits.

To sum up, probing hindered a firm's ability to provide the guarantees
that former collaborators demanded as compensation for curtailing their
own experiments. In turn, firms internalized probing and grew increasingly
isolated from one another. As late as 1994, ten of the twelve interviewed SST
firms reported that in-house production (e.g., mechanical parts, retrofitting,
design, machining, and chroming) accounted for 70 to 80 percent of the costs
for semiautomatic and non-CNC machines and 50 to 60 percent of the costs
for CNC machines.[28] With firms bearing the full costs and risks of probing on
their own, revenues declined and redundancy was widespread throughout
the sector. Thus, given rising financial costs and the inaction by the main
banks, any long-term benefits to probing were threatened by short-term insolvency. One way out of this—buying out one another—was unfeasible
given the uncertainties of probing and the limited funds.

The Failure of SST's External Network
to Facilitate Cooperation

The fragmentation and conflict within SST did not occur overnight but over
four years. Decentralization, geographic dispersion, and infighting had always been aspects of TST. In the past, the common struggle to bargain with
the central government and other VHJs, the legal standing of the TST directorate, and, particularly, the alliances with regional and district councils
served to mediate differences and balance internal power. The Czech depoliticization strategy had fundamentally altered this equation by effectively eliminating the councils from playing viable roles in supporting the network's authority structure and assisting restructuring. Ex-TST members therefore
attempted to build a new support structure of an association (SST) and new
private external partners by combining equity links and past social ties. While
the investment fund, ISB, afforded SST strategic information and seats on the

boards of members and other critical firms, collaboration with the big Czech banks and their investment companies demanded that SST bring in resources to share some of the risks of restructuring. SST, in turn, turned back to its new support structure to gain these resources from Strojimport, Banka Bohemia, ČSOB, and, if necessary, the Ministry of Industry.

In the past, virtually all of TST's export-import activities were conducted through Strojimport (hence, TST's and now SST's 30 to 40 percent ownership of Strojimport). Strojimport had a vast global network of affiliates. The main communist-era trade bank, ČSOB, had provided loans for TST through Strojimport, which arranged them and held them on its own account. The collapse of the CMEA, however, had seriously damaged the solvency of both Strojimport and ČSOB.[29] Through 1994, ČSOB had consistently the worst loan performance and portfolio and capital structures of the five main Czech banks.[30] Given the strict banking policies of the government, ČSOB's weak capital structure and interdependence with Strojimport prevented it from initiating any active restructuring or lending strategy toward Strojimport. This financial instability hindered SST's ability not only to use Strojimport's export financing operations but also to use Strojimport to coordinate the export development of SST firms. As Strojimport could no longer provide needed export credits or insurance, SST members saw little reason to go through the headquarters of Strojimport.

For instance, when Varnsdorf became a finalist for supplying semi-finished boring mills to a U.S. firm and needed development and in-process financing, Strojimport and ČSOB demanded heavy collateral, which Varnsdorf could not provide.[31] In the earlier example of Kovosvit's inability to gain partners for the joint purchase of Japanese CNC parts for the development of a new milling center geared to export markets, Strojimport also failed to facilitate any financing or purchases for the CNC parts. In turn, SST firms increasingly tried to contact foreign firms on their own and through Strojimport affiliates. The former brought short-term work on semi-finished goods, often with little value added. The latter added to the fragmentation of Strojimport. In key markets such as Germany, Spain, Sweden, Switzerland, Taiwan, Brazil, and Argentina, Strojimport was only a minority shareholder, or affiliate managers had left to create their own agencies. In either case, market information became locally guarded and financing was virtually unavailable. SST members reported that by 1994 exports through the Strojimport headquarters accounted for only 5 to 20 percent of total exports. Moreover, when the time came to pay the standard book value for their shares in Strojimport in late 1994, SST firms refused and returned the shares to the government.[32]

The second potential asset of SST was its collective position vis-à-vis the main banks and its links to Banka Bohemia. A key objective of SST was to use group leverage in obtaining restructuring loans from namely IB and KB. Yet in contrast to the holding companies, which had maintained unified accounts with the headquarters or regional directorate of the banks, the loans of individual SST firms had been delimited among the relevant local bank branches. As IB and KB had placed strict lending limits on branches, SST was thus unable to leverage loans for one firm off of the assets or cash flows of another firm. Subsequently, banking relations for SST firms became increasingly dispersed, with SST firms turning often to small new private banks for expensive short-term credits to maintain operations and pay interest rate charges on outstanding loans. SST's links to Banka Bohemia were to help head-off the fragmentation of group finances and provide a partner to share restructuring risks with IB and KB. Although Banka Bohemia initially provided some short-term loans to members, the strategy soon revealed its limits and eventually collapsed. The reasons are another demonstration of the way the government's strategy of depoliticization undermined the risk sharing needed for the management and reorganization of jointly controlled assets.

First, Banka Bohemia did not receive the planned capital increases from its parent companies, the FINOP group and ČSOB. With its weak capital structure and interdependencies with the foreign trade sector, ČSOB, like IB and KB, found it too risky to follow the government's incentive designs to cut off or lead the restructuring of the sector. In turn, FINOP and ČSOB were unwilling finance Banka Bohemia's and SST's projects. Second, as with many new domestic banks, Banka Bohemia then had to offer ever higher interest rates to attract deposits while making more questionable loans.[33] This was a recipe for insolvency. Between January and June 1994, four of the five largest new private banks, including Banka Bohemia, went bankrupt and were seized by regulators in the CNB.[34]

The third main asset in SST's network was its bargaining links to the central government. SST aimed to use its group bargaining strength through its existing relationships to attract the government's attention to the industry's export and R&D needs and influence reforms in the vocational training system. After 1990, the Czech MPO still maintained a department for the machine tool industry whose staff had several former employees of the TST directorate. SST members believed these relationships would help the MPO view them not as disparate, individual firms, but as a group, whose collective impact on the economy was significant. Through mid-1992, the MPO maintained studies on the privatization, export and technology needs of the machine-tool industry.[35] Additionally, contacts to the MPO and the Ministry of Labor were especially critical for vocational training. As opposed to firms like Škoda Plzeň, SST firms used various training centers outside of their boundaries and were thus dependent on national and regional government assistance to coordinate their changes.

Previously, TST firms relied on their directorate and regional councils to bargain with the Ministry of Labor, MPO, and the Ministry of Education about training programs.

Upon taking full control of the Czech government in June 1992, however, the Klaus coalition accelerated the policy of centralizing power and insulating policy organs from economic and social actors. The new minister of industry rationalized his ministry, eliminating the department for the machine tool industry. Interviews in the MPO revealed that although the government reluctantly began to participate in the restructuring of holdings such as Škoda Plzeň, it saw little reason to extend this privilege to SST firms. The government had little remaining equity in them, and as dispersed, medium-sized individual firms, they had little apparent political or economic impact on the national stage. As a testament to this, the MPO and the Ministry of Finance ignored SST's calls to aid an insolvent Strojimport and critical JVs in Hostivař and Kuřim, as well as to address SST's concerns over proposed reforms in vocational training.[36] In 1992–93, the CR government made three major changes: the training centers would be self-financing; their administration was moved to the Ministries of Economy and Education; and the state would subsidize only broad theoretical training. With the elimination and weakening of regional and district councils, SST firms were individually unable to influence the centers and retrain existing workers or replace them with new skilled workers, as discussed previously.[37] With the reorganization of the MPO and removal of training from the Ministries of Labor and Industry, SST firms no longer had the allies to address their personnel needs.

By the end of 1994, SST's new support structure was in disarray and the group was highly fragmented, despite the past network's relatively ideal qualities. One can begin to make sense of the failure of past social relations and equity ties to mediate the disputes among SST firms as well as the impact of depoliticization by understanding social capital and networks as political constructions. On the one hand, the limited number of potential allies shifted the authority structure of SST's network. Whereas previously the polycentric structure and quasi-brokerage positions of various members emanated from ties to district and regional bank branches and councils, after 1990, the new alliances with banks and trade companies were concentrated via the SST directorate. The effectiveness of these new alliances depended in part on a level of cooperation and confluence of interests among SST firms that were strained by the uncertainties of probing and had existed only when firms had their own bases of resources and political leverage via, notably, the councils. On the other hand, the new external allies alone lacked the political and financial capital to credibly mediate intra-SST disputes and share risk with these firms—and thus help reconstruct the social ties and authority structure of the network. The only institutional means available were voluntary contracts, liquidation, and poorly regulated investment funds. As already mentioned, the combination of uncertainty and interdependencies between banks and industrial firms made bank led restructuring via these routes too risky.

Under such conditions, the next best option for a member firm is to forego collaboration, attempt to take full control of network assets, and, ultimately, force the risk back onto the government through financial manipulation. It is this second side of the former TST network to which we now turn.

The Rise of ZPS: Reconstituting Its Local Network

In the midst of the breakdown of SST's cohesion and organization, one member, ZPS Zlin, would not only restructure itself but also attempt a strategy to control the rest of the network that would threaten the stability of the Czech financial system.[38] Viewing ZPS solely in terms of the strength of its inherited production profile, social ties, and control over resources, it would be difficult to account for its rebound relative to other SST members, let alone its ability to impose a new order over the others and attract central government intervention. ZPS was one of the largest members in terms of sales and employment, but so too were Kovosvit, Kuřim, and Čelákovice, all of which lost critical plants during privatization, posted consistent losses, and became targets of ZPS takeovers. Its operations profile of a casting plant and production facilities for a standard set of machine and milling tools was similar to the others, thus offering no relative strategic advantages. (See table 5.1.) ZPS had been a subsidiary of the famous Baťa group in the interwar period, but so too was Kovosvit. Moreover, its performance before and just after the fall of communism was no better, and often worse, than the other TST/SST firms. By 1989, ZPS exports accounted for about 30 percent of its sales (slightly more than the TST average); but whereas 90 percent of its exports were to the former CMEA, the TST average was 62 percent.[39] Between 1989 and the end of 1992, ZPS's exports fell by 30 percent. Its nominal sales increased by only 7 percent. At the same time, it became highly leveraged. Between 1990 and 1992, its total debt/equity ratio rose from .755 to 1.184; its bank debt/equity ratio rose from .525 to .793; and its interest rate coverage ratio fell from 8.33 to a dangerous 1.14.[40]

From the viewpoint of my embedded politics approach, one gains insights not only into the factors that can account for a transformation of networks and institutions but also into the conditions that turn strategies of risk sharing into political and financial instability. First, a distinguishing feature of ZPS's restructuring strategy was its ability to reconstitute its local sociopolitical network and then use it to gain external partners to penetrate export markets and public-private financing. With its new source of economic power, ZPS was in a position to impose its own authority and production structure over the weakening network of SST firms. Second, the government's continued adherence to its depoliticization agenda turned the aims of ZPS and its local allies to bring order to SST into a strategy of exploiting the passiveness of the main banks and the government and taking control of a cornerstone of the financial sector, namely the Czech insurance company, Česká Pojišťovna. Such a strategy would destabilize the sector and leave ZPS and its allies as unavoidable and strong bargaining partners with the government and main banks to restructure SST and Česká Pojišťovna. The rest of the chapter lays out these arguments, with this section first addressing the renewal of ZPS and its local sociopolitical network.

Early in 1990, a group of ZPS managers, centered around Radomir Zbožínek, actively worked to restore the communal and production traditions of Tomáš Baťa to the firm as well as to the city and district of Zlin.[41] Baťa, a rival to the likes of Emil Škoda in Czech industrialization, had built his empire of shoes and machine tools out of Zlin and worked closely with the local and regional governments to support civic associations, entrepreneurs, and some of the first Czech programs for vocational training, engineering, and management.[42] Zbožínek's team became active in the local branch of Civic Forum and in the campaign to return the pre-communist era names to the town, district, streets, and schools (e.g., under communism, Zlin was called *Gottwaldov,* after the Communist party secretary and leader of the 1948 coup). Also, whereas most Czech firms, including those of SST, viewed communist-era social and civic services attached to firms as financial burdens and left them to the municipalities to support, ZPS elected to finance much of their costs and comanage them with the local government.[43] These services included apartments for employees and their families, day care, a health clinic, and a public cafeteria. ZPS maintained facilities for one of Zlin's main civic centers, ZPS Klub, a future subsidiary of ZPS. The Klub provided facilities for new local newspapers, organized business education programs for all citizens, and became a meeting place for local social groups and the local association for entrepreneurs. ZPS brought municipal council members onto the board of the subsidiary Energetika, which provided power to ZPS and part of Zlin. ZPS then upgraded these operations and installed ecologically safe technology in its casting plant. ZPS solidified its relationship with the community by campaigning to have residents use their vouchers to purchase shares in ZPS and form an association of shareholders. This association became one of the largest shareholders in ZPS, with 12 percent, and it had two seats on the supervisory board, including the chairmanship.[44]

Zbožínek's team also followed the Baťa tradition of developing a flexible and loyal workforce. They first worked with Civic Forum to have employees elect new management before this legal provision was eliminated in March 1990.[45] Perhaps unsurprisingly, Zbožínek and his cohort won the election. The new management then set aside in its privatization project 8.25 percent of ZPS shares to be purchased by employees at a discount. ZPS added to these steps by investing in training and decentralizing work practices. For instance, ZPS arranged for the district vocational training center to continue training existing employees at a discount in exchange for the center's use of ZPS facilities for any vocational program and students. Management also took advantage of the disarray in the labor unions by working with its work council to initiate greater worker rotation and a greater percentage of bonuses linked to the performance of respective operating units. In exchange, the unit labor representatives and the foremen managed daily production and kept detailed production and financial accounts, which were reviewed in biweekly meetings with plant and subsidiary managers.[46]

Such actions brought ZPS gains in social peace and finances. On the one hand, the union membership rate at ZPS was above 80 percent as late as 1995, while the national union membership rates fell to about 50 percent in the CR.[47] On the other hand, ZPS converted its sociopolitical capital with employees into financial capital, by tapping directly into employee savings at a time when cash was scarce. For instance, in 1990–91, ZPS raised 17.5 million Kcs through zero-coupon bonds exclusively for employees at a 24 percent discount rate payable in five years. In 1992, ZPS opened an internal bank that offered employees various demand and time deposit accounts. Within the first six months, employees and their families deposited over 60 million Kcs.[48]

ZPS management built on its renewed local sociopolitical capital to develop its own network for exports and financial resources. It immediately solicited the aid of former Baťa employees, including the son of Tomáš Baťa, who were émigrés in Canada and the United States. Baťa took a seat on the ZPS board. Through him and a lifelong associate, ZPS tapped into a global sales network, with which it formed joint trade offices in Asia and North America.[49] ZPS management also worked with former employees of ZPS, Svit (Baťa's former shoe factory in Zlin), and the regional branch of KB to create an investment company, First Privatization Fund (PPF), and a bank, Pragobanka. This group of businessmen became known throughout the CR as the "Zlin Mafia" (connoting a control group and not illegal practices). The main shareholders of Pragobanka included PPF, ZPS, and Česká Pojišťovna.[50] As the former state monopoly for insurance, Pojišťovna was the fourth-largest financial institution in the country. Pojišťovna invested into four new banks, of which Pragobanka was the largest. Between December 1990 and December

1994, Pragobanka's total assets grew from about 2.5 billion Kcs to 18.4 billion Kcs, and its equity capital grew from 60 million Kcs to over 1.3 billion Kcs.[51] Much of the increase came from consistent capital investments, deposits, and subordinated debt by Pojišťovna.[52] At the same time, PPF rose to become one of the most profitable IPCs in the CR.[53] Besides obtaining significant equity stakes in SST firms, PPF developed close ties through the Zlin Mafia with IPCs of the Czech Savings Bank and Pojišťovna to coordinate equity investments and off-market trades in Czech and Slovak industry and create a new fund for Russia. In 1994–95, PPF then began buying Pojišťovna shares, joining the four main Czech banks and the state administrator of property, FNM, as one of the main shareholders of Pojišťovna.[54]

ZPS management used its emerging local sociopolitical and economic capital in two critical ways to stabilize the firm and then expand its growth. First, top management was able to prevent key plants from breaking off during privatization in 1991–92 while offering them greater autonomy within the boundaries of the firm. On the one hand, management's ties to the local banks and privatization council, with which the Ministry of Privatization consulted on spin-off projects, effectively undermined competing privatization projects for ZPS plants.[55] On the other hand, management allowed many upstream plants to become semiautonomous subsidiaries with direct ties to foreign firms. Incorporating them as joint-stock companies that owned their own land and facilities, rather than simple limited-liability companies, offered subsidiaries greater potential access to capital and foreign partners. Independent-minded managers in subsidiaries, such as SM for shoe machines, Elektro-montáže, and Systems for computer design technology and machinery software, were allowed to purchase equity stakes in their subsidiary at a discount and in installments.[56] ZPS management also used its ties through Baťa to develop JVs and product development partnerships for its subsidiaries with firms from China, Austria, Silicon Valley, and Germany.[57]

Second, ZPS kept probing alive by feeding its local order with new export contacts and funds gained through its external network.[58] Foreign partners helped both upstream and downstream operations develop new technologies, product scope, sales, and cash flow. For instance, through its affiliate in the United States and partnership in Germany, ZPS developed two new vertical machining centers from its previously minor production of horizontal centers, and became one of the leading suppliers vertical centers in Europe and the United States by 1995.[59] Its Italian partnership helped ZPS redesign its multispindle lathes for the SAY series and gained several lucrative contracts.[60] Non-machine tool subsidiaries also benefited. For instance, between 1991 and 1993, exports for SM and Slevarna, the castings foundry, increased, respectively, by 40 percent and 280 percent. Accessory subsidiaries developed a new pallet exchanger for machining centers with sales of 500 pieces per year and three new types of containers for horizontal lathes. The results of these efforts were impressive. Between 1992 and 1994, total sales and exports more than doubled, with exports exceeding 1 billion Kcs. 85 percent of sales were exports, virtually all of which was to the West and Asia, and ZPS's leading market became the United States, which accounted for over 30 percent of the firm's exports.

To alleviate the financial distress that had plagued probing in other firms, ZPS built on its employee "loans" by channeling in development funds with the aid of the Zlin Mafia. By the end of 1992, ZPS had already obtained over 80 million Kcs in two and four-year loans from Pragobanka and another 16 million Kcs loan direct from Pojišťovna.[61] These loans functioned mainly as risk-sharing mechanisms to gain additional funds from KB, whose regional manager was brought onto the board of ZPS. By the end of 1993, when Pragobanka became a leading shareholder of ZPS, ZPS management and its allies began simultaneously to push up its share price, revalue its equity capital, and gain more debt financing. Their virtually unimpeded control of the corporate boards allowed them to increase investment and revalue their equity capital by one-third, while their control over Pragobanka facilitated additional loans.[62] Subsequently, ZPS's leverage remained high.[63] The questioned remained as to whether ZPS could generate enough revenues to counter this trend.

Rewriting the Rules of Network Governance and Government Policy

Given the continued rise of the real value of the Czech currency, ZPS management believed that export growth could only come from using the other SST firms to lower production costs and generate new revenue streams.[64] Yet with both the main Czech banks and the government reluctant to share the risks of restructuring and SST firms crumbling, ZPS and its allies faced the stark choice of being dragged down into the morass of insolvency or seize control of the other firms and the necessary financial assets.[65]

This section ties the previous sections together and shows how the need to bring order to an industrial network would ultimately require political negotiations over the control of public-private funds. ZPS's expansion was based not on dissolving network ties but on recombining them—a struggle to impose a new authority structure over the network. However, just as the Czech policy of depoliticization had left the main Czech banks as the primary financiers of restructuring but with few incentives to participate, it also left the central government as the primary public body responsible for fulfilling the dual goals of privatization—clarifying the new ownership rights and maintaining asset value. That is, while the policy created incentives for ZPS and its allies both to control SST and Česká Pojišťovna's funds through force rather than compromise, it demanded that the government fulfill its privatization obligations by negotiating with the only private actors (ZPS and PPF) left in a position to do more damage to the financial system and hopefully stabilize both Česká Pojišťovna and the machine-tool industry.

Controlling the Ties That Bind

Though unknown at the time by outside analysts, ZPS had been expanding export market share by selling much of its products below cost.[66] Through 1993, ZPS was still producing 50 to 70 percent of parts in-house with rising costs from the low economies of scale and reliance on imported CNC technology. Rationalizing production threatened potentially lucrative sources of cash flow and innovation, as its upstream units and subsidiaries were selling 25 to 40 percent of their output to outside customers. Other SST firms, however, still had skilled workshops and needed contracts desperately, but they were reluctant to become beholden to ZPS. To exploit this opportunity, ZPS began to graft its own network onto that of SST. ZPS gained key information and coordination via the SST's meetings; its managing director, who was a board member of ZPS; and PPF, which began accumulating significant stakes in some of the largest members, such as Čelákovice, Kuřim, Kovosvit, and Šmeral; as well as traditional regional collaborators like Zbrojovka Všetín, a producer of textile and drilling machines. Moreover, ZPS managers represented PPF on the boards of these firms. In late 1993, ZPS began "cooperation agreements" with SST firms—small batch orders for components. As ZPS used direct and indirect channels to negotiate production changes, it also facilitated operating loans via Pragobanka and KB, which firms could acquire upon proof of contracts from ZPS. By the end of 1994, no less than nine SST members were subcontracting for ZPS. Six of them confirmed that new loans were linked to ZPS orders. Moreover, these firms confirmed that KB, Pragobanka and its sister bank within the Česká Pojišťovna group, Kreditní Banka, sourced the bulk of new short-term operating loans.

A change in the management of SST firms, however, would demand stronger direct control by ZPS over the network. In mid-1994, the new owners/IPCs of eight leading SST firms fired their top managers, one of whom was the president of SST, after the firms posted consistent losses. Two other firms, Hostivař and Kuřim, also bordered on bankruptcy as their JVs collapsed in the face of resistance by the Ministry of Finance to write off large tax arrears. Foreign firms stood ready to take over their considerable shares (over 50 percent) still in the FNM, which was anxious to rid itself of them. Moreover, Čelákovice and Kovosvit owned two key trademarks, for which other members paid a commission. At the same time, the rebound of the world machine-tool market brought SST firms new short-term orders from foreign firms and thus potentially greater bargaining power to hold up ZPS.[67] The case of Vrchlabí, the hydraulics supplier that had hooked into foreign partners and decreased its production for Czech firms, had already demonstrated the problem of competing customers, especially when one was offering export revenues. ZPS management essentially worried whether it and its allies could continue to make financial guarantees, in turn take the risk, with potentially hostile sub-contractors bound by only vague medium-term agreements. The rebuilding of SST was still incomplete and could thus not supplement the agreements.

ZPS, in turn, began to use its own network and the SST headquarters to assert more direct control over firms while they were still weak. In December 1994 it initiated the creation of a fifty-fifty JV with Zbrojovka for add-on parts and chucks for ZPS machines. While Zbrojovka committed facilities, ZPS provided some start-up finance, access to new loans, and export contracts. This was engineered with the aid of PPF and SST's engineering fund, the two biggest shareholders, and Pragobanka. This deal allowed ZPS to gain virtually full control of key Zbrojovka assets at low cost.[68] The next move came in June 1995 with ZPS's purchase of 44 percent of the failing Čelákovice, the forth-largest SST firm. The minority share was actually a "hidden super majority," since both PPF and SST's engineering fund would vote with ZPS. Demanding that SST's fund sell only 12 percent of its original 20 percent and thus allowing ZPS a strong coalition additionally demonstrated ZPS's sway over SST's fund. In November 1995, ZPS then purchased 62 percent of Kovosvit, the second largest SST firm. PPF and SST's engineering fund again provided additional votes to give ZPS a super majority to wrestle with the FNM over a 15 percent equity stake in Kovosvit that was still unprivatized (see the following).[69]

ZPS's allies also helped financing ZPS's share purchases and debt restructuring of the target firms. The three largest ZPS shareholders, (PPF, Pragobanka, and the IPC of Czech Savings Bank) continued off market trades to push ZPS's equity capital so that the firm and shareholders could acquire greater leveraged finance. The funds were also matched by equity swaps: the IPCs of Czech Savings led other IPCs to swap their shares in target firms for preferred stock in ZPS. Moreover, with their regional directors on ZPS's board, Pragobanka and KB helped restructure some of the debt burdens of Čelákovice and Kovosvit, using ZPS's equity in the target firms as collateral.

Toward the end of 1995, ZPS and its major collaborator, PPF, made plans for completing their hold over the industry and external finances. PPF began to purchase shares of Česká Pojišťovna through off-market trades. ZPS turned its sights onto Kuřim and Hostivař. But both strategies depended on pushing its previous modus operandi to the limit: if the big banks and the government would not share risk voluntarily, ZPS and PPF, whether or not intentionally, would push the risk on them.[70]

Kuřim and Hostivař, the third- and sixth-largest SST firms, still had, respectively, 54 percent and 100 percent of their shares in the FNM, due to failed JVs with foreign firms. Moreover, the FNM had failed to complete a subsequent tender for Hostivař, as the Czech buyers were unable to obtain needed financing. ZPS immediately began discussions with the FNM for a purchase of both firms. ZPS's purchase strategy involved using its financial network to decrease its purchase costs and the aggregate revenues that the FNM would receive, and getting the FNM and the Ministry of Finance to write off much Kuřim's and Hostivař's large tax arrears.[71] Despite two months of negotiations, the parties were at an impasse. The FNM and Ministry of Finance were obviously concerned about effectively subsidizing the purchase. The state clearing house on old trading loans, KOB, had already twice extended Kuřim's and Hostivař's repayment of these loans. Moreover, the government was still negotiating with ZPS and Kovosvit (now a ZPS subsidiary) over some their own shares still in the FNM.[72] The FNM essentially now wanted to tie the two sets of negotiations together, so as to minimize its losses. It saw ZPS as getting a large amount of shares for a discounted price. As talks were postponed, ZPS bargained it could make the government blink, while applying pressure by taking the matter to the press and the courts.[73]

At the same time, PPF had acquired 3.5 percent of Česká Pojišťovna, gained a seat on the board, and now demanded an opportunity to bid on shares predesignated for the FNM and four of the main Czech banks (at book price).[74] As the banks had yet to pay for their shares but were running Pojišťovna's board, PPF reasonably argued that the banks would have to purchase the shares at the higher market price, decrease their stakes, or allow PPF to purchase additional shares at the book price.

Together, the two actions of ZPS and PPF signaled a potential shift in industrial and financial power. Two previously small players in the Czech economy were on the verge of consolidating control over assets for relatively low costs and could challenge the government's policies and the main banks management of the bulk of the country's financial assets. These fears of KB and IB, which controlled the supervisory board of Pojišťovna, even made it to the public press. Throughout January–April 1996, the board tried to block PPF's attempts to gain more control over the insurer, fearing that Pojišťovna would

move its deposits to other banks. During these months the board even authorized several counter attacks at PPF by trying to use Pojišťovna's subsidiary banks to buy controlling stakes in the largest PPF funds.[75] Moreover,
the hitherto strategy of ZPS and PPF had been built less on cooperation with
other firms and more on complete control over others with resources gained
by exploiting the weaknesses of the Czech capital markets. At least in the cases
of the holdings, the government and banks had established a modicum of
monitoring and control over the new owners.

Notice, at this point, how efforts to recombine the network began to extend to public institutions. This may cause one to reconsider conventional
views of networks and institutions in such a way as to integrate both micro-
and macropolitical variables. To a certain degree, one can interpret ZPS actions as generated from its advantageous brokerage position and capital,
which emerged via ZPS's conscious efforts to rebuild and convert its own
local sociopolitical network into a source of sales and financing. These actions were sufficient for ZPS to restructure itself and begin new lines of potentially lucrative products. Yet, brokerage is a two-way profession and depends still on the integration of supporting public institutions. On the one
hand, the broker needs a reasonably stable core network (SST) to put existing assets and information to new uses without taking full responsibility for
them. On the other hand, as the core network collapses and total control becomes paramount to the broker's entrepreneurial aspirations, the broker
(ZPS) demands ever more resources to consolidate its position (and avoid
default). Local public actors could no longer participate, as they lacked resources and a political framework to coordinate actions with other SST localities or the central ministries. Moreover, without institutionalized mechanisms to encourage existing financiers to share the risk in the broker's
consolidation, the broker's private allies must mirror the broker's domination strategy to capture any available financial resources. For ZPS's allies this
meant a short-term strategy of manipulating the values of their own investment portfolios and for ZPS to gain debt-finance via their own banks and
the Czech insurance company. Notice that the brokerage strategy ends in a
domination strategy—over both the broker's former core network and its financial channels—when there are no adequate institutions to facilitate extended negotiation and multiparty risk sharing. Ultimately, the incentives
lead to systemic failure, when the state can no longer ignore the damage.

The Limits of Depoliticization and Complete Asset Control

Since the strategies of ZPS and PPF lent themselves to leveraging their fragile
network on the hope of future revenues, it would only take a proper audit to

expose the weaknesses of their framework and force all parties to negotiate a broader structure of shared control. Just as PPF pressed the banks to justify their positions and reveal their investments into Pojišťovna, the CNB suspended the license of Kreditní Banka, one of Pojišťovna's banks. This triggered a full audit of Pojišťovna that found a weaker than expected capital adequacy of Pragobanka. The FNM, CNB, and Ministry of Finance immediately sacked Pojišťovna's top management and began negotiations with the big banks about how to restructure Pojišťovna and whether to seize Pragobanka as well.[76]

Radical changes in the finances and control structure of Pragobanka and Česká Pojišťovna could seriously threaten the nascent financial control structure of ZPS and PPF. Pragobanka and Pojišťovna had financed and bore the risk of much of ZPS's expansion and its restructuring plans for the SST firms. Indeed, by mid-1996 Pojišťovna's board had begun withdrawing liquidity from Pragobanka, which in turn began having trouble meeting its interbank loan payments to IB and KB.[77] The development of its new acquisitions, purchase strategies for Kuřim and Hostivař, and increasing hold over SST all depended on ZPS's ability to bring in outside financing and risk sharing. This, in turn, depended on the ability of ZPS and PPF to maintain a hold on Pragobanka and cooperation with Pojišťovna.

Three factors, however, played to the advantage of ZPS and PPF in the face of the upheaval surrounding Pojišťovna. First, both PPF and ZPS were already closely involved in Pragobanka, and PPF was a new board member of Pojišťovna. Second, the continued passivity of the main banks and the recent aggressive actions by two nonbank IPCs toward two of the main banks and Czech utilities had already threatened the stability of the Czech financial system. The government did not want a repeat, but preferred less confrontation and more controlled compromise.[78] PPF had been quite successful as a fund manager, rising to become the second-largest nonbank IPC in the Czech Republic. It also had a track record of working with the big bank IPCs. In turn, PPF was brought in to negotiate a restructuring plan for Pojišťovna and its subsidiary banks with the FNM, CNB, and the Ministry of Finance—many of the same people with whom ZPS had just broken off talks over the purchases of Kuřim and Hostivař. But simply allowing quick purchases by ZPS and PPF would have given them relatively unrestricted reign over the machine tool industry and Česká Pojišťovna. Denying them no place at the bargaining table would have destabilized Česká Pojišťovna further and leave the FNM with insolvent firms. By opening up continued negotiations on both fronts, the government could still fulfill the dual goals of privatization but now through a public-private partnership that regulated both the government's policy and the private use of assets.

But a third factor would appear to tilt the relative bargaining power further to ZPS and PPF and potentially undermine any real partnership. In the beginning of 1996, with the government declaring victory in its privatization policies, the Klausians moved the FNM under control of the Ministry of Finance, whose minister was a close associate of Klaus and a loyal, leading member of his party. Previously, the FNM board was comprised of various ministers and even opposition party members, and the chairman had been a leading member of a smaller party (ODA) in the coalition that also controlled the Ministry of Industry. Beginning with the crisis in Škoda Plzeň, the FNM and the Ministry of Industry had been the sources of stronger advocacy, relative to the Klaus's party, of pragmatism, transparency, and an expanded role of public agencies in restructuring and privatization of firms as well as stronger regulatory frameworks for utilities and capital markets. The shift in control over the FNM in 1996 tied the chairman's hands from pushing policy in these directions and moved him and his deputies to follow the Klaus line of a quick resolution to all outstanding privatizations.

Subsequently, the government laid the foundations for an alternative governance order to monitor economic activity and restructuring. The cornerstone was having ZPS and PPF become direct negotiating partners with the government and main banks over the stabilization of a key Czech financial institution and the fulfillment of the two goals of privatization for the machine tool industry. (See figure 5.2.) ZPS and the government (the FNM, Ministry of Finance, and Ministry of Industry) resumed talks over the purchases of Kuřim and Hostivař and the employee shares. In late 1996, ZPS finally agreed to purchase part of Kuřim and was still allowed to negotiate with the state's KOB on the write-off of some of Kuřim's loans. PPF, four of the main banks, and the government (FNM, CNB, and Ministry of Finance) negotiated the restructuring of Pojišťovna and its banks, particularly the size and purchase price of Pojišťovna shares, the division of liabilities to cover the deposits of Kreditní Banka, and the division of managerial responsibilities for various Pojišťovna operations. PPF obtained 20 percent of Pojišťovna and began to run the investment funds of Pojišťovna. ZPS and PPF shared control of the board of Pragobanka with one of the big banks, IB. ZPS, and with it SST, took positions previously reserved for only the largest companies where the government still had large equity stakes (holdings, utilities, and the big banks). In 1995, the Ministry of Industry called on SST to draw up a detailed analysis and policy proposal for boosting exports of the machine-tool industry. In June 1996, the minister of industry began a commission for policies to address problems of interfirm arrears, taxes, and exports. Along with the Czech industrial elite—the energy monopolist CEZ and holdings from engineering, chemicals, and steel—were ZPS and SST.[79]

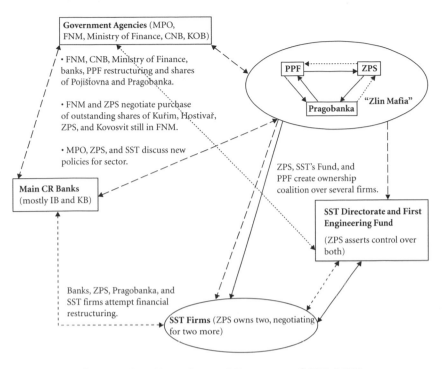

Figure 5.2.   New Control Structure of SST, 1996

Note: Solid lines denote ownership; broken lines denote lines of communication. Thickness of lines and direction of arrows denote relative strength of channel and dyadic control.

This new round of government-backed negotiations allowed contrasting governance orders for restructuring to emerge within the mechanical engineering industry. First, whereas in the governance order for SST critical producers and units for R&D, export, and training remained largely outside the organizational boundaries of a single firm, these activities were within the boundaries of a single firm in the case of Škoda and DDR. Second, and perhaps more importantly, SST's new governance order contrasted significantly from Škoda's in terms of control rights, ownership, and government involvement. Škoda and DDR had dispersed de facto control rights between Škoda's center, the banks, the subsidiaries, and the government (i.e., the MPO and, to a certain degree, the FNM). At the same time, formal ownership was rather concentrated, moving from the government (FNM) to the new management team and the bank consortium. SST moved in the opposite direction. Although ZPS gained significant ownership stakes in some firms, its super majorities depended on the collaboration of PPF and SST's fund, among others.

Similarly, ZPS management did not hold equity in its firm, but rather depended on the collaboration of these same actors (PPF, SST's fund, Pojiš-ťovna's fund, and Pragobanka) to run ZPS, as these actors formed the main coalition of owners. The government held relatively little equity in SST firms and the banks were not to get any. Critical control rights, however, became concentrated in the hands of ZPS management and PPF, while government agencies not involved in DDR and to some degree the main banks participated only indirectly in the privatization and restructuring of SST members. For instance, as the FNM, Ministry of Finance, and CNB negotiated with PPF and the main banks over the stabilization of Česká Pojišťovna, they indirectly opened up financial resources for ZPS and PPF to channel to members. At the same time, the MPO and FNM negotiated with ZPS and the SST directorate over the final privatization of certain members and policies to aid SST with export development.

Notice that I have not elaborated on the details of how the multiparty monitoring worked in this new scheme, as I did in discussing Škoda and DDR. This is not a coincidence, as SST's new governance order was sufficient to avoid immediate systemic crisis but was not able to affect restructuring changes necessary to withstand a revitalization of the firms and an economic downturn in 1998. This weakness came from vital differences between DDR and SST's scheme regarding the nature and composition of public power. In turn it is also no coincidence that these differences became similarities between SST and the post-1995 Škoda, when the government left Škoda to be governed by the existing system of investment funds and banks rather than using the DDR experience to enact changes in financial laws and industrial policy. Recall that in DDR, the ability of the government to affect a dispersion of control rights and to enhance information and risk sharing through iterative deliberations came from its use of significant ownership shares and debt finance as bargaining leverage as well as the discretionary powers afforded to the MPO and the FNM to revise privatization projects and become credible bargaining partners.

In the SST scheme, both of these forms of public power had been significantly diminished. The large majority of shares for ZPS and other SST firms were already privatized to ZPS and investment funds. Moreover, interministerial and interparty disputes about whether to formalize further government participation in the economy and which political actors would control this led Klaus to reclaim his publicly declared mantel of depoliticization and reconsolidate power. This effectively cut off other channels of political power from experimenting with alternative policies. Putting the FNM under Klaus's Minister of Finance in early 1996 effectively removed the FNM from control of ODA and oversight by the opposition parties and the CNB and diluted the

1993 and 1994 decrees that had given the FNM and MPO greater latitude in privatizing and restructuring firms. Hence, the FNM had little independent bargaining room. The KOB, which still represented another source of bargaining power over SST firms—debt refinancing, and was active an application of DDR in the reorganization of Aero Holding, the aircraft manufacturer, was also further constrained. Although the Ministry of Finance had always owned the Consolidation Bank, most of the Bank's financial resources and policy initiatives came from the FNM. The shift in control over the FNM to the Ministry of Finance, in turn, undermined an independent channel of resources and strategy for the KOB.

Concluding Remarks: Network Change and the Stability of an Alternative Governance Order

The attempt to restructure SST and construct an alternative governance order in the mechanical engineering industry highlights two critical issues in the transformation of postcommunist countries. First, the strategies, conflicts, and changes in the relations among the firms of the machine tool sector demonstrate both the continued impact of former network structures and the critical influence of sociopolitical dimensions of industrial networks. While the use of private ownership and contracts as well as old social ties could not resolve restructuring conflicts among the firms, reference simply to resource control or past norms cannot account for the rise of ZPS and the drastic reorganization of the former TST network. Instead, viewing the industry as a sociopolitical network allows one to understand not only the strategies of former TST firms but also the way public power is constitutive of the authority structure of networks and becomes a defining factor of change. ZPS's initial turnaround, for instance, was largely due its ability to reconstitute its local sociopolitical network and use it to tap public-private resources. Moreover, the fragmentation of SST and ZPS's as well as PPF's determination to bring stability to the branch through control—and not cooperation—over other firms and Pojišťovna highlight the way public power is connected network stability. In pursuing depoliticization and thus combining the centralization of power with use of private contracts to regulate resource distribution, the Czech government created not only the conditions for the fragmentation of SST but also the incentives for ZPS and PPF to restructure firms through financial manipulation.

Second, in comparison with the Škoda case, ZPS's subsequent domination of the machine tool sector and its gradual financial insolvency in the wake of the Asian and Russian crises highlight the way political and economic power can shape the revival of an industrial network and the sustainability of needed risk sharing and learning through public-private governance structures. That is, the distribution of power—both the hold-up power within a network and the public power that is bestowed upon constituents—becomes a key factor in determining the sustainability of delegation and deliberation, the two principles at the core of DDR and Škoda's initial revival.

The Škoda and SST cases are similar in their need for public participation in restructuring and in the way the upheaval in the political coalition commanding the government undermined the ability of public agencies to continue to experiment with their new roles in the economy, monitor adequately their private counterparts, and translate these experiences into more general policies and legal reforms. As noted at the end of chapter 4, fights within the coalition on whether to pursue the gains made in DDR and Škoda or treat them as aberrations in the maintenance of depoliticization limited the influence of actors, such as those in the MPO and FNM, to revise securities and bankruptcy laws and export and FDI policies. In this stalemate, the government simply left Škoda to be governed by a weak set of investment funds and a capital market with no new incentives for private actors to reveal information and share the risks of investment or restructuring. By the time the government intervened into the Pojišťovna crisis and into ZPS's activities in SST, the coalition was beyond repair, with Klaus and his party asserting greater control over key public agency's, like the FNM and KOB, and blocking MPO initiatives on export promotion and foreign direct investment. Indeed, central figures for both cases, the minister of industry and the FNM chairman and their teams, resigned from the government and their party (ODA) in, respectively, early 1997 and 1998.

The cases of Škoda and SST are different in the way public authority was delegated and monitored. This distinction also becomes a key variable for comparisons between models of public-private institution-building models as well as for conditions facilitating deliberative governance. Much of the gains in DDR came from the government's ability to use its continued control over equity and debt in Škoda to force a decentralization of control rights and tie private actors into a structure that facilitated frequent deliberations and thus monitoring and learning. The weakness of the new governance order for the machine tool sector emanated partially from the lack of leverage the government had when it finally intervened in Pojišťovna and ZPS's activities. Although the government had control over the distribution of equity in Pojišťovna as bargaining leverage with PPF, it had little debt and equity resources directly linked to ZPS and SST members. An increase in government bargaining leverage would have meant allowing public agencies, like the FNM, MPO, and KOB greater discretion in regulating and generating new resources, such as through new export, bankruptcy, and vocational training policies. But such actions were tantamount to altering the agenda of an already crumbling government coalition. The distribution of power and control over assets within the former TST network had already evolved to a point where variables of public authority endogenous to the network had virtually vanished.

These observations on the distribution of public power in many ways reflect arguments on institution building that focus exclusively on either the coherence of the state or the micro-level distribution of inherited resources.[80] The added value of my embedded politics approach is that it can tie the two arguments together into a more comprehensive framework. For instance, it has taken the insolvency of ZPS and Škoda, the collapse of the capital market, and the formation of a new government controlled by the Czech Social Democrats to allow public actors to gain bargaining leverage via de facto renationalizations of firms and construct a new public-private workout vehicle for firms, once again based on the principles of delegation and deliberation. Interestingly, the substance of the vehicle and the conditions for its creation are in many ways similar to Poland's creation of the Enterprise-Bank Restructuring Program in 1993–96 as well as current efforts to revive several economies in East Asia and Latin America. Moreover, my use of sociopolitical networks as a lens to connect two levels of politics and power distribution and thus compare the governance orders that emerged from the Škoda and SST cases has broader implications in comparing developmental models recently articulated by Sabel about Japan and eastern Germany and Stark and Bruszt about Hungary.[81] These two applications of my embedded politics approach for public-private governance and the comparative analysis of institution building will now be discussed in the concluding chapter of the book.

CHAPTER 6

Conclusion

Governing Institutional Experiments

Any scholar writing on transformations is burdened by the Greek notion that the end of a story can force us to rewrite its earlier chapters.[1] As the upheaval surrounding Russian reforms reminds us, 1989 marked not the "end of history," a "fresh start," nor even a continuation of the "ancien régime," but rather a new chapter in a long, ongoing journey for countries of East Central Europe to reshape the institutions that govern and hopefully improve their lives. The Czech Republic is a case in point. On the one hand, the Czech Republic stood out as a potential success story of transformation even as late as 1997.[2] Indeed, the two dominant approaches to institutional transformation—the tabula rasa view with its emphasis on depoliticization and the continuity view with its emphasis on the unscathed determinacy of past social structures—embraced the Czech case as proof positive of their respective claims. On the other hand, in the wake of the Asian and Russian crises, unemployment almost tripled, growth declined, capital markets collapsed, and many of the leading industrial companies and banks became insolvent. In turn, proponents of the two approaches have been forced to reconsider their first principles or blame it on lack of "political will."[3]

The goal of the comparative scholar is to find a constant among the twists in the story—a constant that can illuminate our understanding of institutional change and define a set of paths for economic and political renovation both within and across countries. A key empirical constant appears to be the continued experimentation by the state with public-private vehicles to help actors share risk, define their claims to assets, and restructure them. The Czechs' attempt to create such vehicles for the holding companies was perhaps a harbinger of their efforts beginning in 1999 to construct an agency—owned by the state, yet managed by private actors—to reorganize the industrial companies, such as Škoda and ZPS, and create new, hybrid ownership structures. Poland initiated privatization by leasing assets to stakeholders, jump-started bank and large firm restructuring with its debt conciliation program of 1993–96, and built capital markets via state-created mutual funds that were managed by private actors. Hungary's experiments with bankruptcy laws that promoted workouts and with regional development agencies can be seen in this light as well.

But what are the conditions under which these experiments turn into durable general laws, policies, and institutions? The inability of proponents of the dominant approaches to support their claims even in their ideal case of the Czech Republic, let alone reconcile the phenomena of public-private institutional experiments with their categories, invites the need for a new set of analytical lenses that can help us focus on both the evolution and governance of institutional change.

This book is an attempt to offer an approach that accounts for both continuity and change in institutions by highlighting the way sociopolitical networks shape the interaction between the micro- and macro-level attempts to create new forms of economic governance. By way of conclusion, in this chapter I will first summarize the main findings and arguments of the book. I then build on this review to offer broader lessons about the comparative study of institutional change and the conditions for the democratic governance of institutional experiments.

Reappraising the Czech Transformation

I have argued that postcommunist political economies, as in the Czech Republic, are composed of distinct sociopolitical networks that tied together core groups of firms with regional and district councils and state bank branches in different ways under communism. By providing members with a definition of associationalism, a set of political and economic resources, channels of communication, and an authority structure, a network shapes the restructuring strategies firms as well as mediates between state and society. The strict continuity of the past industrial networks, however, is broken, not simply from new economic shocks or incentives, but more so from alterations in the political architecture that buttressed the distinct groups of firms, that is, for the Czechs, the system of territorial-party councils. To identify, then, the factors of continuity and change and, in turn, the conditions for institutional renewal, I have further argued that the interaction between the macropolitics of implanting state designs and the micropolitics of intranetwork struggles over asset control can alter state policy, the formation of institutional rules, and the reorganization of networks in two ways. Because the new rules of governance were defined at the same time that asset value was being created, cooperation between members of former VHJ networks required negotiated solutions. These solutions were more likely to occur when public institutional actors became both financial partners and conflict mediators to the particular network. The specific tasks of the public actors are not necessarily permanent, but represent the initiation of experiments to build

public-private institutions that we now take for granted in advanced industrialized nations, such as those facilitating multiparty workouts, risk sharing,
and investment into complex assets and start-ups. Moreover, the patterns of
intranetwork struggles over asset control shaped the conditions of negotiations and thus the variation in the ways institutional rules were rewritten and
resources redistributed.

These arguments were developed incrementally. In chapter 2, I showed
that despite its relatively advanced industrial development and communist orthodoxy, communist Czechoslovakia (CSSR) did not resemble the standard
view of a communist political economy as a Taylorist mass-production system,
in which atomized individuals or firms were vertically commanded by the
Party-state through a strict hierarchy. Rather, the CSSR Party-state attempted
to maintain control and increase industrial growth by creating and strengthening middle-level institutions, such as industrial associations (VHJs), state bank
branches, and regional and district party councils. This policy had two unin-
tended consequences. First, VHJ managers attempted to adapt to the shortage
environment by increasing their self-sufficiency and broadening their production scopes. Second, VHJ managers built direct, horizontal channels with state
bank branches and party councils. These relationships enabled managers to
share political and financial risk and to maintain an authority structure for the
governance of their VHJs. The channels spread financial risk by helping VHJs
access funds to support their autarky and internal production bargaining without soliciting aid continually from central ministries. They spread political risk
by enabling VHJ managers, bank branches, and councils to combine their authority, limit central intervention, and create informal rules for economic coordination and conflict resolution. In turn, a VHJ became the center of a distinct
sociopolitical network or coalition of particular VHJ managers, SBCS branch
officers, and regional or district representatives.

I analyzed the formation of VHJ networks by comparing and contrasting the emergence of two ideal types (hierarchical versus polycentric) represented respectively by the VHJs Škoda Plzeň and TST. Both were mechanical
engineering VHJs, both had the same legal form, and both were subjected to
the same planning reforms in the 1980s. Yet the Škoda and TST networks had
different histories of industrial and planning organization. These histories
shaped the different ways Škoda and TST adapted to the strengthening of
middle-level institutions and shortage. The networks developed different
patterns of formal and informal governance rules, associationalism, authority
distribution, production organization, roles of members, and channels to
councils and bank branches.

In chapter 3, I analyzed the general interaction between the formation
of government policy and the response of old networks after 1989 in the

Czech Republic. Chapter 3 focused on the reorganization of political power and the attempts by the government to fulfill the dual goals of privatization—the delineation of private property rights and the maintenance of asset value. The Czech program of depoliticization aimed to limit rent seeking by eliminating space for deliberations between the state and society about new institutions and restructuring. The government first centralized power in the hands of a group of state technocrats, which were guided by clear rules to implement policies of rapid privatization and financial discipline. It then addressed the dual goals of privatization separately by creating incentives for the resolution of restructuring disputes through complete contracts—for example, buyouts, liquidations, rule-based and one-time debt relief. The view was that private actors, namely the main Czech banks, domestic investment companies, and foreign investors, would have sufficient legal and financial incentives to become the principal agents of restructuring. The failure of this view revealed both the constraints and instability of the inherited networks. The interdependencies between industrial firms and the main banks made the banks view cutting firms off or financing restructuring as highly risky to achieve on their own. In turn, the main investment companies and the stock market in general took on passive roles in corporate governance and restructuring. At the same time, foreign direct investors and Czech managers were unable to reach contractual agreements over division of liabilities and asset control. As they sought third-party guarantees from the government, the Klausians viewed such a role as a threat to their institutional designs, and the proposed joint ventures collapsed.

These failures revealed a key dilemma for restructuring: the combination of inherited socioeconomic ties between firms and banks with the new institutional incentives made investment and workouts highly risky. Given the establishment of hard budget constraints, a new property rights regime, and the strong historical ties among certain firms, why would economic actors be unable to resolve their restructuring conflicts through contractual means or reference to past structures of resource control or norms of reciprocity? Why would the government, and not a private investor, need to become a financial partner and conflict mediator to groups of firms and banks, rather than maintain its distance, offer a new set of resources and incentives, and walk away? In chapters 4 and 5, I examined these issues in detail. In contrast to the tabula rasa and continuity approaches, my *embedded politics* approach emphasized how the initial changes in political institutions undermined collaboration. In turn, the restructuring of networked assets demanded political solutions that intertwined the exploration of new roles of public actors with organizational and production experiments.

Past links created interdependencies and constrained individual discretion over restructuring. But the inability of firm members of both the hierarchical and polycentric networks to cooperate on new definitions of asset control and production strategies as well as gain outside investment grew from two related ways interests and power were changing. On the one hand, decentralized probing (experimentation) not only undermined the use of contracts (be they between members or with outsiders) for typical problems of uncertainty and risk but also broke up the past social order of networks. A firm's or plant's position in a network (e.g., as a critical supplier or customer) was a source of power and goal definition that influenced the bargaining over the definition of formal and informal rules of decision making and resource use.[4] During transformation, members discovered a new set of uncertainties and opportunities that called into question the existing distribution of authority and the goals it imbued in individual members. As members experimented with new forms of organization and product development, the opportunities translated into a reorganization of production that altered their relative positions, discretionary powers, and thus their definition of worldviews (i.e., Am I part of a team or out for myself? Do I remain a supplier for others in the group or should I become an independent firm?). This opened up a set of potential conflicts that made the a priori definition of means and goals indeterminate.[5] These conflicts were about how asset control should be divided and who gets to decide this (i.e., who and how members should decide over their individual or collective future as manufacturers).

On the other hand, the centralization of power and the strict rules for the main banks and liquidation eliminated or severely weakened traditional partners (state bank branches, regional and district councils) of former VHJs from playing their support roles.[6] The authority structure of former VHJ networks was removed and could not resolve the new conflicts between members. These partners had previously helped maintain order within the networks by sharing financial and political risk with VHJ members to resolve internal conflicts—be it through supporting a polycentric authority structure that facilitated consensus or a hierarchical structure that promoted coercion. For instance, with the effective loss of councils as partners, former VHJ networks lost access to public resources, and certain members lost key political allies to support their positions within the group.

In the face of this turmoil, network firms, such as those of Škoda and SST, attempted to use private actors as new external partners, but this failed. The very ambiguity of asset-control rights and production specialties within the networks extended to the new potential partners. Lacking either the financial or local sociopolitical capital to ensure mutual, voluntary commitments, the potential private partners viewed investment into Škoda and SST as too risky. In the collapse of joint ventures, the initial failures of public tenders, and the fragmentation of SST, neither foreign direct investors nor the banks would commit funds without an ex ante clarification of asset control and liabilities.

Because contractual and pure ownership solutions could not resolve the restructuring conflicts surrounding Škoda and SST, the concerned parties required negotiated solutions, in which an external partner could provide credible guarantees for risk sharing. Without the traditional public partners of the networks and no credible institutional mechanisms to support multiparty workouts, the Czech government was forced to take up this role in order to carry out its commitment to the dual goals of privatization (i.e., to delineate property rights and to maintain asset value). Government agencies used their financial and sociopolitical capital to initiate deliberations and then to become both financial and negotiating partners to the former VHJ networks. As shown in the initial progress in the restructuring of Škoda via DDR, the latter role was particularly important since it helped the parties to deliberate about the division of asset control and liabilities and to learn to monitor one another and share information. The government delegated public authority to private actors and committed capital to them under a general agreement. Government agencies no longer imposed governance rules nor simply enforced those given to them by the private actors. Rather, they merged the two goals of privatization and bridged the incomplete contracts by learning to become credible monitors, mediators, and, perhaps most importantly, negotiators with the network actors about the definition of governance rules.

In the next sections, I will discuss the conditions needed for sustaining deliberative forms of restructuring. But before that, consider another key issue suggested in the foregoing discussion: that sociopolitical networks not only demand government-backed negotiated solutions to restructuring but also can impact the course of the negotiations. In turn, the interaction between state policy and network reproduction can shape different formative paths of new governance orders and business organizations.

Scholars have in general tried to explain institutional and organizational outcomes in terms of economic agency or past social structures.[7] For instance, recent research on Latin America, East Asia, and East Central Europe argues that natural endowments of economic and technological resources, say of an industrial sector, determine one's policies and governance structures.[8] Recent work in rational choice theory and economic sociology suggests that the resource distribution and norms of reciprocity from past social structures remain largely unchanged and determine almost unambiguously new institutional and organizational forms.[9] By adhering to either of these approaches, one is usually left to analyze institutional and organizational

transformation in terms of either total discontinuous change or total continuity. However, as matched pairs, the cases of Škoda and TST/SST should
cause one to reconsider these views. They showed evidence of both historical
continuity and significant change in their organizational forms and their relationships to government agencies.

On the one hand, both Škoda and TST/SST were organized by the same
unions, had similar employment size, and employed similar workforces to
produce products in the mechanical engineering sector with more or less
similar technologies. Under communism, both cases had the same owner and
same legal VHJ form; after communism, both were exposed to the same economic shocks and the same privatization policies. Yet they developed starkly
different patterns of conflict, strategic choices, and, eventually, different organizational forms and relationships with government agencies. This variation
in the politics of adjustment and in the formation of economic governance
orders may be difficult to explain if one ignores the historical evolution of the
companies and uses only parameters of economic resources and technologies. The privatization and restructuring strategies of the firms as well as their
ability to employ their machinery and labor for different uses depended as
much, and perhaps more, on the historical social and political relationships
among managers, regional councils, and bank branches as they did on the
technological traits of their assets.[10]

On the other hand, rather than simply reproducing themselves, the former VHJ networks were substantially reconfigured.[11] The clearest example
was the realignment of authority, lines of communication, and commercial
relations. Whereas Škoda previously had a strong centralization of power and
vertical command structure, its restructuring via DDR substantially dispersed power and increased internal horizontal relations by strengthening
subsidiaries' decision-making rights and direct access to external resources,
suppliers, and customers. Whereas TST had a relatively decentralized distribution of authority and resources, its successor, SST, became dominated by a
single member firm, controlling access to key financial resources and export
markets.

In chapters 4 and 5 I have argued that these differences in governance
orders and changes in network relations were due to ways that firms and
plants, like those of Škoda and SST, were embedded in different sociopolitical
networks. These networks shaped the different choices for member firms
about network reproduction and the basic patterns of conflict and internal
power. But because industrial networks were socially as well as *politically* constructed under communism, the Czech depoliticization strategy agenda altered the authority structures of the networks and the ability of members to
resolve the conflicts. In turn, the different patterns of conflicts created differ-

ent conditions for government-backed negotiations about the rewriting of governance rules and the division of resources—that is, the selection and roles of public and private bargaining partners, the relative bargaining power, and the boundaries of the firms themselves.

Hierarchical networks, such as Škoda's, had a history of the tight internal subcontracting links and centralized formal and informal control of resources. The combination of depoliticization policies and tight socioeconomic links led members to try to privatize themselves as a whole through vouchers and joint ventures and to form a holding company that allowed an internal diffusion of authority. When members were unable to resolve the subsequent restructuring conflicts, the potential destabilizing impact of the collapse of a holding company on the economy quickly brought the government and the main banks to the negotiating table. This was actually a benefit to government, as it still had significant bargaining resources to leverage (debt relief and a large equity stake) and a newly elected, strong coalition that afforded agencies the political leeway to pursue an extended, experimental monitoring role. In turn, the MPO and, to a certain degree, the FNM used both the bargaining resources and their discretion to force Škoda and the banks to decentralize decision making and improve information and risk sharing through iterative deliberations. The resulting governance order, DDR (delegated deliberative restructuring), altered the distribution of power within hierarchical networks. Formal ownership was concentrated and critical operational resources remained largely within the formal boundaries of a single firm (the holding). But subsidiaries gained significant decision-making and bargaining powers with the political support of the government and the direct financial links to the banks.

Polycentric networks, such as TST/SST, had a history of decentralized political and production resources at the local and firm levels. Although this history led members to choose full autonomy (privatize individually) and coordinate themselves via a new association and its equity fund, the effective removal of district and regional councils brought a loss of political buttressing for network cohesion. The ensuing fragmentation of the network created conditions for the emergence of a new internal asymmetry of power and for a government-backed negotiated solutions. As ZPS and its allied investment company (PPF) attempted to impose a new production and governance order over SST firms, they ignited a direct confrontation with the main banks and the government over control of national financial institutions and the privatization of some SST members. The government did not react to what it saw as the insolvency of many, small and medium-sized, already privatized firms, but rather to the actions of ZPS and its allies. This delayed reaction left government agencies at a disadvantage. They had relatively few existing bargaining resources under their direct control. And by 1996 Klaus wanted to reconsolidate his power over a contentious governing coalition, leaving the bargaining agencies (FNM, MPO, KOB) with little discretion to pursue extended deliberations and generate new resources to leverage in negotiations. In turn, although the government averted an immediate financial crisis, it simply reified the positions of ZPS and PPF and was unable to alter the behavior of both shareholders and stakeholders. In contrast to Škoda and TST's former structure, formal ownership of SST was relatively dispersed among several investment companies and the critical production, financial, and training resources lay largely outside the confines of a single firm. But de facto power was concentrated in the hands of ZPS management and PPF.

In this account of the institutional transformation of the Czech Republic, I have developed throughout the book an *embedded politics approach* that stresses the role of ongoing sociopolitical relations and structures to influence and remold the conceptions and strategies of economic actors. Rather than deriving the interests and power of actors, and thus the projected institutional designs, from purely structural or economic factors, I have focused on the ways that two levels of politics—the macropolitics of implementing transformation policies and micropolitics of intranetwork asset control—interact and alter the views and resources that public and private actors have at hand. In turn, my approach revises the role of politics in comparative analysis of institutional change and economic renovation in two ways. First, using sociopolitical networks helps specify the relative power and interests of key public and private institutional actors and how changes in policy can shift these variables. Second, this approach focuses attention on the way the distribution of public and private power can impact the ability of transforming societies to sustain and learn from their institutional experiments through deliberative forms of governance. I will now turn to these two issues in the following sections.

Restructuring and Institutional Change in Comparative Perspective

An embedded politics approach attempts to strengthen comparative analysis by drawing on historical institutionalism and economic sociology. First, instead of focusing on individual actors (e.g., firms), national institutional structures, or vague sociological concepts like *field* or *habitus,* using sociopolitical networks as the unit of analysis allows one to identify how different actors are connected to one another and to the broader institutional environment, and thus the context in which the power and goals for both the group and individual are constructed and reconstructed.[12] Sociopolitical networks constitute channels of power, resources, and communication that mediate relations between distinct economic and political actors. In so doing, they help define the contours or membership of a group of actors as well as points of common and potentially conflicting interests.[13]

Second, sociopolitical networks help show how micro-level organizational experiments and macro-level institutional experiments can influence one another, and thus define or change the relative strength and views of participants.[14] An essential aspect of sociopolitical networks is that core members require access to external political and financial resources in order to share the risks of both experimenting with production and organization and maintaining an authority structure.[15] The experiments among core members can create new internal conflicts and thus the need for new types of resources, conflict mediation, and rules. These changes put new demands on both private and public institutions (i.e., banks, commercial and regulatory laws, state economic or administrative bodies) and can bring pressure for a change in the roles of these institutions. In turn, the reorganization of public resources can impact both the responsiveness of government to these pressures and the ability of interconnected public and private actors to experiment with new methods of governance and restructuring.

A first-order extrapolation of this approach is to identify the dominant patterns of sociopolitical networks in which firms were embedded prior to the collapse of the previous regime. One can then identify two key variables: (1) the distribution of power and pattern of associationalism among relevant members; and (2) the public organs that are positioned and disposed to resolve restructuring hold-ups by experimenting with the roles of risk sharer and conflict mediator. With these two variables, one can evaluate how the interaction between the reorganization of certain networked assets and macropolitical approaches to institutional change creates different types of bargaining conditions for the participating public and private actors. My analysis of how hierarchical and polycentric networks shaped contrasting strategies and bargaining conditions within the industrial sector allowed me to control for other explanatory variables. One may find other types or combinations of sociopolitical networks in, say, Hungary and Poland. David Stark's work on Hungary, for instance, suggests that polycentric networks may be the dominant form, and in turn that recent efforts to give local governments more authority and resources for privatization, development, and bankruptcy procedures are helpful.[16] But my emphasis here on how changes in political power can impact the ability public and private actors to initiate and sustain institutional experiments allows us to highlight key differences between countries in their approaches to restructuring and patterns of institutional creation.

Consider first the current efforts to revitalize the Czech economy. I have already analyzed how the Czech government's initiation of, movement away from, and then return to the depoliticization agenda halted, advanced, and stymied restructuring and governance experiments. Consequently, the firms, banks, and investment funds that were able to consolidate control over the different former industrial networks became insolvent, and subnational governments remained relatively weak. In turn, the government's recent re-engagement of industrial actors is largely back at the commanding heights, with central agencies entering into negotiations with the main banks and a few large industrial companies. In 1999, the newly elected Social Democrat government launched the Revitalization Agency, a subsidiary of the state-owned Consolidation Bank (a clearinghouse for bad bank loans) that is managed by a consortium of private turnaround specialists and investment bankers. This was a response to the lack of workout mechanisms available in the Klausian institutional design that led creditors and firms to remain in a stalemate. The agency is attempting to restructure and reprivatize both the largest industrial firms and main banks through a governance structure similar to DDR. Given the severity of the current economic conditions and the change in government, the agency was able to acquire new bargaining power by consolidating the debt of the target firms, for example, Škoda and ZPS, and swapping it for equity to diminish the power of shareholders and exert control over the stakeholders. Similar to DDR, the agency is using limited financial assistance, privatization, and incentive contracts to initiate deliberations among the creditors and different subsidiaries to reorganize assets and resell them to foreign strategic investors.

As of late 2000, there were no indications that government officials were conscious of using this experiment to reform and enhance the institutional infrastructure that would further growth, such as securities and banking laws, vocational training, or the export insurance program. But the government has begun reforming bankruptcy laws to provide workout provisions and emboldening new regional government and small-firm assistance agencies. One could question whether a single agency would be sufficient to facilitate decentralized problem solving and help revive firms embedded in polycentric networks. Probably no single agency can accomplish this. But one may consider how the principles of DDR could be applied to various institutional reforms and what the political conditions may be to advance this process. In this light, a comparative analysis of the relative success of Poland through the lens of an embedded politics approach may offer suggestions.

Figure 6.1 and table 6.1 show the considerable divergence in the growth of industrial output and manufacturing small and medium-sized firms (SMEs). How would one explain this? As discussed in chapter 3, Poland, rela-

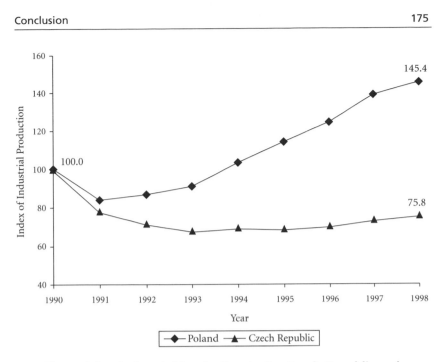

Figure 6.1.   Industrial Production in the Czech Republic and Poland

Source: OECD (1999)

tive to the Czech Republic, had problematic starting conditions, according to the depoliticization view: severe macroeconomic and budgetary imbalances; strong social groups, like Solidarity, that blocked mass privatization until 1995–96 (and even then it was rather limited in scope); and worker-council veto powers over corporate reorganization. Poland did not pour public funds into industries nor did it have significant private and SME participation in manufacturing in the 1980s.[17] Moreover, although Poland's maintenance of industrial foreign trade associations into the mid-1980s created strong socioeconomic linkages within certain groups of firms, recent research has shown that constituent firms had serious cooperation problems in the early 1990s.[18]

My analysis of the Czech case suggested that restructuring was impeded by two factors: (1) the lack of mechanisms in which public and private actors could negotiate iteratively over the restructuring of networked assets; (2) the centralization of power in such ways as to hinder the initiation and sustainability of such deliberations. The Polish approach to transformation, though not always intentionally, sharply contrasted with the Czech approach on both of these issues. The Poles created mechanisms that enabled stakeholders and outsiders as well as public and private actors to negotiate over time the reorganization of

TABLE 6.1.   Divergence in SME Growth in Manufacturing

	Czech Republic (1995)	Poland (1997)
Share of employment (%)	35	52.5
Share of sales (%)	29.5	37

Source: Zemplinerova (1998), Polish Foundation for SME Promotion and Development (1999), and Institute for Small Business Development (1999).

Note: Firms with less than 250 employees. In 1989, the SME share of manufacturing employment for Poland was about 10 percent and for Czechoslovakia about 1 percent. See Acs and Audretsch (1993).

assets and the redefinition of property rights. Rather than focus on rapid mass privatization, the Poles created legal vehicles that tied ownership transformation to the restructuring of assets. Central, regional, and local governments played significant roles in initiating, financially supporting, and monitoring the negotiated transformation of property rights and the restructuring of assets—for both large and small firms. In turn, one could argue that the comparative success of Poland was its ability to restructure by using mechanisms based on delegation and deliberation and to strengthen subnational governments. Consider, briefly, three major areas of Polish policy: stakeholder privatization, the Enterprise-Bank Restructuring Program, and the empowerment of subnational governments.

Stakeholder Privatization through Multiparty Negotiation and Monitoring

The very 1990 law that legalized the worker-council veto powers to block mass privatization enabled the councils to legally dissolve their firms and rent, lease, or sell the assets to a new company. The evolution of this law produced arguably the most important paths (termed *direct privatization* and *liquidation*) of property reform in Poland.[19] As mass privatization languished, by the end of 1996 these two channels had initiated over 2,711, or over two-thirds of, ownership transfers in Poland. By far, the most successful and widespread method of privatization—as measured in terms of project completion, nonbank privatization revenues, number of employees and firms, economic performance, and default rates—was the lease-buy option of direct privation that allowed managers and workers to buy out a set of assets over time through very advantageous state-subsidized financing.[20]

These paths of privatization, particularly the lease-buy option, made two critical contributions toward network reorganization. First, as opposed to focusing on delineation of ownership rights, these routes made asset restructuring and the reordering of property simultaneous and gradual through multi-

party negotiations. For instance, the leasing arrangements effectively were incentive contracts that not only tied the option for full ownership to the reorganization and efficient use of assets but also provided risk sharing for actors to
pursue new production and organizational experiments. Third-party asset
purchases, leasing, and liquidations (which effectively kept assets as going concerns via purchases and leases), all required approvals of employee councils,
management boards, and the relevant public agency. The negotiation mechanisms denied clean break-offs but allowed actors to gradually gain autonomy
for certain assets while maintaining consideration of the strategic interests of
other network members.

Second, public institutional actors, notably the forty-nine *voivodships*
(regional administrations) that received responsibility over most firms as their
founders, became central in facilitating dispute resolutions and consultations
among firms. As the founder of an enterprise, the voivodship could initiate or
block a liquidation petition, was charged with screening and vetting direct privatization projects before they were passed to the central Ministry of Ownership Transformation for final approval, and negotiated with lease-buy candidates about certain terms of repayment. As such, the voivodship was
negotiating with and mediating between the various stakeholders and competing claimants to assets. Moreover, as an agent of the central government
charged with monitoring compliance with the various agreements, it collaborated with other public agencies, firms, and banks to pool information and
learn more about the activities and problems of firms in the region.[21]

Enterprise-Bank Restructuring Program

As a response to the failure of voluntary standstill agreements and the general slowness of standard bankruptcy procedures, the 1993 government-
sponsored workout vehicle (EBRP) mirrored this more micro-level development and provided a broader mechanism for the disciplined flow of
resources to the transforming state firms without abrupt changes in ownership. The policy, namely the "bank conciliation" procedure, provided a
framework for state-owned banks to lead workouts of the largest debtors,
eventually restructuring over 60 percent of outstanding debt. The relatively
positive evaluations of this program, even by the World Bank, highlight a
structure and set of principles that in many ways were similar to those of
DDR.[22] Public-private debt sharing came in the form of rule-based debt relief, government capital injections and back-taxes renegotiations. But in
moving beyond the role of simply first mover, the Polish government combined the principles of delegation and deliberation. While banks received
the authority to restructure firms, general benchmarks for the continuation

or termination of assistance helped government representatives (as senior creditors and owners themselves), the banks and the target firm to monitor one another and share information.

Moreover, government intervention not only broke an existing stalemate between banks and firms, similar to that in the Czech Republic, but also provided a vehicle in which banks could learn more about serving clients and the problems manufacturing firms faced. For instance, in his detailed analysis of the heavily industrialized Lodz region, Dornisch notes that perhaps the most important outcome of EBRP in general, and bank conciliation in particular, was that the regional bank learned how to tap back into interfirm networks and use them to create what he calls "project networks" for more efficient ex ante and ex post monitoring of financing new and existing firms.[23] The project networks were vital to the regional bank's successful development of regional equity and venture capital funds.

Regional and Local Governments

Like the Czechs, the Poles were concerned about the influence of communist apparatchiks at the regional and local levels and the strength of a unitary state. Unlike the Czechs, the Poles delegated to regional (voivodships) and municipal (gminas) governments, not necessarily significantly more resources, but much greater authority over various policy areas and the use of resources.[24] For instance, besides the Klausian efforts to effectively eliminate regional and local power and the establishment of new regional councils only in 1998, the Czechs established (principally at the order of the central government) only two regional development agencies (RDAs) in the regions with the highest unemployment. Polish voivodships and gminas had created sixty-six RDAs by 1996 throughout the country. While privatization and economic restructuring rested solely in the hands of the central government in the CR, voivodships and, to some degree, gminas were from the beginning given significant responsibilities, particularly in becoming the legal founders of many manufacturing firms. Indeed, the Polish gminas have been consistently cited for their improvement in services and their unique ability to create a vibrant municipal bond market. Moreover, recent research in Poland reveals high and strong correlations between the implementation of development policies and the density and diversity of public-private institutions in voivodships, on the one hand, and relatively high rates industrial restructuring, participation in direct privatization (especially via the lease-buy options), SME creation, and the reception of FDI on the other.[25]

One clearly cannot overstate the impact on restructuring of a particular administrative law or budgetary indicator, as continuing criticisms of voivodship accountability and resource capacity.[26] Nonetheless, voivodships and gminas have proven to play important roles, less as profound managers of the economy, but rather as agents of institutional experimentation—to harness their limited, but nonetheless existing, political and organizational capital to revitalize informational, social, and economic links among firms, banks, and one another.[27]

In exploring their legal roles as founders of many state firms and as overseers of regional development, voivodships were most effective when they focused first on becoming an effective monitor of firms in their jurisdictions. To do so, they combined their relative authority and organizational resources with the social, informational, and human resources of regional banks, firms, consultants, gminas, and the local offices of the central tax agency. These initial steps toward pooling diverse sources of knowledge and information became first and foremost a resource for economic actors to expand their portfolios of strategies, collaborators and project screening capabilities. For instance, when EBRP was launched, the regional banks lacked effective monitoring capabilities. In turn, they began to supplement their deficiencies by participating in regular regional council meetings and accessing the voivod database, particularly on the firms that were in EBRP and had the voivodship as its founder. In return, the banks began to consider the strategic goals of the voivodship, regional labor bureau, and the tax authority regarding the firms directly and indirectly under their control.

This interaction via information sharing allowed participants to begin to learn about one another's capabilities and interests and define some basic areas of joint action and risk and resource pooling. For instance, the pilot experience in restructuring firms in EBRP, and in some case becoming co-owners of them, led the Lodz Bank and Voivodship to comanage a closed World Bank investment fund for initially twenty firms. A tie such as this fortified horizontal links among related public and private actors.

These developments were gradual and often initiatives failed. But it was the continued presence and efforts of the voivodships and gminas as well as the impulse coming from programs like EBRP and direct privatization that allowed the actors to learn from the failure and recombine pieces of the potential interorganizational networks. Learning came not simply about how to evaluate a particular project but also from how to define a reasonable set of common projects and how to assess one another's actions and contributions. As Dornisch emphasizes in his analysis of the revitalization of Lodz, a voivodship that went from being a rust belt to one of the most vibrant regions of SME development and restructuring, learning about project selection was intimately connected to learning how to monitor one another and share authority over common assets. Just as private and public actors were assessing the prospects of new projects, they were also gaining experience about what were the most effective roles one another could play.

The foregoing analysis of Poland is naturally incomplete. However, when taken in combination with the findings of the Czech case and my earlier arguments about my embedded politics approach, the comparative analysis makes two strong suggestions about our understanding of economic governance and institutional creation in transforming societies.

First, because of the necessity but indeterminacy of public-private risk-sharing mechanisms, the creation of new rules and institutions governing the public domain is simultaneous to and mutually adaptive with that of the private domain.[28] This process of mutual adaptation and experimentation can make state agencies, however, vulnerable to a variety of moral hazard and adverse selection problems. The standard approaches advocating depoliticization of transformation have tried to avoid these problems by removing or insulating government agencies from society. In contrast, I have argued that mutual adaptation between micro- and macro-level institutional experiments is best maintained through the creation of structures that facilitate disciplined deliberation among public and private actors. Deliberation promotes collective learning by helping actors to compare their different restructuring experiments while defining a set of common goals. It is disciplined in "that at every moment the actors must explain why they are pursuing one course of action as opposed to others, and must announce the measures by which their performance must be judged."[29]

Second, the very notions of the malleability and political construction of power and views that make deliberative governance possible equally expose the fragility of concerted learning. That is, if certain mechanisms and policies can help actors reevaluate their ongoing relationships with one another and share control over resources, then one can imagine that certain political-economic conditions are more or less conducive for initiating and sustaining learning and thus translating multiple public-private experiments into productive legislation and not forays into self-dealing. Solidarity's history in a developing strong grassroots organizational network and strengthening local democracy may well show the importance of well-organized social movements for transforming countries.[30] My brief comparative analysis may be more pragmatic. Public power and resources are necessary for breaking the political economic constraints to deliberative forms of restructuring. Moreover, the creation of multiple channels of political power, in national and subnational governments, is an essential part of governing and adapting to multiple institutional experiments. In the final section of this chapter, I will address these issues by exploring a deliberative and participatory democratic approach to governing institutional experiments in emerging industrial democracies.

The Politics of Governing Institutional Experiments

A central dilemma in the restructuring of East Central Europe is the identification of the public goods to be provided by the government.[31] Identification of a public good includes formulating a role for the government and a set of rules that govern the relationships between public and private institutional actors. As discussed throughout this book, the approaches advocating depoliticization derive ex ante an optimal set of public rules and roles to promote investment by assuming transforming societies are composed of atomized individuals. Once the system of secure ownership rights, as in the economistic view, or clear rules for state intervention into missing markets, as in the developmental statist view, are defined, there is no need for substantive discussions between state and societal actors about the creation and revision of rules of economic governance. Design and implementation of the great leap forward requires mainly a strong government executive that empowers an elite change team to enact reforms without the intervention from social actors and parliament. Approaches focusing on past social structures may view strong states and market liberalization as destabilizing, but they also minimize the role of politics. New public rules and roles emerge from past social capital, in turn preserving the prior bonds of trust and structures of power, which cannot be created but only reinforced.

This book has emphasized an alternative lesson about institutional transformation. I have argued that institutional creation is an ongoing set of experiments in organization and rule-making that are shaped by the ways particular sociopolitical networks mediate between public and private actors. Because these experiments take place at several levels of society, the need for collective learning and monitoring demands structures that facilitate frequent deliberation among the relevant private and public actors. Moreover, these structures are politically initiated since iterative information and risk sharing between interdependent actors requires publicly secured means of voice for participants and initial public resources.

The Czech case showed that because firms were embedded in sociopolitical networks, defining control rights was simultaneous to maintaining asset value. As economically interdependent members experimented with different restructuring strategies, they also had to experiment with different forms of asset control and decision making. The combination of the uncertainties of these experiments with a debilitated authority structure prevented members from deciding on their own how to define control rights and an optimal production strategy. In turn, the resolution of restructuring conflicts through the complete contract methods or prior social capital was hindered. The Czechs began to encourage risk sharing and restructuring via blurred control rights by creating mechanisms that empowered distinct groups of private and public actors to negotiate the terms of restructuring and the division of asset control and liabilities. As government agencies delegated public restructuring authority to private actors and became financial and negotiating partners, they helped connect the ongoing micro- and macroexperiments in institution building. This facilitated two types of learning. First, public and private actors learned how to monitor one another as they shared information and the risk to carry out various restructuring tasks. Second, they learned how to explore different views on goals and means and revise governance rules through joint, iterative evaluations of one another in their new roles.

In this view, the confidence building measures taken to initiate and maintain restructuring experiments are a microcosm of a broader ongoing experiment in democratic institution building via government backed deliberations. Private actors are learning from one another what combination of governance rules can facilitate joint investments and limit opportunistic behavior. As discussed in development of DDR and in restructuring of Polish firms and banks, this was possible mainly through government agencies becoming financial partners and mediators. The government agencies were learning which roles and legal measures could help private actors become more independent and maintain cooperation. At the same time, the agencies were learning which methods could ensure the compliance of private actors in their restructuring tasks and could limit the chances that state participation did not lead to continuous state bailouts. Because of the uncertainty and interactive nature of this learning process between public and private actors about restructuring steps and the redistribution of assets and risk, it is difficult to write ex ante clear and detailed rules (i.e., complete contracts) or depend solely on prior social bonds for governance and cooperation.

The Czech experiments with mechanisms of public-private learning, notably DDR and now the Revitalization Agency, should not be looked at in isolation. For instance, the relative success of Polish restructuring and strength of Polish capital markets can be largely attributed to public-private learning experiments for the development of a strong regulatory system for state founded investment funds, a workout vehicle for large banks and firms, and regional restructuring networks.[32] In all these cases the boundaries of firms and the government remained were blurred and initial institutional designs were rather vague. Advances in rules governing risk sharing and value creation were made rather through the government delegating restructuring authority to

private actors and using mechanisms that forced public and private participants to reveal information and evaluate jointly their success and failures.

This understanding of restructuring and institution building as ongoing
learning experiments is increasingly common in political economy and economic sociology.[33] For instance, recent work that combines political con-
structionism and incomplete markets theory argues that because of the uncertainties from imperfect information one can not a priori determine the
net effect on society of any one combination of rules governing market transactions.[34] This work has shown that societies have created a number of public-private institutions, such as Fannie Mae in the U.S. mortgage markets,
lender of last resort in banking, and workout provisions for bankruptcy, to
help public and private actors share the risk of learning which governance
rules and roles of government can maintain economic stability while promoting investment.[35] In all these institutions, public authority is delegated to
private actors, and a regulatory structure is established to facilitate disciplined deliberations among public and private actors. This combination of
delegation and deliberation allows participants not only to monitor one another but also to evaluate and potentially revise the rules about risk sharing
and the use of public funds.

Another example can be found in the recent convergence between the
development literature that grew out of Hirschman's concept of unbalanced
growth and the more recent literature on disequilibrium learning in business
organizations and product development in advanced industrialized countries.[36] The common observations of relatively successful strategies of economic adjustment and innovation are that public and private actors create
practices that help them: (1) create new ideas to existing and potential problems through provoking changes in static systems and comparing the performance of subsequent organizational and production experiments; and (2) revise anterior performance measures on the basis of the comparisons to push
existing experiments further and develop alternative experiments for failed
ones.[37] In order to induce the risk sharing and the flow of information
needed to build on the experiment, these practices center on the ability of actors to open up the boundaries between the state and society or between private companies. But in doing so, one always runs the risk of individuals or
groups taking advantage of the public externalities, such as shared risk and
information. The result can easily be a breakdown of cooperation or a growth
in collusion, both of which undermine the learning process.

Authors of corporate and policy learning have, in turn, spent a great
amount of energy focusing on ways to reconcile methods of learning with
methods of effective monitoring and accountability. A major outcome of this
work has been the study of both public and private governance structures

based on the delegation of authority and deliberation.[38] Delegation of authority—be it public authority and resources to private associations or private asset control and decision-making powers to suppliers and subordinate units—helps increase flexibility and the generation of multiple organizational experiments by empowering new or previously weak actors and tapping diverse channels of knowledge and resources. For instance, recent work on the reform of social services and product development shows that delegation allows local actors to pursue a number of strategic solutions while forcing them to reveal their results to one another and superior bodies (i.e., central government agencies and corporate headquarters).[39] Even before the transformation in East Central Europe, observers and practitioners of the privatization of public services noted that privatization was not about eliminating the national or local governments from the maintenance of services.[40] Rather, it was about the initiation of institutional experiments that moved the government from the role of administrator to one of overseer or monitor of private actors providing the services. The combination of local experimentation and information disclosure helps the superior bodies learn which more generalized rules and organizational methods may work better under different conditions by comparing performance and behavior of actors over time. The problem for superior bodies is creating a regulatory or monitoring framework at the same time they write a contract with the service or product suppliers. Since one presupposes the other, the initial "sale" contract, as in the cases of Škoda and SST, or the lease-buy contracts with managers and workers and the debt-conciliation agreements with the banks and large firms in Poland are incomplete and become the starting point for developing a new monitoring framework. In turn, the maintenance of learning and the development of a new framework necessitates a mechanism that can help the participants ensure a minimum level of compliance and revise the terms of their relationship as lessons of success and failure arise.

Disciplined deliberation complements delegation by providing methods of rule making that enhance the monitoring of redistributed authority and the learning from a variety of even conflicting approaches to and goals of problem solving. First, since learning disrupts a stable set of enforceable rules and thus undermines the maintenance of cooperation through complete contracts or agreements, disciplined deliberations help actors create rules for evaluating one another when one may not be able to fulfill a prior agreement.[41] That is, deliberations demand that the parties demonstrate the reasons for their choice of strategy and for their successes or failures. In doing so, the parties reveal information that can be used to revise initial governance rules (e.g., performance criteria, the division of decision-making control, etc.) but maintain continued collective participation in a set of projects or ex-

periments. Second, deliberation among several parties enhances the accountability of both participating public agencies and private groups and helps
limit abuse or favoritism.[42] The open lines of communication and information allows participants to judge if they are being treated fairly relative to one
another and a means to voice their concerns. Moreover, scholars note that accountability, and the general stability of deliberative structures, can be improved when parliamentary commissions or the judiciary are empowered to
review regularly the actions of participating public agencies. For instance,
when the Czech government reengaged the restructuring of Škoda and the
Czech insurance company, the alterations in the original privatization plans
incited parliamentary reviews. These reviews aimed to ensure that inappro-
priate use of assets was not occurring and demanded that the Ministry of Industry and the Fund for National Property, for instance, explain the actions
they were taking. Third, in enhancing monitoring deliberation helps individual persons or groups build cohesion and a sense of otherness.[43] That is, frequent negotiation and information disclosure may not necessarily fuse the
interests of different actors, but it can generate greater respect and deference
for competing interests by helping participants learn about one another's
concerns and limitations. In turn, participants can learn to let different
strategies coexist, give one another the benefit of the doubt, and continue cooperation on a basic common goal if they know that they will be able to evaluate one another openly in the near future.

A major benefit of governance through delegation and deliberation in
transforming societies is that societies can avoid the often painful pattern of
setting strict roles and rules only to see their usefulness evaporate under new
circumstances. The result is that society jerks frequently between periods of
profound change and relative stability.[44] And the cost is that rules created to
facilitate short-term adjustment undermine that ability of societies to adapt
themselves over the medium and long term.[45] For instance, in the wake of recent currency crises, countries in Latin America, East Central Europe, and East
Asia are finding themselves setting even stricter rules about government intervention, foreign investment, and the behavior of financial institutions.[46] There
is strong evidence that greater limitations on forms of private lending and the
participation of public agencies in restructuring can lead to decreased investment, product development, and thus a weaker currency again.[47] Governance
through delegation and deliberation may be able to avoid these spasms by
having public and private actors experiment with a variety of financial regulations and public investment programs, learn from these experiments, and
gradually adjust the rules while maintaining confidence in the market. In this
view, institutional change happens continuously and in small steps, not
through precise, one-time plans.

The critical issue currently facing countries of East Central Europe is whether they can continue and expand experiments in deliberative restructuring by generalizing what they have learned to create democratically legitimated laws that help balance private interests and power and further institutional adaptation. The embedded politics approach points to two particularly troubling political impediments but also potential solutions.

The first problem for this form of governance is that by engaging a number of competing groups, the government will become overburdened with conflicting demands.[48] For instance, in the Czech case central government agencies, even the new Revitalization Agency, are participating in restructuring through different governance orders. These orders constitute potentially different governance rules and roles for government agencies. The problem is that the contrasting demands, power distributions, and rules can conflict with one another and overwhelm the government. For instance, the current reorganization of ZPS by the Revitalization Agency will impact other members of SST, who will likely demand different types of export guarantees, financial regulations, and vocational training assistance than those conducive to holding companies like Škoda. With limited political and financial resources, it seems safe to say that the Czech government cannot satisfy all the main demands of Škoda and SST nor necessarily create detailed institutional rules that will stably govern the behavior of the two groups. Students of deliberation would reply that the diversity of participants and information combined with a deepening of the deliberative and participatory principles of governance should help increase government learning and institutional adaptability.[49]

The brief comparative analysis of Poland in the last section showed that the Poles may have averted the problem of overwhelming central government agencies with too many conflicting demands by delegating significant authority on privatization and restructuring issues to the voivodships and gminas. These subnational governments were better positioned than central agencies to respond to emerging problems, pool local information, and develop ex ante and ex post monitoring capabilities. But as recent research has shown in such diverse cases as Italy, Ireland, Brazil, and Russia, decentralizing public power without a responsive national governing framework can also become a recipe for regional disparity and local corruption.[50]

A potential solution to the problems of both overburdening the central government and regional disparity is revealed in the recent work on decentralized development in Latin America. This work shows how national and provincial governments have nurtured collaboration and learning between previously entrenched and hostile subnational and subprovincial governments.[51] For instance, since 1992 the federal government of Argentina, with the aid of the World Bank and Inter-American Development Bank (IDB), has been tried to strengthen provincial governments as part of its program to renew financial stability and growth.[52] Such a process has been hindered by a history of centralism, local clientelism, and open hostility between the various political parties that govern the provincial and federal administrations. Provincial governments are trying to integrate the reforms in public administration, public services, and infrastructure with the creation of public-private consortia for support of small and medium-sized firms. The idea is that financial stability depends as much on prudent national fiscal and monetary policies as it does on increased lending diversification, growth, and decentralized government participation in the often forgotten interior of the country. The policy experiments are closely linked to experiments in federalism and deliberative forms of governance. The World Bank and IDB have made the loans directly to the provincial governments, which are responsible for loan repayment and the actual development and management of the programs. At the same time, a new department, which is governed by both the Ministry of Interior and a council of provincial ministers, acts as a monitor of, provider of technical assistance to, and coordinator of lessons learned from experiments among the provinces. The department utilizes the information revealed through both its own benchmarking and the deliberations over the financing of the diverse provincial projects to improve the monitoring of provinces and cross-provincial learning. Participants within the council have also used this experience for negotiations on a new federal framework of taxation and spending powers. The mechanisms of delegation and deliberation that have governed the provincial reforms have effectively helped federal and provincial public authorities learn how to monitor one another, share revenues and costs, and build mutual respect and confidence—the lack of which had impeded any thought of decentralization in taxing and administrative powers.

Similar to Stark and Bruszt's concept of extended accountability and Cohen and Sabel's model of directly deliberative polyarchy,[53] such an example suggests that the conditions of a separation of powers, secured rights of participation, and an empowerment of local actors are vital for furthering the monitoring and learning process in previously exclusive areas of problem solving. These conditions both enable and constrain actors' discretion in encouraging frequent discussions by diverse groups of related problems that can produce, as discussed already in this section, what Stark and Bruszt call "programmatic pragmatism." But Stark and Bruszt speak of these conditions mainly with respect to the constraints parliamentary democracy places on the executive. Such a focus on the central government may lead to a misinterpretation of these conditions and leads to a second impediment to furthering deliberative governance. That is, these political conditions must apply to private groups and the different levels of government. For instance, even though Stark and Bruszt cite Czech parliamentary democracy meeting these conditions and enabled the Klaus-led governing coalition to become pragmatic, it was this very government that failed to further the gains made from DDR, ignored the fragmentation of SST, and refused to alter the initial bargaining conditions with ZPS and PPF. When analyzed though through the lens of an embedded politics approach, these failures suggest a deeper implication for the aforementioned political conditions.

As discussed in the concluding sections of chapters 4 and 5, Czech parliamentary democracy still produced a coalition that put control over economic policy mainly in the hands of Klaus and his closest allies. This group's interweaving of its hold on power with its determination to fulfill a depoliticized privatization fundamentally conflicted with any discussion of significant changes in the organization of government and its policies that were vital for a public-private collaboration and learning. For instance, after cases like Škoda were back on their feet through DDR, the government diluted reforms in banking and securities regulation and curbed export insurance and financing programs, viewing any such changes as only fanning the flames of the interministerial and intracoalition disputes that emerged during DDR. By the time the ZPS and PPF began negotiating directly with the Consolidation Bank, the Fund for National Property, and the Ministry of Finance, the former two agencies had been put under effective control of the latter, whose minister was a leading member of Klaus' party. In contrast to this rigidity, the Polish government has appeared more responsive to pursuing institutional experiments for the restructuring of large banks and firms, establishing a capital market, and fostering small and medium-size manufacturing firms. Why the difference?

One reason may be that the aforementioned conditions must apply not only to the central government but also to regional and local governments. That is, competing approaches to these issues backed by political power and resources will stimulate and sustain deliberative governance when subnational governments are empowered and secured legitimate channels to voice and press their opinions. This view resonates with the embedded politics approach, which has claimed that those public actors that are most closely positioned to the key nexus points of the sociopolitical networks in which firms are embedded need to have the political and financial resources to take on the roles of risk sharer and conflict mediator for relevant economic actors. In the Czech case, the elimination of regional councils with no replacement (until 1998–99) and the weakening of municipal governments not only led the central government to take on these roles but also eliminated any alternative voice in policy. In contrast, for instance, Poland, however un-evenly, has gradually strengthened provincial and municipal governments, which also became a key political channel for various elements of Solidarity to pursue initiatives often in conflict with central government officials of their parties as well as the reformed communists.[54] It may be no coincidence that it was at these levels of society where public-private development net-works were created, the recombination of asset were gradually negotiated through the policies called *liquidation* and *direct privatization,* and banks and industrial firms beckoned for a government-backed workout vehicle.[55]

The suggestion, then, is that fortification of subnational governments in combination with national frameworks of deliberative democracy will largely determine whether public-private experiments with institution building will be initiated and adequate monitoring and learning will be sustained. Resis-tance toward this direction will not emerge simply from a perceived loss of control at the commanding heights, but particularly from the realization that experimentation may lead to institutional forms of economic and political governance that are not found in our textbooks. Yet when confronting that fear, political, business, and labor leaders as well as academics would be better served if they stopped looking at the diverse governance institutions as they now exist in developed nations and turned instead to an examination of how past public and private actors learned to monitor and share risk to initiate and build those institutions in the first place. I bet those historical agents of change were as nervous as our East European friends are today.

Appendix

List of Interviewees
(Conducted from October 1993
to March 1995)

Zdeněk Bárta, Chief, Sales Section, Škoda TS, Plzeň, s.r.o.
Pavel Bergmann, Director/Chairman of the Board, HYTOS, a.s.
František Bernášek, Member of Executive Committee, FNM
Jiří Bezrouk, Director of Marketing, TOS Kuřim, a.s.
Jiří Bílek, Senior Advisor, Chemapol Group, a.s.
Luděk Blažík, Financial Director, Šmeral, a.s.
Antonie Bočková, Head of Department of Organizational Legislation, Škoda Koncern
     Plzeň, a.s.
Jaroslav Borák, Chief Director, Section of Metallurgy, Engineering, and
     Electrotechnology, MPO
Ladislav Bořek, President/General Director, Šmeral, a.s.
Vladimír Brichta, Managing Director, Škoda Tobacco Machinery, Plzeň, s.r.o.
Karel Brož, Vice President, Technical Director, ČKD Kompresory, a.s.
Miroslav Brychta, Technical Deputy, Metalpres, s.r.o.
Jaromír Černý, Head of Design Department, Sugar Cane Mills, Škoda TS, Plzeň, s.r.o.
Michal Černý, Director, Business Development, AERO Praha, a.s.
Roman Češka, First Deputy Minister, MP (1992–94); Chairman, FNM (1994–98)
Aleš Chytrý, Vice President, Department of Finance, Škoda Jaderné Strojírenství, s.r.o.
Vladimír Cibulka, Director, Department of Economic Administration, MPO
Roman Culík, Investment Banking Division, KB
Oldřich Dědek, Advisor to Governor, ČNB
William Dewey, Advisor to the Chairman, ČSOB
Milan Dolanský, Deputy Director, KB–Tábor
Svatopluk Doležal, International Cooperation Manager, Automotive Industry
     Association
Josef Dráždil, General Manager, TOS Kuřim, a.s.
Karel Dyba, Minister, ME
Pavel Džida, Director, Internal Relations, Union of Industry of the Czech Republic
Otto Emanovský, Director, Economic Policy Department, Union of Industry
Roman Felix, Lawyer, Felix a spol. (Law firm)
Ivan Fišera, Senior Advisor, ČMKOS
Jiří Flidr, General Director, Kovosvit, a.s.
Jan Frána, Deputy Financial Director, Škoda Koncern Plzeň, a.s.
Vladimír Franc, Managing Director, KOB
Miroslav Frolík, Special Projects Department, MPO
Zdeňka Gardasová, Head of Department, KB, Brno-město

Vlastimil Gejdos, Director, Economic Analysis Department, MPO
Michael Gold, Crimson Capital Corp., Investment Bankers to the ME
Milan Haloun, Director, Škoda Dopravní Technika, Plzeň, s.r.o.
Ctibor Hadarič, Statistician, FNM
Jiří Hladík, Secretary, SST
Vladimír Hoffmann, Head of Securities Department, Prvá Slovenská Investičná, a.s.
Josef Horák, Deputy General Director, První Investiční, a.s.
Stanislav Houžvicka, Analyst, SST
Petr Havránek, Chief of Department 3212, Automotive Industry, MPO
Petr Holátko, Director, Regional Branch, KB–Tábor
Petr Hrbáček, Manager, Financial Consulting and Capital Ventures, IB
Terezia Hrnčířová, Chief Director, Department of Privatization and Administration of
      Property, MPO
Jaroslav Hudec, Press Spokesperson, Škoda Koncern Plzeň, a.s.
Robert Irving, White & Case Law Firm, Prague
Pavel Janda, Head of Department, SST
Evžen Jelínek, Deputy Director, Energy Equipment Supplies, Škoda Jaderné
      Strojírenství, Plzeň, s.r.o.
Helena Jensová, Director of Marketing and Information Services, IB
Jaroslav Jirásek, Professor, Czechoslovak Managment Center
Magdalena Jurečkova, Department of Special Operations, KB
Marta Justonová, Economic Policy Department, Union of Industry of the CR
Zdeněk Kadlec, Deputy Director, SST; Director, První Strojírenský Fond
Miroslav Kerouš, Vice-Governor, CNB (1991–93); Executive Chairman, Velkomoravská
      Banka, a.s.
Karel Klíma, Head, Department of Finance, Škoda Koncern Plzeň, a.s.
Jiří Kment, Deputy Director, KB , Brno-město
Josef Knižek, Expert, SST
Miroslav Kolanda, Economic and Organizational Consultant, Praha
Vladimír Kopl, General Director, OSO, s.r.o.
Viktor Korbel, Director of Strategy and Corporate Development, Škoda Koncern
      Plzeň, a.s.
Vladislav Krásný, Consulta Plzeň, s.r.o. (Former manager of Škoda Plzeň for
      thirty years)
Vladislav Krátký, Public Relations Manager, Škoda Koncern Plzeň, a.s.
Zdeněk Kroca, Chief, Department of Economic Planning, ZPS, a.s.
Jindřich Kroupa, Director, Department of Credit Operations, KB
Alice Krsáková, Manager, Prvá Slovanská Investičná, a.s.
František Kubát, Director of Secretariat, IB
Petr Kučera, Financial Advisory and Capital Operations, IB
Vojtěška Kupcová, Press Spokesperson, ZPS, Zlín, a.s.
Hana Lahradníková, KB, Brno-venkov
Miloslav Lanzendorf, Vice President, Sales and Marketing, Škoda Koncern Plzeň, a.s.
Jan Lembas, Resident Manager, Central Europe Trust, PLC
Jan Liška, Director, Department of Credit Operations, KOB
Miloš Lisý, Manager, Financial Advisory and Project Finance, IB
Václav Lobovský, Manageing Director, Škoda Jaderné Strojírenství, Plzeň, s.r.o.
Jaroslav Lopata, Department of Financial Advisory and Projects, IB

Marek Macháček, Head, Department of Credit Limit, KB
Karel Macík, Associate Professor, Faculty of Machanical Engineering, ČVUT Praha
Václav Malý, Voswinkel-Tradex, GmbH
Radovan Martínek, Deputy Director, Investiční Kapitálová Společnost, KB; Member, Board of Directors, ZPS, a.s.
Jan Mládek, Advisor to Minister, MPO
Miloslav Morava, Commercial Director, TOS Hostivař, s.p.
Vladimír Musil, Deputy Director, Department of Financial Restructuring, KB
Ludmila Navrátilová, Head, Department of Labor Market Analysis, Úřad Práce, Plzeň-Sever
Lubomír Netolický, Head of Department, MP
Ivan Neumaier, Executive Director, Credit Rating, a.s.
Jaroslav Nosek, Technical Director, Škoda Automatize/Controls, s.r.o.
Ladislav Novotný, Managing Director (1990–92), Škoda Koncern Plzeň, a.s.
Stanislav Novotný, General Manager/Director, ČKD Choceň, a.s.
Zdeněk Novotný, Director, Úřad Práce, Plzeň
Oldřich Paclík, Technical Director, Kovosvit, a.s.
Břetislav Ondra, Chief of Marketing, Šmeral, a.s.
Milan Otto, Divison Director, KB, Plzeň
Eduard Pálka, Asst. Vice President, IB
Karel Patočka, President, ČKD Dukla, a.s.
Oldřich Paulík, Director of Personnel Department, Škoda Koncern, Plzeň, a.s.
Petr Peca, Vice Chairman, Advisory Board, Škoda Koncern Plzeň, a.s.
Jindřich Pechan, Director, Škoda ETD, Plzeň, s.r.o.
Vladimír Petr, Director, Metallurgical Department, MPO
František Petrášek, Director of Finance, AERO Praha, a.s.
Miloš Podražil, Chief, Department of Petrochemicals and Plastics, MPO
Tomáš Polák, Director of Transaction Department, MP
Zdeněk Polnický, Section Manager, Consultancy and Analysis, KB
Zdeněk Prouza, Director, Úřad Práce, Ostava
Václav Průcha, Professor of Industrial History, VŠE Praha
Thomas Putnam, Manufacturing Specialist, GE Power Generation
Vladimír Rada, President, Škoda Forge Plant, s.r.o.
William Rocca, Relationship Manager, Corporate Finance, Citibank, a.s.
Jaromír Rojar, Director, ČKD Žandov, a.s.
Jan Rollo, Member of the Advisory Board, ZPS, a.s.; Professor, Engineering Faculty, ČVUT Praha
Pavel Rozsypal, Director, Center for Foreign Assistance, ME
Josef Rulička, Member, Management Board, TOS Čelákovice, a.s.
Oldřich Rybařík, Assistant to the General Director; Marketing Department, ZPS, a.s.
Jan Rydl, Director, TOS Varnsdorf, s.r.o.
Radomír Sabela, Deputy Minister, MPO
Ivan Samek, Head of Department, FNM
Lubomír Samuhel, Financial Director, TOS Varnsdorf, s.r.o.
Lumír Šašek, Executive Manager, Škoda ETD, s.r.o.
Petr Schut, Vice President, Spořitelní Investiční Společnost, a.s.
Eugen Sedláček, Chairman, ČKD Kompresory, a.s.
Petr Sedlák, Assistant to the Director, ČKD Kompresory, a.s.

Miloš Sedlecký, Former Manager, TST
Miroslav Singer, Chief Economist, Expandia Finance Group, a.s.
Antonín Šípek, Director, Automotive Industry Association
Jaroslav Skrhák, Director, Finance and Economic Department, ČKD Praha Holding, a.s.
Václav Slesinger, Head, Department of Organization and Management, Škoda Koncern
    Plzeň, a.s.
Jiří Slezák, Financial Advisory and Capital Operations, IB
Václav Smazal, Vice President, Škoda TS, Plzeň, s.r.o.
Josef Snopek, Manager, Loan and Deposit Administration Department, KB
Miroslav Souček, Head of Department, IB
Lubomír Soudek, General Director, Chairman of the Board, Škoda Koncern Plzeň, a.s.
Tomas Spáčil, Director of Branch, KB, Brno–Pod Petrovem
Ladislav Šťastný, Former Manager, TST
Pavel Stejskal, Director, Special Projects Department, MPO
Vít Štěpánek, Chief of Cabinet, ME
Vít Šubert, Director of Employment Service Administration, ML
Štefan Suhada, Deputy Director, Společenství Průmyslových Podniků Moravy a Slezska
Ivana Švadlenková, Department of Privatization, MPO
Pavel Svoboda, Commercial Director, TOS Kuřim, a.s.
Přemysl Svoboda, Director, Department of Economy, Poldi Kladno, a.s. (1990–93)
Luboš Ticháček, Chief, Department of General Support, FNM
Pavel Tomek, President, VUOSO,a.s.
Zdeněk Trinkewitz, Vice President & Executive Director, ČKD Praha Holding, a.s.
Dušan Tříska, Former Advisor the Federal Minister of Finance; Director, RM-System
Miroslav Tuček, Professor of Technology Management, Engineering Faculty, ČVUT
    Praha
Zdeněk Tůma, Adviser to Minister, MPO
Zdeněk Urba, Metallurgical Department, MPO
Miroslav Urban, Director of the Secretariat of the General Director, KOB
Ivan Valenta, Chief, Department of Banking Sales, KB, Plzeň
Ladislav Vaškovič, VUB Invest, i.a.s.
Josef Vejrosta, Former Director of TST
Ivan Vezník, General Manager, EPIC Bohemia & Moravia, s.r.o.
Vlastislav Vičenda, Director, Corporate Sales and Production Coordination, Škoda
    Koncern Plzeň, a.s.
Josef Vichr, General Manager, TOS Hostivař, s.r.o.
Emil Voráček, Professor of Industrial History, Historický ústav AV ČR
Jan Vosejpka, Engineering Manager, Škoda Turbines, Plzeň, s.r.o.
Petr Votoupal, Assistant to the Vice Director, KB
Jan Vrba, Minister, MPO (1990–92); President, USA Style Consulting, s.r.o.
Michael White, Crimson Capital Corp., Investment Bankers to the ME
Nigel Williams, Chairman of the Management Board, Creditanstalt Securities, a.s.
Vlastimil Zahradník, Director, Škoda Ozubená Kola, Plzeň, s.r.o.
David Žák, Vice President Regional Controller, ABB, s.r.o.
Anton Zámečník, Deputy General Manager, International Division, Všeobecna
    Úvěrova Banka, a.s.
Karel Zavadil, Director, Průmyslový zápočtový ústav, a.s.
Antonín Zermeg, Market Department, TOS Čelákovice, a.s.

Notes

Chapter 1

1. In this book, I analyze primarily the Czech Republic. The firms analyzed in this book have always been located in Bohemia and Moravia. Although prior to 1993 the Czech Republic was part of the Czecho-Slovak Federated Republic (CSFR), I refer to government transformation policy (1990–93) as that of both the CR and CSFR. The reason is that CR political leaders were the principal architects of CSFR economic policies. Although Slovakia had some disputes about the reforms and later altered them, the Czech political leaders both at the CR and CSFR levels forcefully implemented them.

2. The general tabula rasa view can be found in the works of Sachs (1990, 1993), Boycko, Shleifer, and Vishny (1995), and even developmental statists such as Amsden (1992), Amsden, Kochanowicz, and Taylor (1994), and Haggard and Kaufman (1992b). For works hailing the Czechs as following this view, see Frydman and Rapaczynski (1994), Frydman, Murphy, and Rapaczynski (1998), and Haggard and Kaufman (1995, concl.). For critiques of this work, see Grindle (1991, 1996) and Moon and Prasad (1994).

3. See Róna-Tas (1997) for an excellent work on the communist-era apparatchiks becoming the new entrepreneurs in Hungary. See also Johnson (1997) on the problematic origins of Russian business groups.

4. Both sets of problematic developments can be found in World Bank (1999a) and Spicer, McDermott, and Kogut (2000).

5. Excellent works on the continuity approach can be found in Ekiert (1996), Stark (1992), Stark and Bruszt (1998), Hausner, Jessop, and Nielson (1995), Chavance and Magnin (1997), and Spenner et al. (1998). Stark and Bruszt (1998) hailed the development of Czech investment funds as a positive case of reproduction of the past networks, while Mlcoch (1994) saw the reproduction of the old networks as pure theft. Rutland (1993) noted that the history of Czech democratic culture was decisive in the peaceful nature of reforms.

6. This approach builds directly on the work in economic sociology on advanced industrial democracies by Sabel (1982, 1993, 1994), Granovetter (1985), and Locke (1995) and on the work on East Central Europe of Stark (1986, 1990, 1996), Grabher and Stark (1997), and Stark and Bruszt (1998). It differs from these works (some more than others) by treating economic networks as social *and* political creations, not autonomous but tied to the broader political-institutional landscape. See, for instance, the work of Locke (1995), Herrigel (1996), Piore and Sabel (1984), Berger (1972, 1981), and Hall (1986) on local sociopolitical orders and historical institutionalism.

7. For economistic approaches to policy choice and the organization of interests in transforming countries, see Frieden (1991) and Shafer (1994); on business organization in general, see Williamson (1985); and on an application of this view in East Europe, see Boycko, Shleifer, and Vishny (1995) and Frydman and Rapaczynski (1994). See Granovetter (1995) and Fligstein and Freeland (1995) for reviews of the debate on business

groups. See also Guillen (2001) for an analysis of business groups in transforming societies based on economic sociological and resource-based approaches.

8. On Russia, see Johnson (1997), Shenk (1998), and Prokop (1996). On Poland, see Dornisch (1997).

9. *Wall Street Journal* (May 8, 1996). The article analyzes five major players, two of which were Škoda Plzeň and ZPS Zlín. ZPS was a member of TST and soon came to dominate the group.

10. See the *Economist* (February 18, 1995).

11. This double challenge has been discussed in two enlightening ways. One has been the discussion of the *orthodox paradox*, whereby utilitarian approaches to reform can easily lead to self-dealing. See Haggard and Kaufman (1992a, chap. 1), Grindle (1991), and Evans (1995, chap. 2) for analyses of this problem. Another way of discussing the double challenge can be found in Elster (1993) and Offe (1991). They argue that reform of several interconnected institutions at the same time is virtually impossible and can easily lead to social instability and antidemocratic practices.

12. For insightful analyses on the development of U.S. institutions for bankruptcy, mortgages, limited liability, deposit insurance, and lender of last resort, see Cui (1994, 1995) and Moss (1996a,b, 1998). See also Sabel (1996a) and Audretsch (2000) on the importance of U.S. public-private programs to support small and medium-sized firms and technological development.

13. I have embraced and adapted Herrigel's concept of *industrial order* here. See Herrigel (1989, 1996) and Locke and Thelen (1995). Note, though, that my understanding of institutions draws on the work of North (1990), March and Olsen (1984), and Thelen and Steinmo (1992).

14. See, most notably, Sachs (1990, 1993), Olson (1992), Boycko, Schleifer, and Vishny (1995), Frydman and Rapaczynski (1994), Camdessus (1995), and World Bank (1996).

15. This work emerges from that of Gershenkron (1966). The most known proponents are Wade (1990), Amsden (1989, 1992), Amsden, Kochanowicz, and Taylor (1994), and Evans (1992, 1995). See Moon and Prasad (1994) for an insightful overview.

16. The obvious candidates are those who wrote on the past and the transformation, such as Kornai (1990a, 1992a,b), Olson (1992), Murrell and Olson (1991), Staniszkis (1991), Klaus (1989), Klaus and Jezek (1991), and Winiecki (1989). See also Lipton and Sachs (1990); Amsden, Kochanowicz, and Taylor (1994, chaps. 1, 3); Przeworski (1991), Huntington (1991), Di Palma (1990), and Karl and Schmitter (1991).

17. I would argue that Krasner, Skocpol, North, Olson, Przeworski, and the strategic choice school on Latin America share these common points and underpin research on transformations and institutional change. See Krasner (1984), Skocpol (1979), North (1990), Olson (1992), Przeworski (1991), Staniszkis (1991, esp. chap. 2), Karl and Schmitter (1991), O'Donnell, Schmitter, and Whitehead (1986), and Haggard and Kaufman (1992b, 1995). Moreover, just as advocates of the economistic approach speak of "leaps" from the institutional designs of communism to those of capitalism, advocates of the statist approach speak of "leaps" from the institutional designs of backwardness to those of the advanced technological frontier. Recent critiques showing the similar faults in structuralist and rational choice theories can be found in Hazbun (1992), Munck (1994), Kitschelt (1992, 1993), Doner (1992), and Moon and Prasad (1994). For a similar line of criticism on the East Central Europe literature, see Levitas (1994) and Stark and Bruszt (1995).

18. See, in particular, David Woodruff's critiques of neoliberal, rent-seeking, positive political economy approaches to reform in Russia (1999a, chap. 1). Good examples of

these can be found in Olson (1992), Frydman, Murphy, and Rapaczynski (1998), and Weimer (1997).

19. Depoliticization has been an explicit aim of the neoliberal or economic approaches to transformation. See Shleifer and Vishny (1994), Boycko, Shleifer, and Vishny (1995), and Frydman and Rapaczynski (1994). Depoliticization has been a more subtle aspect of developmental statists, despite their advocacy of state intervention in the market. In their extensive critique of the developmental statist approach, Moon and Prasad (1994) show that a common fundamental problem for statists and neoliberals is their emphasis on depoliticization as both a positive and normative assumption.

20. This literature is enormous. The clearest discussions can be found in Boycko, Shleifer, and Vishny (1995), Frydman and Rapaczynski (1994), Frydman, Murphy, and Rapaczynski (1998), Olson (1992), and Lipton and Sachs (1990). See also Kornai (1990a), Clague and Rausser (1992, esp. chaps. 1, 3, 4, 5, 13, 15), and Shleifer and Vishny (1994). The works of North (1990), North and Thomas (1982), Buchanan (1980), and Olson (1982) are clearly present in this literature, as will be discussed.

21. The clearest discussions of the importance of consolidating power in legally insulated and autonomous agencies to implement the right solution can be found in Frydman and Rapaczynski (1994, chap. 2), Boycko, Shleifer, and Vishny (1995, chaps. 2, 3), Lipton and Sachs (1990), and Kornai (1990a,b). See Stark and Bruszt (1998, chap. 5) for a summary of this view. As Grindle (1991, 57–62) notes, the neoliberal work stresses that fundamental institutional change will usually come about after a catastrophic event, such as revolution or invasion, and with a benign leadership that controls and insulates critical policy-making powers.

22. This classification may be more controversial. Its prominence is in analysis of Latin American and East Asian development. See Amsden (1989, 1992), Wade (1990), Evans (1992, 1995), and Haggard and Kaufman (1992b, 1995). For its application to East Central Europe, see Amsden, Kochanowicz, and Taylor (1994), Kochanowicz (1994), and Nelson (1993). Kornai (1990b) also has variants of this view, particularly in his stress on bringing state firms under control of the government with clear rules on restructuring before privatization.

23. For a summary of this view, see Moon and Prasad (1994), Doner (1992), and Haggard and Kaufman (1992b, 1995). The extent of political inclusion for Haggard and Kaufman (1992b; 1995, concl.), for instance, is in their advocacy of catchall parties to consolidate policies, although they present little empirical evidence to support the claim. Moreover, their use of catchall parties appears more about ways of gaining mass support while limiting groups from directly influencing policy-making.

24. See Boycko, Shleifer, and Vishny (1995, chap. 2). This is the standard application of the Coase Theorem. For more on this, see Hart (1988), Hart and Moore (1988), and Grossman and Hart (1986). See also Frydman and Rapaczynski (1994). For excellent critiques on these applications in East Central Europe, see Griffin (1993) and Cui (1994).

25. See Amsden (1989, 1992), Amsden and Hikino (1993), and Amsden, Kochanowicz, and Taylor (1994). See also Wade (1990), Evans (1992, 1995), Karl (1990), and Karl and Schmitter (1991). These approaches derive interests either from paths of industrial development, modernization, or positions in the socioeconomic structure of societies. For critical analyses of these approaches, particularly in their portrayal of institutions and the formation of interests, see Moon and Prasad (1994), Doner (1992), Stark and Bruszt (1998, chap. 5), and Herrigel (1996).

26. Evans (1992, 1995) has tried to make up for the shortcomings of the statist approach by arguing for an autonomous state that is embedded in organic social networks between state and societal actors. But how societal groups shape the design of institutions in a positive way is unclear. His reliance on Weberian ideal-type bureaucrats setting the rules of the game lead to a conclusion about depoliticization similar to that in Amsden's work. See Evans (1992; 1995, chap. 2 and concl.), as well as the critiques by Moon and Prasad (1994), and Stark and Bruszt (1998, chap. 4).

27. See, in particular, Frydman, Murphy, and Rapaczynski (1998) and World Bank (1996).

28. That is, Klaus led economic policy from 1990 to 1997. In the first elected government, June 1990 through June 1992, he was minister of finance and rapidly consolidated control over key areas of reform. He was prime minister and head of the largest party for the next two governments. For more on this, see chapter 3.

29. Shafik (1993), OECD (1994, 1998a), World Bank (1996), Svejnar (1993), Mann (1993), Frydman and Rapaczynski (1994), Haggard and Kaufman (1995, particularly 374–75), and Pohl, Jedrzejczak, and Anderson (1995).

30. See McDermott (1997), Hayri and McDermott (1998), Pistor and Turkewitz (1995), and Myant (1993).

31. For a review of state participation in the restructuring of these industries, see Pistor and Turkewitz (1995), Desai (1994, 1995), Brom and Orenstein (1994), and Hayri and McDermott (1998).

32. Two overviews in this vein can be found in Hausner, Jessop, and Nielson (1995) and Chavance and Magnin (1997). A mainstream structuralist approach to explaining the creation and change of market institutions can be found in Fligstein (1996). As will become evident, the continuity approach shares much in common with structuralist and rational choice discussions of whether societies have trust or trustlike behavior. See Putnam, Leonardi, and Nanetti (1993) and Ostrom (1990).

33. See Stark (1990, 1996) and Stark and Bruszt (1998), as well as Ekiert (1996) and Spenner et al. (1998).

34. For excellent discussions of approaches that focus solely on national institutions, see Locke (1995), Locke and Thelen (1995), and Herrigel (1996). According to the economistic/property rights approach, differences between governance institutions are determined by differences in initial factor endowments or asset specificity. See Hart (1988), Grossman and Hart (1986), and Williamson (1985). Frieden (1991) and Shafer (1994) give some of the clearest explications of sectoral determinants of preferences and restructuring strategies in Latin America and East Asia. According to the statist approach, institutional differences are determined by different technological paths of development and positions in the socioeconomic structure of a country. See Gerschenkron (1966) and Amsden (1989, 1992). See also Herrigel (1996) and Friedman (1988) for critiques of the late-development literature as it relates to national or sectoral institutional systems.

35. For excellent works on how alternative patterns of social relations and politics can lead to diverse orders of economic coordination within national political economies, see Locke (1995) and Herrigel (1989, 1996).

36. See, for instance, Powell and DiMaggio (1991) and Nohria and Eccles (1992) for representative volumes on economic sociology and networks, and Powell (1990) for another application of this view towards institutional creation in Eastern Europe. See also Hausner, Jessop, and Nielson (1995) for a discussion of the analytical tensions created by this approach when discussing selection.

37. See, in particular, Stark (1996, 2001) and Stark and Bruszt (1998, chaps. 5, 6).

38. See Coffee (1996), Pistor and Spicer (1997), and World Bank (1999a).

39. It is interesting to note that two former advocates of path dependent approaches have recently written strong critiques of them. See North (1995) and Sabel and Zeitlin (1997).

40. See Stark and Bruszt (1998, chap. 6).

41. One should also note that research on the tripartite industrial relations system—Stark and Bruszt's main evidence for deliberative associations—shows that it did less for sustainable policy adjustment toward restructuring and more to help the government co-opt disgruntled unions and managers and impose wage indexing on these weakly organized groups. See, in particular, Myant (1994) and Buchtíková and Flek (1992, 1993a).

42. This problem reflects also the problem of structure versus agency in the debate about so-called institutionalisms. See, in particular, Immergut (1998), Hay and Wincott (1998), and Woodruff (1999b).

43. To be fair, one could argue that Czech industrial networks and the old institutions of government shaped government policies adopted within the first few years. Yet to avoid an over-determined rent-seeking account of state capture, one would have to specify how legacies led to frequent changes in the rules of the game. I will take up this argument elsewhere. Moreover, even in Stark and Bruszt's most empirically detailed case, Hungary, they argue that the strong social structures and networks led to a bargaining model of privatization, yet they fail to specify the contours of bargaining within their networks or key bargaining variables such as power.

44. Theoretically, this approach does not view actors behaving simply as isolated atoms nor according to a single "script written for them by the social category they happen to occupy." See Granovetter (1985, 487).

45. The two political considerations draw from Berger (1972, 1981), Locke (1995), and Sabel (1982).

46. Polanyi (1944).

47. See Bryant (1994) and, particularly, Woodruff (1999a) for insightful discussions of Polanyi and various interpretations of his work, especially when applied to East Europe and development in general.

48. For an insightful self-criticism about the uses of path dependency and critical junctures, see North (1995). For more on the debate on institutional change, see Immergut (1998), Hay and Wincott (1998), Thelen and Steinmo (1992), and, especially, Woodruff (1999b) for his application of the debate in the Russian context.

49. This view follows the work of Sabel and Zeitlin (1997), Herrigel (1996), and Stark (2001).

50. See, for instance, Sabel and Zeitlin (1997), Locke (1995), Herrigel (1996), Granovetter (1995), and Jacoby (2000).

51. See, for instance, Immergut (1998), Hay and Wincott (1998), Woodruff (1999b), North (1995), Knight (1992), Kitschelt (1993), Sabel and Zeitlin (1997), and Piore (1995).

52. Stark and Bruszt (1998) and Stark (1996, 2001) have written extensively about the network properties of assets and liabilities. Although they clearly believe that networks enable restructuring and constrain government policy, I interpret their use of networks during transformation as relatively free of internal conflict and rather autonomous from the political domain. In building on their work, I am attempting to clarify more

completely how networks affect the development of concrete monitoring mechanisms and how networks are altered through political struggles. Thus, in contrast to their understanding of networks, my approach attempts to link more closely the way government agencies are necessary partners to network reorganization.

53. Ekiert (1991), Stark (1986), Szelenyi (1988), and Stark and Bruszt (1998, 203–8) are noted works that have discussed the opening of previously unforeseen social and political spaces under communism.

54. See Ekiert (1991), Seleny (1993), and Nee and Stark (1989).

55. Issues of the duality of roles, interests, and power as well as of interest mediation and representation under CPEs are especially well examined in Seleny (1993) and Stark and Bruszt (1998, 112–15).

56. The analysis of shortage comes from Kornai's seminal work (1980, 1986). See Nee and Stark (1989, chap. 1) for this discussion. But I particularly draw on sociological analysis on the effects of shortage. See the following discussion.

57. The seminal work of David Stark (1986) is fundamental here. See also Burawoy and Lukacs (1992).

58. Research on the second economy and the emergence of national and religious traditions, for instance, reveal how the dominance of official ideology and rules was undercut both by the corruption of the Party-state ethos and by the opportunities to utilize traditional and new ideas. See Seleny (1993), Ekiert (1991), and Szelenyi (1988, 1989).

59. See Levitas (1989), Nee and Stark (1989), Aven and Shironin (1988), and Szelenyi (1989).

60. See Sabel and Stark (1982), Stark (1986), Voskamp and Wittke (1991), Kogut and Zander (2000), Burawoy and Lukacs (1992), Levitas (1989), Kawalec (1988), Prokop (1995, 1996), Aven and Shironin (1988), Grabher (1997), and Woodruff (1999a).

61. See, for instance, Myant (1989), Rychetnik (1981, 1992), and Rosický (1983). The literal translation is "production economic units."

62. See Premusová (1989a,b) and Illner (1992 a,b).

63. I draw here on Locke's (1995) understanding of using ideal types to analyze alternative patterns of industrial adjustment. See also Watkins (1978) and Ragin (1987), and Ragin and Becker (1992).

64. As Hrnčíř notes (1990, 35): "It seems justified to argue that the decisions made and their implementation do not a priori and unambiguously express the will and intention of central bodies nor of a uniform economic mechanism. In fact, they are the outcome of bargaining among subjects at various levels of the vertical management, the outcome of confrontation of their interests, authority, and economic power. . . . The problem of vertical regulation is not only and not primarily a technical problem, but above all the problem of interest, economic power, and force."

65. See, for instance, Prokop (1995, 1996), Sabel and Prokop (1996), and Woodruff (1999a,b) on the former USSR: Griffin (1993) and Jacoby (2000) on the former GDR: and Dornisch (1997, 1999) on Poland. See also the work on industrial districts and networks in the U.S. and Western Europe, such as Locke (1995), Herrigel (1996), Grabher (1993b), Saxenian (1994), and Deeg (1999).

66. See Berger (1972), Cohen and Rogers (1992), Locke (1995), and Putnam, Leonardi, and Nanetti (1993).

67. For more on networks in political economy and corporate governance, see Nohria and Eccles (1992), Granovetter (1985, 1995), Piore and Sabel (1984), Locke (1995), Grabher (1992), Herrigel (1989), Grabher and Stark (1997), and Stark (1996).

68. See discussions of these issues in Nelson and Winter (1982), Stiglitz and Weiss (1981), Cui (1995), Knight (1992), and Piore et al. (1994).

69. For a Dukheimian perspective, see, for instance, Stark (1990, 1996, 2001), Stark and Bruszt (1998), and Granovetter (1985). For a rational-choice perspective, see North (1990), Ostrom (1990, 1995), Putnam, Leonardi, and Nanetti (1993), Knight (1992), North and Knight (1997), and Bates (1988). To be fair, Knight, for instance, does hypothesize that an external shock to the institutional system could weaken old power asymmetries and allow for the weak to organize greater bargaining power. But the latter issue depends on resolution of collective-action problems via such mechanisms as side payments, forward contracts, cognitive changes, or ideology, each of which either contradicts or is outside his distributional theory.

70. For more on the malleability of social relations and trust, see Sabel (1992, 1993, 1995), Locke (1995), Granovetter (1985), and Coleman (1988). The political constructionist view here draws on the work of Herrigel (1996), Sabel (1982, 1992, 1994), and Sabel and Zeitlin (1997).

71. See, for instance, Berger (1981), Sabel (1982, 1993), Locke (1995), and Piore and Sabel (1984).

72. See Balcerowicz, Gray, and Hoshi (1998) for several works on bankruptcy procedures in East Central Europe, especially the chapter by Hoshi and Mládek on the Czech Republic.

73. Stark and Bruszt (1998) saw the government's attempt to net-out interfirm debts as a significant step toward restructuring networks, but the measure failed. On incomplete markets and statist views to solving these problems, see Cui (1995), Stiglitz (1994, 1996), Stiglitz and Uy (1996), Amsden (1992), and Amsden, Kochanowicz, and Taylor (1994).

74. See, for instance, Granovetter (1995), Piore et al. (1994), Sabel and Zeitlin (1997), Saxenian (1994), Piore (1995), Sabel (1994, 1995), and Sunstein (1995).

75. See also Cui (1995) and Sabel (1994).

76. This was identified by van Wijnbergen (1993) in Polish corporate debt-relief negotiations.

77. In this sense, I embrace David Woodruff's call for comparative scholars of transformations to provide "guidance in how to describe the dimensions along which 'outcomes' might vary, rather than explain the outcome itself." See Woodruff (1999a, epilogue).

78. See, in particular, Sabel (1994, 1995), Piore (1995), Stark and Bruszt (1998, chaps. 4 and 7), and Cohen and Sabel (1997).

79. For more on the role of deliberation for facilitating cooperation and as a core aspect of governance institutions, see Sabel (1993, 1994), Dorf and Sabel (1998), Cohen (1998), and Cohen and Rogers (1992).

80. See Berger (1981), Immergut (1998), Woodruff (1999b), and Locke (1995).

81. See Piore et al. (1994), Piore (1995), Kitschelt (1993), Sabel (1994), and Cohen and Sabel (1997).

82. See, in particular, Katzenstein (1989) and Locke (1995).

83. See Ragin (1987), Ragin and Becker (1992), Locke (1995), Locke and Thelen (1996), Herrigel (1996), and Saxenian (1994).

84. These sectoral groupings are according to the United Nations (UN) International Standard Industrial Classification system. For instance, steel is ISIC 271; mechanical engineering, particularly for Škoda and TST, is ISIC 29 and 292; truck production is ISIC

341; and aircraft production is ISIC 353. Teichova (1997) also classifies the fifty largest industrial VHJs according to the UN ISIC, including my cases.

Chapter 2

1. I will develop this point, but see, in particular, Beissinger (1988) for the use of scientific management as the bases for Soviet planning regimes, and see my discussion of this view in chapter 1. See also Acs and Audretsch (1993), Murrell (1990), Burawoy and Lukacs (1992), and Sylos-Labini (1992) for discussions of using models based on economies of scale to analyze communist political economies. Kornai (1992a) also uses a model of Weberian forms of bureaucracy to analyze the organization of planning in classical or orthodox communist systems.

2. This is also elaborated in chapter 1. But see, in particular, Nee and Stark (1989) and Comisso (1991).

3. See, for instance, OECD (1992), Frydman and Rapaczynski (1994), and Garton Ash (1989).

4. See, in particular, Kornai (1980, 1986).

5. See, especially, Teichova (1974, 1988, 1997) on this point.

6. For both Marxist and neoclassical theories of economic development and modernization theories of political development, mass production has been a defining feature of advancement. See Piore and Sabel (1984), Berger and Piore (1980), and Kerr et al. (1960).

7. Figures are from OECD (1992) and Hasager (1986a).

8. Beissinger (1988, 5). For a comprehensive analysis of Soviet admiration for Taylorism and American mass production and of scientific management and mass production as points of comparative analysis between communism and capitalism, see Beissinger (1988), Erlich (1960), Nove (1984), Berliner (1976), Kornai (1980, 1986, 1992a), Burawoy and Lukacs (1992), Sylos-Labini (1992), Winiecki (1986), Audretsch (1995, chap. 1), Chandler, Amatori, and Hikino (1997), and Acs and Audretsch (1993). See also Lenin (1975), Stalin (1952), and Gramsci (1992). As Beissinger (1988, 60) notes, scientific management was proclaimed as the basis for Bolshevik administrative policy at the Twelfth Party Congress. I do not deny the critical role that the Communist party played in creating "real communism." But like Kornai (1986, 1992a), I understand the Party as an integral part of the planning system in CPEs.

9. For a full exposition of Taylorism, see Chandler (1977) and Piore and Sabel (1984).

10. See Lenin (1975) and Beissinger (1988, 23, 33). See Erlich (1960), Nove (1984), Berliner (1976), Kornai (1980, 1986, 1992a), Burawoy and Lukacs (1992), Sylos-Labini (1992), Winiecki (1986), Audretsch (1995, chap. 1), Chandler, Amatori, and Hikino (1997), and Acs and Audretsch (1993), as well as Aoki (1990) for discussions on the relationship between the organization of mass production and productivity improvements in both capitalist and communist systems.

11. See Nee and Stark (1989, chap. 1) and Beissinger (1988) for discussions of how these issues were reflected in the different theories of communism. On totalitarianism, see also Brzezinski (1956) and Ulam (1963); for the economic theories, see Berliner (1976), Hewett (1988), Murrell (1990), Stefan (1996), Murrell and Olson (1991), and Sylos-Labini (1992); on pluralist and modernization theories, see Richta (1969) and

Field (1976). Moreover, the whole calculation debate and much of neoclassical analysis of CPEs, which takes place within the framework of static efficiency, effectively uses the Taylorist mass-production regime as the reference point. See, for instance, Murrell (1990), Cui (1991), Lavoie (1985), and Asselain (1984).

12. This reflects the classic debate among Marxists about the optimal level of development for achieving communist control. See Lenin (1975) and Beissinger (1988). Convergence and modernation theories also discuss the relation between the stages of industrial development and the adoption of classic mass-production models. See, for example, Kerr et al. (1960). For convergence theories as applied to CPEs explicitly, see Richta (1969) for a good example.

13. Indeed, the two regions accounted for 70 percent of machinery and engineering production in the Austro-Hungarian Empire. See Teichova (1974, 1988, 1997).

14. See, for instance, Teichova (1988, 1997) and Myant (1989). This point was confirmed in an interview with Jaroslav Jirásek, a leading Czech industrial analyst and a participant in industrial planning experiments (see appendix).

15. Holesovsky (1980, 61).

16. As Rosický (1983, 36) quotes the 1956 KSČ conference proceedings, "The decentralization of authority to lower organs is necessarily understood as a systemic creation for the preconditions of fundamental changes in the style and method of the work of the whole state and economic apparatus; as the basic precondition for the development of initiative and independence as well as of the high responsibility of the lower bodies and organs; as the lasting way to harness the experiences and endow the widest mass of workers with the interest of building socialism."

17. See Myant (1989) and Hasager (1986a,b).

18. The issue here was how the communist could impose upon an existing production system a new, integrated system of increasingly subdivided tasks and narrowly specialized producers of standardized inputs and products that could allow, in theory, central authorities to plan and coordinate the balance between throughputs and outputs. See Myant (1989, chaps. 1, 2), Jirásek (1970, 1984), Holesovsky (1980), Holeček (1983), Kaplan (1966), and Rosický (1983).

19. On the development of Czech production methods, including its relationship to the fluctuations in armaments production, see Šťastný (1987b, 1990), Smrček (1980), Teichova (1974, 1988), Jirásek (1970), Janáček et al. (1990), and the following notes.

20. See Jíša (1969, 1980), Lanzendorf (1964), Janáček (1990, chaps. 4, 5), and Jukl and Jíša (1964).

21. See Šťastný (1990) and Smrček (1980) for detailed historical analyses of the Czech machine tool industry.

22. This discussion of the different production methods draws on Jirásek (1970, chap. 3), Šťastný (1990), Jíša (1969, 1980), Řezníčka (1963, chap. 2), and Karmazín (1965), as well as interviews with Jirásek, Vrba, and industrial managers (see appendix).

23. Less than one-third of engineering employees participated in the shock workers program, despite the heavy promotion of the socialist competition by the KSČ. See Myant (1989, 40–42).

24. See Holesovsky (1980), Kaplan (1966, 230–33), Myant (1989, chap. 2), and Rosický (1983) for discussions of this debate. In his theoretical treatment of planning, Asselain (1984, 83–87) draws particular attention to the development of meso-level institutions in Czechoslovakia in 1958 as a major experiment in dealing with the problems of monitoring and adaptation.

25. Baťa had built a shoe empire during interwar Czechoslovakia and influenced the machine tool industry. See Myant (1989, 32–36), Smrček (1980), Lehár (1960), Rosický (1983), Roušar (1967), Pochylý (1990), and Křeček (1992).

26. Rosický (1983), Jirásek (1970), Kaplan (1966), Jukl and Jíša (1964), Žaloudek et al. (1973), Karmazín (1965), and Teichova (1988).

27. For discussion of the 1958 debate, see Myant (1989), Holesovsky (1980), Žaloudek et al. (1973), Vácha (1978), and Rosický (1983).

28. See Jukl and Jíša (1964), Žaloudek et al. (1973), Roušar (1967), Rápoš (1982), and, especially, Kaplan (1966, 225–40) for the relationship of VHJ organization, the aims of mass production, and the influences of the Czech production traditions.

29. Full discussions of rationalization and consolidation in VHJs can be found in Hasager (1986a,b), Rosický (1983), Rychetnik (1981), Vácha (1978), Teichova (1988), and Zemplinerová (1986, 1989).

30. This paragraph draws on Kaplan (1966), Hasager (1986b), Rosický (1983), Nemrava (1982), Haufler (1984), and Myant (1992), and Jíša (1969, 1980).

31. See Rosický (1983), Žaloudek et al. (1973), Vácha (1978), and Smrček (1980). Trusts were first called *federations* in 1958.

32. See Hasager (1986b), Myant (1989), Rosický (1983), and Vácha (1978).

33. The twenty-four general administrations (GAs), which had previously directed whole industries, were abolished. Staff of industrial ministries and the planning commission was cut by two-thirds and was relegated to drafting fewer, broader indices, mainly on five- to ten-year horizons. In turn, VHJs and their members gained greater decision-making independence over drafting one- to three-year indices and managing horizontal relationships and finances, including investment. An example of greater autonomy came in financial management. Because almost all current costs and over 50 percent of investment were to be financed from VHJ and firm funds, firms could retain unused profits and savings, and profit. See Hasager (1986b, chap. 5), Myant (1989, 80–82), and Rosický (1983).

34. See Holesovsky (1980, 59), Vácha (1978), and Rosický (1983).

35. Holesovsky (1980, 61). Campbell (1966) also develops these points more generally about CPEs. On specific changes in VHJs and planning in the 1960s, see Vácha (1978, chap. 3), Rosický (1983, chap. 2), and Rychetnik (1981).

36. See Rosický (1983, 46–49), Hasager (1986b, 115–17), and Myant (1989, chap. 4).

37. The citation is from Rosický (1983, 41, 44). Vácha (1978) and Žaloudek et al. (1973) also discuss this point.

38. Both Rosický (1983, chaps. 2–4) and Vácha (1978, chaps. 2, 3) go into detail about these points and frequently use the expressions in quotation marks. See also Rychetnik (1981).

39. See Rosický (1983), Vácha (1978), Hasager (1986b), Turek (1969, 1983), and Majcher and Valach (1989).

40. See, notably, Ekiert (1996, chaps. 6, 7), and, on planning, see Rychetnik (1981) and Asselain (1984, 85–88).

41. Several authors have studied the problematic relationship between ČSSR trade and its industrial structure. See, for example, Myant (1989, chaps. 3–5), Jirásek (1970), Kosta (1982), Chronc and Siroky (1986), Komárek (1982, 1986), Kolanda (1989), and Šťastný (1990).

42. See Šťastný (1990).

43. Šťastný (1990, 13).

44. Jirásek (1970, 71–74).

45. Jirásek (1970, 142, 175).

46. See, for instance, Nešvera (1979, 11–13), Nešporová (1984, 814), Hasager (1986a, 189), and Šťastný (1990, 15–17).

47. See Jirásek (1970, 79) and Šťastný (1990, 42). Both authors also relate this tendency to the development of a "finalist psychosis" of producers.

48. Jirásek (1970, 80–81).

49. For more on this, see Vácha (1978, chap. 3), Rosický (1983, chap. 2), Hubáček (1986), and Nešvera (1979).

50. It was estimated that by the 1970s, two-thirds of production in heavy engineering went toward supplying such turn-key systems. For instance, in 1959, an associated producer of turbines within Škoda VHJ constructed only one system; by 1970, it had constructed fifty-eight. Indeed, 88 percent of its production was accounted for by complementary supplies to these type of projects. See Jirásek (1970, chap. 2, 3, esp. 81–88).

51. Jirásek (1970, 84).

52. Kareš (1962, 24).

53. This figure was measured in terms of value added and cost. See Jirásek (1970, 84–85).

54. Šafář (1987b, 10).

55. See Jirásek (1970, 87) and Myant (1989, chap. 9).

56. See especially Kornai (1980, 1992a) and Hewett (1988).

57. See Zemplinerová and Stíbal (1995), Zemplinerová (1986, 1987, 1989), McDermott and Mejstřík (1992), and Brown, Ickes, and Ryterman (1994).

58. See Jirásek (1970, 84–85, 153–54, 207) and Kareš (1962, 24–26). For example, only about 25 percent of 485 types of parts (according to the state classification system, or CAN) were produced in large batches.

59. Šťastný (1990, 1–4).

60. See Kareš (1962, 24–26). For instance, data from the third five-year plan showed that of the 143 parts in heavy engineering proposed to be standardized according to CAN, standardization of only 7 was actually realized.

61. Only about 5 percent of specialized and standardized production concerned parts production; in the USSR, it was 15 percent, and in developed capitalist countries, 20 to 25 percent. Specialized plants for standardized products accounted for only 6 percent of total production in the industry. Only 5 to 7 percent of heavy engineering plants were classified as *technologically progressive* (i.e., plants specialized in standardized parts and products). Nonspecialized and nonstandardized production was rising at a rate of 115 percent per annum. Also, only 5 percent of ČSSR engineering exports to the CMEA and 13.1 percent and 16.4 percent of intra-CMEA exports and imports, respectively, were classified as standardized production (very low by international standards). See Jirásek (1970, 49, 84–85, 153–54, 207) and Kareš (1962, 24–26).

62. See Jirásek (1970, 85–89, 142, 154–55, 252–70) and Šťastný (1990, sec. 2) for explicit discussions of the production methods.

63. Jirásek (1970, 88).

64. Jirásek (1970, 116–17).

65. See Jirásek (1970, 116–20; 1983) and Šťastný (1990, 4–10).

66. Analyses of this tendency across several industries can be found in Myant (1989, chaps. 7–9), Komárek (1982, 1986), Šafář (1987a,b), and Kolanda (1989). Discussions on the lack of investment into new technologies, the rise of redundancy and parts

assortment, and declines in capacity utilization and productivity can be found in Rosický (1983, 73), Nešvera (1979), Nešvera et al. (1983), Nešporová (1984), Saska et al. (1981, 1988b), Kotulán et al. (1990), and Filáčková and Štajnerová (1983). Note also that I am not asserting that ČSSR producers had necessarily developed a coherent form of "flexible specialization," as discussed in Piore and Sabel (1984) and Burawoy and Lukacs (1992). My point has been to note that ČSSR producers had adapted universal production methods under communism to produce a variety of production-organizational forms that did not adhere to the ideal form of mass production. See Sabel and Zeitlin (1997) and Grabher and Stark (1997) for discussion of organizational adaptation and hedging strategies for both capitalist and socialist firms in recent history.

67. I draw here on the arguments in Rosický (1983, chaps. 2, 3), Vácha (1978, 29–48), and Nešvera et al. (1983), Saska et al. (1988a,b), Turek (1983), Hubáček (1986), Smrčka (1988), and Mlčoch (1983, 1992a,b). See also the discussions in Jirásek (1970), Šafář (1987a,b, 1988), and Šťastný et al. (1987a,b, 1990) on the increasing redundancy in machine tool production units, forges and foundries, and internal VHJ supply lines.

68. In addition to the materials cited, much of this discussion draws from interviews with former VHJ managers, especially those of Škoda Plzeň and TST. See appendix for list of interviews.

69. See Vácha (1978, 32–39, 44–48) and Rosický (1983, 99–117). Discussions of the development of the banking and territorial administration systems will be discussed in detail.

70. The *koncern* form was first introduced as an experiment in the chemical industry in the 1970s. For details on the reforms, see Rosický (1983, chaps. 2, 3), Vácha (1978, 29–48), Nešvera et al. (1983), Hubáček (1986), Hasager (1986b), Rychetnik (1981, 1992), Smrčka (1988), and Saska et al. (1988). For a detailed analysis of the steel industry, see Spurný and Prokopec (1980) and Dostál et al. (1988).

71. See Vácha (1978, 32–38) and Rosický (1983, chap. 3) for detailed discussions about the qualitative nature of production coordination and its incompatibility with prevailing methods of planning. Further details on changes in planning methods and indicators are in Hasager (1986b), Malý (1979), Malý and Záruba (1986), Federal Ministry of Universal Engineering (1980, 1986), Dürrer and Pachl (1982), and Šourek (1980).

72. See Mlčoch (1983, 1992b), in particular, as well as Asselain (1984), Malý and Záruba (1986), Šťastný (1990), Kotulán et al. (1990), and Filáčková and Štajnerová (1983) for discussions of rule making and bargaining in and around the directorate. The pattern is similar to the types of bargaining discussed in Stark (1986), Burawoy and Lukacs (1992), Aven (1992), and Aven and Shironin (1988).

73. See Hasager (1986b, chap. 7, 8), Rosický (1983, chap. 3), Procházka (1988), Malý (1980), and Veselá (1992). Official governance rules of the *khozraschot* can be found in Federal Ministry of Universal Engineering (1980, 1986).

74. This paragraph draws on Vácha (1978), Jíša (1980), Nemrava (1982), and Škoda Plzeň (1989).

75. See Škoda Plzeň (1989) Rychetnik (1992).

76. See Škoda Plzeň (1989), Nemrava (1982), and Feiferlík (1992). As mentioned previously, see also Škoda interviews in appendix.

77. As trust firms were increasingly tied to the state budget and the state planning commission and the VHJ directorate was increasingly tied to the ministerial budget, internal VHJ relations were incohesive. This point and the rest of the paragraph draw

from Malý (1979), Malý and Záruba (1986), Procházka (1988), Žaloudek et al. (1973), Hubáček (1986), Horský (1988), Haufler (1984), Filáčková and Štajnerová (1983), Mašek (1979), and Šťastný (1990).

78. See Žaloudek et al. (1973, chap. 1, 3), Polák (1987), Mašek (1979), and Malý (1979).

79. As mentioned previously, see TST and SST interviews in appendix. See also Šťastný (1990), Krejčová (1991), TST (1982, 1983, 1984, 1985, 1986, 1987), Smrček (1980), Žaloudek et al. (1973), Mašek (1979), and Malý (1979).

80. For these points, see Jirásek (1989), Krejčová (1991), Šťastný (1990), TST (1982, 1983, 1984, 1985, 1986, 1987), and the *American Machinist* (1983).

81. Extensive analyses of falling capacity utilization, increasing repair costs, and limited standardization of parts and automation can be found in Šťastný (1990), Nešvera et al. (1983), Saska et al. (1988), and VUSTE (1983).

82. In addition to the materials cited, much of the following draws from interviews with former VHJ managers, especially those of Škoda Plzeň and TST, and employees of the main Czech banks and the Ministry of Industry and Trade. I am especially indebted to Vaclav Malý, Josef Valach, and Milan Majcher for their insights on ČSSR corporate finance. See appendix for list of interviews.

83. Between 1980 and 1985 alone state subsidies to firms (noncooperatives) dropped by over 30 percent; in 1986 expenditures to firms (noncooperatives) accounted for only 32 percent of total state budget expenditures. See Petřivalský and Kočárník (1983), Kočárník (1983), Seidenstecher (1975), and Majcher and Valach (1989, 37–40).

84. See McDermott (1998, 82–85) for a detailed analysis of the rule changes regarding these areas. The most important financial and banking reforms came in 1980, 1984, and 1986. Details can be founds in Hasager (1986b), Valach (1988), Majcher and Valach (1989), Malý (1979, 1980), Malý and Záruba (1986), Šourck (1980), Durrer and Pachl (1982), Krejča (1987, 1989), Federal Ministry of Finance CSFR (1990), and Federal Ministry of Universal Engineering (1980, 1986).

85. See, for instance, the zero-sum perspective on bargaining and inflation/budget deficits in Olson (1992), Murrell and Olson (1991), Kornai (1986), and Hewett (1988). Similar Czech views can be found in Klaus (1989), Klaus and Ježek (1991), and Klaus and Tříska (1989, 1994).

86. See, in particular, Kornai (1986), Murrell (1990), and Olson (1992).

87. For details on these trends in finance, see Malý (1980), Majcher and Valach (1989), Krejča (1984), Petřivalský and Kočárník (1983), and Bulíř (1989, 1990). For a general perspective on this pattern, see Mlčoch (1983, 1992b).

88. I draw from the seminal work of Mlčoch (1983, 1992b) and from Bulíř (1989, 1990), Hrnčíř (1990), and Turek (1988).

89. See Bulíř (1989).

90. For an excellent discussion of analyzing finances in terms of flows rather than stocks, see Edwards and Fischer (1994).

91. See Hasager (1986b, 167). Two key reasons for the decrease in state budgetary expenditures to VHJs were that they were prohibited and ministerial funds were exceptional in financing limit investments. For extensive discussions on relations between the SBČS and VHJs and changes in financial flows to industry, see Seidenstecher (1975), Zwass (1979), Malý and Záruba (1986), Makúch (1988), Majcher and Valach (1989), Valach (1988), Kočárník (1983), and Petřivalský and Kočárník (1983).

92. See Makúch (1988, 739). One may argue that operating loans simply went to financing inventories and hoarding of materials by firms, and thus that is evidence that

firms and units, even within VHJs, were essentially isolated from one another. Yet the data suggests otherwise. As current account loans increased, the share of inventory credits fell to 34.4 percent of total operating loans. See table 2.12 and Majcher and Valach (1989, 212–38).

93. See, especially, Mlčoch (1983, 1992a), Hasager (1986b), Malý and Záruba (1986), Zwass (1979), Bulíř (1989, 1990), Valach (1988), and Makúch (1988).

94. See Šourek (1980), Horský (1988), Hasager (1986b), and Majcher and Valach (1989). Unsurprisingly, the share of total investments for machinery and equipment accelerated to over 50 percent in the 1980s.

95. For analyses of corporate and banking finance in these and other VHJs, see Škoda Plzeň (1989), TST (1982–1988), Malý (1980), Malý and Záruba (1986), Nemrava (1982), Horský (1988), Procházka (1988), Feiferlík (1992), Ducheček (1983), ČKD Praha (1989), Zavádil (1992), Filáčková and Štajnerová (1983), and Šafář (1987b). Also see appendix for list of interviews on Škoda and TST.

96. See Kočárník (1983), Petřivalský and Kočárník (1983), Malý and Záruba (1986), Šulcek (1980), Krejča (1984, 1987, 1989), Makúch (1988), Macků (1988), and Kerouš (1985).

97. See, in particular, Nápravník and Tyll (1986), Macků (1988), Ptáček (1984), and Procházka (1988).

98. This paragraph draws on Majcher and Valach (1989), Petřivalský and Kočárník (1983), Konečný (1989), Chrtek (1988), Kerouš (1985), Macků (1988), Ptáček (1984), Rajdl (1988), and Nápravník and Tyll (1986).

99. See, especially, Macků (1988), Nápravník and Tyll (1986), Krejča (1984), and Procházka (1988).

100. See appendix for list of Škoda and TST interviews. See also Horský (1988) and Valentová (1989) for discussions of these and other VHJs.

101. There were also a total of 6,794 municipalities in the ČSSR (4,120 in CSR), yet they had few resources and powers. Note that the cities of Brno, Plzeň, and Ostrava have district status. See Illner (1992a,b), Dostál et al. (1992), and Haufler (1984) for overviews of the territorial administrative system.

102. In the 1980s, regional and national councils received almost 50 percent of their revenues from enterprise transfers and wage taxes. See Illner (1992b, 25), Dostál et al. (1992), and Hanspach, Kostelecký, and Vajdová (1993).

103. In addition to financial and material resources, firms controlled the majority of facilities and infrastructure for councils. See Illner (1992b,c), Dostál et al. 1992, Myant (1992), Premusová (1983a,b, 1989a,b), and Vajrauchová (1985).

104. See Illner (1992b,c), Dostál et al. (1992), Hanspach, Kostelecký, and Vajdová (1993), Premusová (1983a,b, 1989a,b), Vajrauchová (1985), and Vitišký (1985).

105. Premusová (1989b, 26–30).

106. See Dostál et al. (1992) and Vajrauchová (1985). See also appendix for list of interviews.

107. See Žaloudek et al. (1973), Malý and Záruba (1986), and Premusová (1989a,b), as well as appendix for TST interviews. An example of another pattern, one organized around the main city of northern Moravia, can be found in Premusová (1983a,b, 1989b).

108. This analysis of TST is drawn from interviews with former TST managers (see appendix for list of interviews). Note that regional and district councils did not appear to play a direct role in assisting firms with their internal TST production relations, other than supporting the decentralization of discretionary resources.

109. See Rychetnik (1992), Matejka (1989), Smrčka (1988), Zemplinerová (1989), Gregus and Kalisová (1991), Hubáček (1986), and Kysilka (1989a,b).

110. See Rychetnik (1992) and Smrčka (1988).

111. See Škoda Plzeň (1989) and Šafář (1987a,b).

112. See Šafář (1988) and Rychetnik (1992).

Chapter 3

1. See, for instance, the *Economist* (March 13, 1993, 90), the *Financial Times* (September 15, 1992, 15; December 19, 1994, III), the *Wall Street Journal* (October 2, 1995, sec. B, 6), Frydman and Rapaczynski (1994), De Melo, Denizer, and Gelb (1996), European Bank for Reconstruction and Development (1995, 1996), World Bank (1996), Camdessus (1995), Claessens, Djankov, and Pohl (1997), Lieberman et al. (1995), and Boycko, Shliefer, and Vishny (1995).

2. See, for instance, the change of tone in John Coffee's work (1996, 1999) and, especially, in the World Bank analyses (1996, 1999a) and Andrei Shleifer's arguments (Boycko, Shliefer, and Vishny 1995; Johnson and Shleifer, 1999).

3. In 1989, Czechoslovakia was still the ČSSR. After the fall of the communists, it would soon be renamed the Czecho-Slovak Federated Republic (CSFR). Although the creation of policies took place within CSFR, I maintain that the split of the country did little to reshape the fundamental policies and organization of policy-making in the Czech Republic. Indeed, it may have strengthened the approaches to be discussed. This is because the key architects of the policies for the CSFR were Czechs, such as Václav Klaus, Dušan Tříska, Jan Vrba, Roman Češka, Tomáš Ježek, Vladimír Dlouhý, and Petr Miller. The split of the country was largely due to continuous complaints from Slovaks about the shape of the policies and their exclusion from the critical debates. The split of the country in 1993 only reinforced the positions and policies of these Czech officials.

4. Discussions on the formation of policy and the conditions in the CSFR and CR can be found in OECD (1996), World Bank (1996), Svejnar (1993), Mejstřík (1997a), Solimano (1991), and Myant (1993).

5. See OECD (1996), World Bank (1996), Svejnar (1993), Mejstřík (1997a), Solimano (1991), and Myant (1993) for analyses of economic conditions. For a thorough analysis of income distribution in East Central Europe, see Atkinson and Micklewright (1992). Using a variety of methods to estimate and compare income distribution in the regions, the authors show that Czechoslovakia and the Czech Republic consistently had the most equal distribution of income compared to its neighbors and to West European countries. See especially chapter 5. Also, the relative strength of the economy is not meant to mask the country's economic troubles: Czechoslovakia had an average annual net material product (NMP) growth rate of only 1.95 percent in 1985–89, a fall of net fixed investment to 13 percent of NMP, and a distorted price system. The data come from Svejnar (1993) and Dyba and Svejnar (1994).

6. Amsden, Kochanowicz, and Taylor (1994, 184) state "strong and easily perceivable political and economic challenges" as a key precondition for statist policies. For more on the advantages of focusing privatization on a clear goal, see Cui (1994), Corbo, Coricelli, and Bossak (1991), Bohm and Simoneti (1993).

7. See Shafik (1993), Przeworski (1991, chap. 3), Lipton and Sachs (1990), Blanchard et al. (1991), and Frydman and Rapaczynski (1994).

8. The corresponding figures for Hungary and Poland were 65.2 percent, 69.9 percent and 81.7 percent, 71.5 percent, respectively. See OECD (1992) and Milanovic (1989).

9. See Dabrowski, Federowicz, and Levitas (1991), Levitas (1994), Stark (1990, 1996), Mihalyi (1992), and Gabor (1990).

10. Early literature on East Central European reforms discusses the importance of establishing this control over assets. See Blanchard et al. (1991), Corbo, Coricelli, and Bossak (1991), and Kornai (1990b).

11. Haggard and Kaufman (1992b) conclude that the ability to create catch-all political parties is vital for statist and neoliberal policies. Both statist and economistic approaches often argue that weak social groups are essential for implementing sweeping policies for institutional transformation. See, for instance, Haggard and Kaufman (1992b, 1995), Amsden, Kochanowicz, and Taylor (1994, chap. 8), Moon and Prasad (1994), Przeworski (1991), and Karl and Schmitter (1991). See Orenstein (1994), Myant (1993), and Ekiert and Kubik (1999) on the political landscape in the CSFR and CR.

12. See Stark and Bruszt (1998, chaps. 1, 3, 4), Ekiert and Kubik (1999), and Dabrowski, Federowicz, and Levitas (1991).

13. Again, see Haggard and Kaufman (1995) and Amsden, Kochanowicz, and Taylor (1994, chap. 8) on this point. In their concluding chapter, Haggard and Kaufman specifically attribute the relative success of the Czech policies to the legacies of poorly organized social groups and the retained legal and financial powers of the Czech central government.

14. For more on the problems of both Czech and Slovak trade unions and employer associations, see Myant (1993, 1994), Flek (1993), and Buchtíková and Flek (1992, 1993b).

15. See Levitas (1994), Dabrowski, Federowicz, and Levitas (1991), Ekiert and Kubik (1999), Bruszt (1990, 1994, 1996), and Wittenberg (1997, 1999).

16. The depoliticization approaches often cite the following conditions as critical for enabling the formation of a coherent state to create new institutions: economic equality, a stable macroeconomic environment, weak social groups, cultural-social homogeneity, and a high level of education. See, for instance, Amsden, Kochanowicz, and Taylor (1994, 184–85) and Haggard and Kaufman (1992b, 234–35). For a path dependent application, see Stark and Bruszt (1998, chaps. 1, 3).

17. Even if Czechs and Slovaks differed in their cultural histories, the umbrella movements of VPN and Civic Forum were able to forge a consensus for the first stages of transformation. When differences threatened to derail policy, the rapid "velvet divorce," initiated in mid-1992, preserved Czech cultural homogeneity. As we shall see, the 1990 policy framework for reform was ushered in by both Czech and Slovak leading political movements. The most detailed accounts of Czech-Slovak nationalist politics during transformation clearly show that conflict of cultural and national identities did not derail the early years of reform. See Stein (1994, 1995). For the common view about the influence of Czech cultural traditions of consensus, tolerance, social democracy, and moderation, see Rutland (1993). For a further critique of culturalist and preconditions arguments, see Orenstein (1994). For recent data on the relatively high levels of education for Czechs and Slovaks, see the summary of the Third Annual Maths and Science Study in the *Economist* (March 29, 1997, 21–23).

18. Thorough discussions of this reform framework and comparison with other countries in the region can be found in Svejnar (1993), Myant (1993, chaps. 7, 8),

OECD (1996), and World Bank (1996). In addition to price liberalization for virtually all goods on January 1, 1991, trade was liberalized, and the currency (Kcs) was made internally convertible and devalued to help exports. Stabilization gave priority to anti-inflation policies—planned budget surpluses, restrictive monetary policies, and positive real interest rates. I also draw from interviews with such reform architects as Vladimír Dlouhý, Jan Vrba, Karel Dyba, Jan Mládek, Roman Češka, and Dušan Tříska. A list of interviews is provided in the appendix.

19. For discussions of reforms in the organization of the government and public administration, see Myant (1993, chaps. 7, 8), Dostál et al. (1992, chaps. 2–4), Tříska (1993, 1994), Češka (1993), and Svejnar (1993). The Federal Ministry of Industry was maintained but weakened.

20. For a complete discussion of the OF upheavals and their immediate consequences, see Myant (1993, chaps. 7–9), Stein (1994), and the Czech weekly *Respekt* (September–December 1991). Klaus's victory centered on three points: total commitment for his conception of rapid economic transformation, a "debolshivization of society" through lustration legislation, and converting OF into a properly organized, center-right political party. Lustration laws aimed to remove certain former communists and collaborators from high-level government and firm posts. Klaus wanted to show that his reforms would delink the country from its communist past in every possible way.

21. The division of other key ministries were: ODS controlled the all-important MF, which was already designing privatization policy, Federal Ministry of Interior, and the Czech Ministry of Economy; its partner, ODA, controlled the Czech Ministry of Privatization (CMP), the FNM, and the Federal Ministry of Economy (ME); OH controlled the Czech Premiership.

22. This paragraph draws on Myant (1993, chap. 6; 1994), Flek (1993), Buchtíková and Flek (1992, 1993a), Orenstein (1994), Ham, Svejnar, and Terrell (1995), and Svejnar and Terrell (1994).

23. This would be possible for the following reasons: (1) the ML and MF would hold equal policy authority, but subject to budgetary plans of the MF; (2) only general agreements on wage growth, unemployment compensation, pension reform, and limited employment-relocation services would be discussed; (3) labor would receive restrictions on the right to strike; (4) labor and employer association could not make policy proposals; (5) labor councils would be restricted to partial representation on company supervisory boards that held only oversight duties. For details, see Myant (1994), Buchtíková and Flek (1992, 1993b), and Flek (1993).

24. The quote is from Myant (1993, 196). See also pages 193–96. Desai (1995) argues that by 1993, branch unions developed different organizational capacities to influence policy. In contrast, two union activists, Vlačil and Horniak (1992) argue that differences in bargaining leverage for branch unions were marginal under the framework of mass privatization.

25. This paragraph draws on Dostál et al. (1992, chaps. 2–4), Illner (1992a,b,c), OECD (1996), Blažek (1993), and Baldershiem et al. (1996).

26. For overviews of this debate, see Frydman and Rapaczynski (1994), Frydman, Murphy, and Rapaczynski (1998), Mládek (1993), Bohm and Simonetti (1993), Mann (1993), Shafik (1993), Mejstřík (1997, chap. 1), Mejstřík and Berger (1992), and Kotrba and Svejnar (1994). In addition to interviews cited in the appendix, the following paragraphs largely draw from Myant (1993, chaps. 10, 11), who gives a close account of the policy battles; the CERGE Lectures on Practical Aspects of Privatization (1991–93),

which became a well-publicized forum in Prague; the position papers given by independent analysis and government officials at a critical policy summit in Kolodéj, February 2–4, 1990 (on file with the author); the work of some of the more public debaters, such as Klaus (1991, 1992), Češka (1993), Tříska (1993), Svejnar (1989), Mejstřík et al. (1992), Vrba (1991), Komárek (1993), Turek (1993), Kolanda (1989), and Mlčoch (1994).

27. See Vrba (1991), Kolanda (1992, 79–82), OECD (1992, 54–57), and Ministry of Industry (1992).

28. Concise descriptions of large privatization can be found in Mann (1993), Shafik (1993), Kotrba and Svejnar (1994), Brom and Orenstein (1994), Coffee (1996), and Mejstřík (1997a).

29. Various pricing and investment criteria strongly favored foreigners over locals, who could mainly participate in direct purchases of small assets of under 50 million Kcs. But the government would not break up or reorganize firms prior to privatization; this would come from management or in the privatization proposals by purchasers. Other than indemnifying investors against certain specified risks (e.g., restitution, partial environmental damage), the government would not provide any meaningful representations and warranties in the purchase agreements. Purchasers would conduct their own unlimited due diligence and reflect any contingencies and uncertainties in the purchase price. See Mann (1993) for details on these issues. For the debate, see Vrba (1991), Myant (1993, chaps. 10, 11), Tříska (1993), and Češka (1993).

30. This paragraph draws on Mann (1993), Shafik (1993), Kotrba and Svejnar (1994), Brom and Orenstein (1994), Kotrba (1994), Myant (1993, chap. 11), and Fund for National Property (1992, 1993a).

31. On the rules of the council and oversight of the FNM and ministries, see Mann (1993), Fund for National Property (1992, 1993a), Tříska (1990), Act No. 92/1991 Coll., Act 171/1991 Coll., and Resolution No. 568 (1993).

32. See, in particular, Moon and Prasad (1994), Amsden, Kochanowicz, and Taylor (1994, chap. 8), Haggard and Kaufman (1992b).

33. For the most coherent analyses of these, see Begg and Portes (1992), Van Wijnbergen (1992), Corbett and Mayer (1991), Dittus (1994), Anderson (1994), and Roe (1992). For comprehensive overviews and comparative analyses of bank reform in East Central Europe, see the World Bank papers by Borish and Noel (1996) and Borish, Long, and Noel (1995). For details on Czech banking policy, see OECD (1996), Brom and Orenstein (1994), Mejstřík and Berger (1992), Hrnčíř (1993, 1994), Kerouš (1993), and Hlaváček and Tůma (1993).

34. OECD (1992, 1994).

35. The post-1989 growth in exports to the West had largely gone to producers of luxury items, such as glass and porcelain, and low value-added goods. The export analysis here draws on Kolanda (1993) and Buchtíková and Flek (1993a). See also Mertlík (1995), Stíbal (1993), and OECD (1992, 1994). Whereas the CMEA and USSR had accounted for over 60 percent and 30 percent, respectively, of ČSSR exports in 1989, by 1991 their respective shares had dropped to 39.4 percent and 19.6 percent.

36. Buchtíková and Flek (1993a).

37. For instance, the quick ratio for CSFR industry as a whole dropped from 0.94 in 1989 to 0.526 by June 1991 (Krauseová, 1993). According to the Czech Union of Industry, cash flow declined on average by 50 percent in 1992–93 for a sample of 424 of its members, most of which were in machines and equipment. The consulting firm Spring

(1993) estimated that median payables/sales grew from 8.09 to 26.19 in 1990–92 for firms in machines and equipment sectors.

38. Total payment arrears rose by 250 percent in 1991 and 100 percent in 1992. One set of estimates showed that arrears as a percentage of GDP rose from about 1 percent in 1989 to about 25 percent by 1992. See Dyba and Svejnar (1994), Ptáček (1993), Veselý (1992), and Horčicová and Vašková (1992). In interviews at the Fund for Naitonal Property and Ministry of Privatization, I learned that the Ministry of Finance had two estimates. One based on overdue receivables to the government (taxes), banks (loan payments), and firms showed arrears as a percentage of GDP increased to 102.6 percent by 1992 and then fell to 70.1 percent by the third quarter of 1993. Another estimate based on payables owed by firms and banks showed that arrears amounted to 59.6 percent of GDP by the first quarter of 1992 and fell to 45.5 percent of GDP by the end of 1992. Because firms are less willing to divulge their overdue payables, arrears estimates based on payables tend to be understated. The opposite tends to be the case for estimates based on receivables. (Estimations by the Ministry of Finance on file with author.)

39. See Veselý (1992).

40. In 1992 and 1993, engineering accounted for 40.4 percent of industrial arrears, electronics for 6.2 percent, steel for 18.2 percent, and chemicals for 9 percent (from internal documents of the Czech Union of Industry), which are on file with the author. Dolečková (1993) also gives accounts of the Union's estimates and concerns.

41. MPO (1994a,b). By 1992, bank debt as a percentage of total liabilities ranged from 45 percent to 57 percent for steel, engineering, chemicals, and electronics sectors. See also Buchtíková and Čapek (1994), Čapek (1994, 1995), and Hlaváček and Tůma (1993).

42. MPO (1994a,b).

43. For discussions on the formation and privatization of the Czech banking system and its concentration, see Mejstřík (1997) Hrnčíř (1993, 1994), Kerouš (1993), Buchtíková and Čapek (1994), and Matesová and Seďa (1994). The Consolidation Bank (KOB) was established in mid-1991. Under the jurisdiction of the Ministry of Finance, this bank clearinghouse was initially given a six-month license and financed mainly by the CNB, the Czech Savings Bank, and the Czech Insurance Company (Česká Pojiš ťovna). The aim was to assume and restructure only the TOZ, continuously revolving loans for inventories established in the 1970s. Eighty percent of TOZ was transferred to the KOB—worth over 80 billion Kcs for the CR and 20 percent of total loans. TOZ were turned into new eight-year loans with a higher interest rate of 13 percent. By December 1992, KOB loans accounted for 14 percent of total loans in the CR. See Konsolidační Banka (1993).

44. Česká Národní Banka Report (December 1994). The KOB had about 13 percent of total loans.

45. See Tang, Zoli, and Klytchnikova (2000, tab. 2).

46. Discussions of this part of bank policy and the roles of the Ministry of Finance and CNB can be found in Hrnčíř (1993, 1994), Kerouš (1993), and Tříska (1994).

47. The new Central Bank was the Czechoslovak State Bank (SBCS), directed by the fiercely independent and internationally acclaimed Josef Tošovský. After the velvet divorce, the SBCS split into the Czech National Bank (CNB) and Slovak National Bank (SNB). Tošovský stayed on as governor of the CNB. I use the acronym CNB for the sake of simplicity and continuity.

48. Discussions of bank development in Hungary and Poland can be found in Borish, Long, and Noel (1995), Borish and Noel (1996), and OECD (1996). Czech concerns over bailouts and the developments in Poland and Hungary are found in Kerouš (1993) and Hrnčíř (1993, 1994).

49. See Investiční Banka (1993), Kerouš (1993), and SBCS (1992) for details of banking laws and the balance sheets of the main Czech banks.

50. See Hlaváček and Tůma (1993) as well as Tomáš Ježek's explanation for the debt-relief measures in the 1992 Annual Report of the FNM. (After the June 1992 elections, Ježek, a longtime friend of Klaus, moved from running the Ministry of Privatization to become the chairman of the FNM. Josef Skalický then moved from the Ministry of Finance to become the minister of privatization.)

51. I benefited greatly from conversations with Miroslav Kerouš, a former vice governor of the CNB, and Roman Češka, former vice minister for privatization and then the chairman of the FNM. Both Kerouš and Češka were instrumental in revising the bankruptcy law (see appendix for list of interviews). For overviews of the bankruptcy law and its use, see Hlaváček and Tůma (1993), Kerouš (1993), Hoshi, Mládek, and Sinclair (1998), Brom and Orenstein (1994), Fund for National Property (1992, 1993), and Trade Links (1993). The original law is Act No. 328/1991, the authorization for temporary suspension of the law is Act No. 471/1992 Coll., and the amendment is Act No. 122/1993.

52. All these schemes removed loans worth 37.2 billion Kcs (about 7.6 percent of total outstanding loans of the banking sector) from the books of IB and KB.

53. By October of 1993, the FNM had transferred over 38 billion Kcs to the big banks and the KOB—65 percent of large privatization revenues, 77 percent of large privatization expenses, and the equivalent of 5.2 percent of GDP. See Fund for National Property (1993, 1994) and Konsolidační Banka (1993, 1994a,b).

54. For discussions of the rejection of mass write-offs and the formation of the debt relief and capital injection programs, see Holman (1992), Kerouš (1993), Hrnčíř (1994), Brom and Orenstein (1994), Fund for National Property (1992, 1993), and Konsolidační Banka (1993). The alternative scheme, developed by Vrba and Ježek, was told to me in an interview with Vrba (see appendix for list of interviews). Vrba noted that previous delays in privatization, concerning the submission and review of projects as well as the refinements of laws regulating investment funds, had already unsettled Klaus about the devolution of power. For more on these delays, see Češka (1993), Mejstřík et al. (1992), "Czechs Postpone" (1991), and Myant (1993, chap. 11).

55. See Begg and Portes (1992), Van Wijnbergen (1992), Roe (1992), Borish and Noel (1996), and Borish et al. (1995).

56. This view emerged from advocates of the German corporate governance system and the relationship between long-term debt contracts and optimal monitoring structures. For the models and their adaptation to East Central Europe, see Diamond (1984), Jensen (1986), Hart (1988), Hart and Moore (1988), Lipton and Sachs (1990), and Corbet and Mayer (1991); for a rich critical analysis of these views, see Edwards and Fischer (1994) and Sabel, Griffin, and Deeg (1994). Concerns on its adaptation to East Central Europe can be found in Griffin (1993) and Čapek (1994).

57. Some of this argument is similar to McDermott (1997) and Stark and Bruszt (1998, chaps. 5, 6). But the distinction here is on the two components of privatization and the instability of inherited sociopolitical networks.

58. See Hrnčíř (1993) and Kerouš (1993). The general analysis is based largely on interviews conducted with loan officers of Komerční Banka and Investiční Banka. See appendix for list of interviews. See also Komerční Banka (1993).

59. Investiční Banka (1993); Komerční Banka (1993).

60. See Komerční Banka (1993a,b).

61. The problems of firms divulging critical payables data was viewed as major problem for the Czech policy. See Kerouš (1993), Kořínek (1994), and Ministry of Industry and Trade CR (November 1993). For a discussion of similar problems in Russian interfirm debt, see Ickes and Ryterman (1992).

62. See Komerční Banka (1993a,b).

63. Veselý (1992), for instance, analyzes how secondary insolvency revealed a multiplier effect, in which the liquidity problems of an initial group of firms hinder the solvency of firms across industrial sectors.

64. The program, initiated by the MPO, CNB, and FNM, started with 10 billion Kcs and projected that for every 1 Kc spent, interfirm debt would be reduced by 15 Kcs. As the program fell well short of this goal, it was terminated after two rounds of factoring and 1 billion Kcs spent. See Ministry of Industry and Trade CR (November 1993) and Kořínek (1994).

65. In addition to the aforementioned documents about the program, interviews with factoring agencies and firms revealed that main failures of the program were due to: (1) the fact that large firms and trade companies were the main debtors; and (2) the lack of cooperation in divulging corporate payables. In both cases, interlinked firms lacked a third party to facilitate terms of payment and information sharing. See appendix for list of interviews.

66. See Kerouš (1993), Hrnčíř (1994), Buchtíková and Čapek (1994), Mervart (1995), and Hayri and McDermott (1998).

67. This can be found in the Annual Reports of the respective banks as well as in Investiční Banka (1993).

68. On the expectations of lending, see Kerouš (1993). The data come from Česká Nardní Banka (1992, 1993a), Annual Reports of the respective banks, and Investiční Banka (1993).

69. By mid-1994, the additional 2 billion Kcs were returned to the FNM. Fund for National Property (1994).

70. See Česká Nardní Banka (1992, 1993a). The serious burden of interest rate payments on firms can be seen for instance in the jump in interest rate costs as a percentage of gross income. In 1991, this ratio increased in the engineering industry from 15 percent to 21 percent, in electronics from 8.7 percent to 19 percent, and in steel from 6.7 percent to 15 percent. (Based on author's calculations from sectoral data obtained from the Czech Statistical Office.)

71. These recapitalization schemes were in addition to the purchase of old inventory credits (TOZ) made in early 1991 by the clearinghouse, KOB. For a discussion of these schemes, see Kořínek (1994), Kerouš (1993), Hrnčíř (1993, 1994), Fund for National Property (1992, 1993, 1994), and Konsolidační Banka (1993, 1994).

72. For instance, KB wrote off loans for 304 firms, only 33 of which were nonindustrial. The average of the write-offs was 54.9 million Kcs. Division 300 of the Ministry of Industry CR tracked the write-offs of 69 leading firms in mechanical engineering and manufacturing of transportation vehicles and equipment. According to this data, KB

wrote off 3.24 billion Kcs of debts, accounting for over 77 percent of write-offs to these firms. For the KB write-off to these firms, the maximum write-off was 528.2 million Kcs, the minimum was 1.5 million Kcs, the average was 49.1 million Kcs, and the median was 23.38 million Kcs. The leading economic newspaper, *Hospodářské Noviny* (31 Dec. 1991), published a list of the different firms that received write-offs from IB, KB, and CSOB (another major Czech bank). For more on the behavior of the main Czech banks with regard to the write-offs, see Kerouš (1993) and Čapek (1994).

73. By the end of 1994, there were 319 bankruptcies in the Czech Republic. Of these, only 37 were state-owned companies, and 27 were publicly held companies. These include only 10 industrial firms, which were largely small parts (e.g., services) of larger firms. Based on data from Ministry of Industry and Trade CR (1994) and European Business Solutions (1995). By 1997, only 129 joint-stock companies had entered bankruptcy. See Hoshi, Mládek, and Sinclair (1998).

74. First, in 1992–93, the FNM issued 19 billion Kcs of bonds, the receipts of which went to strengthen the capital and reserve fund of the KOB. In 1993, the FNM an additional 9 billion Kcs to KOB to cover bankruptcy losses of the main banks, whose cooperation would be needed to initiate foreclosure proceedings. Second, while table 13 shows the rise in risk loans for total outstanding loans, over 25 percent of KOB loans were classified as risky and an additional 25 to 30 percent of loans were in monthly default. See Fund for National Property (1992, 1993), Kořínek (1994), and Konsolidační Banka (1993, 1994). Analysis of KOB loans is based on internal KOB documents from 1992 and 1993.

75. Deeg (1994) and Griffin (1993) report that the big German banks were similarly reluctant to extend new loans to ailing East German firms. The banks eventually became involved because of political pressure. For analyses on the resistance of Hungarian and Polish banks to lead bankruptcies and restructuring, see Bonin and Shaffer (1999), Balcerowicz, Gray, and Hoshi (1998), and Dornisch (1997).

76. Independent intervention by KOB was not a worry, since the KOB lacked the personnel and information necessary for close monitoring of troubled debtors, and the bankruptcy law required two creditors (mainly senior) to initiate proceedings. In turn, the KOB still depended significantly on cooperation with the main Czech banks. Interviews with officers of the KOB, KB, and IB revealed the frequent attempts to coordinate restructuring strategies. See appendix for list of interviews. See also Hoshi, Mládek, and Sinclair (1998). This positioning by the banks, however, does not necessarily mean the emergence of relational investing. For more on this topic, see Scott (1986) and Sabel, Griffin, and Deeg (1994).

77. World Bank (1999a).

78. I speak of investment privatization companies (IPCs) rather than investment privatization funds (IPFs), since IPCs often manage several IPFs. IPCs are joint-stock companies, often subsidiaries of a bank-sponsor. IPFs were joint-stock companies in the first wave and mainly open- and close-ended unit trusts in the second wave. The owners of an IPF are individual investors. But the owner of an IPC can be the sponsor. The control that a bank sponsor can have over an IPC and indirectly over an IPF is maintained through the equity or debt investment the sponsor makes into the creation of the IPC and the long-term management contracts signed between the IPC and IPF. Anderson (1994) and Coffee (1996) give lucid discussions of these issues as well as the problems related to the use of unit trusts.

79. Lewandowski and Szomberg (1989), for Poland, and Švejnar (1989), for Czechoslovakia, were among the first scholars to put forth a privatization model based on con-

centrating shares to achieve effective corporate governance. For elaborations of these ideas and comparisons between the Czech model and those of other countries in the region, see Lipton and Sachs (1990), Boycko, Shleifer, and Vishny (1995), Frydman and Rapaczynski (1994), Lieberman et al. (1995), Pohl, Jedrzejczak, and Anderson (1995), Claessens, Djankov, and Pohl (1997), Anderson (1994), Coffee (1996), Mejstřík (1997a), Pistor and Spicer (1997), Shafik (1993), Tříska (1993), and Pistor and Turkewitz (1995).

80. Johnson and Shleifer (1999) give a strong critique and evidence for weakness of the Czech stock market and relative strength of the Polish stock market. See also World Bank (1999a).

81. Interview with Dušan Tříska. See appendix for list of interviews. See also Tříska (1993). A similar view can be found in Frydman and Rapaczynski (1994, chaps. 2, 3).

82. For detailed descriptions and analyses of both waves of privatization, see Coffee (1996), Mejstřík (1997a,b), Laštovička, Marcinčin, and Mejstřík (1994), Kotrba (1994), Svejnar and Kotrba (1993), and Mládek (1994).

83. The second wave began in December 1993 and finished in June 1994.

84. Figures vary about the precise amount of property privatized through vouchers or other methods and held in the FNM. The FNM number varies, even if we maintain original book value, since small percentages of assets for all firms were earmarked for restitution and various funds. The impact of the FNM holdings will be addressed in chapter 4. The data is from Kotrba (1994), Mládek (1994), Laštovička, Marcinčin, and Mejstřík (1994), and Mejstřík (1997a,b).

85. Virtually all of the previously cited papers note the importance of the relationship between concentrating ownership in bank-controlled IPCs and corporate governance. Coffee (1996), Pistor and Spicer (1997), Anderson (1994), and Mládek (1994) often take a critical view of the Czech situation. Broader discussions of the importance of such intermediaries in East Central Europe can be found in Corbett and Mayer (1991), Lipton and Sachs (1990), and Amsden, Kochanowicz, and Taylor (1994, chap. 6).

86. The incentive for individuals to invest in funds was not simply their lack of information on the market but particularly the guarantee that most large IPCs offered—a cash payment of over ten times the registration fee for voucher privatization (1,035 Kcs), redeemable within one to three years. See Kotrba (1994), Mládek (1994), Coffee (1996, 24–27), and Vojtěch and Macháček (1993).

87. The analysis of IPC concentration of shares and voucher points comes from Kotrba (1994), Mládek (1994), Mejstřík (1997b), and Laštovička, Marcinčin, and Mejstřík (1994). Detailed analyses of corporate control can be found in Claessens et al. (1997) and Mejstřík (1997b), Laštovička, Marcinčin, and Mejstřík (1994), who define corporate control was defined as controlling over 30 percent of shares, adjusted for small individual shareholders. Analyses of advanced industrialized countries often define corporate control for 10 to 15 percent of shares. See Coffee (1996), Pistor and Spicer (1997), Pohl, Jedrzejczak, and Anderson (1995), and Claessens et al. (1997) on this issue and the debate about whether IPC share concentration actually undermines the influence of shareholders on the boards of Czech firms.

88. In-depth discussions of the following two points can be found in Anderson (1994), Pohl, Jedrzejczak, and Anderson (1995), Lieberman et al. (1995), and Coffee (1996).

89. For instance, the World Bank survey of mass privatization in East Central Europe and the former Soviet Union (Lieberman et al., 1995, 8) notes that during 1994 Czech market capitalization reached U.S.$14 billion, or over 50 percent of GDP, and that estimates

on the level of foreign capital in the Prague Stock Exchange range between 50 percent and 90 percent. Moreover, this study and others (Pohl, Jedrzejczak, and Anderson, 1995; Claessens et al., 1997; Coffee, 1996) note that the relatively high percentage of companies that are publicly held.

90. On this point about the Czech Republic, see Coffee (1996), Pohl, Jedrzejczak, and Anderson (1995), and Claessens et al (1997). Griffin (1993) develops a lucid analysis and criticism of this view as applied to East Central Europe, in general, and the former East Germany, in particular.

91. See, in particular, World Bank (1999a), Coffee (1996, 1999), Johnson and Shleifer (1999), Anderson (1994), Brom and Orenstein (1994), Pistor and Turkewitz (1995), and Pistor and Spicer (1997). Claessens et al. (1997) and Pohl, Jedrzejczak, and Anderson (1995), on the other hand, argue that the increase in share prices and improvements in other corporate indices reveal a positive impact of the Czech model and IPCs on corporate restructuring. Coffee (1996) and Pistor and Spicer (1997) make strong arguments that call into question the institutional assumptions and the causal factors made in these studies.

92. Detailed analyses on crossholdings can be found in Coffee (1996), Mládek (1994), and Pistor and Spicer (1997).

93. See Coffee (1996), Anderson (1994), and Pistor and Spicer (1997) for the problems created by these actions.

94. There have been two notable examples of raids on IPCs and banks. Both occurred in 1995. One case is a takeover of Agrobanka by the independent outsider Motoinvest; there is a current investigation into allegations of fraud and embezzlement by Motoinvest managers. In the other case, Motoinvest raided two unprotected funds of KB's IPC. See World Bank (1999a), Pistor and Spicer (1997), and Coffee (1996).

95. See World Bank (1999a). From June 1994 until February 1998, the Prague Bourse continually underperformed the IFC Global Composite Index.

96. Coffee (1996) and Anderson (1994) give rich discussions of this point. The securities company Wood Company Securities (1994), for instance, revealed that even investment funds that it regarded as the best in the CR were trading at discounts between 25 percent and 45 percent of their net asset value.

97. See, in particular, Coffee (1996), Pistor and Spicer (1997), and Brom and Orenstein (1994). A major nonbank IPC, HC&C, has focused on only a few firms and become an active owner. However, HC&C has largely stayed away from industrial firms. The papers by Coffee and by Pistor and Spicer discuss the actions of HC&C.

98. The debate over the intentions of the banks can be found in Coffee (1996), Pistor and Spicer (1997), Mládek (1994), Matesová and Seďa (1994), and Pohl, Jedrzejczak, and Anderson (1995). Pistor and Spicer (1997) give a lucid analysis of the problems IPCs have exerting influence over Czech corporate boards. But see Coffee (1996, sec. II) for a detailed analysis of the problems of incentives and cooperation for IPCs.

99. See Laštovička, Marcinčin, and Mejstřík (1994, table 11).

100. The previously cited papers discuss this problem at length. But see especially Coffee (1996, secs. IIb2–3).

101. The Czech Republic essentially has two stock markets: the Prague Stock Exchange and the RM-System, an over-the-counter market. Most of these activities are off-market. For analyses of the trading strategies and incentives in the markets, see Coffee (1996, sec. IIb), Matesová and Seďa (1994, 54–72), and Mejstřík (1997a).

102. Virtually all of the papers cited make the assumption that the main banks gain valuable information from their IPCs. This is conventional view of the German model

of corporate governance. See, for instance, Edwards and Fischer (1994) and Sabel, Griffin, and Deeg (1994) for discussions of the evolution of this view and critical analyses of it. Coffee (1996, sec. IIc) is one of the few that calls this relationship into question in the CR. My even stronger claim, that the direction of the flow of information is the complete opposite, is based on extensive interviews with over fifteen managers of KB and IB in their headquarters and regional directorates between December 1993 and March 1995. See appendix for a list of interviews.

103. These are the author's calculations, based on unpublished privatization data obtained from the Ministry of Industry and Trade CR and the Fund for National Property CR. The data is on file with the author. See also Pistor and Turkewitz (1995) for analysis of shares of firms from all sectors still held by the FNM.

104. I am not denying that Industry Minister Vrba prepared a campaign to help advertise Czech industries to foreign investors and also assembled a team of local and foreign advisors to assist him in evaluating projects and counseling firms. The key was that the projects and particularly the use of joint ventures left much of the decision making in the hands of managers.

105. Mann (1993) gives a thorough discussion of these rules and their implications. I benefited also from several discussions with Michael Gold and his colleagues, who acted as the investment bankers for the Ministry of Privatization CR. See appendix for the list of interviews.

106. See Zemplinerová and Stíbal (1995) and Lízal, Singer, and Svejnar (1995) for analyses of the relationship between industrial concentration and privatization. See Svejnar and Singer (1994) and Buchtíková and Čapek (1993) for analyses of the informational advantages firms held over the Ministry of Privatization and investors.

107. See Ministry of Industry CR (1991), Pistor and Turkewitz (1995), and Desai (1995).

108. See Vrba (1991). Michael Gold and his colleagues, who acted as the investment bankers for the Ministry of Privatization CR, also provided critical insights into the strategies of FDI and JVs. See appendix for the list of interviews.

109. That is, foreigners demanded isolating the JV assets in order to protect themselves from assuming the financial and potential environmental liabilities of the holding or other interlinked firms. See Hayri and McDermott (1995, 1998) for thorough discussions of these problems.

110. For instance, once a privatization project was approved, the FNM was simply to realize it. Government participation in a JV meant it could possibly become a negotiating arm of the government, the role previously assigned to the Ministry of Privatization and its team of investment bankers. Moreover, negotiations and any responsibilities/liabilities taken by the Ministry of Privatization on behalf of the government could only come in the case of a direct sale of assets.

111. The most notable failures of JVs were Škoda Plzeň with Siemens, ČKD Praha with AEG and Borsig-Babcock, Aero with Rockwell, Poldi with a steel consortium led by Maison Lazard, Tatra with Iveco, Avia and Liaz with Mercedes, Chemapol with Dow Chemicals, and TOS Kuřim with Thomas Mantzen.

112. As of December 1994, engineering accounted for only 2.5 percent of total FDI in the CR, although it accounts for 24 percent, 30 percent, and 32 percent of industrial production, employment, and value added, respectively, in the CR. Moreover, significant FDI is concentrated in only a few deals. The four largest cases accounted for over 45 percent of total FDI in the CR. The JV analyses are based on author's interviews at these

firms and in the Czech Ministry of Industry. FDI data is from the Czech National Bank and also Hlaváček and Tůma (1993).

Chapter 4

1. See, in particular, Pistor and Turkewitz (1995), Desai (1994,1995), Hayri and Mc-Dermott (1995, 1998). Calculations based on privatization data from the MPO and FNM.

2. Changes in the privatization procedures and the transfer of company management are in Act No. 210/1993; Resolution No. 568; Fund for National Property (1993b, 1994b,c,d), and Ministry of Industry and Trade (1994c). The calculation of equity was based on the MPO memo listing the forty-four firms for transfer (on file with the author).

3. I thank an anonymous reviewer of the manuscript for suggesting this acronym.

4. The case of Škoda Plzeň will be contrasted with former machine tool *koncern*, TST, in chapter 5. Despite their shared legal heritage, industrial sectors, technologies, skill level, labor union, and end-markets, Škoda Plzeň and TST ended up with fundamentally different patterns of restructuring and governance orders. This difference, I argue, is the result of contrasting network politics.

5. Discussions about mass privatization breaking the stake-holder powers of Czech managers and breaking up firms can be found in Hlaváček and Mejstřík (1991), Mejstřík and Berger (1992), Klaus (1991), Tříska (1993), Frydman and Rapaczynski (1994), and Mlčoch (1994).

6. Buchtíková and Flek (1993a, 9) show marginal changes in the industrial structure. For instance, between December 1989 and December 1991, the number of Czech firms in mechanical machinery increased only from 148 to 189, in electrical machinery from 38 to 44, and in steel from 35 to 43. Employment decreased on average 20 to 30 percent. Analysis of the structure of Czech industrial product markets between 1989 and 1992 shows a continuation of high two and four firm sales concentration ratios at the three-digit level. See Zemplinerová and Stíbal (1995).

7. For instance, in a 1991–92 survey of managers in over sixty major manufacturing firms, 85 percent of the firms continued to produce only for their past few customers, and 25 percent devoted all of their production to a single customer. In addition, 80 percent of the firms had almost fully internalized R&D, input and parts production, and distribution and marketing activities, but could no longer support such integration. Seventy percent said that the only alternative was to cooperate with their past customer to develop new processes and products. The survey included firms mainly from the engineering, metal working and steel sectors. Their size ranged from 500 to 20,000 employees. Together the firms accounted for over 5 percent of industrial employment, 5 percent of turnover, and 8 percent of capital assets in the CSFR. Forty percent of firms were located in Bohemia, 30 percent in Moravia, and 30 percent in Slovakia. See Mihola, Havlín, and Skála (1991), Mihola and Havlín (1992), and Havlín (1991).

8. See McDermott and Mejstřík (1992), Mlčoch (1994), Frydman and Rapaczynski (1993), and McDermott (1997).

9. For instance, the aforementioned survey indicated that only 6.5 percent and 8 percent of managers believed that vouchers would, respectively, improve production and

financial health of the firm and help generate investment capital. Over 50 percent of the managers surveyed asserted their primary interest was to maintain or increase their independence and decision-making rights over wages and disposal of assets vis-à-vis the center. Only 10 percent believed that privatization and vouchers would allow "the influence and interests of new outside owners to felt." At the same time, over 70 percent said they could gain needed financing and know-how, which vouchers lacked, by creating partnerships with foreign firms. See also Vrba (1991) and Mann (1993) on this subject.

10. See Buchtíková and Čapek (1993), Svejnar and Singer (1994), and Mejstřík et al. (1992) on the problems of information asymmetries during the approval of projects and the voucher bidding. For analyses of ownership and methods used, see Kotrba (1994), Mejstřík (1997), and Laštovička, Marcinčin, and Mejstřík (1994).

11. Much of this draws from interviews made with managers. See Appendix for list of interviews. But see also Smrčka (1988) and Škoda, Koncernový Podnik, Plzeň (1989). Šafář et al. (1987b, 1988) are indeed documents that debate various options for reorganization. Law No. 88/1988 Sb. of the CSSR set out the new basic forms that firms could take under communism. See Federal Ministry of Steel, Engineering, and Electronics of the ČSSR (1989a,b).

12. Much of this is also based on interviews with managers. But see also Mihola and Havlín (1992), Havlín (1991), Valenta (1992), Mihola and Batšová (1992), and McDermott (1997). Holdings appeared largely to escape the of view the academics analyzing the Czech Republic and CSFR, but not the lens of many journalists. The local papers, namely *Hospodářské Noviny* and *Ekonom*, carried regular articles on the subject of holdings in 1992 and 1993. For a nice sample, see Dolečková (1993), Brabec and Klein (1993), Turek (1993), and Oswald (1993a). See also regular pieces by Alena Adámková and Václav Prokoš in both of these publications.

13. Here are a few details on the original and revised privatization projects. First, the government made initial changes because of unsold equity in the first wave of vouchers and the decline of the holdings. Six and nine-tenths percent of equity for Škoda Plzeň was unsold and returned to the FNM. ČKD originally earmarked 28 percent for vouchers and about 65 percent in FNM for potential foreign partners. After selling only 25 percent in first wave, the MPO initiated the following changes in the project: an average of 20 percent of equity of each ČKD subsidiary would be sold in a second wave, thus lowering equity capital of ČKD Holding. This still left over 10 percent of ČKD Holding equity unsold, leaving the FNM with over 51 percent. Aero sold only 35 percent of equity in the first wave, leaving the FNM with over 60 percent of equity. Second, government interventions and tenders as of 1995 (column 4 of the table 4.1) resulted as follows. For Škoda Plzeň, the Czech firm Nero, headed by Lubomír Soudek, would receive 20 percent of equity and the consortium of the Czech banks, IB and KB, would receive 17 percent. Restrictions were placed on the resale of equity and the bankruptcy of Škoda. For ČKD Praha, the Czech firm INPRO, won the 1994 tender for 51 percent of the equity of the ČKD Holding, while IB and KB financed part of INPRO's purchase and partially restructured ČKD debt. Restrictions were placed on the resale of equity and bankruptcy of ČKD. For Aero, the FNM retained 60 percent of the equity of the holding, while the Czech banks, ČSOB, IB, and KB as well as the state-owned bank clearing house, KOB, all did debt equity swaps in the largest subsidiaries for controlling minority equity stakes. For Poldi, the Czech firm Bohemia Art won the 1993 tender for 51 to 66 percent of equity of Poldi I & II. The final price and quantity were to be determined based on certain restructuring steps. The FNM retained 97 percent of the equity of Poldi Holding. KB was

the principle creditor of Poldi and Bohemia Art. After a series of fights over the actions of Bohemia Art and related liabilities, KB and FNM initiated lawsuits against Bohemia Art in 1995–96, resulting in the FNM retaking control of Poldi I & II. For Tatra, in 1993 the IPCs, under pressure from the government, created a manager-owner (a former director of Chrysler) with 15 percent equity in Tatra. Internal fights led to his departure less than twelve months later.

14. These groups roughly correspond to the three-digit level of the Standard Industrial Classification system. See chapter 2 for more details. Šafář (1987b) gives a discussion of the number of different product groups in Škoda, ČKD, etc. See also the relevant annual reports.

15. The author made the calculations from Škoda Plzeň data with the help of Škoda's Deputy Financial Director, Jan Frána. We used only Škoda VHJ and Koncern level data—sales and output data about production sold to firms within Škoda and outside Škoda. Discussions of internal subcontracting densities can also be found in Šafář (1987b, 1988) and Feiferlik (1992).

16. The following is based on interviews conducted with plant managers. This included sets of structured questions about outsourcing (within and outside of Škoda Plzeň) and in-house production expressed as percentages of costs and output. Supplementary analyses were done with Jan Frána, Deputy Finance Director of Škoda Koncern, Plzeň, using output and payables/receivables data.

17. For instance, in their report to the former Federal Ministry of Steel and Heavy Engineering, Šafář (1987a) estimated that 14 percent to 34 percent of various base steel products in the ČSSR was produced in firms/VHJs outside of the main domestic VHJ for steel production. According to data compiled by the industrial research institute, VUSTE, which was attached to the Federal Ministry of Steel and Heavy Engineering, there were thirty-two firms in ferrous metallurgy and fifteen in nonferrous metallurgy in July 1989 (after the dissolution of the VHJ system).

18. Its main production areas are rail transport (diesel locomotives and trams), industrial engines (diesel, electric, and combustion), compressors, electrical engineering, metallurgy, and industrial plant systems. See Šafář (1987b) and ČKD's Annual Reports (1991a, 1992a, 1993a). The calculations that follow are based on output and internal supply data of ČKD, broken down by plant/subsidiary, provided by the Special Projects Department of the MPO and from the annual economic and production report of ČKD Praha for 1989 (February 1990). The following is based on interviews at ČKD and the MPO, the original ČKD privatization project (October 1991), three extensive analyses of ČKD done by the MPO (1992c,d; 1993iČKD) and the MPO (1994e,f) analyses that accompanied the government decree authorizing the tender of 51 percent of ČKD in June 1994 (Usnesení No. 334, 15 June 1994).

19. ČKD data indicates that the large majority of unit output (on average) was sold outside the firm while less than 20 percent of inputs (on average) were bought from external suppliers. The exception was the plant Trakce, which produced traction components. Over 90 percent of Trakce's output were for the ČKD units Locomotivka and Tatra. See previous footnote for data references.

20. The conflicts and confusion over the formation of new divisions and JVs eventually made their way to the press in October and November 1992. See, for instance, articles on ČKD in *Prostor* (6 Oct. 1992), *Svobodné Slovo* (9 Oct., 4 Nov. 1992), *Hospodářské Noviny* (9 Oct. 1992), and *Český Deník* (6 Nov. 1992). See also Zavadil (1992) and Veselá

(1992) for case studies on the reorganization, product development, and joint-venture proposals of ČKD Kompressory.

21. In addition to interviews with Aero managers and relevant officials at the MPO, I draw on the Annual Reports of Aero (1991b, 1992, 1993), a draft of a restructuring proposal for Aero made by the Department for Special Projects of the MPO in March 1993 (MPO-Aero, 1993) and the restructuring proposal for Aero made by this department in February 1994 (Doc. No. 447/94/3230/1000).

22. This fight also became public. See, for instance, the article on reorganizing Aero's production links in *Hospodářské Noviny* (27 Jan. 1993).

23. In addition to the interviews with managers and relevant officials in the MPO, I draw on the case studies of the truck industry by Jirásek (1991, 1992, 1993a, 1993), Jirásek, Svoboda, and Varcop (1993), Mihola and Batšová (1992), and the MPO analysis of Tatra Kopřivnice (MPO CR 1992b).

24. Prior to 1989, top management of the respective VHJs had ensured that Motorpal, CZM, and Meotopa would meet the needs of both Tatra and Liaz. After 1989, these common component producers became independent, pursued new production areas and joint ventures, and fell into financial difficulties as well. For case studies of the truck industry under communism, see Zavadil (1990), Vordová-Havelcová (1986), Wittlerová (1987), and Plechatá (1986). For the subsequent coordination problems and their relation to proposed joint ventures with Iveco and Mercedes, see Jirásek (1991, 1992), Bautzová (1992), and the articles in *Hospodářské Noviny* by Martin Hejral (24 July 1992; 12 March 1993; 2 April 1993).

25. Discussions of the organization, production and financial lines, and restructuring of the steel industry can be found in Slámová-Formandlová (1986), MPO-Steel (1993d), and Sofres Conseil/Roland Berger (1992). Besides interviews with Poldi Managers and relevant officials of the MPO, I draw on BBDS Servis (1994a,b), extracts internal privatization documents of Poldi (on file with author), interview notes from Michal Mejstřík, the report attached to the government decree authorizing the partial sale of Poldi I and Poldi II (Usnesení No. 431, 11 Aug. 1993; on file with the author), MPO-Steel (1994b), and internal memorandum for MPO Minister Dlouhý discussing problems with the deal between Poldi and Maison Lazard (MPO-Steel 1993a), a report to the Council of Economic Ministers (MPO-Steel 1993c) on the restructuring and privatization of Poldi (cerca 1993), and the MPO document 89/93.

26. Poldi wanted to keep 34 percent of equity of the subsidiaries, which was unattractive for potential buyers. The Conversion Division included over 2,000 employees. The Kladno Municipality received a seat on the supervisory board and Poldi proposed a transfer to Kladno of 5 percent of Poldi Holding equity. Kladno was to gain subsidies for the Conversion Division and the Energetické Centrum, as both were vital for maintaining employment and power for the city.

27. Analysis of the growth in interfirm debt shows a strong rise in secondary insolvency and the number of firms caught in the webs of arrears, while primary insolvency increased and then plateaued. As end producers' sales and liquidity dropped, they created a financial cushion by simply passing on their insolvency to other members of the network. See Veselý (1992).

28. An indirect form of cross-collateralization was using equity still in the FNM as security and tying debt repayment to future revenues from the sale of the equity. This was possible since the original privatization law made the FNM, as holder of the equity, the

bearer of liabilities. In practice, equity to be sold, and thus its revenues, was earmarked by the banks as collateral for loans. This part of the law was removed in the amendments made by the Czech government in August 1993.

29. The financial data comes from the Annual Reports of Škoda, koncern, Plzeň (1991a, 1992a, 1993a), interunit debt data from Škoda's Department of Finance, the draft of the report attached to the decree authorizing the tender for Škoda (13 Sept. 1992), the MPO document A1/4865/92 (29 Oct. 1992), and the Investiční Banka internal memo on the restructuring of Škoda, ČKD, Aero, and Tatra.

30. The financial data and analyses come from ČKD Annual Reports (1991a, 1992a, 1993a, 1994a) and the MPO documents cited previously. See also the Investiční Banka internal memo on the restructuring of Škoda, ČKD, Aero, and Tatra. For the following five subsidiaries, overdue payables exceeded overdue receivables by over 1.2 billion Kcs, or 45 percent of total overdue payables for all of ČKD.

31. ČKD avoided shutdown with the help of a loan guarantee from the Czech government made in June 1993. Discussions of the closure and the loan guarantee can be found in the MPO documents on ČKD cited previously as well as numerous articles in the press. See for instance articles on ČKD in *Rudé Pravo* (24 Oct. 1992), *Zemědělské Noviny* (23 Oct., 3, 4 Nov. 1992), *Český Deník* (6 Nov. 1992), *Svobodné Slovo* (4 Nov. 1992), *Hospodářské Noviny* (16, 28 Dec. 1992; 6 Jan., 25, 26 Feb. 1993).

32. The data comes from the Aero Annual Reports and related MPO documents cited previously. See also the Investiční Banka internal memo on the restructuring of Škoda, ČKD, Aero, and Tatra.

33. In addition to interviews with Aero managers and relevant officials at the MPO, a draft of a restructuring proposal for Aero made by the Department for Special Projects of the MPO in March 1993 (MPO-Aero, 1993) and the restructuring proposal for Aero made by this department in February 1994 (Doc. No. 447/94/3230/1000) contain in depth discussions of the JVs and the attempts at debt restructuring.

34. See Jirásek (1991, 1992) and the MPO documents on Tatra cited previously. See also the Investiční Banka internal memo on the restructuring of Škoda, ČKD, Aero, and Tatra. I also benefited from interviews with Jaroslav Jirásek, a former member of the supervisory board of Tatra. See also Bautzová (1992) and articles in *Hospodářské Noviny* by Martin Hejral (24 July 1992; 12 March 1993; 2 April 1993) for public discussions of these cases.

35. I draw particularly on excerpts of internal privatization documents of Poldi (on file with author), the report attached to the government decree authorizing the partial sale of Poldi I and Poldi II (Usnesení No. 431, 11 Aug. 1993), MPO-Steel (1994b), and internal memorandum for MPO Minister Dlouhý discussing problems with the deal between Poldi and Maison Lazard (MPO-Steel 1993a), a report to the Council of Economic Ministers (MPO-Steel 1993c) on the restructuring and privatization of Poldi (cerca 1993), and the MPO document 89/93.

36. See, for instance, articles in *Telegraf* and *Práce* (7 Jan. 1994).

37. Right before the deal with Maison Lazard collapsed, Poldi had its electricity turned off for lack of payment. This set off a broad coverage of the problems at Poldi. See, for instance, articles on Poldi in *Hospodářské Noviny* (12 Feb. 1993), *Mladá Fronta Dnes* (11 Feb. 1993), and *Rudé Právo* (10, 11 Feb. 1993). At this time, Poldi had total debts of 5.1 billion Kcs, receivables of 2.8 billion Kcs, and inventory of 2.5 billion Kcs. For 1993, Poldi was scheduled to pay over 1.5 billion Kcs for bank debts (mainly to KB and KOB), yet they projected enough cash for only about 570 million Kcs. On 9 February

1993, SEZ cut off the electricity to Poldi because of 260 million Kcs of unpaid electricity bills. Despite a tender for majority control of Poldi in June (see concluding section of this chapter), SEZ again reduced the supply of electricity to Poldi at the beginning of November 1993. SPZ cut the gas two weeks later. See, for instance, *Telegraf* (13, 15, 16 Nov. 1993) and *Práce* (16 Nov. 1993). ECK, a former subsidiary of Poldi, cut off the supply of steam and some electricity to Poldi in February 1994. See, for instance, *Mladá Fronta Dnes* (11, 19 Feb. 1994), *Lidové Noviny* (15 Feb. 1994), *Hospodářské Noviny* (15 Feb. 1994).

38. Examples are Huť and Kovárna in Škoda; Hradec Králové, Trakce, Žandov, Slévarny, and Hořovice in ČKD; Mesit and Motorlet in Aero; and Strojírny, Energetické Centrum, KND, and SID in Poldi.

39. In 1989–90, such units as Škoda Export and Škoda Praha of Škoda Plzeň, Jihostroj, Jihlavan, Mikrotechnica, and Technometra of Aero, Slaný, Naftový Motor, Slavia, and Kutná Hora of ČKD Praha, and Motorpal in trucks all had strong production and sales programs outside of their respective groups and decided to become independent firms.

40. Notable cases are those of Škoda Praha, Mikrotechna, and Jihostroj.

41. See Kotrba (1994) and Lízal, Singer, and Svejnar (1995).

42. See, for instance, Ostrom (1995), Knight (1992), Ellickson (1991), Coleman (1990, 1993), and Bates (1988).

43. The work of Piore et al. (1994) on product development was critical in formulating the concept of probing. See also White's (1992) discussion of "gaming." Aydin Hayri and I (1995, 1998) developed the concept of probing to understand the contractual and commitment problems transforming firms face in attempting to restructure and build a new governance structure. See Helper et al. (2000) for a similar discussion.

44. The data on changes in production programs and output can be found in the Annual Reports of Škoda (1991a, 1992a, 1993a). The MPO documents cited previously on Škoda give extensive discussions of the different JV in process. Insightful discussions of the problems of developing multiunit product development and JVs in Škoda can be found in the series of articles by Prokoš (1993a,b,c,d) in the leading economics daily *Hospodářské Noviny*. This discussion of probing in general and in each of the firms mentioned in this section is based especially on extensive interviews with relevant managers. See appendix for list of interviews.

45. Detailed discussions of product development and JV projects at both the holding and subsidiary levels are found in the three extensive analyses of ČKD done by the MPO (1992c,d; 1993i) and the MPO (1994a,b) analysis that accompanied the government decree authorizing the tender of 51 percent of ČKD in June 1994 (Usnesení No. 334, 15 June 1994).

46. See, for instance, the article on reorganizing Aero's production links in *Hospodářské Noviny* (27 Jan. 1993). I also draw heavily from a draft of a restructuring proposal for Aero made by the Department for Special Projects of the MPO in March 1993 (MPO-Aero, 1993) and the restructuring proposal for Aero made by this Department in February 1994 (Doc. No. 447/94/3230/1000).

47. Probing in Tatra and Liaz emanates from their modular vehicle designs. In these designs, the vehicle is conceived as comprised of various modules (engines, brakes, axles, chassis, frames, etc.), each of which is produced semi-independently by a specific plant. Evidence from Jirásek (1991, 1992) and the MPO analysis of Tatra Kopřivnice ("Zprava MPO" No. 200/92—C.j. 3000/3259/92) shows that plants were pursuing modifications in

existing designs and development of new components, particularly in engine, antilock brake systems, and axle parts. In Tatra, this process was amplified by attempts to create a new luxury car. These sources also show that each plant/subsidiary was attempting to form JVs with a foreign partner in its particular area. In Poldi, Poldi I and II began experimenting with new types of high-grade rolled steel, while Anticorro, Strojírny, KND, SID, Autech, and Thermosondy were all increasing the external subcontracting relations. During 1990–92, Poldi subsidiaries were pursuing no less than nine separate JVs. See, for instance, the MPO report attached to the government decree authorizing the partial sale of Poldi I and Poldi II (Usnesení No. 431, 11 August 1993), an internal memorandum for MPO Minister Dlouhý discussing problems with the deal between Poldi and Maison Lazard, a report to the Council of Economic Ministers on the restructuring and privatization of Poldi (cerca 1993), and the MPO document 89/93.

48. For a full, related discussion on the benefits and pitfalls of probing, see Hayri and McDermott (1998).

49. See, for instance, Piore et al. (1994), Cui (1991), Helper, MacDuffie, and Sabel (2000), and Sabel (1994, 1995).

50. Incomplete contracts leading to underinvestment by the contracting parties have been suggested in different contexts by Williamson (1985), Klein, Crawford, and Alchian (1978), Grout (1984), and more recently by Hart and Moore (1988).

51. See Grabher (1992) and Grabher and Stark (1997, chap. 1) for enlightening discussions of the relationship between redundancy and organizational experiments.

52. In particular, the data show a lack of lay-offs (except in administration), labor cost cutting through shorter working hours and attrition, and an increased age of employees. For instance, internal data of the holdings showed that they all cut working hours almost in half, eliminating night shifts while increasing the use of part-time workers by about 15 percent per annum. Škoda data shows that lay-offs accounted for only 18 percent of the decrease in full-time employees during 1991–93; manual production workers continued to account for over 60 percent of the workforce; and the average age of workers increased from about 40 to 42 years old between 1990 and 1993. The new conversion and design units were self-financed units with start-up capital and spare facilities from the holding that could be spun off over time and would offer workers of various production areas part-time employment for diversified internal and external subcontracting services. Discussions of conversion units and employment practices can be found in all the MPO document previously cited.

53. The widening gap between productivity per worker per day and per working hour (1990–93) suggests that shorter working hours were becoming the norm across industrial enterprises. (See the Český Statistický Úřad, 1994b.) See Svejnar et al. (1993, 1994) for discussions of changes in employment practices in the CR. Interviews reveal that the holdings were effectively shortening the working week to thirty-five hours. Concerns of so-called brain drain were widespread. For instance, Škoda data reveals that voluntary departures accounted for over 60 percent of the decrease in full-time employment during 1991–93. The strong concerns about brain drain can be found in MPO analyses on holding, especially in the report to the Council of Economic Ministers on the restructuring and privatization of Poldi (cerca 1993), MPO document 89/93, and in three extensive analyses of ČKD done by the MPO (1992c,d; 1993i).

54. See Granovetter (1985) and Sabel (1994) on the similarities between rational choice and structuralist views of social structures. The relationship between past social structures/social capital and cooperation is well discussed in Ostrom (1995), Knight (1992), Putnam, Leonardi, and Nanetti (1993), and Bates (1988).

55. See, for instance, Amsden (1992), Amsden, Kochanowicz, and Taylor (1994, chaps. 6–8), and Evans (1995) for their conceptualizations of the problems of underinvestment and the way policy tools like technology standards and subsidies get defined and resolve these problems. A similar analysis can be made about Durkheimian approaches that often point to the needs of specific forms of worker training. See Sabel (1994, 1995).

56. In addition to the works of Ostrom, Knight, Putnam, and Bates, cited previously, see North (1990) on how preexisting social networks set a narrow path of economic development and Williamson (1991) on how long term contracting relationships are sufficient to overcome contracting problems in the face of external changes.

57. Data on the first wave of privatization projects for joint-stock companies shows that 11 percent of equity (on average) was proposed as free transfers to local municipalities (making it the third-largest category, behind vouchers and FNM holdings). See Kotrba (1994) and Laštovička, Marcinčin, and Mejstřík (1994). Holdings such as Škoda Plzeň and Poldi Kladno, had originally proposed 5 percent of equity to be transferred to their respective municipalities.

58. Note that 1990–91 municipal elections reveal that most council members did come from the old structures and were independents. See McDermott (1997), Herzmann (1992), and Janiška (1990).

59. In addition to the sources to be cited, the following is based on interviews listed in the appendix. In the case of Škoda, holding and plants managers, IB and KB managers, and relevant officials from the MPO, Ministry of Privatization CR, and the Fund for National Property were interviewed at least twice from September 1993 to March 1995.

60. As of December 1994, engineering accounted for only 2.5 percent of total FDI in the CR, although it accounts for 24 percent, 30 percent, and 32 percent of industrial production, employment, and value added, respectively, in the CR. Moreover, significant FDI is concentrated in only a few deals. The four largest cases accounted for over 45 percent of total FDI in the CR. FDI data is from the Czech National Bank and also Hlaváček and Tůma (1993).

61. Five percent was originally proposed as a free transfer to the Plzeň Municipality. The rest of the equity is held, by law, in two public compensation funds (RIF and DIF) in the FNM. Data on Škoda's privatization and JV projects were obtained from: the privatization database of the Ministry of Privatization CR, Annual Reports of Škoda, koncern, Plzeň (1991a; 1992a; 1993a); MPO CR (1993a); the MPO crisis restructuring analysis of Škoda Plzeň (MPO CR 1992e), and the MPO document preparing Škoda for a public tender (MPO CR 1992f).

62. The quote and concerns of plant managers were repeated to me in several interviews with both Škoda managers and MPO officials. I am especially indebted to Ladislav Novotný, the former general director, and Jan Vrba, the former minister of industry. The quote can also be found in the article on Škoda in Lidové Noviny (4 Dec. 1991). The disputes over the selection of Siemens and competing JV projects from Škoda managers, particularly the project developed by managers of units involved in the nuclear power plant equipment program, can also be found in the popular press. See, for instance, Mladá Fronta Dnes (26 June 1991; 27 Nov. 1991); Rudé Právo (15 Nov. 1991); Lidové Noviny (8, 16 Nov.; 5, 17 Dec. 1991); and Svobodné Slovo (6, 25 Nov. 1991).

63. See MPO documents cited previously for JVs in other holdings and Vrba (1991). I am indebted especially to Michael Gold, head of the USAID-sponsored investment banking advisory team to the Ministry of Privatization CR.

64. One can also find insightful discussions of these problems in Prokoš (1992a,b,c,d,e).

65. For instance, if it were to cancel or decrease already agreed-to purchases by the Energo or Transport groups, Siemens would have to cover the difference between expected profit and sales income for in-progress production. These views were provided to me by the managers of Škoda themselves. See appendix for list of interviews. See also the article by a longtime employee of Škoda, Vladislav Krasný (1992), on the JV controversies.

66. Moreover, the main banks, especially KB and IB, were not very helpful in resolving the potential conflicts in this arrangement, since, in their view, the JV would start working with foreign banks, leaving KB and IB with unprofitable units. The views of the these banks toward JVs were clarified in interviews as well as in internal documents. See Komerční Banka (1993b) and the internal memo from Investiční a Poštovní Banka (1993b).

67. Similar to Škoda Plzeň, Škoda MB had considerable debts, most of which VW was unwilling to assume. The Czechs created a shell company, Prisko, which held the old debts of Škoda MB and the shares in the JV. Prisko had an initial 70 percent stake in the JV from the Škoda MB assets included in the JV. As VW made investments into the JV over the next six years, Prisko's stake would fall to 30 percent and VW's would rise to 70 percent. The equity of Prisko would then be sold on the market and be used to pay off the old debts. The catch was that the FNM would continue to hold the equity of Prisko. The Klaus government, elected in June 1992, wanted nothing to do with the government continuing to hold significant stakes in Czech companies, and thus being responsible for its corporate governance. This view eventually backfired for the Klaus government in the VW deal itself. Realizing that the new government was an absent shareholder, VW failed to meet its investment schedule and reneged on the planned investment for Škoda MB in September 1993. The government has since reversed its policy, renegotiated the terms of the JV with VW, and has taken an active role in the management of the JV and the support of the regional subcontracting networks. A detailed account of this JV and its problems were given to me in interviews with Vrba, Jaroslav Borák, former director of the Division for Engineering, Steel, and Chemicals in the MPO, and Michael Gold, head of the USAID-sponsored investment banking advisory team to the Ministry of Privatization CR. See also the case study of Škoda MB–VW by Feiferlik (1992).

68. Škoda had finished production of sixty locomotives for CSD, the state railway company, which had refused payment (1.2 billion Kcs) for them in early 1992 because budget cutbacks. Energo also had an outstanding debt of 1.9 billion Kcs from the previously state-mandated development of nuclear plant technology. Škoda and its unions argued that since the terms of the finance were dictated by the former government and the government was still the principal shareholder of Škoda, this debt was still the responsibility of the new government. In addition, Siemens needed environmental indemnities on existing environmental damage, which only the government could grant as the holder of Škoda equity. See the MPO documents on Škoda cited previously for detailed discussions of the debt problems of Škoda and the government's changing role with them.

69. In addition to the sources to be cited, the following is based on interviews listed in the Appendix. In the case of Škoda, holding and plants managers, IB and KB managers, and relevant officials from the MPO, Ministry of Privatization CR, and the Fund for National Property were interviewed at least twice from September 1993 to March 1995.

Discussions of the government's aims with the formation of the new privatization project on Škoda Plzeň can be found in the MPO crisis restructuring analysis of Škoda Plzeň (MPO CR 1992e); the MPO document preparing Škoda for a public tender (MPO CR 1992f); and the review of Škoda's new privatization/restructuring process by the Ministry of Privatization CR (Ministry of Administration of National Property and Its Privatization of the Czech Republic 1993c, 1994a). The tender was officialized on 21 October 1992 by the Decree No. 601.

70. Only 41.6 percent of shares were sold in the first wave of vouchers, leaving 6.9 percent unsold. The three largest private shareholders (IPCs) held only 6.8 percent, 4.4 percent, and 2.5 percent, respectively. Three to 4 percent of shares for each firm would be held in the FNM to cover restitution cost. For Škoda Plzeň, 5 percent was transferred free of charge to the Plzeň municipality. About 4 percent was reserved for public compensation funds (DIF and RIF). Eventually, the 6.9 percent unsold from the first wave plus 5 percent unused in the tender were distributed to the public in the second wave of voucher privatization. See the MPO documents cited previously on Škoda.

71. More specifically, Soudek had to create legally independent units out of the existing units, clarify the financial accounts of each, renew negotiations with potential JV partners, and make concrete steps toward recouping uncollected receivables in Russia. The banks had to grant Škoda a six-month moratorium on debt service, decrease penalties on arrears, lengthen payment periods, decrease the interest rates of outstanding debts, and delimit debts among units.

72. For the 1 billion Kcs bond, KB bought 454 million Kcs, IB bought 400 million Kcs, and the Czech Savings Bank bough the remaining 146 million Kcs. Five hundred million Kcs and 1.4 billion Kcs of Škoda outstanding loans were payable to IB and KB, respectively. Their restructuring of the loan maturities, interest rates, six-month payment moratorium, and dissolution of outstanding penalties cost IB and KB over 110 million Kcs and over 550 million Kcs, respectively. Four hundred million Kcs of the KB loss is still in dispute since it was related to the sale of the CSD locomotives, the full payment for which by the government still has yet to resolved. This is based on the review of Škoda's new privatization/restructuring process by the Ministry of Privatization CR (Ministry of the Administration of National Property and Its Privatization of the Czech Republic 1993c, 1994a); a draft of the agreement on loan restructuring between IB and Škoda Plzeň (cerca Dec. 1992/Jan. 1993); and a memo from the USAID investment banking advisory team to IB (19 Jan. 1994).

73. The government already believed that Škoda, along with other N-firms, had to be atomized to facilitate bankruptcies. It was restrained from being so, however, for two reasons. First, such a move could have created a reputation of disregard of ownership rights (new owners created via voucher privatization also opposed atomization). Second, managing the ensuing chaos would bring great financial burdens. If cross-subsidies were as problematic as the government thought they were, several spin-offs would quickly find themselves in default after atomization. Since this could set off a domino effect, the government would be dragged into bailing out the banks and/or some of the spin-offs. The rapid insolvencies of several potentially strong former units of Aero and ČKD holdings were ominous examples of such a process. In addition to the government documents on Škoda just cited, see also MPO CR (1993a), which details this approach.

74. Details of the agreement were given in the review of Škoda's new privatization/restructuring process by the Ministry of Privatization CR (Ministry of the Administration of National Property and Its Privatization of the Czech Republic 1993c, 1994a) and a

draft of the memorandum of understanding to be signed by the parties on 4 November 1992. The signing was then delayed for two weeks. A new agreement was signed between all parties on 16 June 1993, pursuant to the government Decree No. 327 of 16 June 1993, which made the selection of the private parties (Soudek, IB, and KB) official. Copies of both this new agreement and the decree can be found attached to final sale contracts, on file with the author.

75. Soudek received a two-year moratorium on the resale of his shares to a third party for more than the purchase price. IB received a five-year moratorium on the resale of its shares and on any bankruptcy actions taken on its part against Škoda. Any profits made by the banks from the liquidation of any Škoda assets would have to be ceded to the CR government. As of December 1994, the equity involved in the tender was still held in FNM. Soudek signed his sale/purchase contract on 4 November 1994, KB on 2 May 1994, and IB on 8 November 1994. Copies of the contracts are on file with the author.

76. For revealing insights into the limitations of understanding Japanese subcontracting systems from a contractual perspective, see Sabel (1994).

77. Enlightening discussions of privatization of public services and infrastructure in the U.S. and Latin America as a problem of creating a new regulatory structure and oversight role for government as it delegates responsibility to private actors can be found in Hula (1988, particularly chap. 5, 6) and Engel, Rischer, and Galetovic (1997).

78. In addition to Hula (1988) and Engel, Rischer, and Galetovic (1997), see Melumad and Mookherjee (1989) and Hayri (1993). The government may solve its commitment (time-consistency) problem. Even if the government could credibly limit the aggregate amount of subsidies, it faces an adverse selection problem in deciding a priori how to reorganization assets (e.g., breakups or closures) and which technologies to prioritize. With delegation, for the same amount of money the government gets Soudek and the banks to learn about more profitable production projects and combinations of subsidiaries.

79. Sabel (1993, 1994, 1995) gives an extensive discussion of this process in public-private governance structures.

80. Interviews were conducted in the following subsidiaries: Kovárny, TS, Jaderné Strojírenství, Turbíny, ETD, Controls, Dopravní Technika, Tabákové Strojírny, Ozubená Kola, and Hutě.

81. The best accounts of this problem in the press are headline articles in two leading Czech dailies: *Svobodné Slovo* (6 Aug. 1993) and *Hospodářské Noviny* (15 Sept. 1993).

82. These are the necessary conditions identified by Riordan and Sappington (1989) to rule out second sourcing. See also Piore et al. (1994) and Helper et al. (2000).

83. This framework was formalized early on in Škoda's rules and by-laws ("Soubor pravidel holdingových vztahů," passed in the shareholders meeting Decree No. 36/PAS 6/93, signed in meeting no. 6, 29 April 1993). A copy is on file with the author.

84. In understanding the principles used by the banks here, I have gained valuable insight from Sabel, Griffin, and Deeg (1994) on the transformation of German banking practices.

85. Through this channel, the banks offer short-term credits secured with liens on the subsidiaries' receivables. In combining reintermediation with experimental direct lending, the relationship developed between the banks and Škoda bears strong resemblance to the network functions of the Japanese Keiretsu as described in Gilson and Roe (1993) and Sabel (1994).

86. Recent work by Van Wijnbergen on Poland suggest that the first-mover role of the state (via debt forgiveness on back taxes) is sufficient. See Van Wijnbergen (1993).

87. See Cui (1994, 1995) for insightful discussions of the principle of lender of last resort, which demands building both close relations between public and private actors as well as a regulatory framework that permits monitoring through frequent negotiations.

88. For an enlightening discussion on the role of the state in new forms of public-private governance institutions for development, see Sabel (1994, 1995) and Stark and Bruszt (1998, chap. 5). See also Grabher and Stark (1997, chap. 1) on the problem of setting strict short-term rules at the expense of long-term adaptability.

89. This is implicit in Sabel (1995) and more direct in Stark and Bruszt (1998). For further discussion on accountability through deliberation, see Cohen and Rogers (1992), Nino (1996), and Cohen (1998).

90. These views were continually mentioned by the parties when discussing disputes on debt restructuring and the resolution of nuclear and train debts. See the following section for examples.

91. As noted in the amended privatization law (Act No. 210/1993; Resolution No. 568), review is first taken by the multimember board of directors of the FNM and then the parliament. See also Stark and Bruszt (1998, chaps. 6, 8) for the role of the Czech parliamentary system in economic reform.

92. See the *Economist* (18 February 1995); the *Wall Street Journal* (8 May 1996), and the Annual Report of Škoda, koncern, Plzeň (1995).

93. See, for instance, Sabel (1994) and Cui and Gan (1996).

94. See the concluding chapters in Sabel (1996b) and Tendler (1997).

Chapter 5

1. In addition to the case discussed here, that of TST/SST, former VHJs, such as Sigma in industrial pumping systems and Tesla in electronics, also broke themselves up and attempted to resolve some their collective problems through creating close relationships with new, small banks and investment companies. By 1995, the CNB closed and brought eight new banks under forced administration. The hostile takeovers of Agrobanka and the two KB funds sounded the strongest alarms. For discussions of these issues and the activities of the groups led by Motoinvest and Plženská Banka, see Mládek (1995), Pistor and Spicer (1997), and World Bank (1999a).

2. The case of Česká Pojišťovna became fully public in July–August 1996. Daily reports in English can be found over the Internet from Radio Prague. Weekly accounts in English can be found from Internet news service Carolina, particularly Carolina, Nos. 211, 212, 213, and 215. On 17 October 1996, the Czech National Bank announced a plan to help restructure small banks with the assistance of a new entity within the state clearing house for old, nonperforming loans (KOB). See Carolina, No. 220.

3. In 1986, both Škoda and TST had about 60,000 employees. By 1990, both had about 35,000. The decrease is due to organizational changes during the breakup of the VHJ system in 1988–89. Main production unit sizes ranged from 300 to 5,000. Sources: Škoda (1989), Ministry of Industry CR (1992), TST Statistical-Economic Survey (1987), SST (1991).

4. See, in particular, Rowley, Behrens, and Krackhardt (2000), Kogut (2000), Larson (1992), Uzzi (1996), Locke (1995), and Burt (1992, 2000). See Sedatis (1997) for an application of this view on Russian entrepreneurs.

5. This is measured as a percentage of cost and output. See TST (1989) and Šťastný et al. (1990).

6. For instance, hydraulics and pneumatics were consolidated in Rakovník and Vrchlabí, whose intra-TST sales reached 25 to 30 percent of their output. Kuřim became the TST specialist for ball-bearing screws, which accounted for 15 percent of its output. The description of TST in this and the following paragraph is based on interviews with former TST managers (see appendix for list of interviews) and data acquired from Šťastný et al. (1990), TST (1989), SST (1991), and the annual TST Statistical-Economic Survey (1984–1987).

7. SST converted the procurement department of the former headquarters into a firm, TST Servis, which was also jointly owned by the members.

8. See TST (1989), VUOSO (1990), and appendix for list of interviews.

9. State foreign trade houses were converted into a state-owned joint-stock company in the late 1980s, and part of their shares were transferred to the main "customer" VHJs. Strojimport was the principle foreign trade firms for TST. The amount of shares, however, has decreased over time. Initially, TST had about 70 percent of Strojimport shares. During privatization, the Czech government decided that the shares of foreign trade houses that had been transferred onto the books of former VHJ firms would have to be purchased by the firms. This action set off disputes about the amount and price of the shares to be made available for the former VHJ firms and the valuation of assets of the foreign trade houses. These disputes caused discrepancies in the value and the amount of shares that former TST firms were able and willing to buy. According to interviews with former TST firms and officials in the Ministry of Privatization, former TST firms were to buy 30 to 40 percent of Strojimport shares. During these disputes, the former TST firms still acted as collective owners of these shares, at least in terms of voting rights, and sat on the board of Strojimport.

10. See also Grabher and Stark (1997, chap. 1) and Stark and Bruszt (1998, chaps. 5, 6) for discussions of firm and network restructuring in East Central Europe in terms of balancing autonomy and associationalism.

11. This account of SST's strategies is based on extensive interviews with managers of SST member firms and in the directorate of SST. See appendix for list of interviews.

12. As part of the ČSSR's plan to integrate foreign trade operations in the 1980s (recall TST's acquisition of shares in Strojimport), the state created FINOP, the so-called owners of which were the Foreign Trade Ministry and ČSOB. The Ministry of Foreign Trade had 55 percent ownership in FINOP. This stake was privatized through vouchers. Source: Privatization Data Base of the Fund for National Property CR and ČSOB Annual Report (1992).

13. The following is based on ČSOB Annual Report (1992) and data provided by the directorate of SST.

14. A few other leading Czech industrial firms also participated in ISB. The other principal firms were Aero, Škoda Praha, and the agricultural firm OS. These firms eventually sold their shares to ISB management in 1993–94. Data provided by the directorate of SST and ISB (1993).

15. Information on ISB and its funds was obtained from ISB (1993) and interviews with managers in the directorate of SST. See appendix for list of interviews.

16. Similar to German corporate governance laws, Czech law allowed for the creation of a management board and supervisory board. The powers and composition of the boards could vary with changes in the corporate bylaws, decided in general shareholders meetings. For more on Czech corporate governance laws, see Anderson (1994), Coffee (1996), and Pistor and Spicer (1997).

17. In addition to the sources to be cited, this section draws on extensive interviews the author made with managers of the twelve leading SST member firms (according to employment, sales, and historical importance), of the directorate of SST, and of the headquarters and district branches of Komerční Banka and Investiční Banka. Each manager was interviewed at least twice between November 1993 and March 1995. See appendix for list of interviews.

18. The nine largest members has exported 35 to 50 percent of output during the 1980s, about 70 to 75 percent of which was oriented to the CMEA market. see TST Statistical Economic Survey (1983–1987). For an analysis of output, sales, exports, and production practices of SST members, see SST (1994). In surveying the annual reports and financial accounts of the six largest SST firms (ZPS, Kovosvit, Čelákovice, Hostivař, Kuřim, Šmeral) for 1991–1993, one finds the following:

(a) total debt/equity ratios ranging from .5 to 1.3;
(b) time interest earned (EBIT/interest) ranging from 1.2 to 2.08;
(c) decreases in nominal sales ranging from 40 percent to 57 percent.

19. TST Statistical-Economic Survey (1983–1987); firm-level data after 1990 come from interviews, Annual Reports, and prospects of securities of the firms. See ZPS Zlín (1991, 1992a, 1992b, 1993a, 1993b, 1994a, 1994b, 1994c, 1995), Kovosvit (1991, 1992, 1993a, 1993b, 1994, 1995), TOS Čclákovice (1992, 1993a, 1994), HYTOS (1994), TOS Kuřim (1991, 1993a, 1993b, 1994), Šmeral Brno (1993, 1993), TOS Hostivař (1989), Krejcova (1991), and Grcco (1993).

20. See, for instance, Riordan and Sappington (1989).

21. For instance, Hostivař's former plant Mělník had produced gear-making machinery for Hostivař. Yet after Mělník arranged a buyout for itself by the German firm Erwin Junker, Mělník focused production on grinders for Junker. Vrchlabí was TST's main supplier of customized hydraulics. After it formed its JV with an Austrian firm, Vrchlabí reduced its assortment of hydraulics and expanded into new power packs and valves for its partner. Subsequently, sales to SST firms fell from 30 percent of total Vrchlabí sales to just over 10 percent.

22. For instance, Varnsdorf gave a long-term lease for its foundry to a French company. The contract guaranteed the casting needs of Vansdorf's own production but not any other SST firm. The cases involving the foundries of Kovosvit and ZPS will be discussed.

23. Firms expanded assortment mainly in size, tool selection, and set-up (e.g., vertical vs. horizontal machines, universal vs. single-purpose machines).

24. This discussion of the vocational training system and its use by TST/SST is based on the author's interviews with SST firm managers and the study by Vláčil et al. (1996).

25. See Vláčil et al. (1996) and SST (1994).

26. SST (1994, 3–6); Vláčil et al. (1996, chap. 6).

27. Vláčil et al. (1996, 76).

28. The remaining share of costs concerned inputs they had never been able to produce alone: hydraulics from Vrchlabí and Rakovník, ball-bearing screws from Kuřim,

and specific castings from SST forges and Ferrona. But the bulk of purchase costs for CNC machines came in imports for CNC controls.

29. Strojimport had large uncollectible receivables in the former USSR and third world CMEA countries, and it was unable to repay its loans from ČSOB.

30. The comparison is based on the analysis made by Investiční Banka (1993) and the author's calculations from Annual Reports of the big Czech banks (1993, 1994). Note also that the situation in ČSOB became so worrisome that the Czech government (via the FNM) continued to own 90 percent of ČSOB equity in 1995.

31. Similar to other Czech banks, Strojimport and ČSOB were demanding fixed assets of substantial value as collateral, which Varnsdorf did not have available. A common, but slightly more risky, alternative is a lien on the goods to be produced and sold. In export finance, bonding of the actual products for sale is the most common form of collateral. In general, the banks and trade houses are the principal actors who bear most of the risk of the export contract and insurance. In this case, the U.S. customer eventually arranged for a U.S. bank to provide 70 percent of the finance, but at a substantial cut into Varnsdorf's profit margin.

32. Because of the transfer of Strojimport shares to TST under communism, the Czech government declared that SST firms would have to pay for them at the nominal price given for the some remaining shares privatized through vouchers (1,000 Kcs per share). As the firms delayed, the market value of Strojimport dropped to 200 Kcs per share.

33. New banks could be started with only 300 million Kcs of start-up capital. Within eighteen months, thirty-six new, small banks were created in the CR. Yet the new banks faced a squeeze: they were required by law to immediately meet international capital adequacy standards but lacked a branch network and government deposit insurance, both of which the existing big banks inherited. The main CR banks implicitly had government insurance because of their continued large state-ownership stakes. See chapter 3, Kerouš (1993), and Hrnčíř (1994) for discussions of these points.

34. Discussions of the Czech bank failures can be found in Desai (1994) and the *Economist* (1997). Note also that ČSOB was so reluctant to take restructuring initiatives that only after pressure and a subsidy from the CNB did ČSOB take over receivership of Banka Bohemia's deposits.

35. This information was conveyed to the author through interviews with managers of the directorate of SST and officials in the MPO. After the reorganization of the MPO, the employees within the department on the machine-tool industry were laid off and most of the documents were discarded.

36. I greatly benefited from discussions with members of the USAID-sponsored Investment Banking Team for the Ministry of Privatization CR, who worked on these cases, and their internal memos on these cases.

37. See Vláčil et al. (1996, chaps. 6, 7).

38. In addition to the sources to be cited, this section draws mainly on extensive interviews the author made with managers of ZPS Zlín, PPF, of the directorate of SST, and of the headquarters and district branches of Komerční Banka and Investiční Banka. Each manager was interviewed at least twice between November 1993 and March 1995. See appendix for list of interviews.

39. Author's calculations, based on data from the TST Statistical-Economic Survey (1983–87).

40. Author's calculations based on data from ZPS Zlín (1991, 1991b, 1992a, 1992b, 1993a, 1993b, 1994a, 1994b, 1994c, 1995). Interest rate burden is calculated using the standard equation for times interest earned: EBIT / Interest payable.

41. For in depth histories of the SST firms and the business-political practices of Baťa, see Křeček (1992), Lehár (1960), Pochylý (1990), and Smrček (1980).

42. ZPS was the lead machine tool plant, adjacent to ZPS were the shoe manufacturing operations (now called Svit), and down the road was the shoe machinery plant, Malenovice (part of ZPS after 1950). In addition to supporting numerous civic associations and a local cooperative bank to help small firms, Baťa worked closely with local and regional governments to build one of the first Czech vocational training programs and to improve the engineering and management programs in the university in nearby Brno (the capital of Moravia).

43. As discussed in chapter 2, these services were part of a firm's assets but jointly managed with the district and regional councils. See also Locke (1995) and Putnam, Leonardi, and Nanetti (1993) for discussions of the importance of civic associations on economic performance and democracy.

44. In 1995, the Association of Shareholders controlled about 6 percent of ZPS Zlín, still one of the leading shareholders and with a seat on the supervisory board.

45. See Myant (1993, chap. 8) for a discussion of this legal provision and its removal.

46. The workers council also took over the management of conversion units, which advise laid-off employees on developing a new firm and rent excess facilities to them.

47. See Myant (1994) on national industry membership rates.

48. Data on the bond issue and the internal savings bank can be found in ZPS Zlín (1992b, 1994b). The novelty and initial success of the internal bank even made the popular press. See, for instance, the article on ZPS Zlín in *Hospodářské Noviny* (8 Sept. 1992).

49. Baťa had continued the family footwear business in Canada. The associate had worked for thirty years in the U.S. machine tool industry and at Boeing. One of the most critical ventures would be the formation of ZPS Machinery, Inc. in California. Although the author could not obtain full documentation on the ownership of this subsidiary, ZPS managers maintain that Baťa and his associate owned approximately 20 percent of it.

50. Top managers of ZPS, PPF, and Pojišťovna would all serve on, and sometimes chair, the managing and supervisory boards of Pragobanka. The other main shareholders were Třinec Steel Holding and the Czech Savings Bank. Both sold their shares in 1993 to PPF and Pojišťovna. Information on PPF and Pragobanka was obtained in interviews and from PPF (1995) and Pragobanka (1993, 1994, 1996, 1997).

51. Based on data obtained from Annual Reports of Pragobanka (1993, 1994, 1996) and Česká Pojišťovna (1992, 1993, 1994, 1995).

52. Between 1993 and 1995, Pojišťovna's capital investments in Pragobanka grew from 384 million Kcs to 1.48 billion Kcs. Between 1992 and 1995, its direct deposits into Pragobanka grew from 1.2 billion Kcs to 3.625 billion Kcs, making Pragobanka the largest recipient of Pojišťovna's bank investments. Source: Annual Reports of Česká Pojišťovna (1993, 1994, 1995).

53. Information on the actions of PPF was obtained from interviews with managers of PPF, ZPS Zlín, and the directorate of SST and from PPF (1995). The strong position and performance of PPF was noted in Mládek (1993, 1994, 1995) and Lieberman et al. (1995). See Coffee (1996), Kogut and Spicer (1998), and Pistor and Spicer (1997) for discussions of the prevalence of off-market trades and close links between the largest IPCs.

54. See Annual Report of Česká Pojišťovna (1995) and PPF (1995).

55. For discussions of the roles of local privatization councils, see Mejstřík and Berger (1992) and Kotrba and Svejnar (1994).

56. In SM, management owned 15 percent, and in Systems, management had a 51 percent stake. The management of Elektro-montáže, a supplier of heavy-current systems and transformers, had left to form its own company. Rather than simply rent the facilities to this company, ZPS had it purchase a 33 percent equity stake in Elektro-montáže.

57. For instance, SM had direct access to Baťa trade offices throughout the world and formed JVs in China. ZPS facilitated a sales and product development partnership between Systems and a consortium from Silicon Valley. ZPS developed a fifty-fifty partnership between its high-speed milling tool producer and the Austrian firm Kestag. ZPS also helped revive the sales and product assortment for its casting foundry subsidiary, Slévárna, through a partnership with the German firm Deckel.

58. It is worth noting that according to ZPS Zlín (1992a, 1993a, 1993b), Strojimport accounted for less than 20 percent of ZPS exports by the end of 1992.

59. See, for instance, the press reports in the *Wall Street Journal* (27 May 1996), *Ekonom* (1996, No. 21), and *Hospodářské Noviny* (15 June 1995), as well as Annual Reports of ZPS Zlín (1994a, 1995).

60. By 1993, horizontal centers were all but fazed out and vertical centers grew to account for 60 percent of machine tool output. By the end of 1994, ZPS had sold almost 400 vertical centers to the United States and over 240 V-type centers via Deckel. With the Italian-American firm Nuova Tajmac, ZPS redesigned its multispindle lathes for the SAY series and gained a U.S.$15 million contract for its Say 6/16, which led to a contract with Delco's Austrian subsidiary for its Say 6/25–42. Between 1989 and 1993, multispindle lathes' share in machine tool output rose from 15 percent to 30 percent. In addition to sales data and production information obtained through interviews with ZPS managers, information on product development, sales, and exports for ZPS as a whole and its subsidiaries can be found in ZPS Zlín (1992a, 1993a, 1993b, 1994a).

61. See ZPS Zlín (1992b, 1994b).

62. Of the nine members of the board of directors, six were ZPS employees and allies (two from management, one from the local association of shareholders, one from Pragobanka, one from PPF, and one from SST's engineering fund); five of the six members of the supervisory board were ZPS employees or allies. With a two-thirds majority, they had substantial leeway to make such changes as asset revaluations. As ZPS assets began to rise, ZPS management and its allies led the board to revalue its equity capital by one-third, which the board of directors had the right to do. Data on the composition of the board of directors and supervisory board can be found in the Annual Reports of ZPS Zlín (1993a, 1994a, 1995). For analyses of Czech corporate governance laws see Coffee (1996), Anderson (1994), and Pistor and Spicer (1997).

63. Despite growing sales ZPS's debt/equity ratio was still just over parity and its interest rate coverage remained about 1.2 to 1.5 by the end of 1994. Interest rate coverage is calculated using the standard times interest earned equation: EBIT/interest-rate payable. It is worth noting that ZPS's profit to earnings was only 7.5 percent in 1994. Author's calculations based ZPS Zlín (1994a, 1994b). Also, ZPS's aggressive strategy and its problematic financial health grabbed the attention of the popular press eventually. See for instance articles in *Bankové Noviny* (11 Nov. 1995) and *Ekonom* (1996, No. 21).

64. In addition to the sources to be cited, this section draws on extensive interviews the author made with managers of SST member firms, particularly of ZPS Zlín, of the directorate of SST, PPF, and of the headquarters and district branches of Komerční Banka and Investiční Banka. Each manager was interviewed at least twice between

November 1993 and March 1995. Several managers of Zlín and the directorate of SST were reinterviewed in June–September 1996 to discuss the acquisitions and the case of Pojišťovna to be analyzed. See appendix for list of interviews.

65. One obvious option was to hire more workers. ZPS employment data shows employment actually decreased during 1992–94. The main reason was the prohibitive time and money needed to find and train new skilled workers. Despite ZPS's efforts to retrain existing employees through the local vocational training centers, it was unable to attract a new generation. To do so, ZPS would need many new highly qualified machinists and craftspeople. These were, however, in short supply. As discussed earlier in the chapter, the fragmentation of SST and government reforms had undermined the vocational training system, particularly the ability of SST firms to influence and support the development of new skilled trainees. While ZPS's local alliances had helped it use local training centers to maintain its own skill levels and retrain existing employees, it was still unable to do little about attracting a new generation of workers. Therefore, ZPS had to outsource components.

66. This was revealed only after the Asian and Russian crises, when ZPS was put under government receivership.

67. For instance, Kovosvit was also using its component plants and forge for ever more cooperation work for foreign firms, which surpassed 35 percent of total sales in 1994. In addition to interviews, data on the developments of SST firms was obtained through their annual reports. See also press reports on the improved performance and awards received by these firms, such as those in *Bankové Noviny* (22 Mar. 1995) and *Hospodářské Noviny* (30 Aug. 1995, 13 Sept. 1995).

68. ZPS gained substantial control over Zbrojovka's assets in the following ways: the JV utilized most of Zbrojovka's facilities, particularly their largest production hall that was build in the late 1980s; the JV would be under the name of ZPS; a PPF representative, ZPS's technical director, would be the chairman of the board of Zbrojovka; the bylaws of the company were changed to alter the powers of the supervisory board; and ZPS reserved the option to increase its investment in the future to take a majority stake in the JV. Press reports on the increasing control over the JV and Zbrojovka can be found in CTK News Service (20 Feb. 1995) and *Ekonom* (1996, No. 21).

69. These acquisitions and even the behavior of SST's fund was widely covered in the press. See articles for instance in *Hospodářské Noviny* (11 Jan. 1996, 5 Feb. 1996, 8 Feb. 1996), *Bankové Noviny* (7 Nov. 1995, 22 Jan. 1996), *Ekonom* (1996, No. 21), CTK News Service (23 Jan. 1995, 27 June 1995).

70. In addition to the interviews already mentioned, interviews with officials in the FNM and MPO contributed to the following discussion.

71. ZPS planned debt-equity swaps with KB, with Pragobanka refinancing part of the debts as well. The condition of KB's swap was backed by ZPS shares, which KB could exchange for ZPS shares (with ZPS getting KB's shares in Kuřim or Hostivař) at a later date.

72. Over 8 percent of ZPS shares had been reserved as employee shares, to be purchased at a discount. Over 15 percent of Kovosvit shares were reserved for employees as well as for future purchase by an outside investor (originally a foreign partner). The FNM demanded that employee shares be purchased at there book price.

73. For press reports on the difficulties the FNM had with the sales of Hostivař and Kuřim as well as on the subsequent fights with ZPS, see CTK News Service (16 Aug. 1995), *Hospodářské Noviny* (6 Sept. 1995, 3 Apr. 1996, 24 May 1996, 3 June 1996, 19 June 1996).

74. According to the 1995 Annual Report of Česká Pojišťovna, the FNM had retained 26.3 percent, four of the five big Czech banks divided 42 percent between themselves, a small Hungarian bank received 7.7 percent, and 17.5 percent had been privatized in the first wave of vouchers.

75. See, for instance, "Česká pojištovna zatím nezná své nové majitele (Česká Pojiš tovna does not know its owners yet)," *Mladá Fronta Dnes* (16 Jan. 1996, 14); "PPF požádala o svolání valné hromady České pojištovny (PPF asked for a meeting of shareholders of Česká Pojištovna)," *Právo* (17 Jan. 1996); "Fond PPF údajně vykupuje Česká pojištovna (Česká Pojištovna is allegedly buying out stock of the PPF fund)," *Hospodářské Noviny* (26 Feb. 1996).

76. The cases of Česká Pojišťovna, Pragobanka, and Kreditní Banka became fully public in July–August 1996. Daily reports in English can be found over the Internet from Radio Prague. Daily front page reports in Czech can be found in *Hospodářské Noviny*. Weekly accounts in English can be found from Internet news service Carolina, particularly Carolina, Nos. 211, 212, 213, and 215.

77. See, for instance, Roman Pospíšil, "Pragobanka oznámila věřitelùm, že jim vypůjcené peníze nevrátí (Pragobanka annouced to its creditors and it will not return the borrowed funds)," *Pravo* (18 July 1996, 2); and "Dluhy se musí platit včas (Loans have to paid back on time)," *Hospodářské Noviny* (25 July 1996).

78. In addition to interviews with ZPS managers and the FNM, government statements can be found in the press reports mentioned previously.

79. This development was even announced in the press. See, for instance, *Hospodářské Noviny* (12 June 1996).

80. See, for instance, Stark and Bruszt (1998), Evans (1992, 1995), Moon and Prasad (1994), Amsden (1992), Haggard and Kaufman (1992b, 1995), and Knight (1992).

81. See Sabel (1994), Stark (1996), and Stark and Bruszt (1998, particularly chaps. 5, 6).

Chapter 6

1. See Jonathan Schell's insightful essay on the political history of the twentieth century. (Schell, 2000).

2. As the CR entered 1997, it was unique in the region for achieving the following: the sustained electoral success of a single, noncommunist, nonauthoritarian party coalition, relatively few strikes or open protests, unemployment of about 4.1 percent, annual inflation of about 8 percent, annual GNP growth of about 4 percent, and a Standard and Poor's debt rating of "single A." No transforming country in East Central Europe, Latin America, or East Asia can boast such a combination of political and economic achievements.

3. See the recent work of Nellis (1999) and World Bank (1998a) for thoughtful reflections and self-criticisms. A curious case is the recent attempt by Shleifer to stress the importance of capital markets regulations, particularly of small shareholders (Johnson and Shleifer 1999). Shleifer uses the Polish case as proof, while hardly acknowledging not only their past claims about rapid privatization but also the fact that Poland rejected rapid, mass privatization for years and that the state continued to be heavily involved in firms and investment funds during the rise of its capital market and sustained growth.

4. See White (1992, chaps. 1, 2) on the relationship between the shifting positions of network members and power. Knight (1992) and Ostrom (1995) also address the issue of bargaining power of members with respect to their position in a network. But in their models, changes in position and power come largely from external actors providing resources to a particular member and not from members creating new positions on their own within the existing social structure.

5. The reader should note that this conception of worldviews is not new but can be found in Bourdieu (1977), Sabel (1982), and Granovetter (1985), with applications in political economy by, among others, Locke (1995), Herrigel (1996), Saxenian (1994), Cui (1995), and Grabher (1992).

6. As I will discuss further, I want to draw an important distinction between external shocks and external partners. In much of the work on social capital and institutional change, such as that of Coleman (1990), Ostrom (1990), Knight (1992), Burt (1992), Stark and Bruszt (1998), Spenner, Leonardi, and Nanetti (1997), and Putnam et al. (1993), changes in external policies or resources are analyzed in terms of the effects they may have on changing the social capital and structure. But in these models, networks are still viewed as independent and self-governing, making changes in policies and resources understood as exogenous shocks to a network. In contrast, I am arguing that networks are political constructions, whereby the creation and evolution of a network is derived from the sociopolitical relationships built between core network members and outside public actors. Changes in policies and resources are not viewed as exogenous shocks but as part of reconstructing the network and its alliances.

7. Kitschelt (1992, 1993), Munck (1994), and Moon and Prasad (1994) offer good overviews of both approaches; Woodruff (1999a,b) offers excellent insight into the weaknesses of both as applied to contemporary Russia. North (1990) also gives a lengthy discussion of integrating economic and historical factors into the analysis of transformation, though he ends up illustrating an argument based mainly on techno logical and market structure variables. O'Donnell, Schmitter, and Whitehead (1986) made a major contribution in the study of transition by stressing the importance of contingency and actors' resources. But Knight's (1992) work on distributional theory has clearly had a major impact on recent work on transformations. See, for instance, Knight and Sened (1995), Weimer (1997), and Benoit and Scheimann (2001). Frieden (1991), Boycko, Shleifer, and Vishny (1995), and Haggard and Kaufman (1995) offer careful analysis of the problems of policy-making and organization based on models of agency and economic factors. See Grindle (1991, 1996) and Grabher and Stark (1997) enlightening uses of past social structures to analyze transformation. Also in this vein, see Ekiert (1996) for a historical-structuralist analysis of periods of political and social upheaval in East Central Europe during communism. See also Sabel and Zeitlin (1997) and Granovetter (1995) for discussions of change and continuity regarding the formation of business groups and forms of industrial organization.

8. Frieden (1991) and Shafer (1994) are two of the clearest examples of this view in their work, respectively on Latin America and East Asia. Boycko, Shleifer, and Vishny (1995) is exemplary for East Europe. See also Martinelli and Tomassi (1997), Tomassi and Velasco (1996), and Haggard and Kaufman (1992a,b).

9. See Bates (1988), Ostrom (1995), Knight (1992), and Ellickson (1991) for a rational-choice use of past social structures affecting institutional change. Stark and Bruszt (1998), notably in chapters 5 and 6, tend to treat past social networks as unchanging and free of internal conflict in their analysis of East Central Europe.

10. See Frieden (1991), chapter 1, for a detailed discussion calculating actors' preferences and organization according to the asset specificity of certain industries. With respect to industrial organization, these ideas are well developed in Williamson (1985) and Chandler (1977, 1990). For discussions of the importance of sociopolitical factors and historical context shaping industrial strategies and organization, see Locke (1995), Herrigel (1996), Sabel and Zeitlin (1997), and Granovetter (1995).

11. For instance, Putnam et al. (1993, 182–85) admit that a potential drawback of their analysis of local socioeconomic networks is that it fails to address how the actions of local or national actors may alter local social structures over time. For Knight (1992), rules may change, but the existing internal power asymmetries do not. See also DiMaggio and Powell (1991) and DiMaggio (1988) on the problems of integrating change into their models of social structures.

12. For discussions of terms such as field or habitus see Bourdieu (1977), DiMaggio and Powell (1983, 1991), and Stark and Bruszt (1998). For problems on micro-level diversity within national institutional models and historical institutionalism, see Locke (1995), Locke and Thelen (1995), Herrigel (1996), and Thelen and Steinmo (1992).

13. See, in particular, Locke (1995), Herrigel (1996), Grabher (1992), and Grabher and Stark (1997, chap. 1).

14. See Locke (1995, chap. 6), and Locke and Thelen (1995).

15. This discussion of the maintenance of experiments and authority structures will be elaborated and draws on Sabel's concept of "learning by monitoring" (Sabel, 1994, 1995). Sabel derives his understanding of the relationship between monitoring and learning from new methods in production. As a point of distinction, I am trying to show that the reorganization of any social structure is a continual experiment that is intimately related to the political and economic governance of a nation.

16. See Stark (1996, 1999) and Stark and Bruszt (1998).

17. For comparisons of private sector and SME participation in manufacturing across East European countries by the late 1980s, see Acs and Audretsch (1993).

18. See Dornisch (1997, 1999, 2000).

19. For detailed analyses of these privatization mechanisms, see Levitas (1994), OECD (1998b), Jarosz (1999), Nuti (1999), and McDermott (2002).

20. See Blaszczyk and Woodward (1999) and Jarosz (1999) for analyses.

21. See Jarosz (1999, chaps. 2, 4, 10), Dornisch (1997, 1999), and Hausner, Kudlacz, and Szlachta (1995, 1997, 1998). Note that even the liquidation path provided an initial experiment for firms to receive debt relief and banks and voivodships to follow the results.

22. See Van Wijnbergen (1997), Gray and Holle (1998b), Dornisch (1997, 2000), and Montes-Negret and Papi (1996).

23. See Dornisch (1997, 2000).

24. See OECD (1996), Hausner, Kudlacz, and Szlachta (1995, 1998), Baldersheim et al. (1996), Blazek (1993), and Levitas (1999). The basic structural differences are stark. For instance, the number of Czech municipalities grew by 50 percent by 1991 to 6,237 with an average size of 1,700 inhabitants, while Polish gminas maintained most of there integrity (2,466 gminas with average size of 15, 000 inhabitants). While Czech and Polish municipalities have similar, proportional financial data, the Polish gminas were given significantly more autonomy on the use of funds and organizational resources to pursue, that is, investment, infrastructure, regional development, and so on. For analyses of regional development agencies in the region, see Halkier, Danson, and Damborg (1998).

25. On these issues, see OECD (1996), Hausner, Kudlacz, and Sclachta (1995, 1997, 1998), Dornisch (1997, 1999, 2000), and Jarosz (1999).

26. For instance, voivodships are in many ways extensions of the central government, which appoints the governor, controls its budget, and restricts autonomy in the use of funds. See Hausner, Kudlacz, and Sclachta (1995, 1997), Levitas (1999), OECD (1996), and Dornisch (1999, 2000).

27. For the following discussion, see Hausner, Kudlacz, and Sclachta (1995, 1997), and Dornisch (1997, 1999).

28. A similar suggestion has been made by Elster (1993) and Offe (1991) on the problems of achieving multiple reforms simultaneously.

29. Sabel (1995, 35).

30. This is suggested in the work of Levitas (1999). For more on this issue, see Ekiert and Kubík (1999).

31. For an overview of various perspectives on the definition and provision of public goods, particularly with respect to economic institutions, see Coleman (1993), North (1990), Olson (1965), Cui (1995), Amsden (1992), Evans (1995), and Eggertsson (1990). On East Central Europe, see Boycko, Shleifer, and Vishny (1995), Frydman and Rapaczynski (1994), Amsden, Kochanowicz, and Taylor (1994), Kornai (1990b), and Cui (1994, 1995).

32. For the development of rules regulating Polish capital markets, see Coffee (1999). For an analysis of the Polish debt conciliation program, see Gray and Holle (1998). On regional restructuring network and the role of local governments, see Dornisch (1997, 1999), Hausner, Kudlacz, and Szlachta (1995, 1997, 1998), and Levitas (1999).

33. See Sabel (1994, 1995, 1996a,b), Piore et al. (1994), Cohen and Rogers (1992), Grabher and Stark (1997, chap. 1), and Dewey (1927, particularly chaps. 2–4).

34. Although Stiglitz is the father of incomplete markets theory, see Cui (1995, 1996) for an innovative connection between this theory and institution building.

35. For an analysis of these institutions, see Cui (1994, 1995).

36. This connection is most clearly made in Sabel (1994). On industrial development and learning, see Hirschman (1973, 1981), Cui and Gan (1997), Amsden and Hikino (1993), Evans (1995), and Stark and Bruszt (1998, chaps. 5,6). On learning and experiments in firms, see, for instance, Sabel (1993, 1995), Helper et al. (2000), Grabher (1993a), Aoki (1988), and Eccles and Crane (1988).

37. Again these ideas are most clearly developed in Sabel (1994, 1995) and Helper et al. (2000). See also Aoki (1988, 1990), Piore et al. (1994), Shapiro (1994, chap. 5), Cui and Gan (1997), and Hayri and McDermott (1998).

38. Delegation in and of itself has been discussed widely in the literature on regulation and the development of corporatist types of governance. See, for instance, Offe (1981), Lowi (1979), Streeck and Schmitter (1985), and O'Donnell (1994). What is distinctive is the development of work on deliberative forms of governance to address the monitoring problems of decentralization and delegation. In general, see Sabel (1993, 1994, 1995), Cohen (1998), Cohen and Rogers (1992), and Piore (1995). On East Central Europe, see Stark and Bruszt (1998); on Latin America, see Nino (1996); on China, see Cui and Gan (1997) and Oi (1992).

39. See Cohen and Rogers (1992, sec. 3), Cohen (1998), Sabel (1995), Piore (1995), Liebman (1991), and Parks and Oakerson (1993).

40. See Hula (1988, particularly chaps. 5, 6). A good discussion of the dilemmas facing Latin American governments in franchising infrastructure development can be found in Engel, Rischer, and Galetovic (1997).

41. Again this and other points are best developed in Sabel (1993, 1994, 1995). For similar discussions on this point see Piore et al. (1994), Piore (1995), Cui (1995, 1996), Sunstein (1995), and Cohen and Rogers (1992).

42. In addition to the previous citations of Sabel and Piore, see Cui (1996), Stark and Bruszt (1998, chap. 8), Nino (1996, chaps. 6, 7), Cohen and Rogers (1992), and Cohen (1998).

43. This point is also related to debates on the general will. See Cohen (1998), Cohen and Rogers (1992), Nino (1996), Sample (1996), Piore (1995, particularly chap. 7), Dewey (1927), Stark and Bruszt (1998, chaps. 5, 8), and Sabel's discussion of trust (1993).

44. See, for instance, Stark and Bruszt's (1998, chap. 5) discussion of East Central European countries running between neoliberal and developmental statist models of reform.

45. See Grabher and Stark (1997, 1–3).

46. See the *Economist*'s (1997) survey of emerging market banking for an excellent overview. A typical example of this problem is the dilemmas of dealing with different types of capital inflows. See Agosin and Ffrench-Davis (1996), and Corbo and Hernandez (1996). For some excellent cases on Latin America, particularly Argentina, see Guidotti et al. (1996), Powell and Balzarotti (1996), Powell, Broda, and Burdisso (1997), and Torre (1997).

47. The idea is that currency instability also comes from problems in the way bank lending affects productivity and export growth. See supra note 46 for cites.

48. See Locke(1995) and Herrigel (1996) on the problems of contrasting institutional orders within a nation. See also Piore (1995), Berger (1981), Offe (1981), Meier (1991), and Huntington (1975) on the problems of increasing and diverse demands on government.

49. See Piore (1995, chap. 7), Cohen (1996), Cohen and Rogers (1994), Nino (1995), and Stark and Bruszt (1998, chap. 7).

50. On Italy, see Locke (1995) and Putnam, Leonardi, and Nanetti (1993); on Ireland, see Sabel (1996b); on Brazil, see Tendler (1997); on Russia, see Woodruff (1999a) and Prokop (1996).

51. See, for instance, Tendler (1997) and McDermott (2000).

52. A detailed account can be found in McDermott (2000).

53. See Stark and Bruszt (1998, chaps. 6, 7) and Cohen and Sabel (1997).

54. See, particularly, Levitas (1999) and Hausner, Kudlacz, and Szlachta (1995, 1998).

55. For more on these issues, see Levitas (1999), Dornisch (1997, 1999), and Gray and Holle (1998).

References

Books, Articles, Working Papers

Ackerman, Bruce. 1991. *We the People: Foundations.* Cambridge: Harvard University Press.

Acs, Zoltan, and David Audretsch, eds. 1993. *Small Firms and Entrepreneurship: An East-West Comparison.* Cambridge: Cambridge University Press.

Adámková, Alena. 1992. "Konverze bez cizí pomoci." *Ekonom* 44: 41.

———. 1993a. "Díky bance nové šance?" *Ekonom* 26: 41–42.

———. 1993b. "Léčba se protahuje." *Ekonom* 9: 30–33.

———. 1993c. "Tradice zavazuje." *Ekonom* 7: 33–34.

Agosin, Manuel, and Ricardo Ffrench-Davis. 1996. Managing Capital Inflows in Latin America. In *The Tobin Tax: Coping with Financial Volatility*, edited by M. ul Haq, I. Kaul, and I. Grunberg. New York: Oxford University Press.

Agosin, Manuel, Ricardo Ffrench-Davis, and A. Uthoff. 1995. Capital Movements, Export Strategy, and Macroeconomic Stability in Chile. In *Coping with Capital Surges: The Return of Finance to Latin America*, edited by R. Ffrench-Davis and M. Agosin. Boulder, Colo.: Lynne Reinner.

American Machinist. 1983. "Manufacturing Systems: Czechoslovak Machine Tools." 127(2): 35.

Amsden, Alice H. 1989. *Asia's Next Giant: South Korea and Late Industrialization.* New York: Oxford University Press.

———. 1992. A Theory of Government Intervention in Late Industrialization. In *State and Market in Development: Synergy or Rivalry?* edited by Dietrich Rueschemeyer and Louis Putterman. Boulder, Colo.: Lynne Reiner.

Amsden, Alice H., and Takashi Hikino. 1993. Innovating or Borrowing Technology: Exploration of Two Paths Toward Industrial Development. In *Learning and Technological Change*, edited by Ross Thompson. London: Macmillan.

Amsden, Alice H., Jacek Kochanowicz, and Lance Taylor. 1994. *The Market Meets Its Match: Restructuring the Economies of Eastern Europe.* Cambridge: Harvard University Press.

Anderson, Robert. 1994. Voucher Funds in the Transition Economies: The Czech and Slovak Examples. The World Bank Technical Department ECA/MNA Regions, 11 May. Mimeograph.

"Anketa k plánu na rok." 1978. *Plánované Hospodářství* 10: 20–29.

Antal-Mokos, Z. 1998. *Privatisation, Politics and Economic Performance in Hungary.* Cambridge: Cambridge University Press.

Aoki, M. 1988. *Information, Incentives, and Bargaining in the Japanese Economy.* Cambridge: Cambridge University Press.

———. 1990. "Toward an Economic Model of the Japanese Firm." *Journal of Economic Literature* 28: 1–27.

Arbess, Daniel. 1992. "One-Stop Shopping in Czech Privatization." *Financial Times*, September 15: 15.

Arendt, Hannah. 1951. *The Origins of Totalitarianism.* New York: Harcourt, Brace and World.

Asselain, Jean-Charles. 1984. *Planning and Profits in Socialist Economies.* Boston: Routledge and Kegan Paul.

Atkinson, Anthony, and John Micklewright. 1992. *Economic Transformation in Eastern Europe and the Distribution of Income.* Cambridge: Cambridge University Press.

Aucoin, P. 1990. "Administrative Reform in Public Management: Paradigms, Principles, Paradoxes, and Pendulums." *Governance: An International Journal of Public Administration* 3(2): 115–37.

Audretsch, David. 1995. *Innovation and Industry Evolution.* Cambridge: MIT Press.

———. 2000. Globalization, Entrepreneurship and the Strategic Management of Places, Institute for Development Strategies, Indiana University. Working Paper.

Aven, Petr. 1991. "Economic Reform: Different Results from Similar Actions." *Communist Economies and Economic Transformation* 3(4): 417–38.

———. 1992. Economic Reform in a Bargaining Economy. In *Reform and Transformation in Eastern Europe,* edited by Janos Matyas Kovacs and Marton Tardos. London: Routledge.

Aven, Petr, and V. Shironin. 1988. "The Reform of the Economic Mechanism." *Problems of Economics* (June): 33–48.

BBDS Servis. 1994a. Privatizace a současná ekonomická pozice podniků hutnictví železa. Prague, April. Mimeograph.

———. 1994b. Průmyslová politika, ingerence, státu k hutnímu průmyslu. Prague, April. Mimeograph.

Balcerowicz, Eva, Cheryl Gray, and Iraj Hoshi. 1998. *Enterprise Exit Processes in Transition Economies.* Budapest: Central European University Press.

Baldersheim, H., M. Illner, A. Offerdal, L. Rose, and P. Swianiewicz, eds. 1996. *Local Democracy and the Processes of Transformation in East-Central Europe.* Boulder, Colo.: Westview Press.

Barzel, Yoram. 1989. *Economic Analysis of Property Rights.* Cambridge: Cambridge University Press.

Bates, Robert. 1988. "Contra Contractarianism: Some Reflections on the New Institutionalism." *Politics and Society* 16: 387–401.

Bautzová, L. 1992. "Tatra Kopřivnice—zrcadlo doby." *Ekonom* 49: 30–33.

Bautzová, L., and A. Adámková. 1993. "(Nejen) Tramvaj pro Manilu." *Ekonom* 14: 36–38.

Begg, David, and Richard Portes. 1992. Enterpriase Debt and Economic Transformation in Central and Eastern Europe. London, CEPR Discussion Paper No. 695.

Beissinger, Mark. 1988. *Scientific Management, Socialist Discipline, and Soviet Power.* Cambridge: Harvard University Press.

Benáček, Vladimír. 1992. Market Failure versus Government Failure—The Ways of the Emerging Market Economies. Prague, CERGE, unpublished manuscript.

Benoit, Kenneth, and John W. Schiemann. 2001. "Institutional Choice in New Democracies: Bargaining over Hungary's 1989 Electoral Law." *Journal of Theoretical Politics* 13(April): 153–82.

Berger, Suzanne. 1972. *Peasants against Politics: Rural Organization in Brittany 1911–1967.* Cambrige: Harvard University Press.

———, ed. 1981. *Organizing Interest Groups in Western Europe.* New York: Cambridge University Press.

Berger, Suzanne, and Michael Piore. 1980. *Dualism and Discontinuities in Industrial Societies.* New York: Cambridge University Press.

Berliner, Joseph. 1976. *The Innovation Decision in the Soviet Union.* Cambridge: MIT Press.

———. 1988. *Soviet Industry.* Ithaca, N.Y.: Cornell University Press.

Blanchard, Olivier, Rudiger Dornbusch, Paul Krugman, Richard Layard, and Lawrence Summers. 1991. *Reform in Eastern Europe.* Cambridge: MIT Press.

Blaszczyk, B. 2000. The Privatization Program and Post-Privatization Ownership Evolution in Poland. Warsaw, the CASE Foundation, unpublished manuscript from the project Secondary Privatization: The Evolution of Ownership Structure of Privatized Companies.

Blaszczyk, B., and R. Woodward, eds. 1999. Privatization and Company Restructuring in Poland. Poland, Center for Social and Economic Research. Case Report No. 18.

Blažek, Jiří. 1993. Changing Local Budgets in the Czech Republic—Half Way Over? Paper presented for the conference, Regional Organization and Administrative Performance in Central Europe, 27–30 September, Prague.

Blecha, Adam. 1993. "AKčionáři a dividendy: Co všechno přináší vlastnictví aKčií." *Respekt* (April): 5–18.

Blejer, Mario, and Fabrizio Coricelli, eds. 1996. *The Making of Economic Reform in Eastern Europe: Conversations with Reformers in Poland, Hungary, and the Czech Republic.* London: Edward Elgar.

Bohm, Andrea, and Marko Simoneti, eds. 1993. *Privatization in Central and Eastern Europe.* Ljubljana:Central and Eastern Europe Privatization Network.

Bolton, P., and M.D. Whinston. 1993. "Incomplete Contracts, Vertical Integration, and Supply Assurance." *Review of Economic Studies* 60: 121–48.

Borish, Micahel, Millard Long, and Michel Noel. 1995. Restructuring Banks and Enterprises: Recent Lessons from Transition Countries. World Bank Discussion Paper, Series 279.

Borish, Michael, and Michel Noel, eds. 1996. Private Sector Development During Transition. World Bank Discussion Paper, Series 318.

Bourdieu, Pierre. 1977. *Outline of a Theory of Practice.* Cambridge: Cambridge University Press.

Boycko, Maxim, Andrei Shleifer, and Robert Vishny. 1993. "Privatizing Russia." *Brookings Papers on Economic Activity* 2: 139–81.

———. 1995. *Privatizing Russia.* Cambridge: MIT Press.

Brabec, Vladimír, and Karel Klein. 1993. "Holding u nás—ano, či ne?" *Hospodářské noviny,* 25 May: 16–18.

Brealey, Richard, and Stuart Myers. 1991. *Principles of Corporate Finance.* New York: McGraw-Hill.

Brom, Karla, and Mitchell Orenstein. 1994. "The Privatized Sector in the Czech Republic." *Europe-Asia Studies* 4(6): 893–928.

Brown, Annette N., Barry W. Ickes, and Randi Ryterman. 1994. The Myth of Monopoly: A New View of Industrial Structure in Russia. Transition Economics Division, The World Bank. Policy Research Working Paper No. 1331.

Bruszt, Laszlo. 1990. "Hungary's Neogtiated Revolution." *Social Research* 57(2): 365–87.

———. 1994. Reforming Alliances: Labor, Management, and State Bureaucracy in Hungary's Economic Transformation. In *Strategic Choice and Path Dependency in Post-Socialism: Institutional Dynamics in the Transformation Process,* edited by J. Hausner, B. Jessop, and K. Nielsen. London: Edward Elgar.

————. 1996. The Antall Government, the Labor Unions, and the Employers' Associations. In *Lawful Revolution in Hungary, 1989–1994,* edited by B. Kiraly and A. Bozoki. Boulder, Colo.: Atlantic Research and Publications Social Science Monographs.

Bryant, Chistopher G.A. 1994. Economic Utopianism and Sociological Realism: Strategies for Transformation in East-Central Europe. In *The New Great Transformation? Change and Continuity in East-Central Europe,* edited by Christopher G.A. Bryant and Edmund Mokrzycki. New York: Routledge.

Brzezinski, Zbigniew K. 1956. *Totalitarian Dictatorship and Autocracy.* Cambridge: Harvard University Press.

Buchanan, James. 1980. Rent-Seeking and Profit-Seeking. In *Toward a Theory of the Rent-Seeking Society,* edited by J. Buchanan and R. Tollison. College Station: Texas A&M University Press.

Buchtíková, Alena, and Aleš Čapek. 1993. Privatization in the Czech Republic: Privatization Strategies and Priorities. Paper presented at the Conference on Sources of Privatization in Eastern Europe, 21–22 May, Budapest.

————. 1994. Financial Structure, Performance, and Banks. Institute of Economics, Czech National Bank. Working Paper No. 18.

Buchtíková, Alena, Aleš Čapek, and Eva Macourkova. 1992. Statistical Analysis of the Privatization Projects. Institute of Economics, Prague. Mimeograph.

Buchtíková, Alena, and Vladislav Flek. 1992. Wage Determination in Czechoslovakia: Government Power versus Trade Union Power. Institut Ekonomie, Czech National Bank. Working Paper No. 2.

————. 1993a. The Impact of Deconcentration and Indirect Industrial Policy on Structural Development and Export Performance in Czech Republic (1989–1992). Paper presented for the ACE Workshop in Vienna.

————. 1993b. Income Policy and Wage Development in the Czech Republic. Institut Ekonomie, Czech National Bank. Working Paper No. 12.

————. 1995. "Enterprise Behavior, Wage Decisions, and Employment in the Czech Industry." Institute of Economics, Czech National Bank, Working Paper No. 32.

Budina, Nina, Jan Hanousek, and Zdeněk Tůma. 1994. Money Demand and Seignorage in Transition. CERGE-EI. Working Paper No. 48.

Bulíř, Aleš. 1989. "Money and the Behaviour of Firms in Centrally Planned Economy." Department of Finance and Credit, Vysoká Škola Ekonomická. February. Mimeograph.

————. 1990. "Mikroekonomické souvislosti peněžní politiky v ekonomice složené z koalic." Prague, May. Mimeograph.

Burawoy, Michael, and Janos Lukacs. 1992. *The Radiant Past: Ideology and Reality in Hungary's Road to Capitalism.* Chicago and London: Chicago University Press.

Burt, R. 1992. *Structural Holes: The Social Structure of Competition.* Cambridge: Harvard University Press.

————. 2000. "The Network Structure of Social Capital." *Research in Organizational Behavior* 22: 345–423.

Camdessus, M. 1995. *Russia's Transformation at a Turning Point.* Address presented at the Conference of the U.S.-Russia Business Council, 29 March, Washington, DC.

Campbell, Robert W. 1966. On the Theory of Economic Administration. In *Industrialization in Two Systems: Essays in Honor of Alexander Gerschenkron,* edited by Henry Rosovsky. New York: John Wiley and Sons.

Čapek, Aleš. 1994. The Bad Debts Problem in the Czech Economy. Institute of Economics, Czech National Bank. Mimeograph.

———. 1995. The Bad Loans and the Commercial Banks' Policies in the Czech Republic. Paper prepared for the ACE Conference, Corporate Adjustment, Market Failures, and Industrial Policy in the Transition, 5–6 May, Prague.

Casey, Cornelius, and Norman Bartczak. 1985. "Using Operating Cash Flow Data to Predict Financial Distress: Some Extension." *Journal of Accounting Research* (spring): 384–401.

Češka, Roman. 1993. Privatization in the Czech Republic—1992. In *Privatization in Central and Eastern Europe*, edited by Andreja Bohm and Marko Simoneti. Ljubliana: Central and Eastern Europe Privatization Network.

Chandler, Alfred. 1977. *The Visible Hand: The Managerial Revolution in American Business*. Cambridge: Harvard University Press.

———. 1990. *Scale and Scope: The Dynamics of Industrial Capitalism*. Cambridge, Mass.: Belknap Press.

Chandler, Alfred, Franco Amatori, and Takashi Hikino, eds. 1997. *Big Business and the Wealth of Nations*. New York: Cambridge University Press.

Charap, Joshua, and Alena Zempinerová. 1993. Management Buyouts in the Privatisation of Programme of the Czech Republic. Paper presented at the Organization for Economic Cooperation and Development Advisory Group on Privatisation, Third Plenary Meeting, 31 March–2 April, Paris.

Chavance, B., and E. Magnin. 1997. Emergence of Path-Dependent Mixed Economies in Central Europe. In *Beyond Market and Hierarchy: Interactive Governance and Social Complexity*, edited by Ash Amin and Jerzy Hausner. Cheltenham, England: Edward Elgar.

Chronc, Oldřich, and Bohumil Široký. 1986. *Československé strojírenství v mezinarodní dělbě práce*. Praha: Nakladatelstvi svoboda.

Chrtek, Milan. 1988. "Působení finančních a úvěrových nástrojů na vývoj zásob." *Finance a úvěr* 38(3): 186–89.

Claessens, Stijn, Simeon Djankov, and Gerhard Pohl. 1997. Ownership and Corporate Governance: Evidence from the Czech Republic. World Bank Policy Research Working Paper No. 1737.

Clague, Christopher, and Gordon C. Rausser, eds. 1992. *The Emergence of Market Economies in Eastern Europe*. Cambridge: Blackwell Publishers.

Coffee, John. 1995. Investment Privatization Funds: The Czech Experience. Conference on Corporate Governance in Central Europe and Russia, The World Bank. Mimeograph.

Coffee, J. C. 1996. Institutional Investors in Transitional Economies: Lessons from the Czech Experience. In *Corporate Governance in Central Europe and Russia*, vol. 1, edited by R. Frydman, C. W. Gray, and A. Rapaczynski. Budapest: Central European University Press.

Coffee, J. 1999. Privatization and Corporate Governance: The Lessons from Securitites Market Failure. The Center for Law and Economic Studies, Columbia Law School. Working Paper No. 158.

Cohen, Joshua. 1998. Fundamental of Deliberative Democracy. Department of Political Science, MIT, unpublished manuscript.

Cohen, Joshua, and Joel Rogers. 1992. "Secondary Associations and Democratic Governance." *Politics and Society* 20(4): 393–472.

Cohen, Joshua, and Charles Sabel. 1997. "Directly-Deliberative Polyarchy." *European Law Journal* 3(4): 313–40.

Coleman, James. 1988. "Social Capital and the Creation of Human Capital." *American Journal of Sociology* 94 (Suppl.): S95–S120.

———. 1990. *Foundations of Social Theory.* Cambridge: Harvard University Press.

———. 1993. A Rational Choice Perspective on Economic Sociology. Department of Sociology, University of Chicago, unpublished manuscript.

Comisso, Ellen. 1991. Where Have We Been and Where Are We Going? Analyzing Post-Socialist Politics in the 1990s. In *Political Science: Looking to the Future,* edited by William Crotty. Evanston, Ill.: Northwestern University Press.

Corbett, Jenny, and Colin Mayer. 1991. "Financial Reform in Eastern Europe: Progress with the Wrong Model." *Oxford Review of Economic Policy* 7(4): 57–75.

Corbo, Vittorio, Fabrizio Coricelli, and Jan Bossak, eds. 1991. *Reforming Central and Eastern European Economies: Initial Result and Challenges.* Washington, D.C.: The World Bank.

Corbo, Vittorio, and Leonardo de Hernandez. 1996. "Macroeconomic Adjustment to Capital Inflows: Lessons from Recent Latin American and Asian Lessons." *The World Bank Research Observer* 11(1): 61–85.

Csaki, G., and A. Macher. 1997. *Ten Years of Privatization in Hungary.* Budapest, English-language manuscript.

Cui, Zhiyuan. 1991. "Market Incompleteness, Innovation, and Reform: A Commentary on Adam Przeworski's Article." *Politics and Society* 19(1): 59–70.

———. 1994. Can Privatization Solve the Problem of the Soft Budget Constraint? In *Changing Political Economies,* edited by Vĕdat Milors. New York: Lyne Reiner.

———. 1995. The Dilemmas of the Soft Budget Constraint: Three Insitutions that Challenge the 'Invisible Hand' Paradigm. Ph.D. diss., Department of Political Science, University of Chicago.

———. 1996. "Privatization and the Consolidation of Democratic Regimes: An Analysis and an Alternative." *Journal of International Affairs* 50(2): 675–93.

Cui, Z., and Y. Gan, eds. 1997. *China: A Reformable Socialist Giant?* Hong Kong: Oxford University Press.

"Czechs Postpone their Programme." 1991. *Eastern European Privatization Network.* November, 2.

Dabrowski, Janusz M., Michal Federowicz, and Anthony Levitas. 1991. "Polish State Enterprises and the Properties of Performance: Stabilization, Marketization, Privatization." *Politics and Society* 19(4): 430–37.

Davidson, Sidney, Clyde Stickney, and Roman Weil. 1988. *Financial Accounting: An Introduction to Concepts, Methods, and Uses.* Chicago: Dryden Press.

De Melo, Martha, Cevdet Denizer, and Alan Gelb. 1996. From Plan to Market: Patterns of Transition. Transition Economics Division, Policy Research Department, World Bank. Working Paper No. 1564.

Deeg, Richard. 1994. Banking on the East: The Political Economy of Investment Finance in Eastern Germany. Wissenschaftszentrum Berlin für Sozialforschung Working Paper No. 94-303.

———. 1999. *Finance Capitalism Unveiled: Banks and the German Political Economy.* Ann Arbor: University of Michigan Press.

Denton, Nicholas. 1994. "Survey of the Czech Republic." *Financial Times,* December 19: 9.

Desai, Padma, ed. 1983. *Marxism, Central Planning, and the Soviet Economy: Economic Essays in Honor of Alexander Erlich*. Cambridge: MIT Press.

Desai, Raj. 1994. The Politics of Credit-Based Adjustment in Czechoslovakia: Economic Interest and Financial Repression in a Post-Communist State. Paper presented at the 1994 Annual APSA Meetings, 1–4 September, at the New York Hilton.

———. 1995. Governing Enterprises in Transition Economies: The Problem of Mixed Ownership in the Czech Republic. Paper presented at the Workshop on East European Politics, October, at the Center for European Studies, Harvard University.

———. 1996. Organizing Markets: The Politics of Privatization in a Post-Communist Economy. Ph.D. diss., Department of Government, Harvard University.

Dewey, John. 1927. *The Public and its Problems*. New York: H. Holt.

DiMaggio, Paul. 1988. Interest and Agency in Institutional Theory. In *Institutional Patterns and Organizations*, edited by Lynne Zucker. Cambridge: Balinger Publishing Company.

DiMaggio, Paul, and Walter Powell. 1983. "The Iron Cage Revisited: Institutional Isomorphism and Collective Rationality in Organizational Fields." *American Sociological Review* 48: 147–60.

———. 1991. Introduction. In *The New Institutionalism in Organizational Analysis*, edited by W. Powell and P. DiMaggio. Chicago: University of Chicago Press.

Di Palma, Giuseppe. 1990. *To Craft Democracies: An Essay on Democratic Transitions*. Berkeley and Los Angeles: University of California Press.

Dittus, Peter. 1994. "Bank Reform and Behavior in Central Europe." *Journal of Comparative Economics* 19(3): 335–61.

Dolečková, M. 1993. "Svaz průmyslu: Chceme stabilitu; Sdružení podnikatelů: Chceme zvýhodnit." *Hospodářské noviny*, 22 February.

Doner, Richard F. 1992. "Limits of State Strength: Toward an Institutional View of Economic Development." *World Politics* 44: 398–431.

Dorf, Michal C., and Charles F. Sabel. 1998. "A Constitution of Democratic Experimentalism." *Columbia Law Review* 98(2): 267–473.

Dornisch, David. 1997. An Ecology of Projects: Economic Restructuring and Network Recombination in Post-Socialist Poland. Ph.D. diss., Department of Sociology, Cornell University.

———. 1999. "Project Networks vs. Networks of Cooperation: Regional Restructuring and Governance in Post-Socialist Poland." *BISS Public* 27: 73–103.

———. 2000. The Social Embeddedness of Polish Regional Development: Representative Institutions, Path Dependencies, and Network Formation. Sussex, England, Mimeograph.

Dostál, Petr, Michal Illner, Jan Kára, and Max Barlow, eds. 1992. *Changing Territorial Administration in Czechoslovakia*. Amsterdam: Instituut voor Sociale Geografie.

Dostál, Vladimír, Zdeněk Jadrný, Jan Josif, Václav Prucha, and Zdeněk Volf. 1988. *Dějiny hutnictvi zeleza v Československu (1945–80)* Vol. 3. Praha: Nakladatelstvi Československé akademie věd.

Duchecek, Frantisek. 1983. "Některé tendence vývoje financi podnikove sféry." *Finance a úvěr* 33(5): 104–21.

Durrer, Jiří, and Ladislav Pachl. 1982. "Pohled na některé názory pracovníků chozrasotní sféry." *Finance a úvěr* 32(5): 65–85.

Dyba, Karel, and Jan Svejnar. 1994. An Overview of Recent Economic Developments in the Czech Republic. CERGE-EI Working Paper No. 61.

"East European Privatization: Making it Work." 1993. *Economist*, March 13: 90.

Eccles, Robert, and Dwight Crane. 1988. *Doing Deals: Investment Banks at Work.* Boston: Harvard Business School Press.

Edwards, Jeremy. 1993. "The Financing of Industry, 1970–80: An International Comparison." Contribution to the CEPR project, International Study of the Financing of Industry, London. Mimeograph.

Edwards, Jeremy, and Klaus Fischer. 1994. *Banks, Finance, and Investment in Germany.* Cambridge: Cambridge University Press.

Eggertsson, Thrainn. 1990. *Economic Behavior and Institutions.* Cambridge: Cambridge University Press.

Ekiert, Grzegorz. 1991. Democratization Processes in East Central Europe: A Theoretical Reconsideration." *British Journal of Political Science* 21: 285–313.

———. 1996. *The State Against Society: Political Crises and their Aftermath in East Central Europe.* Princeton, N.J.: Princeton University Press.

Ekiert, Grzegorz, and Jan Kubik. 1999. *Rebellious Civil Society: Popular Protest and Democratic Consolidation in Poland, 1989–1993.* Ann Arbor: University of Michigan Press.

Ellerman, D. 1998. Voucher Privatization with Investment Funds: An Institutional Analysis. Development Economics Unit, World Bank. Working Paper No. 1924.

Ellickson, Robert. 1991. *Order without Law: How Neighbors Settle Disputes.* Cambridge: Harvard University Press.

Elster, Jon. 1993. The Necessity and Impossibility of Simultaneous Economic and Political Reform. In *Constitutionalism and Democracy,* edited by Douglas Greenberg, et. al. Oxford: Oxford University Press.

———, ed. 1996. *The Roundtable Talks and the Breakdown of Communism.* Chicago: University of Chicago Press.

Engel, Eduardo, Ronald Rischer, and Alexander Galetovic. 1997. Infrastructure Franchising and Government Liabilities. Paper prepared for the World Bank Conference, Managing Government Exposure to Private Infrastructure Projects, 29–30 May, in Cartagena, Columbia.

Erlich, Alexander. 1960. *The Soviet Industrialization Debate, 1924–1928.* Cambridge: Harvard University Press.

European Bank for Reconstruction and Development (EBRD). 1994, 1995, 1996, 1997, 1998. *Transition Report.* London: European Bank for Reconstruction and Development.

European Business Solutions. 1995. "Bankruptcy: State Behemoths Manage to Put Off Day of Reckoning." *Czech and Slovak Market Watch,* Year 2, Issue 1: 15–19.

Evans, Peter B. 1992. The State as the Problem and Solution. In *The Politics of Economic Adjustment,* edited by S. Haggard and R. Kaufman. Princeton, N.J.: Princeton University Press.

———. 1995. *Embedded Autonomy: States and Industrial Transformation.* Princeton, N.J.: Princeton University Press.

Evans, Peter B., Dietrich Reuschemeyer, and Theda Skocpol. 1985. *Bringing the State Back In.* Cambridge: Cambridge University Press.

Federal Ministry of Finance CSFR. 1990. *Dlouhodobý vývoj finančních ukazatelů ČSFR do roku 1989.* Praha: Federal Ministry of Finance CSFR.

Federal Ministry of Universal Engineering. 1980. "Zásady pro rozvíjení chozrasčotu VHJ a podniků rozpracované na podmínky resortu všeobecného strojírenství." Prague, December.

Federal Ministry of Universal Engineering. 1986. "Hlavní směry a zásady: rozvíjení chozrasotu VHJ a podniků v 8. Pětiletce." Praha, December.

Feiferlík, Radek. 1992. Organizační kultura firem v tržní ekonomice. Diploma Thesis, Fakulta podnikohospodářská, Vysoká Škola Ekonomická, April.

Field, Mark, ed. 1976. Social Consequences of Modernization in Communist Societies. Baltimore: Johns Hopkins University Press.

Filačková, Jana, and Marie Štajnerová. 1983. Empirický průzkum vlivu vybraných faktorů a současných stimulačních nástrojů na dlouhodobost rozvoje VHJ. VUSTE, Praha, October. Research report 1 45/104/0.037.

Flek, Vladislav. 1993. Employer's Unions in the Czech Republic. Friedrich Ebert Foundation, Prague. Mimeograph.

Fligstein, Neil. 1996. "Markets as Politics: A Political Approach to Market Institutions." American Sociological Review 61: 656–73.

Fligstein, Neil, and Robert Freeland. 1995. "Theoretical and Comparative Perspectives on Corporate Organization." Annual Review of Sociology 21: 21–43.

Francis, Arthur, and Peter Grootings, eds. 1989. New Technolgies and Work: Capitalist and Socialist Perspectives. New York: Routledge.

Frieden, Jeffry. 1991. Debt, Development, and Democracy: Modern Political Economy and Latin America, 1965–1985. Princeton, N.J.: Princeton University Press.

Friedman, Daved. 1988. The Misunderstood Miracle. Ithaca, N.Y.: Cornell University Press.

Friedman, Milton. 1962. Capitalism and Freedom. Chicago: University of Chicago Press.

Frydman, Roman, and Andrzej Rapaczynski. 1993. "Insiders and the State: Overview of Responses to Agency Problems in East European Privatizations." Economics of Transition 1(1): 9 59.

———. 1994. Privatization in Eastern Europe: Is the State Withering Away? London: Central European University Press.

Frydman, Roman, Kenneth Murphy, and Andrzej Rapaczynski. 1998. Capitalism with a Comrade's Face: Studies in the Postcommunist Transition. Budapest: Central European University Press.

Gabor, Istvan R. 1990. On the Immediate Prospects for Private Enrpreneurship and Reembourgoisement in Hungary. Cornell Working Paper No. 90.3.

Galík, Rudolf. 1993a. The Transformation of TV Sets Producer. CIS—Middle Europe Centre, London Business School, October. Discussion Paper Series No. 3.

———. 1993. Firm's Adaptability in the Transition Period. CIS -Middle Europe Centre, London Business School, October. Discussion Paper Series No. 3.

Garton Ash, Timothy. 1989. The Uses of Adversity: Essays on the Fate of Central Europe. New York: Random House.

Geertz, Clifford. 1973. The Interpretation of Cultures. New York: Basic Books.

Gerschenkron, Alexander. 1966. Economic Backwardness in Historical Perspective. Cambridge: Harvard University Press.

Gilson, Ronald, and Mark Roe. 1993. "Understanding the Japanese Keiretsu: Overlaps Between Corporate Governance and Industrial Organization." Yale Law Journal 102: 871–906.

Grabher, Gernot. 1992. Eastern Conquista: The Truncated Industrialization of East European Regions by Large West European Corporation. In Regional Development and Contemporary Industrial Response: Extending Flexible Specialization, edited by H. Ernste and V. Meier. Oxford: Belhave Press.

————. 1993a. Rediscovering the Social in the Economics of Interfirm Relations. In *The Embedded Firm: On the Socioeconomics of Industrial Networks*, edited by Gernot Grabher. London: Routledge.

————. ed. 1993b. *The Embedded Firm: On the Socioeconomics of Industrial Networks*. London: Routledge.

————. 1997. Adaption at the Cost of Adaptability? Restructuring the Eastern German Regional Economy. In *Restructuring Networks in Post-Socialism: Legacies, Linkages, and Localities*, edited by Gernot Grabher and David Stark. Oxford: Oxford University Press.

Grabher, Gernot, and David Stark, eds. 1997. *Restructuring Networks in Post-Socialism: Legacies, Linkages, and Localities*. Oxford: Oxford University Press.

Gramsci, Antonio. 1992. *Prison Notebooks*. New York: Columbia University Press.

Granovetter, Mark. 1985. "Economic Action and Social Structure: The Problem of Embeddedness." *American Journal of Sociology* 91: 481–510.

————. 1995. "Coase Revisited: Business Groups in the Modern Economy." *Industrial and Corporate Change* 4(1): 93–130.

Gray, C., and A. Holle. 1998a. Classical Exit Processes in Poland: Court Conciliation, Bankruptcy, and State Enterprise Liquidation. In *Enterprise Exit Processes in Transition Economies*, edited by L. Balcerowicz, C. Gray, and I. Hoshi. Budapest: Central European University Press.

————. 1998b. Poland's Bank-led Conciliation Process. In *Enterprise Exit Processes in Transition Economies*, edited by L. Balcerowicz, C. Gray, and I. Hoshi. Budapest: Central European University Press.

Greenberg, Douglas, S. Katz, and M. B. Oliviero. 1993. *Constitutionalism and Democracy: Transitions in the Contemporary World (The American Council of Learned Societies Comparative Constitutionalism Papers)*. New York: Oxford University Press.

Greguš, Miroslav, and Lenka Kališová. 1991. Economic Reforms and Enterprise Behavior in Czechoslovakia: 1945–1989. Prague, Central European University Working Paper, mimeograph.

Griffin, John. 1993. Privatization and Financial Capitalism in East Germany. Paper presented at the conference, Rethinking Western Europe, 25–27 March at Columbia University, New York.

Grindle, Merilee. 1991. The New Political Economy: Positive Economics and Negative Politics. In *Politics and Policy Making in Developing Countries: Perspectives on the New Political Economy*, edited by Gerald M. Meier. San Francisco: ICS Press.

————. 1996. *Challenging the State: Crisis and Innovation in Latin America and Africa*. Cambridge: Cambridge University Press.

Grossman, Sanford, and Oliver Hart. 1986. "The Costs and Benefits of Ownership: A Theory of Vertical and Lateral Integration." *Journal of Political Economy* 94(4): 691–719.

Grout, Paul A. 1984. "Investment and Wages in the Absence of Binding Contracts: A Nash Bargaining Approach." *Econometrica* 52(2): 449–60.

Guidotti, Pablo, Andrew Powell, Martin Kaufman, and Andrea Broda. 1996. Experience and Lessons From Financial Market Instability: The Argentine Experience. Paper prepared as the Argentine contribution to the G10 Working Party on Emerging Market Instability, Paris, December.

Guillen, Mauro. 2001. *The Limits of Convergence: Globalization and Organizational Change in Argentina, South Korea, and Spain*. Princeton, N.J.: Princeton University Press.

Haggard, Stephan, and Robert R. Kaufman, eds. 1992a. *The Politics of Economic Adjustment.* Princeton, N.J.: Princeton University Press.

———. 1992b. The State in the Initiation and Consolidation of Market-Oriented Reforms. In *State and Market in Development: Synergy or Rivalry?*, edited by D. Rueschemeyer and L. Putterman. Boulder, Colo.: Lynne Reiner.

———. 1995. *The Political Economy of Democratic Transitions.* Princeton, N.J.: Princeton University Press.

Halkier, Henrik, Mike Danson, and Charlotte Damborg. 1998. *Regional Development Agencies in Europe.* Philadelphia: Jessica Kingsley Publishers.

Hall, Peter. 1986. *Governing the Economy.* Oxford: Oxford University Press.

Ham, John, Jan Svejnar, and Katherine Terrell. 1995. Czech Republic and Slovakia. In *Unemployment, Restructuring, and the Labor Market in Eastern Europe and Russia,* edited by Simon Commander and Fabrizio Coricelli. Washington DC: The World Bank.

Hanousek, Jan, Vratislav Izák, and Otakar Klokočník. 1994. Monetary Policy During Transformation. CERGE-EI Working Paper No. 47.

Hanspach, Daniel, Tomáš Kostelecký, and Zdeňka Vajdová. 1993. Local Government in the Czech Republic. In *East Central Europe 2000: The Czech Republic.* Praha: Institute of Sociology, Academy of Sciences of the Czech Republic.

Hart, Oliver. 1988. "Incomplete Contracts and the Theory of the Firm." *Journal of Law, Economics, and Organization* 4(1): 119–39.

Hart, O., and J. Moore. 1988. "Incomplete Contracts and Renegotiation." *Econometrica* 56(4): 755–85.

Hasager, Leif. 1986a. *The Economic Development of Czechoslovakia, 1620–1985.* Copenhagen: Institute of Finance, Copenhagen School of Economics and Business Administration.

———. 1986b. *The Czechoslovak Planning System.* Copenhagen: Institute of Finance, Copenhagen School of Economics and Business Administration.

Häufler, Vlastislav. 1984. *Ekonomická geografie Československa.* Praha: Academia.

Hausner, J., B. Jessop, and K. Nielsen. 1995. *Strategic Choice and Path-Dependency in Post-Socialism: Institutional Dynamics in the Transformation Process.* Aldershot: Edward Elgar.

Hausner, J., T. Kudlacz, and J. Szlachta. 1995. *Regional and Local Factors in the Restructuring of Poland's Economy.* Krakow: Krakow Academy of Economics.

———. 1997. Restructuring in South-Eastern Poland. In *Restructuring Networks in Postsocialism: Legacies, Linkages, and Localities,* edited by G. Grabher and D. Stark. Oxford: Oxford University Press.

———. 1998. Regional Differentiation of Factors Conditioning the Growth of Innovativeness in Poland's Economy. In *Emerging Spatial and Regional Structures of an Economy in Transition,* edited by Ryszard Domanski. Warszawa: Wydawnictwo Naukowe PWN.

Havlín, Václav. 1991. "Podniky před velkou privatizací." *Národní Hospodářství* 10: 29–32.

Hay, Colin, and Daniel Wincott. 1998. "Structure and Agency in Historical Institutionalism." *Political Studies* 46(5): 951–57.

Hayri, A. 1993. Timing of and Selection among Restructuring Options under Uncertainty. In *Three Essays on the Reforms in Post-Socialist Economies,* Ph.D. diss., Princeton University.

Hayri, Aydin, and Gerald McDermott. 1995. Beyond Restructuring and Bankruptcy: Restructuring in the Czech Republic. Program for the Study of East-Central Europe, Center for European Studies, Harvard University. Working Paper No. 36.

———. 1998. "The Network Properties of Corporate Governance and Industrial Restructuring: A Post-Socialist Lesson." *Industrial and Corporate Change* 7(1): 153–93.

Hazbun, Waleed A. 1992. Defining and Restructuring Frameworks for Political Science Discourse. Department of Political Science, MIT. Mimeograph.

Helper, Susan, John Paul MacDuffie, and Charles Sabel. 2000. "Pragmatic Collaborations: Advancing Knowledge While Controlling Opportunism." *Industrial and Corporate Change* 9(3): 443–88.

Hendrych, Dušan. 1993. Transforming Czechoslovakian Public Administration: Traditions and New Challenges. In *Administrative Transformation in Central and Eastern Europe,* edited by Joachim Jens Hesse. Cambridge: Blackwell Publishers.

Herrigel, Gary B. 1989. Industrial Order and the Politics of Industrial Change: Mechanical Engineering. In *Industry and Politics in West Germany,* edited by Peter Katzenstein. Ithaca, N.Y.: Cornell University Press.

———. 1996. *Industrial Constructions: The Sources of German Industrial Power.* Cambridge: Cambridge University Press.

Herzmann, Jan. 1992. "Volby v kontextu vývoje veřejného mínění 1989–1991." *Sociologický časopis* 28: 165–83.

Hewett, Ed. 1988. *Reforming the Soviet Economy.* Washington, D.C.: The Brookings Institution.

Hirschman, Albert. 1963. *A Journey toward Progress.* New York: Twentieth Century Fund.

———. 1973. *Journeys toward Progress: Studies of Economic Policy-Making in Latin America.* New York: Norton.

———. 1981. *Essays in Trespassing.* Cambridge: Cambridge University Press.

Hirst, Paul. 1991. "The State, Civil Society, and the Collapse of Soviet Communism." *Economy and Society* 20(2): 217–42.

Hlaváček, Jiří. 1986. "Homo se assecurans." *Politická ekonomie* 34(6): 37–52.

Hlaváček, Jiří, and Michal Mejstřík. 1991. Preconditions for Privatization in Czechoslovakia in 1991. Central European University, Prague. Working Paper, mimeograph.

Hlaváček, Jiří, and Dušan Tříska. 1987. "The Planning Authority and Its Marginal Rate of Substitution." *Ekonomicko-matematicky obzor* 23(1): 38–54.

Hlaváček, J., and Z. Tůma. 1993. Bankruptcy in the Czech Economy. Faculty of Social Sciences, Charles University, Prague, April. Mimeograph.

Holeček, Ludvík. 1983. *Průmyslové integrace.* Praha: SNTL.

Holešovský, Václav. 1980. Czechoslovakia: Economic Reforms. In *Economic Reforms in Eastern Europe and Prospects for the 1980s,* edited by NATO Economics Directorate. New York: Pergamon Press.

Holman, Robert. 1992. Insolvency of State Enterprises in Czechoslovakia. Liberalní Institut Praha. Working Paper, mimeograph.

Hořčicová, Milena, and Drahomíra Vašková. 1992. "Insolvency in the Transformation Period of the Czechoslovak Economy." *Eastern European Economics* (fall): 5–24.

Horský, Milan. 1988. Možnosti prohloubení vlivu financí na investiční výstavbu v průmyslu. Diploma Thesis, Department of Finance and Credit, Vysoká Škola Ekonomická, March.

Hoshi, I., J. Mládek, and A. Sinclair. 1998. Bankruptcy and Owner-Led Liquidation in the Czech Republic. In *Enterprise Exit Processes in Transition Economies,* edited by Gray Balcerowicz, and I. Hoshi. Budapest: Central European University Press.

Hough, Jerry. 1969. *The Soviet Prefects.* Cambridge: Harvard University Press.

———. 1977. *The Soviet Union and Social Science Theory.* Cambridge: Harvard University Press.

Hrnčíř, Miroslav. 1988. "Central Regulation and the Parametricity of Prices." *Czechoslovak Economic Papers,* 26: 7–38.

———. 1990. "From Traditional to Reform Planned Economy: The Case of Czechoslovakia." *Czechoslovak Economic Papers,* 28: 25–45.

———. 1992. "Financial Institutions and Monetary Policies in Czechoslovakia." Institut Ekonomie, Czechoslovak State Bank. Mimeograph.

———. 1993. "Financial Intermediation in Former Czechoslovakia and in the Czech Republic: Lessons and Progress Evaluation." *Economic Systems* 17(4): 301–27.

———. 1994. "Reform of the Banking Sector in the Czech Republic." Revised version of paper presented at the Conference on Development and Reform of the Financial System in Central and Eastern Europe, 28–30 October, 1993, Vienna, Austria.

Hubáček, Josef. 1986. "K pojetí základního článku podnikové hospodářské sféry." *Politická ekonomie* 34: 505–14.

Hula, R. C., ed. 1988. *Market-Based Public Policy.* New York: St. Martin's Press.

Huntington, Samuel. 1975. "The Democratic Distemper." *Public Interest* 41(fall): 9–38.

———. 1991. *The Third Wave: Democratization in the Late Twentieth Century.* Norman: University of Oklahoma Press.

Ickes, Barry W., and Randi Ryterman. 1992. "The Interenterprise Arrears Crisis in Russia." *Post-Soviet Affairs* 8(4): 331–61.

Illner, Michael. 1992a. "K sociologickým otázkám místní samosprávy (Sociological Questions About Local Independence)." *Sociologický časopis* 28: 480–92.

———. 1992b. Overview of Local Government in the Czech Republic. Institute of Sociology, Ceskoslovenská Akademie Věd, Prague. Mimeograph.

———. 1992c. "Continuity and Discontinuity: Political Change in a Czech Village after 1989." *Czechoslovak Sociological Review* 28: 79–91.

Immergut, Ellen. 1998. "The Theoretical Core of the New Institutionalism." *Politics and Society* 26(1): 5–34.

ISB (Investiční Společnost Bohemia a.s.). 1993. Zpráva o činnosti. Prague.

Jacoby, W. 2000. *Imitation and Politics: Redesigning Germany.* Ithaca, N.Y.: Cornell University Press.

Janáček, František, Marie Bauerová, Antonín Klimek, and Vladislav Krátký. 1990. *Největší zbrojovka monarchie.* Praha: Novinář.

Janáček, Karel. 1993. Unemployment and Labour Market in Czechoslovakia (Czech Republic). Institut Ekonomie, Czech National Bank. Working Paper No. 8.

Janiška, Petr. 1990. "Co řekly volby." *Respekt* 39: 4–5.

Jarosz, M., ed. 1996. *Polish Employee-Owned Companies in 1995.* Warsaw: Institute of Political Studies, Polish Academy of Sciences.

———. 1999. *Direct Privatization: Investors, Managers, and Employees.* Warsaw: Institute of Political Studies, Polish Academy of Sciences.

Jensen, Michael. 1986. "Agency Costs of Free Cash Flow, Corporate Finance, and Takeovers." *American Economic Review* 72(2): 323–29.

Ježek, Tomáš. 1989. The Assumptions of Symmetry as a Methodological Problem of Comparative Organizational and Society Analysis. Prognostický ústav, Ceskoslovenská Akademie Věd. Internal Working Papers, mimeograph.

Jirásek, Jaroslav. 1970. *Technickoorganizační rozvoj výroby: Výrobní základ podnikové racionalizace.* Praha: Institut řízení.

————. 1984. *Vědecké prameny výroby.* Prague: Institut řízení.

————. 1989. Flexible Machining Systems in Czechoslovakia. In *New Technolgies and Work: Capitalist and Socialist Perspectives,* edited by Arthur Francis and Peter Grootings. New York: Routledge.

————. 1991. The Czechoslovak Truck and Bus Industry in Transition. Czechoslovak Management Center, August/September. Mimeograph.

————. 1992. LIAZ: Between Survival and Buyout. Czechoslovak Management Center, January. Mimeograph.

————. 1993. Industry Case Study Czech and Slovak Federal Republic—Vehicles, DESTA. CIS—Middle Europe Centre, London Business School, October. Discussion Paper Series No. 3.

Jirásek, Jaroslav, Vratislav Svoboda, and Tomáš Varcop. 1993. Industry Case Study Czechoslovakia—Automotive Parts. CIS—Middle Europe Centre, London Business School, October. Discussion Paper Series No. 3.

Jisa, Václav. 1969. *Škodovy závody, 1859–1965.* Praha: Práce.

————. 1980. *Dějiny závodu—významný činitel výchovy socialistického člověka.* Praha: Ústřední škola Revolučního odborového hnutí Antonína Zápotockého.

Johnson, J. 1997. "Understanding Russia's Emerging Financial-Industrial Groups," *Post-Soviet Affairs* 13(4): 333–65.

Johnson, S., and G. Loveman. 1995. *Starting over in Eastern Europe: Entrepreneurship and Economic Renewal.* Boston: Harvard Business School Press.

Johnson, S., and A. Shleifer. 1999. Coase vs. the Coasians: The Regulation and Development of Securities Markets in Poland and the Czech Republic. Social Science Research Network. Working Paper.

Jukl, Eduard, and Václav Jisa, eds. 1964. *K dějinám Závodu V.I. Lenina Plzeň.* Plzeň: Krajské Nakladatelství.

Kaplan, Karel. 1966. *Utváření generalní linie výstavby socialismu v Československu.* Prague: Czechoslovak Academy of Sciences.

Kareš, Jiří. 1962. "Úkoly specializace strojírenské výroby." *Plánované Hosopodářství,* 15(7): 21–31.

Karl, Terry Lynn. 1990. "Dilemmas of Democratization in Latin America." *Comparative Politics,* 23(1): 1–21.

Karl, Terry Lynn, and Philippe C. Schmitter. 1991. "Modes of Transition and Types of Democracy in Latin America and Eastern Europe." *International Social Science Journal* 128: 269–84.

Karmazín, Václav. 1965. Vývoj řízení ve Škodových závodech před znárodněním. Diploma Thesis, Institut národohospodářského plánování, Vysoká Škola Ekonomická.

Kaser, Michael C. 1986. *The Economic History of Eastern Europe, 1919–1975,* vol. 3. New York: Oxford University Press.

Katzenstein, Peter. 1985. *Small States in World Markets.* Ithaca, N.Y.: Cornell University Press.

————. 1989. Stability and Change in the Emerging Third Republic. In *Industry and Politics in West Germany,* edited by Peter Katzenstein. Ithaca, N.Y.: Cornell University Press.

Kawalec, Stefan. 1988. Obituary for Central Control. SPGiS, Warsaw, unpublished manuscript.

Kerouš, Miroslav. 1985. "Tendence vývoje zásob v ČSSR od počátku 70. let." *Plánované Hosopodářství* 6: 49–60.

———. 1993. Czech and Slovak Banking in the Transition Period. Paper presented for the Institute of Development Studies at the Univeristy of Sussex. Mimeograph.

Kerr, Clark, John Dunlop, Frederick Harbison, and Charles Meyer. 1960. *Industrialism and Industrial Man.* Cambridge: Harvard University Press.

King, Neil. 1995. "How it Works—Faster, Faster, the Czech Voucher System Had One Overriding Aim: Get it Done Quickly." *Wall Street Journal,* October 2: B6.

Kitschelt, Herbert. 1992. "Political Regime Change: Structure and Process-Driven Explanations?" *American Political Science Review* 86(4): 1028–34.

———. 1993. "Comparative Historical Research and Rational Choice Theory: The Case of Transitions to Democracy." *Theory and Society* 22: 413–27.

Klaus, Václav. 1989. "Socialist Economies, Economic Reforms, and Economists: Reflections of a Czechoslovak Economist." *Communist Economies* 1(1): 89–96.

———. 1991. *Ekonomická věda a ekonomická reforma.* Praha: Gennex and Top Agency.

———. 1992. The Adam Smith Address. Delivered to the 34th Meeting of the National Association of Business Economists, 13 September, Dallas, Texas.

———. 1993. "The Ten Commandments Revisited." *International Economy* (September/October): 36–39, 70–72.

Klaus, Václav, and Tomáš Ježek. 1991. "Social Criticism, False Liberalism, and Recent Changes of Czechoslovakia." *East European Politics and Society* 5(1): 26–40.

Klaus, Václav, and Dušan Tříska. 1989. "The Economic Center, Reform and Equilibrium." *Czechoslovak Economic Digest* 2: 34–56.

———. 1994. "Korani Janoses a poszt-socialista atalakitas (Janos Kornai and the Post-socialist Transformation)." *BUKSZ,* 6(4): 480–83.

Klein, B., R. Crawford, and A. Alchain. 1978. "Vertical Integration, Appropriable Rents and the Competitive Contracting Process." *Journal of Law and Economics* 21: 297–326.

Klvačová, Eva. 1993. "Komu stát pomůže? (Whom Will the State Help?)." *Ekonom* 21: 15–17.

Knight, Jack. 1992. *Institutions and Social Conflict.* Cambridge: Cambridge University Press.

Knight, Jack, and Itai Sened. 1995. *Explaining Social Institutions.* Ann Arbor: University of Michigan Press.

Kočárník, Ivan. 1983. "Ke vztahu mezi dynamikou úvěrového fondu a dynamikou narodohospodářských agregátů." *Finance a úvěr* 33(5): 65–80.

Kočárník, Ivan, and Jiří Petřivalský. 1983. "K některým otázkám měnového vývoje, měnového plánování a měnové politiky ve vztahu k efektivnosti reprodukčního procesu." *Finance a úvěr* 33(8): 145–55.

Kochanowicz, Jacek. 1994. "Reforming Weak States and Deficient Bureaucracies." In *Intricate Links: Democratization and Market Reforms in Latin America and Eastern Europe,* edited by Joan M. Nelson, Jacek Kochanowicz, Kalman Mizsei, and Oscar Munoz. New Brunswick: Transaction Books.

Kogut, Bruce. 2000. "The Network as Knowledge: Generative Rules and the Emergence of Structure." *Strategic Management Journal* 21: 405–25.

Kogut, B., and A. Spicer. 1998. *Chains of Embedded Trust: Institutions and Capital Market Formation in Russia and the Czech Republic.* Wharton School, Philadelphia, unpublished manuscript.

Kogut, Bruce, and Udo Zander. 2000. "Did Socialism Fail to Innovate? A Natural Experiment of the Two Zeiss Companies." *American Sociological Review* 65: 169–90.

Kolanda, Miroslav. 1989. "Strategie rozvoje strojírenského a elektrotechnického průmyslu." *Politická ekonomie* 37: 635–45.

———. 1992. Čs. průmysl a jeho národohospodářské okolí v první etapě reformy 1991–1992. Prognostický ústav, Prague. Mimeograph.

———. 1993. Enterprises in the Czechoslovak Manufacturing Industries in the First Phase of Economic Reform—Production Performance, Dependence on Exports and Profitability 1988–1992. Institute of Economic Forecasting, Prague. Mimeograph.

Komárek, Valtr. 1982. *Technika a ekonomika investic.* Praha: SNTL.

———. 1986. *Inovace a intenzifikace v hospodářství.* Praha: SNTL.

———. 1993. Czech and Slovak Federal Republic: A New Approach. In *Economic Transformation in Central Europe: A Progress Report,* edited by Richard Portes. London: CEPR.

Konečný, Michal. 1989. "Příčiny platební neschopnosti a možnosti jejího řešení." *Finance a úvěr* 39(10): 659–72.

Kořínek, F. 1994. Platební Neschopnost a Bankroty. Master's thesis, Faculty of Social Sciences, Charles University, Prague.

Kornai, Janos. 1980. *Economics of Shortage.* New York: North-Holland.

———. 1986. "The Hungarian Reform Process: Visions, Hopes, and Reality." *Journal of Economic Literature* 24: 1687–1737.

———. 1990a. "The Affinity between Ownership Forms and Coordiantion Mechanisms: The Common Experience of Reform in Socialist Countries." *Journal of Economic Perspectives* 4: 307–37.

———. 1990b. *The Road to Economic Freedom.* New York: Norton.

———. 1992a. *The Socialist System.* Princeton, N.J.: Princeton University Press.

———. 1992b. "The Post-Socialist Transition and the State: Reflections in the Light of Hungarian Fiscal Problems." *American Economic Review* 82(2): 1–21.

Kosta, Jiří. 1982. Aims and Methods of Economic Policy in Czechoslovakia 1970–78. In *The East European Economies in the 1970s,* edited by A. Nove, H.-H. Hohmann, and G. Seidenstecher. London: Butterworths.

Kotrba, J. 1994. Czech Privatization: Players and Winners. CERGE-EI. Working Paper No. 58.

Kotrba, J., and J. Svejnar. 1994. "Rapid and Multifaceted Privatization: Experience of the Czech and Slovak Republics." *MOCT-MOST* 4: 147–85.

Kotulán, Antonín, J. Hlaváček, J. Seják, and D. Tříska. 1990. Přestavba hospodářského mechanismu, ekonomické klima a institucionálné uspořádání ekonomiky. Ekonomický ústav Ceskoslovenská Akademie Věd, Praha. Working Paper collection No. 364.

Krasner, Stephen. 1984. "Approaches to the State." *Comparative Politics* (January): 223–45.

Krásný, Vladislav. 1992. "Třetí konverze Škodovy říše" *Respekt,* (January): 13–19.

Krausová, Jaruše. 1993. "Likvidita českých podniků na počátku renesance tržné ekonomiky." *Finance a úvěr* 43(1): 25–39.

Křeček, Stanislav. 1992. *Pracoval jsem u Batů.* Praha: Dům Techniky.

Krejča, František. 1984. "Účinnost úvěrové diferenciace v roce 1983." *Finance a úvěr* 34(7): 441–49.

————. 1987. "Bankovní měnová politika v přestavbě hospodářského mechanismu." *Finance a úvěr* 37(11): 756–69.

————. 1989. "Bankovní opatření k podpoře činnosti státních podniků." *Finance a úvěr* 39(2): 78–82.

Krejčová, Lenka. 1991. Strategické aspekty zavadení automatizace ve s.p. TOS Hostivař. Diploma Thesis, Fakulta Výrobně ekonomická, Vysoká Škola Ekonomická Praha.

Křovák, Jiří, Alena Buchtíková, and Eva Macourková. 1992. Enterprise Sector Behavior and Performance. Institute of Economics, ČSAS, May. Mimeograph.

Kubeš, Tomáš. 1993a. "Partneři zákazníci požadují víc než podnikové záruky." *Hospodářské noviny,* 6 May.

————. 1993b. "Porsche zřejmě odejde z Českého Krumlova." *Hospodářské noviny,* 7 May.

Kuznetsov, Evgenii. 1993. "How Can an Economy Adjust to Simultaneous Market and Government Failure? Lessons from the Soviet Union, Contemporary Russia and Countries of Late-late Industrialization." *Communist Economies and Economic Transformation* 5(4): 473–97.

Kysilka, Pavel. 1988. Stručný přehled Čs. poválečných ekonomických reforem. Ekonomický ústav, Praha. Working Paper No. 205.

————. 1989a. Stínové řídící systémy a reforma. Ekonomický ústav, Praha. Working Paper No. 341.

————. 1989b. "Počátky úsilí o ekonomické reformy." *Politická ekonomie* 37: 219–33.

Lanzendorf, Miroslav. 1964. Obchod a obchodní organizace Škodovky v letech 1918–1938. Diploma Thesis, Department of Foreign Trade, Vysoká Škola Ekonomická.

Larson, Andrea. 1992. "Network Dyads in Entrepreneurial Settings: A Study of the Governance of Exchange Relationships." *Administrative Science Quarterly* 37: 76–104.

Laštovička, R, A. Marcinčin, and M. Mejstřík. 1994. Privatization and Opening the Capital Markets in the Czech and Slovak Republics. CERGE-EI Working Paper No. 54.

Lavoie, Don. 1985. *Rivalry and Central Planning.* Cambridge: Cambridge University Press.

Leff, Carol. 1988. *National Conflict in Czechoslovakia: The Making and Remaking of the State, 1918–1987.* Princeton, N.J.: Princeton University Press.

Lehár, Bohumil. 1960. *Dějiny Baťova koncernu 1894–1945.* Praha: Státní nakladatelství politické literatury.

Lenin, Vladimír. 1975. *The Lenin Anthology,* edited by Robert Tucker. New York: Norton.

Levcik, Friedrich. 1989. Economic Reforms in Czechoslovakia. In *Economic Reforms in Eastrn Europe and the Soviet Union,* edited by Hubert Gabrisch. Boulder, Colo.: Westview Press.

Levitas, Anthony. 1989. "An Open Letter to Solidarity." *Res Publica.* Mimeograph.

————. 1994. Rethinking Reform: Lessons from Polish Privatization. In *Changing Political Economies: Privatization in Post-Communist and Reforming Communist States,* edited by V. Milor. London: Lynne Rienner.

————. 1999. The Political Economy of Fiscal Decentralization and Local Government Finance Reform in Poland 1989–99. Research Triangle Institute, Warsaw, unpublished manuscript.

Lewandowski, Janus, and Jan Szomberg. 1989. "Property Rights as a Basis for Social and Economic Reform." *Communist Economies* 3: 257–68.

Lieberman, I. 1997. "Mass Privatization in Comparative Perspective." In *Between State and Market: Mass Privatization in Transition Economies,* edited by I. Lieberman, S. Nestor, and R. Desai. Washington, DC: World Bank.

Lieberman, Ira, Andre Ewing, Michal Mejstřík, Joyita Mukherjee, and Peter Fidler. 1995. Mass Privatization in Central and Eastern Europe and the Former Soviet Union: A Comparative Analysis. World Bank Studies of Economies in Transition No. 16.

Liebman, J. S. 1991. "Voice Not Choice: A Review of *Politics, Markets, and America's Schools* by J. Chub and T. Moe." *Yale Law Journal* 101(1): 259–314.

Lipton, David, and Jeffrey Sachs. 1990. "Privatization in Eastern Europe: The Case of Poland." *Brookings Papers on Economic Activity* 2: 293–341.

Lízal, Lubomír, Miroslav Singer, and Jan Svejnar. 1995. Manager Interests, Breakups, and Performance of State Enterprises in Transition. In *The Czech Republic and Economic Transition in Eastern Europe,* edited by J. Svejnar. San Diego: Academic Press.

Locke, Richard M. 1995. *Remaking the Italian Economy: Local Politics and Industrial Change in Contemporary Italy.* Ithaca, N.Y.: Cornell University Press.

Locke, Richard M., and Kathleen Thelen. 1995. "Apples and Oranges Revisited: Contextualized Comparisons and the Study of Comparative Labor Politics." *Politics and Society* 22(2): 337–68.

Lowi, Theodore. 1979. *The End of Liberalism.* New York: Norton.

Lukavská, L. 1992. "Poldi si nechce kleknout." *Hospodářské noviny,* 17 February.

Macků, Mojmír. 1988. "Působení pobočky banky na vývoj zásob." *Finance a úvěr* 38(10): 692–94.

Majcher, Milan, and Josef Valach. 1989. *Financie podnikov a odvětví.* Praha: SNTL.

Makuch, Jozef. 1988. "Bankovní úvěr v podmínkách intezifikace ekonomiky." *Finance a úvěr* 38(11): 737.

Malý, Milan, and Petr Záruba. 1986. *Organizace a řízení průmyslových podniků a VHJ v podmínkách automatizace.* Praha: SNTL.

Malý, Václav. 1979. *Využívání ekonomických nástrojů v řízení strojírenství.* Praha: Knižnice VUSTE.

———. 1980. "Některé problémy finanční politiky odevětvového ministerstva," Finance a úvěr, 30(8): 395–404.

Manikkalingam, Ramanujam. 1992. Learning for Success. Second year paper, Department of Political Science, MIT.

Mann, Bruce A. 1993. "Privatization in the Czech Republic." *The Business Lawyer* 48(May): 963–73.

March, James, and Johan Olsen. 1984. "The New Institutionalism: Organizing Factors in Political Life." *American Political Science Review* 78(September): 734–49.

———. 1995. *Democratic Governance.* New York: The Free Press.

Marcinčin, Anton. 1993. Ownership Concentration and Evaluation Issues: First Wave of Voucher Privatization in the Czech Republic. CERGE-EI. Prague. Mimeograph.

Martinelli, Cesar, and Mariano Tommasi. 1997. "Sequencing of Economic Reforms in the Presence of Political Constraints." *Economics and Politics* 9(2): 115–32.

Mašek, Bohumil. 1979. *Náměty VHJ na nové roypracování záasad dotační a úvěrové politiky, redistribuce finančních prostředků a financování investic z vlastních prostředků s důrazem na návratnost investic (Studie o zkušenostech VHJ TST Praha).* Prague: Institut řízení.

Matějka, Jaromír. 1989. "The Next Phase of the Restructuring of the Czechoslovak Economy." *Czechoslovak Economic Digest* 3: 46–51.

Matesová, Jana. 1993a. The King of the Declining Industry (Veba Broumov). CIS— Middle Europe Centre, London Business School, October. Discussion Paper Series No. 3.

————. 1993b. Intelligent Transformation of the Communist Bulwark (PSP). CIS— Middle Europe Centre, London Business School, October. Discussion Paper Series No.3.

Matesová, Jana, and Richard Šeda. 1994. Financial Markets in the Czech Republic as a Means of Corporate Governance in Voucher Privatized Companies. CERGE-EI Working Paper No. 62.

McDermott, Gerald. 1997. Renegotiating the Ties that Bind: The Limits of Privatization in the Czech Republic. In *Restructuring Networks in Postsocialism: Legacies, Linkages, and Localities*, edited by Gernot Grabher and David Stark. Oxford: Oxford University Press.

————. 1998. *The Communist Aftermath: Industrial Networks and the Politics of Institution-Building in the Czech Republic.* Doctoral diss., MIT, Cambridge, Mass.

————. 2000. Reinventing Federalism: Governing Decentralized Institutional Experiments in Latin America. Policy Paper for the Finance, Private Sector, and Infrastructure Division, World Bank. Documento de Trabajo No. 19, Depto. de Humanidades, Universidad de San Andres.

————. 2002. Network Restructuring and Firm Creation in East-Central Europe: A Public-Private Venture. In *The New Entrepreneurs of Europe and Asia*, edited by Victoria E. Bonnell and Thomas B. Gold. New York: M.E. Sharpe. Forthcoming.

McDermott, Gerald, and Michal Mejstřík. 1992. "The Role of Small Firms in the Industrial Development and Transformation of Czechoslovakia." *Small Business Economics* 4(3): 179–200.

McKinsey and Company, Inc. Czech Republic. 1994. Making International Partnerships Work: The Role of Corporate Governance. Paper presented at Conference Bohemiae, 11 October, Prague.

Meier, Gerald A. 1991. *Politics and Policy Making in Developing Countries: Perspectives on the New Political Economy.* San Francisco: ICS Press.

Mejstřík, Michal. 1986. "Ekonomická problematika vědeckotechnického rozvoje." *Politická ekonomie* 34: 611–22.

————, ed. 1997a. *The Privatization Process in East-Central Europe: Evolutionary Process of Czech Privatizations.* Boston: Kluwer.

————. 1997b. The Emergence of Institutional Owners: The Role of Banks and Non-banking Financial Institutions in the Privatization of the Economy and the Banks. In *The Privatization Process in East-Central Europe: Evolutionary Process of Czech Privatizations*, edited by Michal Mejstřík. Boston: Kluwer.

Mejstřík, Michal, and Vladimír Benáček. 1992. Czechoslovak Textile and Clothing Industry. Study prepared at CERGE, Prague, November.

Mejstřík, Michal, and James Berger. 1992. Voucher, Buyouts, Auctions: The Battle for Privatization in Czechoslovakia. Paper presented at the Center for European Studies at Harvard University, December.

Mejstřík, Michal, Oldřich Kýn, Zdeněk Bláha, and Jan Mládek. 1992. "The Three Knots of Voucher Privatization." *Respekt* 5: 12.

Mejstřík, Michal, Anton Marcinčin, and Radek Laštovička. 1997. Large Privatization: Theory and Practice. In *The Privatization Process in East-Central Europe: Evolutionary Process of Czech Privatizations*, edited by Michal Mejstřík. Boston: Kluwer.

Melumad, N.D., and D. Mookherjee. 1989. "Delegation as Commitment: The Case of Income Tax Audits." *RAND Journal of Economics* 20(2): 139–63.

Mertlík, Pavel. 1995. Future of Industry in Central and Eastern Europe: The Czech Industry. Paper prepared for the Research Project on Future of Industry in Central and Eastern Europe (STD-2 EC Programme), March.

Mervart, Josef. 1995. Český bankovní sektor v období sbližování podmínek s evropskou unii. Institut Ekonomie, Czech National Bank. Working Paper No. 47.

Mihalyi, Peter. 1992. "Property Rights and Privatization: The Three Agent Model (A Case Study on Hungary)." *Eastern Europe Economics,* (winter): 5–64.

Mihola, Jiří, and Milada Batšová. 1992. Zpráva z terénního výzkumu pro IFW. Prague. Mimeograph.

Mihola, Jiří, and Václav Havlín. 1992. "Volné ruce pro rozhodování." *Hospodářské noviny,* January, 31.

Mihola, Jiří, Václav Havlín, and Miroslav Skála. 1991. Adaptace podniku v prvních měsících transformace čs. ekonomiky. Ústřední ústav národohospodářského výzkumu, Prague. Mimeograph.

Milanovic, Branko. 1989. *Liberalization and Entrepreneurship: Dynamics of Reform in Socialism and Capitalism.* Armonk, N.Y.: M.E. Sharpe.

Mládek, Jan. 1993. Czech Privatization Process: Time for Corporate Governance. Paper presented at the Conference on Output Decline in Eastern Europe—Prospects for Recovery at IIASA, 18–20 November, Austria.

———. 1994. *Privatization in the Czech Republic.* Seminar Bulletin No. 4. Centre for Economic Development, 12 December, Bratislava.

———. 1995. Third Wave of Privatization in the Czech Republic. In *Mapping and Support of Privatization in the Slovak Republic,* Seminar Bulletin No. 9. Centre for Economic Development, 12 December, Bratislava.

Mlčoch, Lubomír, 1983. Analýza procesu plánování v podnikové sféře. (Analysis of the Planning Process in the Enterprise Sphere). VUVTR, Prague. Mimeograph.

———. 1992a. "A Synthesis of Descriptive Analysis of a Traditional Model." *Prague Economic Papers* 4(1): 311–32.

———. 1992b. *The Behavior of the Czechoslovak Enterprise Sphere: A Survey of Microeconomic Work, 1968–89.* Prague: Economics Institute of the Czechoslovak Academy of Sciences.

———. 1994. The Political Economy of the Transition. Department of Economics, Charles University, Prague. Mimeograph.

Montes-Negret, F., and Papi, L. 1996. The Polish Experience in Bank and Enterprise Restructuring. Financial Sector Development Department, World Bank, unpublished manuscript.

Moon, Chung-in, and Rashemi Prasad. 1994. "Beyond the Development State: Networks, Politics, and Institutions." *Governance: An International Journal of Policy and Administration* 7(4): 360–86.

Moss, D. A. 1996a. *Socializing Security: Progressive-Era Economists and the Origins of American Social Policy.* Cambridge: Harvard University Press.

———. 1996b. Government, Markets, and Uncertainty: An Historical Approach to Public Risk Management in the United States. Harvard Business School Working Paper No. 97-025, October.

———. 1998. Limited Liability and the Birth of American Industry: Theory Meets History. Harvard Business School Working Paper No. 98-079, March.

Munck, Gerardo. 1994. "Democratic Transitions in Comparative Perspective." *Comparative Politics*, (April): 355–75.

Murrell, Peter. 1990. *The Nature of Socialist Economies: Lessons from Eastern European Foreign Trade*. Princeton, N.J.: Princeton University Press.

———. 1993. Evolutionary and Radical Approaches to Economic Reform. In *Stabilization and Privatization in Poland*, edited by Kazimierz Poznanski. New York: Kluwer.

Murrell, Peter, and Mancur Olson. 1991. "The Devolution of Centrally Planned Economies." *Journal of Comparative Economics* 15: 239–65.

Myant, Martin. 1989. *The Czechoslovak Economy, 1948–1988: The Battle for Economic Reform*. Cambridge: Cambridge University Press.

———. 1992. "Centre and Periphery Relations in Czechoslovakia." *The Journal of Interdisciplinary Economics* 4: 269–80.

———. 1993. *Transforming Socialist Economies: The Case of Poland and Czechoslovakia*. Aldershot: Edward Elgar.

———. 1994. Czech and Slovak Trade Unions. In *Parties, Trade Unions, and Society in East-Central Europe*, edited by Michael Waller and Martin Myant. Essex, England: Fank Cass.

Naishul, V. A. 1990. "Problems of Creating a Market in the USSR." *Communist Economies* 2(3): 275 90.

Nápravník, Josef, and Josef Tyl. 1986. "Efektivní využití zásob a působení regulačních nástrojů na jejich vývoj." *Finance a úvěr* 36(5): 299–304.

Nee, Victor, and David Stark. 1989. *Remaking the Economic Institutions of Socialism*. Stanford, Calif.: Stanford University Press.

Nellis, J. 1999. "Time to Rethink Privatization in Transition Economics?" *Finance and Development*, (June): 16–19.

Nelson, Joan M. 1993. "The Politics of Economic Transformation: Is the Third World Experience Relevant for Eastern Europe." *World Politics* 45(3): 434–65.

Nelson, R., and S. Winter. 1982. *An Evolutionary Theory of the Firm*. Cambridge, Mass.: Belknap Press.

Nemrava, Antonín, ed. 1982. *120 let výroby v elektrotechnickém závodě Škoda*. Praha: Národní technické muzeum.

Nesporová, Alena. 1984. "Kvantifikace ekonomického potenciálu základních fondů a pracovních sil a odhad jejich vzájemného vztahu pro strojírenství ČSSR." *Politická Ekonomie* 32: 27–45.

Nešvera, Václav. 1979. Rozvoj strojírenství a jeho úloha v intenzifikaci národního hospodářství. VUSTE Praha. Research report 1 41/005/2.

Nešvera, Václav, et al. 1983. Náměty na progresivní změny v odvětví strojírenství a elektrotechniky. VUSTE, Praha. Research report 41/277/83/Nes/Do.

Nino, Carlos Santiago. 1996. *The Constitution of Deliberative Democracy*. New Haven, Conn.: Yale University Press.

Nohria, Nitin, and Robert G. Eccles, eds. 1992. *Networks and Organizations: Structure, Form, and Action*. Boston: Harvard University Press.

North, Douglass. 1990. *Institutions, Institutional Change, and Economic Performance*. Cambridge: Cambridge University Press.

———. 1995. Five Propositions about Institutional Change. In *Explaining Social Institutions* edited by Jack Knight and Itai Sened. Ann Arbor: University of Michigan Press.

North, Douglass, and Jack Knight. 1997. Explaining the Complexity of Institutional Change. In *The Political Economy of Property Rights: Institutional Change and Cred-*

ibility in the Reform of Centrally Planned Economies edited by David Weimer. Cambridge: Cambridge University Press.

North, Douglass, and Robert Thomas. 1982. *The Rise of the Western World: A New Economic History.* Cambridge: Cambridge University Press.

Nove, Alec. 1984. *An Economic History of the U.S.S.R.* New York: Penguin Books.

Nuti, D. M. 1999. Employee Ownership in Polish Privatizations. In *Reconstituting the Market: The Political Economy of Microeconomic Transformation,* edited by P. Hare, J. Batt, and S. Estrin. Amsterdam: Harwood Academic Publishers.

Očková, Alena. 1993. Industry Case Study Czech and Slovak Federal Republic—Pharmaceuticals. CIS—Middle Europe Centre, London Business School, October. Discussion Paper Series No. 3.

O'Donnell, Guillermo. 1994. "Delegative Democracy." *Journal of Democracy* 5(1): 55–69.

O'Donnell, Guillermo, Philippe C. Schmitter, and Lawrence Whitehead, eds. 1986. *Transitions from Authoritarian Rule.* Baltimore: Johns Hopkins University Press.

OECD (Organization for Economic Cooperation and Development). 1994. *Prumysl v České republice a Slovenske republice (Industry in the Czech and Slovak Republics.* Paris: Organization for Economic Cooperation and Development.

———. 1996. *Transition at the local level : the Czech Republic, Hungary, Poland, and the Slovak Republic.* Paris: Organization for Economic Cooperation and Development.

———. 1998a. *Czech Republic.* Paris: Organization for Economic Cooperation and Development.

———. 1998b. *Economic surveys: Poland 1997–1998.* Paris: Organization for Economic Cooperation and Development.

———. 1999. *Main economic indicators.* CD-ROM, Paris: Organization for Economic Cooperation and Development.

OECD Economic Surveys. 1996. *The Czech Republic.* Paris: Organization for Economic Cooperation and Development.

OECD Industry Division. 1992. Industry Review of Czechoslovakia. December. Paris. Mimeograph.

Offe, Claus. 1981. The Attribution of Public Status to Interest Groups: Observations on the West German Case. In *Organizing Interest Groups in Western Europe,* edited by Suzanne Berger. Cambridge: Cambridge University Press.

———. 1991. "Capitalism by Democratic Design? Democratic Theory Facing the Triple Transition in East Central Europe." *Social Research* 58(4): 865–92.

Oi, Jean. 1992. "Fiscal Reform and the Economic Foundations of Local State Corporatism in China." *World Politics* 45: 99–126.

Olson, Mancur. 1965. *The Logic of Collective Action.* Cambridge: Harvard University Press.

———. 1982. *The Rise and Decline of Nations: Economic Growth, Stagflation, and Social Rigidities.* New Haven, Conn.: Yale University Press.

———. 1992. The Hidden Path to a Successful Economy. In *The Emergence of Market Economies in Eastern Europe,* edited by Christopher Clague and Gordon C. Rausser. Cambridge: Blackwell Publishers.

Orenstein, Mitchell. 1994. The Political Success of Neo-Liberalism in the Czech Republic. Institute for East-West Studies, Prague. Mimeograph.

Ostrom, Elinor. 1990. *Governing the Commons: The Evolution of Institutions for Collective Action.* Cambridge: Cambridge University Press.

————. 1995. "Self-organization and Social Capital." *Industrial and Corporate Change* 4(1): 131–59.

Oswald, Eduard. 1993a. "Důvody pro holding." *Ekonom* 29: 39.

————. 1993b. "Předimenzovaná nabídka: Hutnictví železa, (Excess supply: Ferrous Metallurgy)." *Ekonom* 53: 37–38.

Parks, R., and R. Oakerson. 1993. "Comparative Metropolitan Organization: Service Production and Governance Structures in St. Louis (MO) and Allegheny County (PA)." *Publius* 23: 19–39.

Pávek, Jan. 1993. Industry Case Study Czech and Slovak Federal Republic—Plastics. CIS—Middle Europe Centre, London Business School, October. Discussion Paper Series No. 3.

Pickel, Andreas. 1993. Authoritarianism or Democracy? Marketization as a Political Problem. Paper presented at the Fifth Annual International Conference of the Society for the Advancement of Socio-Economics, 26–28 March, New York.

Piore, Michael. 1995. *Beyond Individualism.* Cambridge: Harvard University Press.

Piore, Michael, and Charles Sabel. 1984. *The Second Industrial Divide: Possibilities for Prosperity.* New York: Basic Books.

Piore, Michael, Richard Lester, Fred Kofman, and Kamal Malek. 1994. "The Organization of Product Development." *Industrial and Corporate Change* 2(3): 405–35.

Pistor, K. 1999. The Regulatory Framework for Equity Markets in Transition Economies. Social Science Research Network.

Pistor, Katharina, and Andrew Spicer. 1997. Investment Funds in Mass Privatization and Beyond. In *Between State and Market: Mass Privatization in Transition Economies,* edited by I. Lieberman, S. Nelson, and R. Desai. Washington DC: World Bank.

Pistor, Katharina, and Joel Turkewitz. 1995. Coping With Hydra—State Ownership After Privatization. Revised version of paper presented at the Conference on Corporate Governance in Central Europe and Russia, The World Bank, December 1994. Central Europe University. Mimeograph.

Plechata, Jiří. 1986. Normování početního stavu technickohospodářských pracovníků v technickém rozvoji se zaměřením na konstrukční výzkum a vývoj. Diploma Thesis, Fakulta výrobně ekonomická, Vysoká Škola Ekonomická Praha.

Pochylý, Jaroslav. 1990. *Baťova průmyslová demokracie.* Praha: UTRIN.

Pohl, G., R. Anderson, S. Claessens, and S. Djankov. 1997. Privatization and Restructuring in Central and Eastern Europe: Evidence and Policy Options. Washington, D.C.: The World Bank.World Bank Technical Paper No. 368.

Pohl, Gerhard, Gregory T. Jedrzejczak, and Robert E. Anderson. 1995. Creating Capital Markets in Central and Eastern Europe. Washington, DC: The World Bank. World Bank Technical Paper No. 295.

Polák, Jaroslav. 1987. Zdokonalování řízení vyšších dodavatelských funKčí s možností aplikace počítače. Diploma Thesis, Department of Industry Economy, Vysoká Škola Ekonomická, Praha.

Polanyi, Karl. 1944. *The Great Transformation: The Political and Economic Origins of Our Time.* Boston: Beacon.

Pollert, Anna, and Irena Hradecká. 1993. Privatization in Transition: The Czech Experience. Prague. Mimeograph.

Powell, Andrew. 1996. On Central Banks and their Lender of Last Resort Function: 'Constructive Ambiguity' and 'Cheap Talk.' Central Bank of Argentina, June. Mimeograph.

Powell, Andrew, and Veronica Balzarotti. 1996. Capital Requirements for Latin American Banks in Relation to their Market Risks: The Relevance of the Basle 1996 Amendment to Latin America. Paper presented at Jornadas Monetarias y Bancarias, 21–22 August, Central Bank of Argentina.

Powell, Andrew, Andrea Broda, and T. Burdisso. 1997. An Analysis of Lending Interest Rates in Argentina: A Panel Interpretation of a Search Model with Bargaining. Central Bank of Argentina, April. Mimeograph.

Powell, W. 1990. Neither Market nor Hierarchy: Network Forms of Organization. In *Research in Organizational Behavior,* edited by L. L. Cummings and B. M. Staw. Greenwich, Conn.: JAT Press.

Powell, W., and P. DiMaggio. 1991. Introduction. In *The New Institutionalism in Organizational Analysis,* eidted by W. Powell and P. DiMaggio. Chicago: University of Chicago Press.

Pražák, Josef. 1989. "O pokusu racionalizace výroby automobilů v ASAP v Mladé Boleslavi před více než padesáti lety." October. Prague. Mimeograph.

Přemusová, Jarmila. 1983a. Výzkum způsobu spolupráce mezi podniky koncernu SHD a Národními výbory. VUPEK (Výzkumný ústav palivoenergetického komplexu), Praha, Ostrava, August. Research report 440-03-03-1.

———. 1983b. Výsledky empirického šetření spolupráce podniku koncernu SHD s Národními výbory. Appendix 1 and 2. VUPEK (Výzkumný ústav palivoenergetického komplexu), Praha, Ostrava, August. Research report 440-03-03-1.

———. 1989a. "Vazby mezi podniky a územím v lokálním rámci." (Links Between Firms and the Local Region). *Sociologický časopis* 25: 171–82.

———. 1989b. Podíl neformálních sociálních aktivit na tvorbě sociální infrastruktury měst v podmínkách přestavby. VUPEK (Výzkumný ústav palivoenergetického komplexu), Praha, Ostrava, December. Research report 846-00-02-3.

Privatization Newsletter of the Czech Republic and Slovakia. January 1992–December 1994. CERGE-EI/IES, Prague.

Procházka, Jaromír. 1988. "Finanční dopady z hospodaření se zásobami při přechodu na podmínky komplexního experimentu ve VHJ Tesla MLP." *Finance a úvěr* 38(3): 175–78.

Prokop, Jane. 1995. "Industrial Conglomerates, Risk Spreading, and the Transition in Russia." *Communist Economies and Economic Transformation* 7(1): 35–50.

———. 1996. Marketization in Russia's Regions, 1990–1994. Doctoral diss., Department of Government, Harvard University.

Prokoš, Václav. 1993a. "Škoda Ostrov pracuje samostatně." *Hospodářské noviny,* 15 February.

———. 1993b. "Škoda a Dorries konečně svoji." *Hospodářské noviny,* 19 February.

———. 1993c. "Joint Venture Škoda Secheron neziskový." *Hospodářské noviny,* 13 March.

———. 1993d." Škoda Plzeň míří do Ruska." *Hospodářské noviny,* 19 April.

———. 1993e. "Úspora energie zatím není argument." *Hospodářské noviny,* 12 May.

Przeworski, Adam. 1985. "Marxism and Rational Choice." *Politics and Society* 14(4): 379–409.

———. 1991. *Democracy and the Market.* Cambridge: Cambridge University Press.

Ptáček, Jiří. 1993. Platební neschopnost části českých podniků a možnosti jejího řešení. Institut Ekonomie, Czech National Bank. Working Paper No. 9.

Ptáček, Milan. 1984. "Kam mizí zásoby koncem čtvrtletí?" *Finance a úvěr* 34(8): 550–54.

Putnam, Robert, R. Leonardi, and R. Nanetti. 1993. *Making Democracy Work: Civic Traditions in Modern Italy.* Princeton, N.J.: Princeton University Press.

Ragin, C. 1987. *The Comparative Method: Moving beyond Qualitative and Quantitative Strategies.* Berkeley and Los Angeles: University of California Press.

Ragin, Charles C., and Howard S. Becker. 1992. *What is a Case?* New York: Cambridge University Press.

Rajdl, Lubomír. 1988. "Zásoby—překážka i rezerva." PH 4: 49–61.

Rapaczynski, Andrzej. 1996. "The Roles of the State and the Market in Establishing Property Rights." *Journal of Economic Perspectives* 10(2): 87–103.

Rapoš, Jaroslav. 1982. *Integrované výrobní úseky.* Praha: Institut řízení.

Řeznička, Jiří. 1963. *Ekonomika československého průmyslu a průmyslových podniků.* Praha: Nakladatelství politické literatury.

Richta, Radova. 1969. *Civilization at the Crossroads: Social and Human Implications of the Scientific and Technical Revolution.* White Plains, N.Y.: International Arts and Sciences Press.

Riordan, M. H., and D. E. M. Sappington. 1989. "Second Sourcing." *RAND Journal of Economics* 20(1): 41–58.

Roe, Alan. 1992. "Financial Sector Reform in Transitional Socialist Economies." Economic Development Institute, The World Bank. EDI Policy Seminar Report No. 29.

Roman, Zoltan. 1989. "The Size of the Small Firm Sector in Hungary." *Small Business Economics* 1(4): 37–54.

Róna-Tas, Ákos. 1997. *The Great Surprise of the Small Transformation: The Demise of Communism and the Rise of the Private Sector in Hungary.* Ann Arbor: University Of Michigan Press.

Rosický, Miroslav. 1983. *Organizace výrobní základny a plánovité řízení ekonomiky.* Praha: Academia.

Rousar, Přcmysl. 1967. *Dějiny národního podniku Svit.* Praha: Práce.

Rowley, T., D. Behrens, and D. Krackhardt. 2000. "Redundant Governance Structures: An Analysis of Structural and Relational Embeddedness in the Steel and Semiconductor Industries." *Strategic Management Journal* 21: 369–86.

Rutland, Peter. 1993. "Thatcherism, Czech Style: Transition to Capitalism in the Czech Republic." *Telos* 94 (winter): 103–29.

Rychetník, Luděk. 1981. The Industrial Enterprise in Czechoslovakia. In *The Industrial Enterprise in Eastern Europe,* edited by Ian Jeffries. New York: Praeger.

———. 1992. Industrial Reform in Czechoslovakia. In *Industrial Reform in Socialist Countries,* edited by Ian Jeffries. Hants, England: Edward Elgar.

Sabel, Charles F. 1982. *Work and Politics: The Division of Labor in Industry.* Cambridge: Cambridge University Press.

———. 1992. Studied Trust: Building New Forms of Co-operation in a Volatile Economy. In *Industrial Districts and Local Economic Regeneration,* edited by Frank Pyke and Werner Sengenberger. Geneva: Institute for Labour Studies.

———. 1993. Constitutional Ordering in Historical Perspective. In *Games in Hierarchies and Markets,* edited by Fritz Scharpf. Boulder, Colo.: Westview Press.

———. 1994. Learning by Monitoring: The Institutions of Economic Development. In *The Handbook of Economic Sociology,* edited by N. Smesler and R. Swedberg. Princeton, N.J.: Princeton University Press.

———. 1995. Design, Deliberation, and Democracy: On the New Pragmatism of Firms and Public Institutions. Paper presented at the conference on Liberal Institutions,

Economic Constitutional Rights, and the Role of Organization. European University Institute, 15–16 December, Florence, Italy.

———. 1996a. "A Measure of Federalism: Assessing Manufacturing Technology Centers." *Research Policy* 25: 281–307.

———. 1996b. *Local Partnerships and Social Innovation: Ireland.* Dublin: Organization for Economic Cooperation and Development.

Sabel, Charles, and Jane Prokop. 1996. Stabilization through Reorganization? Some Preliminary Implications of Russia's Entry into World Markets in the Age of Discursive Quality Standards. In *Corporate Governance in Central Europe and Russia.* vol. 2. Insiders and the State, edited by Roman Frydman, Cheryl Gray, and Andrzej Rapaczinski. Budapest: Central European University Press.

Sabel, Charles, and David Stark. 1982. "Planning, Politics, and Shop-floor Power: Hidden Forms of Bargaining in Soviet-Imposed State Socialist Societies." *Politics and Society* 11(4): 439–75.

Sabel, Charles, and Jonathan Zeitlin. 1997. Stories, Strategies, Structures: Rething Historical Alternatives to Mass Production. In *Worlds of Possibility: Flexibility and Mass Production in Western Industrialization,* edited by C. Sabel and J. Zeitlin. Cambridge: Cambridge University Press.

Sabel, Charles, John Griffin, and Richard Deeg. 1994. Making Money Talk: Towards a New Debtor-Creditor Relation in German Banking. In *Relational Investing,* edited by J. Coffee, R. Gilson, and L. Lowenstein. Oxford: Oxford University Press.

Sachs, Jeffrey. 1990. "Eastern Europe's Economies." *Economist,* 13 January: 21–26.

———. 1993. *Poland's Jump to the Market Economy.* Cambridge, Mass.: MIT Press.

Šafář, Josef. 1987. Rozvoj organizace řízení hutního průmyslu. TEVUH, Praha, September. Research project 903 123 204.02.

———. 1987. Rozvoj organizace řízení a uspořádání výrobně technické základny v resortu FMHTS. TEVUH, Praha, October. Research project 903 123 204.

———. 1988. Principy, pravidla a způsoby sdružování hospodařských organizací. TEVUH, Praha, May. Research project 903 123 204.02.

Sajo, Andras. 1990. "Diffuse Rights in Search of an Agent: A Property Rights Analysis of the Firm in the Socialist Market Economy." *International Review of Law and Economics* 10: 41–59.

Sample, Thomas. 1996. The Federalist Conception of Constitutional Governance: A Reconstruction. Department of Political Science, MIT. Mimeograph.

Saska, Josef, et al. 1981. Komplexní rozvoje řízení ve strojírenství. Strojírenský institut, VUSTE. Internal paper.

———. 1988a. Technickoekonomická studie k unifikaci strojírenských výrobků. VUSTE Praha. Part 1 of research report 901/124/311.

———. 1988b. Kvalitativní posuny ve struktuře konstrukčních materiálů pro strojírenství. VUSTE Praha. Part 2 of research report 901/124/311.

Sauer, Martin. 1993. Industry Case Study Czechoslovakia—Heavy Chemistry, SPOLANA. CIS—Middle Europe Centre, London Business School, October. Discussion Paper Series No. 3.

Saxenian, AnnaLee. 1994. *Regional Advantage: Culture and Competition in Silicon Valley and Route 128.* Cambridge: Harvard University Press.

Scarrow, Susan, and Jonathan Stein. 1995. The Politics of Retrospective Justice in Germany and the Czech Republic. Program on Germany and Europe, Center for European Studies, Harvard University. Working Paper No. 5.4.

Schell, Jonathan. 2000. "The Unfinished Twentieth Century: What We Have Forgotten about Nuclear Weapons," *Harper's Magazine*. January: 41–56.

Schumpeter, J. 1934. *The Theory of Economic Development: An Inquiry into Profits, Capital, Credit, Interest, and the Business Cycle*. Cambridge: Harvard University Press.

Schwarz, Jiří. 1991. Privatization from the Public Choice Perspective: The Case of Czechoslovakia. Central Europe University, Prague, July. Mimeograph.

Scott, R. E. 1986. "A Relational Theory of Secured Financing." *Columbia Law Review* 86(5): 901–77.

Sedatis, Judith. 1997. Network Dynamics of New Firm Formation: Developing Russian Commodity Markets, In *Restructuring Networks in Postsocialism: Legacies, Linkages, and Localities*, edited by Gernot Grabher and David Stark. Oxford: Oxford University Press.

Seidenstecher, Gertraud. 1975. Capital Finance. In *The New Economic Systems of Eastern Europe*, edited by Hans-Hermann Hohmann, Michael Kaser, and Karl C. Thalheim. Berkeley and Los Angeles: University of California Press.

Seleny, Annamaria. 1993. The Long Transformation: Hungarian Socialism, 1949–1989. Ph.D. diss., Department of Political Science, MIT.

Shafer, D. M. 1994. *Winners and Losers: How Sectors Shape the Developmental Prospects of States*. Ithaca, N.Y.: Cornell University Press.

Shafik, N. 1993. Making a Market, Mass Privatization in the Czech and Slovak Republics. World Bank Policy Research Paper No. 1321.

Shapiro, Helen. 1994. *Engines of Growth: The State and Transnational Auto Companies in Brazil*. Cambridge: Cambridge University Press.

Shenk, Gary. 1998. Financial-Industrial Conglomeration and Effective Corporate Management in Transition Economies: A Case Study of the Russian Automotive Industry. The Wharton School, Philadelphia, unpublished manuscript.

Shleifer, Andrei, and Rober W. Vishny. 1994. Privatization in Russia: First Steps. In *The Transition in Eastern Europe: Restructuring*, vol. 2, edited by O. Blanchard, K. Froot, and J. Sachs. Chicago: University of Chicago Press.

———. 1995. A Survey of Corporate Governance. Paper prepared for the Nobel Symposium on Law and Finance, August, Stockholm.

Skilling, Gordon H., and Franklyn Griffiths, eds. 1971. *Interest Groups in Soviet Politics*. Princeton, N.J.: Princeton University Press.

Skocpol, Theda. 1979. *States and Social Revolutions: A Comparative Analysis of France, Russia, and China*. Cambridge: Cambridge University Press.

Slámová-Formandlová, Kateřina. 1986. Organizace výrobně technické základny výrobně hospodářské jednotky hutnictví železa. Diploma Thesis, Fakulta výrobně ekonomická, Vysoká Škola Ekonomická Praha.

Smrček, Otto, ed. 1980. *Historie výroby obráběcích strojů u nás*. Liberec: Dům Techniky ČSVTS.

Smrčka, Jaroslav. 1988. "The Prospects of Development of Organization Structures of Enterprises." *Czechoslovak Economic Papers*, 27–39.

Solimano, Andes. 1991. The Economies of Central and Eastern Europe: An Historical and International Perspective. In *Reforming Central and Eastern European Economies: Initial Results and Challenges*, edited by Vittorio Corbo, Fabrizio Coricelli, and Jan Bossak. Washington DC: World Bank.

"Something Clunky Out East." 1995. *Economist*, 18 February.

Šourek, Stanislav. 1980. "Rozvoj chozrascotu a úloha financí." *Finance a úvěr.* 30(6): 370–79.

Spenner, Kenneth I., Olga O. Suhomlinova, Sten A. Thore, Kenneth C. Land, and Derek C. Jones. 1998. "Strong Legacies and Weak Markets: Bulgarian State-owned Enterprises during Early Transition." *American Sociological Review* 63(4): 599–618.

Spicer, A., G. McDermott, and B. Kogut. 2000. "Entrepreneurship and Privatization in Central Europe: The Tenuous Balance between Destruction and Creation." *Academy of Management Review* 25(3): 630–49.

Spring, s.r.o. 1993. *Sector Trends in the Economy of the Czech Republic.* Prague: String, s.r.o.

Spurný, Milan, and Josef Prokopec. 1980. Organizační struktury a organizačně právní formy VHJ hutního průmyslu. Technickoekonomický výzkumný ústav hutního průmyslu (TEVUH), Praha, June. Research report 4439.

Stalin, Joseph. 1952. *Economic Problems of Socialism in the USSR.* New York: International Publishers.

Staniszkis, Jadwiga. 1991. *The Dynamics of Breakthrough in Eastern Europe.* Berkeley: University of California Berkeley Press.

Stark, David. 1986. "Rethinking Internal Labor Markets: New Insights From a Comparative Perspective." *Amercian Sociolgical Review* 51: 492–504.

———. 1989. Coexisting Organizational Forms in Hungary's Emerging Mixed Economy. In *Remaking the Economic Institutions of Socialism,* edited by Victor Nee and David Stark. Stanford, Calif.: Stanford University Press.

———. 1990. "Privatization in Hungary: From Plan to Market or From Plan to Clan?" *East European Politics and Society* 4: 351–92.

———. 1992. "Path Dependence and Privatizations Strategies in East Central Europe." *East European Politics and Society* 6: 17–51.

———. 1996. "Recombining Property in East European Capitalism." *American Journal of Sociology* 101: 993–1027.

———. 2001. Ambiguous Assets for Uncertain Environments: Heterarchy in Postsocialist Firms. In *The Twenty-First Century Firm: Changing Economic Organization in International Perspective,* edited by Paul DiMaggio. Princeton, N.J.: Princeton University Press.

Stark, David, and Laszlo Bruszt. 1991. "Remaking the Political Field in Hungary." *Journal of International Affairs* 45(1): 201–46.

———. 1995. Network Properties of Assets and Liabilities: Patterns of Inter-Entrprise Ownership in the Post-Socialist Transformation. Paper presented at the Workshop on the Dynamics of Industrial Transformation: East Central European and East Asian Comparisons, May, at Budapest University of Economic Sciences, Budapest.

———. 1998. *Post-Socialist Pathways: Transforming Politics and Property in Eastern Europe.* Cambridge: Cambridge University Press.

Šťastný, Ladislav, et al. 1987a. Klasifikace kapacit pro změny výrobkových programů. VUSTE Report. Mimeograph.

———. 1987b. Klasifikace kapacit pro změny výrobkových programů: Příloha. VUSTE Report, June.

———. 1990. Prognóza modernizace výrobně technické základny strojírenství a elektrotechniky a možnost jejího zajištění. Policy paper, Prognostický ústav Ceskoslovenská Akademie Věd a UPV ČSFR, Praha.

Stefan, Paul B. 1996. "Towards a Positive Theory of Privatization—Lessons from Soviet-Type Economies." *International Review of Law and Economics* 16: 173–93.

Stein, Jonathan. 1994. Internal Opposition and the Development of Parties in the Czechoslovak Federal Assembly. Paper presented to the Workshop of Parliamentary Scholars and Parliamentarians, International Political Science Association, August 19–20, Berlin.

———. 1995. The Politics of Retrospective Justice in Germany and the Czech Republic. Program on Central and Eastern Europe, Center for European Studies, Harvard Univeristy. Working Paper No. 35.

Stern, Richard E. 1992. Access to Capital, Incentives, and Information Problems: A Study of Financial Market Formation in Post-Socialist Economies. Department of Economic, University of California Berkeley and Central European University Prague. Mimeograph.

Stíbal, Josef. 1993. "Exportní výkonnost zpracovatelského průmyslu České republiky v letech 1989 až 1992." Centrum vnějších ekonomických vztahů. *Ekonomická studie* č. 5 (June): 37–54.

Stiglitz, Joseph. 1982. "The Inefficiency of the Stock Market Equilibrium." *Review of Economic Studies*, 49(2): 241–57.

———. 1992a. "Capital Markets and Economic Fluctuations in Capitalist Economics." *European Economic Review* 36: 269–306.

———. 1992b. The Design of Financial Systems for the Newly Emerging Deomocracies of Eastern Europe. In *The Emergence of Market Economies in Eastern Europe*, edited by Christopher Clague and Gordon C. Rausser. Cambridge: Blackwell Publishers.

———. 1994. *Whither Socialism?* Cambridge, Mass.: MIT Press.

———. 1996. "Some Lessons from the East Asian Miracle." *World Bank Research Observer* 11(2): 151–77.

———. 1999. "Whither Reform? Ten Years of the Transition." Keynote address, World Bank Annual Conference on Development Economics, 28–30 April, Washington, DC.

Stiglitz, Joseph, and Marilou Uy. 1996. "Financial Markets, Public Policy, and the East Asian Miracle." *World Bank Research Observer* 11(2): 249–76.

Stiglitz, Joseph, and Andrew Weiss. 1981. "Credit Rationing in Markets with Incomplete Information." *American Economic Review* 71: 393–410.

Streeck, Wolfgang, and Philippe Schmitter. 1985. Community, Market, State—and Associations? The Prospective Contribution of Interest Governance to Social Order. In *Private Interest Governance: Beyond Market and State*, edited by Wolfgang Streeck and Philippe C. Schmitter. Beverly Hills, Calif.: Sage.

Sulček, Emanuel. 1980. "Účast SBCS na přípravě a realizaci plánu." *Finance a úvěr* 30(7): 479–81.

Sunstein, Cass R. 1995. "Incompletely Theorized Agreements." *Harvard Law Review* 108: 1733–72.

Svejnar, Jan. 1989. "A Framework for the Economic Transformation of Czechoslovakia." *PlanEcon Report* 5(52): 1–18.

———. 1993. Czech and Slovak Federal Republic: A Solid Foundation. In *Economic Transformation in Central Europe: A Progress Report*, edited by Richard Portes. London: CEPR.

Svejnar, Jan, and Miroslav Singer. 1994. "Using Vouchers to Privatize an Economy: The Czech and Slovak Case." *Economics of Transition* 2(1): 43–69.

Svejnar, Jan, and Katherine Terrell. 1994. Explaining Unemployment Dynamics in the Czech and Slovak Republics. CERGE-EI Working Paper No. 64.

Sylos-Labini, Paolo. 1992. Capitalism, Socialism, and Democracy in Large Scale Firms. In *Entrepreneurship, Technological Innovation, and Growth,* edited by F. M. Scherer and Mark Perlman. Ann Arbor: University of Michigan Press.

Szelenyi, Ivan. 1988. *Socialist Entrepreneurs.* Cambridge: Polity Press.

———. 1989. Eastern Europe in an Epoch of Transition: Toward a Socialist Mixed Economy? In *Remaking the Economic Institutions of Socialism,* edited by Victor Nee and David Stark. Stanford, Calif.: Stanford University Press.

Szelenyi, Ivan, Eva Fodor, and E. Hanley. 1997. "Left Turn in Postcommunist Politics: Bringing the Class Back In?" *East European Politics and Society* 11(1): 190–224.

Szelenyi, Szonja, Ivan Szelenyi, and Winifred Poster. 1996. "Interests and Symbols in Post-Communist Political Culture: The Case of Hungary." *American Sociological Review* 61(3): 446–58.

Talíř, Václav. 1980. "Zkušenosti s efektivností využívání úvěru a náměty k jejímu zvyšování." *Finance a úvěr.* 30(8): 543–46.

Tang, Helena, Edda Zoli, and Irina Klytchnikova. 2000. Banking Crises in Transition Economies: Fiscal Costs and Related Issues. World Bank Policy Research Working Paper No. 2484.

Teichová, Alice. 1974. *An Economic Background to Munich.* Cambridge: Cambridge University Press.

———. 1988. *The Czechoslovak Economy 1918–1980.* New York: Routledge.

———. 1997. Czechoslovakia: The Halting Pace to Scope and Scale. In *Big Business and the Wealth of Nations,* edited by A. Chandler, F. Amatori, and T. Hikino. Cambridge: Cambridge University Press.

Teichová, Alice, and P. L. Cottrell, eds. 1983. *International Business and Central Europe, 1918–1939.* New York: St. Martin's Press.

Tendler, Judith. 1997. *Good Government in the Tropics.* Baltimore: Johns Hopkins University Press.

Thelen, Kathleen, and Sven Steinmo. 1992. Historical Institutionalism in Comparative Context. In *Structuring Politics: Historical Institutionalism in Comparative Analysis,* edited by S. Steinmo, K. Thelen, and F. Longstreth. Cambridge: Cambridge University Press.

Tommasi, Mariano, and Andres Velasco. 1996. "Where Are We in the Political Economy of Reform?" *Journal of Policy Reform* 1: 187–238.

Torre, Juan Carlos. 1997. Las Dimensiones Politicas e Institucionales de las Reformas Estructurales en America Latina. Instituto Torcuato Di Tella, Buenos Aires, unpublished manuscript.

Trade Links. 1992. *The Commercial Code (Act No. 513/1991 Coll.).* Prague: Trade Links.

———. 1993. *The Bankruptcy and Composition Act.* Prague: Trade Links.

Tříska, Dušan. 1990. "Dočasná správa a denacionalizace národního majetku." Czechoslovak Ministry of Finance. Mimeograph.

———. 1993. Investment Privatization Funds on Securities Markets in the Czech Republic. Paper presented at the Fourth Annual CEEPN Conference on Privatization in Central and Eastern Europe, 15–17 September, Ljubljana.

———. 1994. Central Bank Independence: The Theory and Practice in the Czech Republic. Paper prepared for the conference, Central Banks in Eastern Europe, 21–23 April, Chicago.

Turek, Otakar. 1969. Czechoslovak Economic Reform as a Process of Social Conflict Resolution. Praha, unpublished manuscript.

———. 1983. Centralistický systém fungování socialistické ekonomiky. Ekonomický Ustav, Praha. Mimeograph.

———. 1988. "Hospodářská politika v období přestavby hospodářského mechanismu." Politická ekonomie 36: 575–92.

———. 1989. Direktivně-přídělový systém. (Directive-Assignment System). Prague, unpublished manuscript.

———. 1993. "Státní podniky v agonii." Ekonom 8: 23.

———. 1995. Příspěvek disfunKčí ekonomického systému k pádu komunismu v Československu. Praha. Mimeograph.

Tyson, Laura D'Andrea, and Tea Petrin. 1994. "Promoting Entrepreneurship in Eastern Europe." Small Business Economics 6(3): 165–84.

Ulam, Adam. 1963. The New Face of Soviet Totalitarianism. Cambridge: Harvard University Press.

Unger, Roboerto Mangabeira. 1987. Social Theory: Its Situation and its Task. Cambridge: Cambridge University Press.

Uzzi, B. 1996. "The Sources and Consequences of Embeddedness for the Economic Performance of Organizations: The Network Effect." American Sociological Review 61: 674–98.

———. 1997. "Social Structure and Competition in Interfirm Networks: The Paradox of Embeddedness." Administrative Science Quarterly 42: 35–67.

Vácha, Jan. 1992. Organizační změny v a.s. Škoda—Volkswagen. Diploma Thesis, Fakulta Podnikohospodářská, Vysoká Škola Ekonomická Praha.

Vácha, Stanislav. 1978. Koncepční řízení VHJ. Praha: SNTL.

Vajrauchová, Věra. 1985. "Vztahy mezi podnikovou a územní sférou v oblasti sociálního rozvoje." Expertní šetření, Dům techniky ČSVTS Pardubice, April.

Valach, Josef. 1988. "Některé otázky samofinancování, rozdělování zisku a kriteria efektivnosti při přestavbě hospodářského mechanismu." Finance a úvěr 38(1): 34–44.

Valencia, Matthew. 1997. "Banking in Emerging Markets." Economist, Special Survey, 12 April.

Valenta, František. 1992. AKčiové společnosti v první vlně kuponové privatizace. Ekonomický ústav, Ceskoslovenská Akademie Věd, Prague. Mimeograph.

Valentová, Zuzana. 1989. Analýza působení banky na vývoj zásob na příkladě st. podniku ČKD Praha Kombinát. Diploma Thesis, Fakulta podnikohospodářská, Vysoká Škola Ekonomická, May.

Van Wijnbergen, Sweder. 1992. Enterprise Reform in Eastern Europe. London, CEPR Discussion Paper No. 738.

———. 1993. On the Role of Banks in Enterprise Restructuring: The Polish Example. CEPR Discussion Paper No 898.

———. 1997. "On the Role of Banks in Enterprise Restructuring: The Polish Example." Journal of Comparative Economics 24: 44–64.

Vavříkova, J. 1987. "Některé aspekty spolupráce oblastních a odvětvových orgánů." Plánované hospodářství 8: 87–90.

Veselá, Romana. 1992. Změny organizační struktury v ČKD Kompresory. Diploma Thesis, Department of Industry Economy, Vysoká Škola Ekonomická.

Veselý, Zdeněk. 1992. "Platební neschopnost v roce 1991." Finance a úvěr 42(8): 61–69.

Vintrová, Růžena. 1993. "The General Recession and the Structural Adaptation Crisis." *Eastern European Economics* (spring): 78–93.

Vitiský, Josef, ed. 1985. *Vývoj průmyslových oblastí Československa v období budovaní socialismu.* Opava: Slezský ústav Ceskoslovenská Akademie Věd.

―――, ed. 1986. *Studie z dějin průmyslových oblastí v období výstavby socialismu v Československu.* Opava: Slezský ústav Ceskoslovenská Akademie Věd.

Vláčil, Jan, and Václav Horniak. 1992. Velká privatizace: Sociální konflikt a konsensus v pluralitě podnikatelskyých organizací. Sociologický ústav, Ceskoslovenská Akademie Věd, Prague. Mimeograph.

Vláčil, Jan, Irena Hradecká, Ivana Mazelková, and Gerald McDermott. 1996. Politics, Skills, and Industrial Restructuring. Sociologický ústav, AV ČR. Working Paper 96:8.

Vlašek, Josef, Vlasta Nigrinová, and Libuše Šafránková. 1992. Financování investic se zaměřením na veřejné investice. Československý statistický Úřad, 30 October. Mimeograph.

Vojtěch, Ondřej. 1993. "Privatizační poločas." *Respekt,* April, 8: 5–18.

Vojtěch, Ondřej, and Jan Macháček. 1993. "Investiční fondy: jak si stojí nejmocnější hráči na ekonomické šachovnici." *Respekt,* April, 8–9: 19–25.

Vordová-Havelcová, Helena. 1986. Normování počtu technickohospodařských pracovníků v podmínkách automatizace. Diploma Thesis, Fakulta výrobně ekonomická, Vysoká Škola Ekonomická Praha.

Voskamp, Ulrich, and Volker Wittke. 1991. "Industrial Restructuring in the Former GDR." *Politics and Society* 19(3): 341–71.

Voszka, Eva. 1993. Spontaneous Privatization in Hungary. In *Privatization in the Transition to a Market Economy,* edited by Earle, Frydman, and Rapaczynski. New York: St. Martin's Press.

Vrba, Jan. 1991. Comments on Privatization in Czechoslovakia. Czech Ministry of Industry, Prague. Mimeograph.

VUSTE. 1983. Rozvoj strojírenství a elektrotechniky do r. 2000 a v 8. 5LP. VUSTE Praha, April. Internal report.

Wade, Robert. 1990. *Governing the Market: Economic Theory and the Role of the Government in East Asian Industrialization.* Princeton, N.J.: Princeton University Press.

Walder, Andrew. 1992a. Local Bargaining Relationships and Urban Industrial Finance. In *Bureaucracy, Politics, and Decision-Making in Post-Mao China,* edited by K. Lieberthal and D. Lampton. Berkeley and Los Angeles: University California Press.

―――. 1992b. Corporate Organization and Local State Property Rights: The Chinese Alternative to Privatization. Paper presented at the Conference, The Political Economy of Privatization and Public Enterprise in Eastern Europe, Asia, and Latin America, 24–25 April at the Thomas J. Watson Institute for International Studies, Brown University.

―――. 1994. Corporate organization and local government property rights in China. In *Changing Political Economies: Privatization in Post-Communist and Reforming Communist States,* edited by V. Milor. London: Lynne Rienner.

Wall Street Journal. 1996. "Czechs Offer Peek at New Corporate East." 8 May.

Watkins, J. W. N. 1978. Ideal Types and Historical Explanation. In *The Philosophy of Social Explanation,* edited by Alan Ryan. Oxford: Oxford University Press.

Weimer, David, ed. 1997. *The Political Economy of Property Rights: Institutional Change and Credibility in the Reform of Centrally Planned Economies.* Cambridge: Cambridge University Press.

White, Harrison. 1992. *Identity and Control*. Princeton, N.J.: Princeton University Press.

"Who's Top?" 1997. *The Economist*, March 29: 21–23.

Williamson, O. 1985. *Economic Institutions of Capitalism*. New York: Free Press.

———. 1991. "Comparative Economic Organization: The Analysis of Discrete Structural Alternatives." *Administrative Science Quarterly* 36: 269–96.

———. 1992. "Markets, Hierarchies, and the Modern Perspective." *Journal of Economic Behavior and Organization* 17(3): 335–52.

Winiecki, Jan. 1986. "Distorted Macroeconomies of Central Planning." *Banca Nazionale del Lavoro Quarterly Review,* 157 (June): 192–224.

———. 1989. "Large Industrial Enterprises in Soviet-Type Economies: The Ruling Stratum's Main Rent-Seeking Area." *Communist Economies* 1(4): 363–83.

———. 1990. "Why Economic Reforms Fail in the Soviet System—A Property Rights-Based Approach." *Economic Inquiry* 28(2): 195–221.

———. 1997. Religious Institutions and the Resilience of Conservatism in Hungary, 1945–1994. Paper presented at the Annual Meeting of the APSA, 28–31 August, Washington DC.

Wittenberg, Jason. 1999. The 1994 Hungarian Election in Historical Perspective. In *The 1994 Election to the Hungarian National Assembly*, edited by G. Toka and Z. Enyedi. Berlin: Sigma. Forthcoming.

Wittlerová, Jana. 1987. Vliv automatizace na organizační řízení. (Avia) Diploma Thesis, Fakulta výrobně ekonomická, Vysoká Škola Ekonomická Praha.

Wood Company Securities. 1994. Creditanstalt Investment Privatization Fund. Czech Equity Research Department, May. Internal Report.

Woodruff, D. 1999a. *Money Unmade: Barter and the Fate of Russian Capitalism*. Ithaca, N.Y.: Cornell University Press.

———. 1999b. Rules for Followers: Institutional Theory, Russia, and the New Politics of Economic Backwardness. Paper prepared for the conference Ten Years After the Fall, 21–22 May at the University of California Davis.

World Bank. 1996. *From Plan to Market*. New York: Oxford University Press.

———. 1999a. *Czech Republic: Capital Market Review*. Washington, D.C.: World Bank.

———. 1999b. *Global Development Finance: Country Tables*. Washington, D.C.: World Bank.

Wroblewski, Andrzej. 1988. Control, Influence and Money in the Socialist Economy. Warsaw, SPGiS. Mimeograph.

Žaloudek, Věroslav. 1973. *Integrovaná soustava řízení vyrobní hospodářské jednotky*. Praha: Institut řízení.

Zavadil, Jan. 1992. Ekonomické aspekty zavádění automatizace. Diploma Thesis, Department of Industry Economy, Vysoká Škola Ekonomická.

Zavadil, Pavel. 1990. Organizace a její změny při přechodu na tržní mechanismus. Diploma Thesis, Fakulta podnikohospodářská, Vysoká Škola Ekonomická Praha.

Zemplinerová, Alena. 1986. "Velikost průmyslových výrobních jednotek v ČSSR a metodika měření koncentrace výroby." *Politická ekonomie* 34: 49–58.

———. 1987. "Dynamika a efektivnost koncentrace výroby." *Politická ekonomie* 35: 69–78.

———. 1989. "Míra a zdroje monopolizace čs. průmyslu." *Politická ekonomie* 37: 1453–64.

Zemplinerová, Alena, and Josef Stíbal. 1995. Evolution and Efficiency of Concentration in Manufacturing. In *The Czech Republic and Economic Transition in Eastern Europe*, edited by Jan Svejnar. San Diego: Academic Press.

Zwass, Adam. 1979. *Money, Banking, and Credit in the Soviet Union and Eastern Europe.* White Plains: M.E. Sharpe.

Zysman, John. 1983. *Government Markets, and Growth.* Ithaca, N.Y.: Cornell University Press.

Czech Government Documents

Act No. 92/1991 Coll. (Act on the Conditions of Transfér of State Owned Property to Other Persons).

Act No. 210/1993 (June); Resolution No. 568 of October 6 1993 (Additional Procedures in the Privatization Process).

Act No. 171/1991 Coll. (Act of the Czech National Council on the Authority of the Governing Bodies of the Czech Republic in Matters Concerning Transfer of State Property to Other Persons).

Act No. 328/1991 Coll. (The Bankruptcy and Composition Act).

Act No. 471/1992 Coll. (Act on the temporary Restriction of Procedure Under the Bankruptcy and Composition Act).

Act No. 122/1993 Coll. (Amendments and Supplements to the Bankruptcy and Composition).

Act No. 248/1992 (Investment Fund Act).

Resolution No. 334/1994 (O rozhodnutí o privatizaci 51% aKčií aKčiové společnosti ČKD Holding).

Česká Národní Banka (Czech National Bank). 1991, 1992, 1993a, 1994. *Úvěry a vklady bankovní soustavy.* Monthly Reports.

————. 1993b. "Indikátory měnového a hospodářského vývoje České republiky v roce 1993." Statistical Department, No. 24, December.

Český Statistický Úřad (Czech Statistical Agency). 1993a. "Ekonomické výsledky nefinančních podniků a korporací na území ČR za 4. čtvrtletí 1992." Finanční statistika, 14 June.

————. 1993b. "Vývoj pohledávek a závazků na území ČR k 31.12.1992." Finanční statistika, 2 July.

————. 1993c. "Ekonomické výsledky nefinančních podniků a korporací za 1. pololetí 1993." Finanční statisitika, 15 October.

————. 1993d, 1994a. *Statistical Yearbook of the Czech Republic.* Prague: Český Spisovatel.

————. 1994b. "Ekonomické výsledky nefinančních podniků a korporací za 3. čtvrtletí 1993." Finanční statistika, 21 January.

Federal Ministry of Steel, Engineering, and Electronics of the CSSR. 1989a. Návrh Nařízení vlády ČSSR o finančním hospodaření statních podniků a některých dalších socialistických organizací (Proposal for a CSSR Government Statute About the Financial Management of State Enterprises and Some Other Socialist Organizations). Mimeograph (revised version).

————. 1989b. "Státní podniky a ostatní organizace resortu FMHSE." October. Mimeograph. (Compiled with Dept. 431 of VUSTE.)

Fund for National Property of the Czech Republic (FNM CR). 1992, 1993a, 1994a. *Výroční zpráva (Annual Report).*

————. 1993b, 1994b. "Roční účetní závěrka a výroční zpráva." Mimeograph.

————. 1993c. Standard Form of the Share Purchase Agreement.

————. 1994c. "Materiál pro jednání výkonného výboru Fondu Národního Majetku: Informace o realizacích privatizačních projektu k 31.12.1993." 19 January.

————. 1994d. "Materiál pro jednání výkonného výboru Fondu Národního Majetku: Depozitní politika FNM ČR." Financial Evidence Sector, 7 September.

————. 1994e. "Smlouva o prodeji a koupi akcií mezi FNM ČR a NERO s.r.o." 11 April.

————. 1994f. "Smlouva o prodeji a koupi akcií mezi FNM ČR a Komerční Bankou, a.s." 2 May.

————. 1994g. "Smlouva o koupi akcií mezi FNM ČR a Investiční a Poštovní Bankou, a.s." 8 November.

Konsolidační Banka, s.p.u. (Consolidation Bank). 1992, 1993, 1994a, 1995. *Výroční zpráva (Annual Report)*.

————. 1994b. "Směrnice pro odkupování pohledávek za úpadci." Úsek úvěrových obchodů, 25 January.

Ministry of the Administration of National Property and Its Privatization of the Czech Republic. 1993a. "Rozbor hospodaření Fondu Národního Majetku České republiky za rok 1992." 7 June.

————. *Report on the Privatization Process for the Years 1989 to 1992*.

————. 1992. Důvodová zpráva ke způsobu privatizace aKčiové společnosti TOS Kuřim. 15 April. Mimeograph.

————. 1993b. Report on Proposed Investment by Thomas J. C. Matzen GmbH in TOS Kurim a.s. Internal memo from USAID Advisory Team to Deputy Ministers, exact date unknown.

————. 1993c. Internal memo from USAID Advisory Team to Deputy Ministers, 11 November.

————. 1994a. Zásady, podle kterých by měly být odkoupeny aKčie Škoda Plzeň. Memo from USAID Advisory Team to Investiční Banka, 19 January.

————. 1994b. Conclusion of TOS Kurim Privatization Negotiations with Thomas J.C. Matzen. Internal memo from USAID Advisory Team to Deputy Ministers, 1 July.

Ministry of Industry of the Czech Republic. 1991. *Profile of Enterprises*. Prague: Ministry of Industry of the Czech Republic.

————. 1992. Register of Companies within the Ministry of Industry of the Czech Republic. Prague: Ministry of Industry of the Czech Republic.

State Bank of Czechoslovakia. 1992. Czechoslovak Bank Acts, Prague.

"Záznam z jednání MPO ČR, FNM ČR, KB a IB a NERo, reprezentované ing. Lubomírem SOUDKEM," Agreement prepared 4 November 1992.

Restructuring Documents from the Ministry of Industry and Trade of the Czech Republic (MPO CR)

Ministry of Industry and Trade of the Czech Republic (MPO CR). 1992a. "Návrh privatizace s.p. Modřanské strojírny." Zpráva pro poradu vedeni MPO ČR No. 172/92; C.j. 3 200/159/92, 27 October.

————. 1993a. Modelový projekt transformace holdingových společností na samostatné akciové společnosti. February. Mimeograph.

————. 1993b. Souhrnné vyhodnocení vzájemných zápočtů závazků a pohledávek. 12 November. Mimeograph.

————. 1993c, 1994a. *Analýza ekonomiky ČR a odvětví v působnosti MPO*. Department of Economic Analysis. Prague: MPO CR.

————. 1993d, 1994b, 1996. *Analysis of Economic Development in the Czech Republic and in MIT Organizations*. Prague: MPO CR.

————. 1994c. Informace o rozvojových projektech k poskytnutí statních záruk, resp. využití účelových vládních úvěrů. Internal memo with appendices.

On Aero a.s. and the Aircraft Industry

MPO CR. 1993e, Současná situace leteckého průmyslu ČR, program jeho restrukturalizace a problematika uzavírání společných podniků se zahraničními partnery. Document prepared by the Department of Aircraft Manufacturing, with appendices. Prague.

————. 1994d. "Informace k postupu realizace projektu restrukturalizace Aero Holding a.s." Materiál pro poradu ministrů vlády České republiky, No. 42; C.j. 4447/94/3230/1000; 22 February.

On the Automotive and Truck Industry

MPO CR. 1992b. "Zpráva o situaci v a.s. Tatra Kopřivnice, a návrhy na její řešení." Zpráva pro poradu vedení MPO ČR No. 200/92; C.j. 3000/3259/92; 10 October.

————. 1993f. Progress of Restructuring in Automotive Industry of the Czech Republic. August. Mimeograph.

On ČKD Praha a.s.

MPO CR. 1992c. "Současná situace ČKD Praha a návrhy vedení holdingu na její řešení." Zpráva pro vedení MPO ČR, No. 179/92; C.j. 3200/120/145/92, 19 October.

————. 1992d. Důvodová zpráva. Department 3230, 17 December. (A 50 page memo detailing the developments of ČKD Praha.)

————. 1993g. Přednosti výrobní základny společenství ČKD Praha, a.s. Mimeograph. (exact date unkown).

————. 1993h. Postup a některé výrazné aspekty privatizace ČKD Praha. Mimeograph. (exact date unkown).

————. 1993i. Přehled výrobních aktivit ČKD Praha v r. 1992. Memo prepared by Ing. Srp, 25 March.

————. 1994e. "Privatizace akcií ČKD Praha Holding a.s. uložených na FNM ČR." Materiál pro poradu ministrů vlády České republiky; C.j. 8207/94/3230/1000; (exact date unkown).

————. 1994f. Důvodová zpráva: k návrhu privatizace 51% akcií společnosti ČKD Praha Holding, a.s. Mimeograph. (exact date unkown).

On the Chemical Industry

————. 1994g. "Chemický průmysl: souhrnné zhodnocení." Department of Petro-Chemicals and Plastics, March-April, internal report.

————. 1994h. "Důvodová zpráva: rafinersko-petrochemického komplexu." Department of Petro-Chemicals and Plastics, March-April, internal report.

On the Steel Industry and Poldi Kladno a.s.

MPO CR. 1993j. "Jednání o vstupu zahraničního kapitálu firmy Maison Lazard do POLDI Kladno a.s." Information for Minister V. Dlouhý. Internal memo.

————. 1993k. "Privatizace a restrukturalizace POLDI Kladno a.s." Informace pro poradu vedení MPO ČR, No. 89/93; C.j. 21889/93/3210; 14 May.

————. 1993l. "Privatizace a restrukturalizace POLDI Kladno a.s." Zpráva pro jednání porady ekonomických ministrů vlády ČR, May.

―――. 1993m. "Současný stav hutnictví železa České republiky." Materiál pro poradu ministrů vlády České republiky No. 25; C.j. 44301/93/3210/1000; 22 November.

―――. 1994i. "Restrukturalizace hutního průmyslu severomoravského regionu—bankovní úvěry na výstavbu kontility." Materiál pro schůzi vlády České republiky, No. 46, C.j. 87/94/3210–1000; 26 January.

―――. 1994j. "Informace o přípravě projektu minihutě na výrobu plochých výrobků v severomoravském regionu—výsledky jednání se zahraničními partnery." Materiál pro poradu ministrů vlády České republiky; C.j. 15466/94/3210/1000; 3 June.

―――. 1994k. "Současná situace ve vztazích mezi holdingem POLDI, a.s. a POLDI OCEL, resp. BOHEMIA ART a její řežení." Information for Minister V. Dlouhý, No. 19536/94; with appendices.

Federal Ministry of the Economy. 1992. Program restrukturalizace čs. hutnictví. Document prepared by Sofres Conseil, Roland Berger a Partner, Sofresid, June. Mimeograph.

On Škoda Plzeň a.s.
MPO CR. 1992e. "K problematice Škoda, *koncern* Plzeň, a.s." Návrh usnesení vlády České republiky, 13 September.

―――. 1992f. "Podklady pro vyhodnocení veřejné soutěže pro přímý prodej 34% akcií společnosti Škoda, *koncern* Plzeň, a.s." Informace pro poradu ekonomických ministrů vlády České republiky; C.j. A1/4865/92; 29 October.

―――. 1993n. "Privatizace akcií a.s. Škoda, *koncern*, Plzeň dočasně ponechaných ve FNM ČR." Materiál pro schůzi vlády České republiky, June.

Škoda, Plzeň. 1968a. Vývoj organizace řízení ve Škodových závodech v období první republiky. Internal document.

―――. 1968b. Jak byly řízeny Škodovy závody jako aKčiové společnosti. Internal document.

Škoda, Koncernový Podnik, Plzeň. 1989. Historický vývoj právního základu Škodových závodů. Plzeň, May.

Documents From Joint-Stock Companies (Firms, Banks, Investment Companies)
Aero, a.s. 1991a. Zpráva o hospodářských výsledcích a podnikatelské činnosti a.s. Aero—holding za I. pololetí 1991. Document prepared by the Department of Economic Development and Financial Policy, 23 July.

―――. 1991b, 1992, 1993, 1994, 1995. *Výroční Zpráva (Annual Report).*

Česká Pojišťovna, a.s. 1992, 1993, 1994, 1995. *Výroční Zpráva (Annual Report).*

Česká Spořitelna, a.s. 1992, 1993, 1994, 1995. *Výroční Zpráva (Annual Report).*

―――. 1993, 1994. *Pololetní Zpráva (Half-Year Report).*

Chemapol. 1993, 1994. *Výroční Zpráva (Annual Report).*

ČKD Dukla, a.s. 1993. Information Memorandum: ČKD Dukla, a.s. Document prepared by the European Privatization and Investment Corporation, Vienna, March.

ČKD Praha. 1989. "Roční rozbor." 15 February.

ČKD Praha, Kombinát. 1990. Roční rozbor výsledků hospodářské činnosti za rok 1989. Department of Economy, 15 February. Mimeograph.

ČKD Praha, a.s. 1991a, 1992a, 1993, 1994, 1995. *Výroční Zpráva (Annual Report).*

―――. 1991b. "Strategická cílová orientace a koncept struktury pro ČKD-*koncern*." Extract of Analysis of ČKD Praha written by A. T Kearney, 13 September.

―――. 1992b. "Privatizační Projekt." (includes original project of 1991 and amendments), February.

ČSOB (Československá Obchodní Banka), a.s. 1992, 1993, 1994, 1995. *Výroční Zpráva (Annual Report).*

HYTOS. 1994. *Vyrobni program.*

Investiční Banka, a.s. 1991, 1992, 1993. *Výroční Zpráva (Annual Report).*

Investiční a Poštovní Banka, a.s. 1994, 1995, 1996. *Výroční Zpráva (Annual Report).*

————. 1992–1993a. Aktualizovaný propočet majetkové ujmy IB, a.s. vyplývající z restrukturalizace závazku Škoda Plzeň a.s. vůči IB, a.s. a jejího podílu na odkupu emitovaných dluhopisů Škoda Plzeň. Internal memo, (exact date unknown, c. December 1992–January 1993).

————. 1992–1993b. Dohoda o restrukturalizaci závazku a.s. Škoda, *koncern* Plzeň, vůči Investiční bance, a.s., Praha a chystané kapitalizaci části úvěru. Draft of agreement, (date unknown, c. December 1992–January 1993).

————. 1993a. Financial Statement Comparison for the Major Czech Banks. Department 14. Mimeograph.

————. 1993b. Strategie restrukturalizace velkých holdingových uskupení ŠKODA *koncern* Plzeň, a.s. (ŠKODA), ČKD Praha, a.s. (ČKD) a Aero a.s. Praha (Aero) a připravovaného holdingu TATRA, a.s. Internal memo, (exact date unkown, c. April–May).

Komerční Banka, a.s. 1992a, 1993a, 1994a, 1995. *Výroční Zpráva (Annual Report).*

————. 1992b. Analýza odvětví hutnictví železa. Department 613, October. Mimeograph.

————. 1993b. Analýza odvětví investiční strojírenství. Department 613, April. Mimeograph.

————. 1993c. Analýza oboru výroba strojů a přístrojů. Department 613, September. Mimeograph.

————. 1993d. Portfolio úvěru Komerční banky, a.s., z hlediska zadlužení klientů od pololetí roku 1992 do 30. 6. 1993 s očekávaným výhledem do konce roku. Mimeograph.

————. 1994b. Rozdělení komerčních úvěru podle jednotlivých odvětví. Department 622, 12 August. Mimeograph.

Kovosvit, a.s. 1992, 1993a, 1994, 1995. *Výroční Zpráva (Annual Report).*

————. 1990, 1991. Profit and Loss Account, Balance Sheet. Internal mimeograph.

————. 1993b. *Prospekt na 729 510 akcií na doručitele v nominální hodnotě Kč 1000.* December.

LIAZ, a.s. 1994, 1995. *Výroční Zpráva (Annual Report).*

Pragobanka, a.s. 1993, 1994. *Výroční Zpráva (Annual Report).*

První Privatizační Fond (PPF). 1995, 1996. *Výroční Zpráva (Annual Report).*

Škoda, *koncern*, Plzeň. 1991a, 1992a, 1993a, 1994, 1995a. *Výroční Zpráva (Annual Report).*

————. 1990, 1991b, 1992b, 1993b. Přehled o odchodech pracovníků podle důvodu. Internal analysis on personnel. Mimeograph.

————. 1993c. Souhrná charakteristika. Internal memo, (exact date unknown, c. June).

————. 1993d. "Soubor Pravidel holdingových vztahů." Rules passed by the Management Board as set forth in Resolution No. 36/PAS 6/93 of the Shareholder Meeting, 3 May.

————. 1993e. Pohledávky a závazky. Internal financial table. Mimeograph.

————. 1993f, 1995b. Vnitroholdingové pohledávky a závazky (údaje dle s.r.o.). Internal financial tables. Mimeograph.

Šmeral Brno, a.s. 1993. *Prospekt Cenného Papíru.* June.

————. 1994. "Zpravodaj zaměstnanců." June. Internal report.

SST (Svaz výrobců a dodavatelů strojírenské techniky). 1991. Charakteristika organizace svazu. Mimeograph.

————. 1992. *Katalog obráběcích a tvařecích strojů.* Praha: Realizace Studio Typo Tisk Typografie.

————. 1994. Dílčí oborová studie o obráběcích strojích. 2d draft, December. Mimeograph.

Tatra, a.s. 1994, 1995. *Výroční Zpráva (Annual Report).*

TOS Čelákovice, a.s. 1992, 1993a, 1994. *Výroční Zpráva (Annual Report).*

————. 1993b. *Prospekt emitenta cenných papírů.* 20 December.

TOS Hostivař. 1989. Financial Statements for Hostivar Division. McDowell CPAs.

TOS Kuřim, a.s. 1993a. *Prospekt cenného papíru.* 17 December.

————. 1993b. Průvodní list privatizačního projektu. Mimeograph.

————. 1994. Zápis z jednání valné hromady. 20 June. Mimeograph.

TST (Továrny Strojírenské Techniky) *koncern.* 1982, 1983, 1984, 1985, 1986, 1987. *Statiticko-ekonomický přehled.* Odbor informační soustavy.

————. 1989. Společný materiál koncernu generálního ředitelství TST a PZO Strojimport Praha k řežení koncepčních otázek rozvoje výroby vyrobní techniky po roce 1990. Internal memo, 14 March.

VUOSO. 1990. "Koncepce technického rozvoje oboru 512 od roku 1995 az 2000." Odbor 210, June.

ZPS Zlin, a.s. 1991, 1992a, 1993a, 1994a, 1995, 1996, 1997. *Výroční Zpráva (Annual Report).*

————. 1992b. *Prospekt dluhopisu: obligace 50 Mill, 17%, 1992–1997.* 1 February.

————. 1993b. *Podnikatelský Záměr.*

————. 1993c. *Prospekt dluhopisu: obligace 250 Mill Kč, 18,5%, 1993–1998.* 1 March.

————. 1994b. *Basic Information.*

————. 1994c. *Prospekt cenného papíru (Emise akcií hodnoty 364 Mill Kč.* 16 June.

Index

Page numbers for tables and figures are in italics